D1083998

ANCIENT JUDAISM

Number 64

ANCIENT JUDAISM
Debates and Disputes

by
Jacob Neusner

ANCIENT JUDAISM
Debates and Disputes

by
Jacob Neusner

Scholars Press
Chico, California

ANCIENT JUDAISM
Debates and Disputes

by
Jacob Neusner

© 1984
Brown University

BM
.73
.N48
1984

Library of Congress Cataloging in Publication Data

Neusner, Jacob, 1932–
  Ancient Judaism

  (Brown Judaic studies ; 64)
  Includes index.
  1. Judaism—History—To 70 A.D.—Book reviews.
2. Judaism—History—Talmudic period, 10–425—Book
reviews. 3. Jews—History—Book reviews.
  I. Title. II. Series
BM173.N48   1984   296'.09'015   84–5532
ISBN 0-89130-755-9
ISBN 0-89130-746-X (pbk.)

Printed in the United States of America

For

Kent Richards

For the upright will inhabit the land,
and men of integrity will remain in it.

Proverbs 2:21

CONTENTS

PREFACE

A primary mode of scholarly expression takes the form of argument, debate and discussion about both substantive results and methods. Argument goes forward in two modes. First, one's own books and articles present statements of method and accounts of the result of learning, hence arguments on how a given scholar holds we should think and what conclusions we should reach. These, in the nature of things, constitute also criticisms of the methods and conclusions of others. Second, when we read and respond in book reviews to the work of others, we advance debate and discussion still further. By dealing with the ideas of others, by constructing arguments for, or against, their results, by sustained attention to the issues important to colleagues, we make a statement of our own. We exemplify our views by what we say on others' results. That statement may express still more vividly and succinctly than our own articles and books the larger theory of method and the major results of that method characteristic of one's own ouevre. That is so for anyone who pursues scholarship for a long time, and it is certainly the case for me.

In this book I propose to explain my work by systematically reviewing books of others, both of our own day and in times past. In the debates and disputes at hand, I aim to advance the understanding of how I believe we should study the history of the formation of Judaism in the first seven centuries of the Common Era (= A.D.). In this book I present nearly two dozen reviews, some brief, many long, as well as bibliographical essays on three of the major topics on which I have worked. In presenting the papers at hand, I mean to introduce my own work as well.

The reviews are divided into five parts, moving from the most general to the most particular questions and from matters of method and theory to issues of fact. These divisions correspond to the principal categories of my inquiry. I started life thinking of myself as a "Jewish historian," but very rapidly discovered that that category proved too narrow. My work required me to enter the field of history of religions, trying to learn from and apply the issues of that discipline to the history of Judaism, and the discipline of literary and exegetical criticism as well. I furthermore have had to translate principal texts of formative Judaism so as to confront the sources in acute detail. I also have had to stand very far back and attempt to characterize the totality of the social culture of Judaism as the rabbis of late antiquity created it. I have attempted to distinguish from one another the literary components of our picture of that Judaism. Finally, I have undertaken the reconstruction of the history of critical and definitive ideas of that same Judaism, as that history unfolded across the distinct literary compositions. The subject at hand demanded that I follow the work of historians of earliest Christianity and also gain knowledge of the languages and histories of Armenia and Iran, on the East, and the Greco-Roman and Byzantine world on the West.

Still, the reason for following the subject where it led me remained one and the same: an interest in how the Jews made the transition from antiquity and the Land of Israel to medieval and modern times and the West. Why did the Judaism that took shape in late antiquity serve so well, when it did, and so poorly, when it did? As a believing and (imperfectly) practicing Jew, I pursued a theological motive as well: How can that same Judaism be made to serve once more? My conviction was that if I could take things apart and put them together again, I might know how they once worked and so learn how they might work again.

The book therefore starts with the theoretical question of whether there is such a thing as "Jewish history," and, if so, how do colleagues practice it. I begin with my own most current methodological statement, written to be presented to the Historical Society of Israel in July, 1984, but presented only in this book. The themes of that statement recur throughout the reviews at hand. But I wish to begin with a constructive and positive view of what I think people should do and why I think they should do it. Clearly, what to me is self-evident proves offensive to others, who would deny a hearing to these ideas. That is why book reviews and bibliographical essays are important vehicles of scholarly discourse. Most of what follows explains why I think what people have done is wrong and why they should not have done it. From the theoretical beginning, I proceed to specific comments on how biblical and talmudic historians have practiced their craft. As is clear, I find more enduring the results of the historians who study literary sources and pursue questions of cultural analysis and description.

From history I proceed to religion, the historical study of ancient Judaism, from the first century onward. Here I review four books that follow a single line of work, systematically answering questions of historical and dogmatic theology: Bonsirven, Moore, Urbach, and Sanders. Not of the same quality -- Moore stands head and shoulders above the others -- they concur on the same incorrect agenda of categories. They ask the wrong questions. Even if they asked the right questions, moreover, their answers rest upon false methodological premises. I include, also, my review of Heschel's work on the theology of revelation in Talmudic Judaism, different in idiom, but alike in premise.

From the general history of Judaism, I move on to a very specific debate, between Goodenough and Kraeling on what the symbolic evidence of synagogue art means for the interpretation of ancient Judaism.

In part five I reach the most specific issues of all: the Pharisees, Jesus, Paul, and other matters of intense scholarly and theological interest.

Finally, part six consists of three bibliographical essays, which, though not strictly speaking book reviews, seemed to me important specimens of argument and criticism. The bibliographical essays cover their subjects to the date of their original publication; I have not continued to work in these areas and so did not bring them up to date. It seemed to me that this book would prove far more useful and comprehensive if I included these bibliographical studies, even though the first of them, on the use of the Talmud as a historical source, and the second, on the Pharisees in modern historiography, are available in Method and Meaning in Ancient Judaism (I, 1979, and III, 1981, respectively). By contrast, book reviews and essay-reviews in various volumes of my series, <u>Formative Judaism I-II</u>, as well as <u>Major Trends in Formative Judaism I-II</u> do not demand inclusion here, since they treat single items and do not so advance the argument of this work that reprinting them might be called for.

It goes without saying that over the past quarter-century I have reviewed many more books than are represented here. I chose the items that seemed to me to exhibit broadest general interest or to raise the most suggestive and stimulating issues.

I have printed the reviews as they originally appeared, making deletions only to remove views I no longer hold. I thank the copyright holders of all items for permission to reprint my work here.

Twenty-five years ago, with Honi as my model, I drew a circle and stood there, exploring the limits of the matters I had chosen as my own. Today I find many others standing with me in that same circle of criticism and controversy, teaching and learning from one another. Outside of the circle are yet others, with whom debate and dispute may prove equally stimulating and suggestive. No issue is settled, no question closed, no road forward barricaded. I joyfully argue with anyone about any pertinent question, <u>sine ira et studio.</u>

J.N.

Program in Judaic Studies
Brown University
Providence, Rhode Island, U.S.A.

14 Adar II, 5744
March 18, 1984

INTRODUCTION

METHODOLOGY IN TALMUDIC HISTORY

[Written for the Historical Society of Israel. Conference in celebration of its journal, Zion, on the occasion of its fiftieth volume. Jerusalem, Israel. Scheduled for July 2, 1984. This paper was mailed to Jerusalem on January 27, 1984, and the invitation to present it was withdrawn in a letter dated March 5, 1984. The facts speak for themselves, but I prefer not to suggest what they say.]

I

METHODOLOGY

When we speak of methodology, we may mean many things. To specify the very few things under discussion here, let us begin with the simplest possible definition. The method by which we work tells us the questions we choose to pose and the means we use to find the answers. Our method tells us what we want to know and how we can find it out. Method then testifies to the point at which we begin, the purpose for which we work. A sound method will guide us to questions both pertinent to the sources under study and also relevant to broader issues of the day. The one without the other is merely formal, on the one side, or impressionistic and journalistic, on the other. Proper method will tell us what sources we must read and how to interpret them. Above all, sound method will match the issues we raise to the information at hand, that is, will attend especially to questions of historical epistemology: what we know and how we know it.

We cannot raise in the abstract the issues of historical methodology in Talmudic history. Talmudic history is a field that people practice. We cannot ignore what people actually do in favor of some preferred theory of what we think they should do. It furthermore would defy the honorable occasion at hand, to speak about Talmudic history without paying appropriate attention to the journal we celebrate here and now. Accordingly, let us first of all turn our attention to Zion itself and ask how Talmudic history is practiced in its pages: the methodology demonstrated here.

The answer is in three parts. First, Talmudic history constitutes a strikingly unimportant field in Zion. From 1935 (Vol. 1) to 1983 (Vol. 48), the journal published 476 articles, at the rate of approximately 10 per volume. Of these, no more than 28 in all fall into the category of Talmudic history, approximately one article for every two volumes. Talmudic history accounts, in all, for little more than 5% of all articles published in the 50 years we celebrate -- a strikingly small proportion.[1] Yet, in fact, these figures overstate the importance accorded to Talmudic history in the journal. How so? Of the 28 articles at hand, seven deal with Second Temple times, using rabbinic literature for the

treatment of the period before 70 (five of the seven by Y. Baer, as a matter of fact).
Now since a vast range of sources, outside of the Talmud, pertain to the period before 70,
and since the bulk of the Talmudic writings do not speak of that period, we can hardly
concur that that period falls into Talmudic history at all. Strictly speaking, Talmudic
history encompasses the period from the second century A.D. onward. Accordingly, when
we ask how many articles in Zion dealt with problems on which the Talmuds and related
documents provide first-hand evidence, rather than merely referring to things that
happened long ago of which the authors have no direct knowledge of their own, and on
which (by definition) the Talmuds constitute the principal corpus of evidence, the figures
change. Specifically, only 21 of the 476 articles -- four percent of the total, at the rate
of somewhat less than one article every two years -- attend to the field at hand. So we
see in a rather dramatic way that Talmudic history -- the history of the Jewish people in
its formative centuries beyond 70 and up to the rise of Islam -- enjoys little attention in
Zion.[2] I need hardly add that were we to examine other scholarly journals[3] in this country
[viz., the State of Israel, where the paper was supposed to be presented] and overseas, the
proportions might change somewhat, but the picture would emerge pretty much the same.

The second and third observations about the status and methodology of Talmudic
history in Zion require less exposition.

The second is that when people practice Talmudic history in Zion, they limit their
discussion to Talmudic history in particular. The field does not encompass its period, but
only one set of sources emergent from its period. While many of the scholars represented
in Zion draw upon sources outside the Talmud, none of the articles deals with a problem
outside the Talmud. Accordingly, Talmudic history in the journal at hand finds definition
as the study of historical problems pertinent to a given source, rather than to a chronological period to which that source attests.[4] (In this regard, Baer's articles form an
exception to the rule.) It follows that Talmudic history severely limits itself, in Zion, to
literary evidence. While, once again, we may find allusion to archeological data, no
article in the past half-century has entered the category of inquiry in which archeology,
as much as literature, defines the problem or contributes to its solution.

The third observation is that the methodology of reading the literary sources, which
define the problems and solutions of Talmudic history in Zion, begins in an assumption
universally adopted by the scholars of the journal (and not only there). Whatever the
Talmud says happened happened. If the Talmud attributes something to a rabbi, he really
said it. If the Talmud maintains that a rabbi did something, he really did it. So among the
21 articles under discussion, I find not a single one that asks the basic critical questions
with which historical study normally commences: how does the writer of this source know
what he tells me? How do I know that he is right? On the contrary, the two Talmuds
serve, in Zion, as encyclopedias of facts about rabbis and other Jews in the Land of Israel
and Babylonia. The task of the historian is to mine the encyclopedias and come up with
important observations on the basis of the facts at hand. The work of the historian then is
the collection and arrangement of facts, the analysis of facts, the synthesis of facts. It is

not in the inquiry into the source and character of the facts at hand. Just as, for the literary scholar, the text constitutes the starting point of inquiry, so for the historian, the text at hand defines the facts and dictates the character of inquiry upon them. This is the case, beginning and end, from Allon to Kimelman.

Whether it is Allon, telling us what Yohanan ben Zakkai meant in his conversation with Vespasian in August 70, on the assumption that Vespasian and Yohanan were attended by secretaries who wrote down their every word, or whether it is Kimelman, telling us about the politics of the priesthood and exilarchate as reported by a story in Yerushalmi Shabbat 12:3, the method is the same. Now I hasten to add that the prevailing assumption need not deprive of all interest and value a given study in Zion. For instance, where the meaning of a story is subject to interpretation, without attention to whether or not the story took place, the article stands on its own, as in the case of Wasserstein on Gamaliel and Proclus and Israi on Abbahu's saying. Again, when the author deals with events on which the Talmud by definition constitutes a primary source, as in the case of Goodblatt's study of the Babylonian Yeshivot, we deal with a very high level of critical acumen. But the bulk of the articles could not have been written in the way that they were written had the authors first of all taken up the critical program of contemporary historical scholarship.

II

THE FIRST CENTURY OF TALMUDIC HISTORY

No one should suppose that the work of Zion met a lower standard of critical acumen than articles and books published elsewhere. The contrary is the case. My impression is that the great Gedaliahu Allon, to name the premier Israeli Talmudic historian of all time, published his best work in Zion. In fact, from the beginning of Talmudic history in modern times, things scarcely have changed. The work of Talmudic history began with three books, all of them completed within approximately one decade, from 1850 to 1860: A. Geiger's Urschrift und Uebersetzungen der Bibel (1857), an effort to correlate the history of biblical translation with the history of Israelite sects in the period at hand; Z. Frankel's Darkhei HaMishnah (1859), a collection of thumb-nail biographies of Talmudic rabbis and some other historical observations; and H. Graetz's History of the Jews, volume 4, on the Talmudic period (the first book to be published of his general history of the Jews) (1853). These were the first systematic inquiries into the Talmud as a historical document, as distinct from an interest in the Talmud as a source of law for Judaism.

From the very beginnings of Talmudic history, the critical program of ancient history and of biblical studies remained remote. By the 1850s, biblical studies had attained a quite critical program. From the time of Geiger, Graetz, and Frankel, down to nearly our own time, by contrast, it has been taken for granted that a story in a holy book about an event accurately portrays exactly what happened. The story itself has no history, but it is history. No special interests or viewpoints are revealed in a given historical account. Everything is taken at face value. Since historians and story-tellers stand together within the same system of values, it was unthinkable that anyone would either lie or make up a story for his own partisan purposes. No one ever would wonder, Cui bono? To whose interest is it to tell a given story? Obviously, if a learned rabbi told a story, he said it because he knew it to be so, not because he wanted to make up evidence to support his own viewpoint.

In modern times -- beginning long before the Enlightenment -- by contrast, people learned to take a skeptical position vis-à-vis the sacred histories and holy biographies of the earlier generations. They asked about the tendencies of stories, the point the storyteller wished to make, and wondered not about whether a story "really" happened, but rather, about the situation to which a given story actually supplies accurate testimony. They asked how the storyteller knew the facts of the case. Who told him? If he was an eye-witness, on whose side did he stand in a situation of conflict? No reporters were present to take down verbatim what was said and done at the various incidents recorded in the rabbinic traditions. If that is so, then all we have are traditions about such events, given both form and substance on some other, later occasion than that of which they speak. But often we have not traditions but mere legends, fabrications quite unrelated to the events they purport to report.

Such a skeptical attitude had been well established in biblical studies done by non-Jews by the early nineteenth century. Western scholarship in these and related fields had furthermore shown the necessity of analyzing the components of stories and asking how each element took shape and where and when the several elements were put together. But with rabbinic materials, aside from some reservations about obvious miracles, one rarely discerns among nineteenth or even most twentieth century scholars an appreciation of the necessity to understand the historical background of texts in a manner other than that narrated in the texts themselves. And when the rabbinic scholars tried to stand outside the presuppositions of the texts, they did so chiefly for exegetical, not historical purposes.

III

EXAMPLES OF ESTABLISHED METHODOLOGIES

One cannot, however, attempt to refute histories made up on the basis of Talmudic tales. One can only point out that such histories are seriously deficient, because they are wholly uncritical and gullible, omit all reference to the internal evidence revealed by the Talmudic sources, and exclude from discussion the literary evidence available in cognate literature. Nor need one refute the nineteenth- and twentieth-century historians, who, using the Talmudic materials, go on to reinterpret them, to posit new "postulates" about their meaning, to reject one detail of a story in favor of another -- in all, to lay claim to a "critical" position toward a literature whose historical usefulness is never in the end called into question. In such histories we have the pretense of critical scholarship but not its substance. The bulk of the work of nineteenth and twentieth century historians must be regarded as pseudo-critical, critical in rhetoric but wholly traditional in all its presuppositions; and in the main, primitive and puerile. Like the "critical" fundamentalists, who agree that the whale did not really swallow Jonah, but only kept him in his cheek, or like the pseudo-orthodox who say it was for three hours, not three days, the "critical" scholars of the modern period have scarcely improved upon the traditional picture. They have merely rearranged some of its elements. "Plus ça change, plus c'est la même chose." Nothing has changed, but much is made of the changes.

Two specific examples of the primitivism of the scholarship of so-called "scientific" scholars will suffice.

First, Zecharias Frankel, the founder of the modern study of the Mishnah, the first component of the Talmud, is still taken seriously, as shown by the reprinting of his books and their use in contemporary Israeli scholarship to this day. But Frankel operates in a world of private definitions, circular reasoning, and capricious postulates. For him it is unnecessary to prove much, for one may, through defining things properly, obviate the need for proof. For Frankel medieval commentaries constitute primary sources for the study of the Mishnah. He furthermore claims that Seder Toharot is old because it is the largest order (!); that the ancient Jews were all students of the rabbinic Torah; that the structure of the Mishnah was revealed by divine inspiration; and numerous other marvels. In what way then is he to be regarded as "modern"? The reception of his book supplies the answer. His enemies accused him of treating the Mishnah in a secular spirit and not as a divinely revealed document, the Oral Torah. They said he regarded the Mishnah as the work of men and as a time-bound document. He even explained Mishnaic laws otherwise than through the Babylonian Talmud. For this Frankel was condemned by the tradition- alists of his day. That his work today is taken seriously among traditionalists tells us that what is said in the name of tradition changes from one century to the next. But scarcely a line of his Darkhei Hammishnah can be taken seriously as history.

Second, H. Albeck, in his Mabo Lammishnah (1959) looks upon the Mishnah and Talmud as the culmination of the process of "oral tradition" beginning in ancient times. He takes for granted that anything reflective of non-Scriptural (= oral) tradition, whether in biblical or apocryphal, pseudepigraphic, or Septuagintal literature, is The Oral Tradition of Pharisaic-Rabbinic Judaism. While Albeck is critical of earlier students of the history of the Oral Torah, he does not depart from their frame of reference. Indeed, Albeck takes pretty much the position of Sherira Gaon, founder of Talmudic history in the ninth century, altering details but not the main points. What is striking is that for Albeck the scholarly agenda formulated by Sherira remain uncriticized and unchanged: "When was the Mishnah written?" He extensively reviews and criticizes the ideas of earlier scholars, as if they had supplied him with viable agenda. So we find ourselves once again in the midst of debates on the work of the Men of the Great Assembly, although we have not the slightest shred of evidence about what they had actually done, let alone a document produced by them or in their days. While Y.N. Epstein demonstrated for example, in his Introduction to Tannaite Literature (1957) that the tractate Eduyyot was produced by the disciples of Aqiba at Usha -- they are explicitly named throughout -- Albeck takes seriously what the traditions from Talmudic times assert, that Eduyyot was produced at Yavneh: "It was ordered according to the names of the sages and the work was done at

Yavneh." But he never proves this is so. One may easily show that Eduyyot is <u>different</u> from other tractates, but that difference does not mean it is <u>earlier</u> than the others. Whatever a Talmudic tradition alleges about a tractate is taken as fact. Albeck seldom looks in a thorough and critical way for internal evidence. Again and again one finds circular reasoning. For example, Albeck holds that Rabbi Judah the Patriarch, author of the Mishnah, arranged the material he had received according to a single principle, content, and he did not change anything he had received. How do we know this? Because Judah ordered the material only according to the content of the laws and any material not collected according to this principle was formed into units before Judah received them. We know that they were formed into units in Judah's sources because Judah ordered his material only according to the content of the laws. Likewise, Judah did not change any of the material he received because the sources are not changed. We know the sources are not changed because Judah did not change any of the sources. And so forth. Albeck further disputes the view of Epstein that the Mishnah yielded numerous variations in texts. He says once the Mishnah was edited, it was never again changed. I am not clear on how Albeck understands the work of the early Amoraim, for they seem not only to have changed the Mishnah, but to have stated explicitly that they changed the Mishnah.

Though separated by a century, Frankel and Albeck exhibit the same credulousness and lack of critical acumen. Considering the achievements of scholarship in the intervening hundred years, one may be astonished at how little Albeck's perception of the critical task and definition of the problems has been affected. But Frankel, too, exhibits little mastery of the critical conceptions of his own day.

IV
PRINCIPAL ERRORS OF PREVAILING METHODOLOGIES
IN TALMUDIC HISTORY

Let me now generalize from these two examples. I focus discussion on the concrete errors that render useless for historical purposes nearly all work on the Talmud, with the two exceptions specified earlier, namely, interpretation of Talmudic texts in historical context, typified by Wasserstrom's splendid article, and study of Talmudic institutions in historical reality, exemplified by that of Goodblatt. The bulk of the articles in <u>Zion</u>, as well as elsewhere, have taken for granted that the numerous specific stories concerning what given rabbis and other Jews actually said and did under specific circumstances -- on a given day, at a given place, in a given setting -- tell us <u>exactly the way things were</u>. I speak, then, of a species of the genus, fundamentalism.

The philological fundamentalists have generally supposed that once we have established a correct text of a rabbinic work and properly interpreted its language, we then know a set of historical facts. The facticity will be proportionately greater the earlier the manuscript and the better its condition. These suppositions are correct. But these facts will concern <u>only</u> what the compiler of the text wished to tell us. Whether or not the original text was veracious is to be settled neither by textual criticism nor by philological research, valuable though both of these ancillary sciences are for the historical inquiry.

The fundamentalists further suppose that any story, whether occurring early or late in the corpus of rabbinic literature, may well contain valuable information, handed on orally from generation to generation, until it was finally written down. I cannot accept the unexamined opinion held in rabbinical circles, both scholarly and traditional, that all rabbinical material was somehow sent floating into the air, if not by Moses, then by someone in remote antiquity (the Men of the Great Assembly, the generation of Yavneh); that it then remained universally available until some authority snatched it down from on high, placed his name on it, and so made it a named tradition and introduced it into the perilous processes of transmission. By this thesis nothing is older than anything else: "there is neither earlier nor later in the Torah."

Synoptic studies of the traditions of Yohanan b. Zakkai and of the Pharisees before 70[5] indicate that versions of a story or saying appearing in later documents normally are demonstrably later than, and literarily dependent upon, versions of the same story or saying appearing in earlier documents. This is important, for it shows that what comes late is apt to be late, and what comes in an early compilation is apt to be early. Admittedly, these are no more than probabilities -- extrapolations from a small number of demonstrable cases to a large number in which no demonstration is possible. But at least there are grounds for such extrapolation.

I therefore suggest that the fundamentalists' convictions about the nature of the historical evidence contained in the Babylonian Talmud are likely to be false. Whether true or false, the primary conviction of fundamentalism is that the story supplies an accurate account of what actually happened. It is difficult to argue with that conviction. A study of rabbinic sources will provide little, if any, evidence that we have eyewitness accounts of great events or stenographic records of what people actually said. On the contrary, it is anachronistic to suppose the Talmudic rabbis cared to supply such information to begin with. Since they did not, and since they asserted that people had said things of which they had no sure knowledge, we are led to wonder about the pseudepigraphic mentality. By the time we hear about a speech or an event, it has already been reshaped for the purpose of transmission in the traditions. It is rarely possible to know just what, if anything, originally was said or done. Sometimes we have an obvious gloss, which tells us the tradition originated before the time the glossator made his addition. But knowing that a tradition was shaped within half a century of the life of the man to whom it was attributed helps only a little bit. It is very difficult to build a bridge from the tradition to the event, still more difficult to cross that bridge. The fact is that the entire Babylonian Talmud is a completely accurate record of the history of those who are responsible for it. But the specification of those people, the recognition of the viewpoint of a particular group, place, and time to which the Talmud's various facts pertain -- these remain the fundamental task still facing us.

V

TOWARD A RECONSIDERATION OF APPROPRIATE METHODOLOGY

I now wish to offer an alternative set of problems and solutions, a program of inquiry in my judgment more appropriate to the sources under study and to the sort of information we may ask those sources to supply us. In order to offer such a fresh program, I naturally have to begin at the beginning. Let us start with the character of historical study -- the field of history itself, the place of Talmudic history within the historical field. History is the noun, the genus, Talmudic history the adjective, the species. Before we can deal with the species, we surely must first attend to the genus.

A subdivision of the vast realm of historical learning marked off solely by information contained in a particular book finds the definition of its program and tasks in the pages of that book. The field of historical study bearing the adjective "Talmudic" covers the age in which the Talmudic canon took shape and to which it refers. That field of history attends to the places in which the people of that document flourished. So the time and place conform to the limits set by the principal source of historical study. The boundaries of topics, too, fall within the bindings of one book. Now to those who study other realms of historical learning, the one at hand must appear artificial, merely theological. In general people define a range of historical inquiry through limits posed by geography, political change to denote beginnings and endings, surely in addition national or ethnic traits that include some and exclude others. More to the point, the pertinent historical information will derive from many different sources, not from a single book. Accordingly, anyone opening a book of history will find puzzling the particular sort of historical study under way here. Specifically, such a person will ask what sort of history may bear the adjective "Talmudic," as distinct from "American," "medieval," or "African," thus national, chronological, or regional, not to mention economic, social, or political. Indeed, who has ever heard of a field of historical study defined by a particular book, unless it is what is in the book that is studied, e.g., constitutional history or the history of New England as seen through Cotton Mather's sermons!

By "the Talmud," all agree, we mean the entire canon of writings of the Jewish sages of Babylonia and the Land of Israel ("Palestine"), a canonical corpus beginning with the Mishnah, closed at ca. A.D. 200, and ending with the Talmud of Babylonia, completed at ca. A.D. 600. These documents to be sure refer to events spread over a longer period of time, specifically from the creation of the world onward to the end of history. They cover, in their scope of commentary, things that are supposed to have happened throughout much of the known world of their day. But in chronology, the account becomes particular to the first-hand knowledge of its authors and editors at ca. A.D. 70 or so, and, in geographical area, it covers the affairs of the Jews in the specified provinces, the one under Iranian, the other under Roman, rule.

In all, Talmudic history cannot be said to deal with great affairs, vast territories, movements of men and nations, much that really mattered then. Even the bulk of the women and men of Israel, the Jewish nation, in the time of the composition of the canonical writings at hand, by the testimony of the authors themselves fall outside of the frame of reference. Most Jews appeared to the sages at hand to ignore -- in the active sense of willfully not knowing -- exactly those teachings that seemed to the authors critical. To use the mythic language, when God revealed the Torah to Moses at Mount Sinai, he wrote down one part, which we now have in the Hebrew Scripture ("the Old

Testament"), and he repeated the other part in oral form, so that Moses memorized it and handed it on to Joshua, and then, generation by generation, to the contemporary sages. Now, to the point, the contemporaries of the sages at hand did not know this oral half of the Torah, only sages did, and that by definition. Only sages knew the whole of the Torah of Moses. So, it follows, the Talmudic corpus preserves the perspective of a rather modest component of the nation under discussion.

How could we define a subject less likely to attract broad interest, than the opinions of a tiny minority of a nation, about the affairs of an unimportant national group living in two frontier provinces on either side of a contested frontier? Apart from learning, from the modest folk at hand, some facts about life on the contested frontier of the ancient world -- and that was only the one that separated Rome from Iran, the others being scarcely frontiers in any political sense -- what is to be learned here that anyone would want to know must seem puzzling.

VI

LATENT AND MANIFEST HISTORY IN THE TALMUD

Self-evidently, no one can expect to find stories of great events, a continuous narrative of things that happened to a nation in war and in politics. The Jews, as it happens, both constituted a nation and sustained a vigorous political life. But the documents of the age under discussion treat these matters only tangentially and as part of the periphery of a vision of quite other things. But if manifest history scarcely passes before us, a rich and complex world of latent history -- the long-term trends and issues of a society and its life in imagination and emotion -- does lie ready at hand. For the Talmudic canon reports to us a great deal about what a distinctive group of people were thinking about issues that turn out to prove perennial and universal, and, still more inviting, the documents tell us not only what people thought but how they reasoned.

That is something to which few historians gain access, I mean, the philosophical processes behind political and social and religious policy, class struggle and popular contention. For people do think things out and reach conclusions, and for the most part, long after the fact, we know only the decisions they made. Here, by contrast, we hear extended discussions, of a most rigorous and philosophical character, on issues of theory and of thought. In these same discussions, at the end, we discover how people decided what to do and why. That sort of history — the history of how people made up their minds — proves particularly interesting, when we consider the substance of the story. The Jews in the provinces and age at hand adopted the policies put forward by the sages who wrote the sources we consider. The entire subsequent world history of the Jews -- their politics, social and religious world, the character of the inner life and struggle of their com-munity-nation -- refers back to the decisions made at just this time and recorded in the Talmud.

A further aspect of the character of the principal sources for Talmudic history, moreover, will attract attention even among people not especially concerned with how a weak and scattered nation explained how to endure its condition. The Talmudic canon bears the mark of no individual authorship. It is collective, official, authoritative. Now were it to hand on decisions but no discussion, that collective character would not mark the literature as special. We have, from diverse places and times, extensive records of what legislative or ecclesiastical bodies decided. But if these same bodies had recorded in detail how they reached their decisions, including a rich portrait of their modes of thought, then we should have something like what the Talmud gives us.

But the points of interest scarcely end there. The Talmudic corpus stands in a long continuum of thought and culture, stretching back, through the biblical literature, for well over a thousand years. Seeing how a collegium of active intellectuals mediated between their own age and its problems and the authority and legacy of a vivid past teaches lessons about continuities of culture and society not readily available elsewhere. For their culture had endured, prior to their own day, for a longer span of time than separates us in the West from the Magna Charta, on the one side, and Beowulf, on the other. If these revered documents of our politics and culture enjoyed power to define politics and culture today, we should grasp the sort of problem confronting the Talmud's sages. For, after all, the Talmud imagined as normative a society having little in common with that confronting the sages -- isolated, independent, free-standing, and not -- as the sages' Israel was -- assimilated in a vast world-empire, autonomous yet subordinate, and dependent upon others near and far.

VII
TOPICS FOR TALMUDIC HISTORY

Proceeding from the explanation of why the species Talmudic belongs in the genus history to the logical next question, we ask ourselves just what sort of history we may expect to compose. The Babylonian Talmud and related literature contain two sorts of historical information: first, stories about events occurring within an estate of clerks; second, data on the debates of those who produced the Talmud. How are these to be used for historical purposes? It is important to specify what those purposes are. We must at the outset recognize that there are many kinds of information we simply do not have, and never shall have, on Jews and Judaism in late antiquity. The Talmud contains very little information on such questions, for instance, as the nature of the inner life, the consciousness and personal hopes of Jews of the day. It has no autobiographical materials, no record of what people thought and felt as private individuals. No one person stands behind a simple sentence. All has been refracted through a shared prism. The whole is a public record, publicly redacted and communally, hence politically, transmitted. Few individuals play a manifest part in the redaction of their own thoughts, much less in their transmission. This seems to me a significant fact: autobiography, letters, the records of individual life are simply not present. It means at the outset that we cannot ask questions about the motives of individuals, their feelings and intentions -- the essence of historical inquiry. But there is, in compensation, the record of the collectivity of sages, and, as I have argued, that permits a remarkably contemporary kind of historical study.

Our information on various kinds or groups of Jews, moreover, is limited. The Talmud is not a historical document and was never intended as such. It is the record of the laws and logic, exegesis and episodic theology, of a relatively small group of Jews. One may estimate that about three hundred names of Babylonian Amoraim are mentioned, yet we may guess that a minimum of two hundred thousand, and probably more like half a million, Jews lived in Babylonia and Mesopotamia in Parthian and Sasanian times. Whatever judgments one may make about the rabbis' being "normative" or "more significant" than others are fundamentally theological, not historical. Moreover, when we take seriously the facts of rabbinical life -- that the rabbis lived within a relatively limited institutional framework, somewhat like the contemporary monastic communities of Mesopotamian and Babylonian Christianity -- we may wonder how far what we do know represents what we do not know. Whatever archaeological data we have of the same place and period -- the Dura synagogue and the magical bowls -- bear little obvious relationship to what we learn in the Babylonian Talmud. So we cannot ask a great many questions about Jews who are other than rabbis, except in relationship to the rabbis themselves.

The third and most important specification is this: We must at the outset isolate and identify the viewpoint of the texts we study and attempt to separate ourselves from that viewpoint for the purposes of historical inquiry. As I said earlier, we must always wonder, Cui bono? Who is served? What interest advanced? If we neglect to do so, we simply repeat, in modern language, the viewpoint of our sources, rather than attempt to understand and evaluate that viewpoint. When, for example, we concentrate attention on the issues set by the texts, when we merely generalize in historical language the specific stories and ideas presented by the text, then we are doing little more than repeating what is before us in the same propagandistic, tendentious, and partisan spirit in which it was originally composed. This will not serve any useful purpose, for if all we hope for from history is to participate in the world-view of the documents that supply us with information, why study history at all? Why not remain in the tradition of the classical and modern exegetes, who may add their episodic philological hiddushim (artificial refinements, fictional distinctions that make no difference, and other artifices) but contribute nothing new and comprehend nothing more than they are told by the discrete texts they study?

What purposes then do we have in reading the Babylonian Talmud for the writing of history? It will not suffice, alas, to say we want to know just how things were. This is naive, since "things" encompasses information about trivialities as well as important matters. We must acknowledge at the outset the values and interests shaping our mind and imagination and isolate what we regard as important issues. We must criticize those values and interests. And then we may proceed to the historical problems. What we must seek to know is not just how things were, but just how those things were which interest us, and which the documents in their present state may reveal. What interests us is, naturally, a reflection of our, and not their, situation. So the we is decisive. And we who read the Babylonian Talmud for historical purposes are modern historians, who want to know things of no interest whatever to classical Jews, or who want to know the same things but in different ways, in ways congruent to our knowledge and understanding of all aspects of reality.

What I want to know, first, is how a community actually functioned: the dynamics of the relationships among various power-groups, and between those groups and the inchoate masses. In many ways my History of the Jews in Babylonia[6] is an essay not merely in historical knowledge -- though that lies at the foundation of everything historians do -- but an essay in power. What earlier interpreters saw as ethics I see as power. What they saw as objective and eternal truths I see as statements of a particular viewpoint, serving a particular group and its interest; statements reflecting the values and ideals, the imagination, of the special interest groups represented in the documents available to us.

Alongside concern for power is an interest in myth: namely, the stories people told, the beliefs they held, to verify and justify the power-relationships they experienced. Why did people do what they did? Earlier, I denied that we can investigate individual motivation. But we can ask many questions about ideas widely held, characteristics of specific groups; issues investigated by historians of religion: What were the beliefs that people referred to in order to understand and explain reality? What were the fundamental convictions about reality that underlay all their actions? How did they justify themselves to other people -- Israel, gentiles -- and before God? In line with my earlier emphasis on the record of the collective consensus of individuals, I further want to know what happened to many people so as to present as self-evident the mythic world at hand. How do we account for the formation of the consensus of myth and of power, expressed in a distinctive mode of powerful discourse, achieved in an iron consensus within the estate of the clerks, but then, among the nation at large.

These two, then, power and myth, represent the theoretical interests of our day, these and still a third -- function: How did things work? Granted the existence of power, the ability of some men to coerce others to say and do their will, either by force or, more amiably, by moving them through an internalization of values; and granted the knowledge of the imagination of those men and their community, knowledge of their mythic life -- granted these two, we ask ourselves, how did the system work? What defined adaptive behavior in such a power-structure? What sort of history took place? What institutions embodied the power and the myth, what programs carried them forward, what was their thrust and dynamism, and what were the events that at specific times and places embodied these abstract forces of power and of myth in historical facts?

These then are the questions in my mind as I do my work. I should confess that at the outset I could not have specified them. On the contrary, it was in response to the materials I found pertinent to my History that I began to discern what I wanted to know. I began with chaos, the chaos of the texts and of my own limited historical understanding. Whatever order and sense emerged came forth unanticipated and uninvited.

VIII
FOUNDATIONS OF TALMUDIC HISTORY

But does the Babylonian Talmud serve to answer these questions, and if so, how? What are the principles of historical knowledge by which I can justify historical results? First, it seems to me important to form a view of the whole, rather than to allow oneself to be paralyzed by the exegesis and eisegesis of the discrete texts within the whole that historians supposed were historical, primarily because of their contents and themes. Earlier historians of the Talmud took for granted that what a man was said to have done is what actually was done. What was attributed to him is what he really said. What people claimed happened actually took place. And the record before us is the accurate, detailed, account of what _really_ was said and done. The legal scholar or textual exegesis is interested in the content of the texts; it would not matter to him whether a man _really_ said what is attributed to him, for he wants only to know the legal principles at issue and to trace the rabbis' discussion of those principles through legal literature. The literary critic -- and the classical scholars produced brilliant literary criticism of a kind -- takes at face value the text before him. He so concentrates on the meaning of words and sentences and their relationships to other words and sentences, that he cannot but accept their content as true. The exegesis and explication of texts, whether by Talmudists or by Biblical scholars, in the very nature of things, tend to produce a fundamentalist spirit.

But if it is time to attempt a critical characterization of the whole, not merely a gullible reprise of suggestive parts, what to characterize? Here, as I said earlier, we need to locate questions both pertinent to our own imagination _and_ appropriate to the Talmud. These questions obviously could not concern what the Talmud purports to tell: Was Aqiba really ignorant until he was forty? Did Rabbah b. Nahmani really get taken up to heaven because his Torah was needed in the heavenly academy? On the other hand, the Talmud does accurately tell what those responsible for compiling it thought about the world around them. It contains substantial materials given _en passant_, not in a polemical or tendentious spirit. For example, it preserves numerous reports of what rabbinical courts decided in specific cases. These seem to me to possess great historical value, for, while we may never know whether such a decision was actually made on a given day concerning a given litigation, the fact that the tradents certainly believed such decisions _could_ be made is of some sociological interest. The shape of such beliefs, after all, cannot have greatly diverged from the configuration of everyday life, if no polemical or theological interest intervenes.

While the beliefs of the rabbis about times past may be of slight consequence for the description of those times, the belief of the rabbis about what they themselves did every day in their courts seems to me very important in analyzing what the courts actually did. So I do not know whether a man named Samuel really decided thus-and-so in court. But I think the conviction of the generation and school responsible for shaping the story that he had done so accurately portrays how _they_ saw things, and therefore provides us with valuable information on how they viewed the state of their courts and the range of their authority and power. And if, further, we find evidence of a consistent picture, extending for several hundred years, we may then conclude that the courts in general could accomplish pretty much what the rabbis claimed in their behalf. If a picture of an effective court-system emerges, we may then proceed to speculate on the basis for the ability of a group of men to force others to do what they wanted. Obviously, we must take into account not only how the rabbis explained things, but also the facts known to us from quite separate sources of information. In the case of Babylonian Jewry, we need to know about the policies of successive Iranian governments toward the minority communities and their government, and also about other groups and institutions within the Jewish community likely to be able to exercise authority, which are not described in much detail in rabbinical sources.

When it comes to the mythic life of the rabbinical group, we are on still firmer ground, for the Talmud is a rich resource for information on how the rabbinical circles in particular viewed reality. Here again, we may well have the record only of the final period of Talmudic literature. Only through specific and careful investigation can we distinguish what is peculiarly characteristic of the last group of Talmudic tradents and redactors, and what also characterized earlier groups in sequence.

IX
THE PROMISE AND PROSPECTS OF TALMUDIC HISTORY

What will persuade someone primarily interested in historical study, rather than in continuities and changes in culture and society, that the document at hand demands sustained attention in particular as a problem for historians? It is the simple fact that the Talmud provides a striking example, for close analysis, of a problem of acute interest in historical debates even in our own day. I refer to the debates on how we study not the individual but human societies, organized groups, that engage historians from the Annales of the 1920s through Social Science History today. Let me explain.

In describing and interpreting the life of peoples, we seek to generalize about attitudes and shared conceptions, using the French word, "mentalité," for example, to explain that about which we speak. Specifically, we want to know how people form a shared conception of themselves, so as to see themselves as a group, and how, further, what they conceive in common relates to how they each, as individuals, confront and experience life. Louise A. Tilly, writing on "People's History and Social Science History"[7] frames matters in terms of shared emotions and, citing Lucien Febvre, founder, with Marc Bloch, of the Annales, quotes Febvre as follows:

> [Emotions] imply relations between men, collective relationships. They are doubtless born within the organic depths specific to a given individual... [B]ut their expression is the result of a series of experiences of common life, or similar and contemporaneous reactions to the shock of identical situations and encounters of the same nature... [L]ittle by little... by linking many participants in turn as initiators and followers -- [these] end by becoming a system of interindividual motivations that differ according to circumstances and situations... [and] a true system of emotions is built. They become something like an institution.

Febvre copes with the deep problems of how peoples' emotions so take shape as to fit a common pattern. That is why he speaks of experiences of common life, identical situations, encounters of the same nature. Now if we take up the same issue framed in terms not of feelings but of the ideas and doctrines that give expression to attitudes and feelings, we find ourselves raising exactly the same questions. The thesis at hand, that collective relationships expressed through mutually comprehensible emotions emerge, not from what is specific to the given individual, but from what is shared and common, becomes all the more pertinent. Specifically, we take up the social expression of attitudes. We turn then to matters of doctrines and institutions, and issues of governance of groups based on a compact of common values. These all together constitute politics, for the secular world, and theology, for the religious one. In the setting of Judaism, with its interest in what people do as much as in what they think, the whole reaches the surface of everyday life in what we call halakhah, the rules and laws of life. If, then, we can trace the context of consensus and the progress through which consensus is achieved, we find ourselves providing an exceptionally suggestive example for the inquiry into the interplay between the individual and the group, specifically the formation of collective attitudes out of individual experiences.

In the Talmudic corpus we have the end result of half a millennium of the process of attaining concurrence, the achievement of what was at first a caste and class consensus but what was at the end a national compact and agreement. Israel, the Jewish people, in late antiquity produced a minority, the sages under discussion, which to begin with coalesced on its own, and then won adherence to its views, through coercion and persuasion alike, among the nation as a whole. So when we ask what sort of history we may expect from the sources at hand, we find a remarkably relevant sort of discourse. We deal with an example of the long-term formation of collective doctrine, social theory shared among people in diverse times and places, subject to transmission, moreover, from the special circumstances in which the theory took shape to distant and wholly other conditions confronted by the Jewish nation later on. The sources at hand come down from late antiquity because people agreed to copy and preserve them. They came to that agreement because what they found in the sources laid claim to truth and authority. The fundamental thesis of the sources attained that status of utter self-evidence that made possible debate on everything but the fundamental issues. These were settled in late antiquity. Where, when, how they were settled, what sort of "experiences of common life, of similar and contemporaneous reactions to the shock of identical situations and encounters of the same nature," in Febvre's language, produced these components of a common consensus and endowed them with self-evidence -- these are the issues at hand.

In the conditions of contemporary debate on the nature of historical study, the interest in generalization and the analysis of collectivities, the concern for comparison of group to group, the interest in small details and how these typify large trends, the concern for politics and the influence of ideology -- in these conditions the Talmudic historian finds remarkably relevant what in itself is remote, particular, and rather special. What we have is a collective biography of a well-organized political and religious estate. But the constant reference to individual opinion characteristic of the sources at hand allows for attention to the individual as well. The vigorous debate, the close study of modes of argument as much as of substance, likewise allow us to address the formation of shared modes of thought. Self-evidence, in the documents at hand, is not conferred by politics alone but achieved by argument. Professor Tilly concludes her article with the following words:

> The genius of social science history is twofold. First, its central method -- collective biography of one kind or another -- preserves individual variability while identifying dominant social patterns. Second, its focus on social relationships rather than psychological states remains our surest guarantee of reconstructing how ordinary people of the past lived out their days and made the choices that cumulate into history. Social science history, properly conceived, is the ultimate people's history.

So far as we wish to trace collective biography, our documents exemplify precisely the sort of sources that make that work feasible. So far as we take up the issues of social relationships, both within a social group and also between that group and the outsider, the sources of the Talmudic canon address precisely the issue at hand. That is why I claim that, by criteria of contemporary historical debate, the kind of history that bears the adjective "Talmudic" and that emerges from a rather circumscribed body of sources indeed falls smack in the center of historical learning today.

X

MY OWN PROGRAM

Let me close with a few remarks about how I have tried to carry out the program outlined here. Since my work has never been read and reviewed in this particular setting -- in Zion, I mean -- or indeed in any other journal in this important center of Jewish learning, it is surely appropriate to introduce it to people who do not know it.[8] My work began with precisely the methodology I have rejected, with a history of the Jews in Babylonia and some parallel studies, all of which rest upon the givens that the sources mark the beginning of study, not the focus, and that their facts define the task at hand.

From all that has been said, the reader will realize that there is not a page, not a paragraph, not a sentence in my early books that I could write today exactly as I did twenty-five or even fifteen years ago. The very fundamental category at hand -- "the Jews in Babylonia" -- yields a program that stands entirely asymmetrical with the characteristics of the sources. The division by particular periods, for instance, is simply implausible. In order to speak of "the Parthian period" or "the early Sasanian period," I have to take for granted that stories told about events before the rise of Sasanian rule, in the early third century, really took place in the time and circumstances in which the story teller narrates them. What is attributed to rabbis of the period before 200 really was said, before 200, by those rabbis. None of this has been or can be either demonstrated or disproved. And, it goes without saying, in those early studies everything Josephus tells us is fact, pure and simple. But Josephus was not eye-witness to the stories cited here, and we do not know how he found out about these events. To state matters simply, I here assume as data for the composition of manifest history what in fact serve as constituents for that very different, latent history I described earlier.

More to the point, the sources at hand -- stories and sayings -- cannot be read distinct from the documents that contain those sources. We begin from the whole and work back to the parts. We start with, not the Jews in Babylonia in Parthian or Sasanian times, but Josephus, the Mishnah, the Tosefta, the Talmud of the Land of Israel ("Yerushalmi") and the Talmud of Babylonia ("Bavli"). Let me state with appropriate emphasis. Each of the components, the documents, of the Talmudic canon requires attention as a whole and on its own terms. And if we pay attention to the documents, we shall not find interesting the remnants and shards that these documents contain on the history of the Jews in Babylonia in Parthian times. The documents tell their own story. It is to that story that we must teach ourselves to listen. The documents (except for Josephus) constitute artifacts of culture, testimonies to the inner life of people who expressed their consensus through them -- facts of politics, indicators of collective doctrine and dogma, expressions of a small community of clerks and their imagination.

So I think it quite correct to say that we need to find out just what happened, what came first and what came afterward. But what happened is not what I described, analyzed, and interpreted in my earlier books. It is the documents that constitute the principal events: social events, cultural and intellectual events. The history must then be the history of the cultural life of a well defined social group and its encounter with the politics and condition of the larger nation of which it formed an active and aggressive component. When we know how the community of sages framed its ideas in the context of its historical and social setting, we shall have learned from the books that community endorsed and transmitted precisely the kind of history they allow us to recover. And, as I argued at the outset, that is exactly the sort of historical inquiry that in our own day proves urgent and compelling.

Let me conclude by referring to the two trilogies that bring to fruition twenty years of reflection and further study of exactly the same texts and problems of historical description, analysis, and interpretation, on which I worked at the outset.

These are, first, the trilogy on the reading of each of three individual documents as historical testimonies: Judaism: The Evidence of the Mishnah, Judaism in Society: The Evidence of the Yerushalmi and Judaism and Scripture: The Evidence of Leviticus Rabbah (all: Chicago, The University of Chicago Press, 1981, 1983, and 1985, respectively). Second is the trilogy in which, reading documents as a whole on critical issues, I carry out the first work of stage-by-stage restoration and renewal: Foundations of Judaism: Method, Teleology, Doctrine, as follows: I. Midrash in Context: Exegesis in Formative Judaism, II. Messiah in Context: Israel's History and Destiny in Formative Judaism, and III. Torah: From Scroll to Symbol in Formative Judaism (all: Philadelphia, Fortress Press: 1983, 1984, and 1985, respectively). The double trilogy shows rather strikingly that Talmudic history enjoys prospects unimagined in its first century, the one that began with Geiger, Graetz, and Frankel, and ended with my History. So let the old -- whether in

Zion or in my History -- find its way as a model, not of what to do, but of what not to do. Alas, since most of the historical work on the documents at hand even now remains bound to the old ways, the claim that my History of the Jews in Babylonia marks the epitaph may appear premature. But in fact it is where things indeed did end, and it marks the point from which the future began.[9]

Notes

[1]My student, Paul Flesher, supplied the following footnote:

A list of all the articles of Talmudic History appearing in the journal, Zion, since its inception. I have divided the articles into two categories, General Talmudic history, and the use of the Rabbinic literature for the study of the second Temple period.

I.   Talmudic History

1.   E. Bickermann, "Notes on the Megillath Taanith," vol. 1.
2.   G. Allon, "How Yabneh became Rabbi Johanan ben Zakkai's Residence," vol. 3.
3.   M. Stein, "Yabneh and her Scholars," vol. 3.
4.   A. Kaminka, "Rabbi Johanan ben Zaccai and his Disciples," vol. 9.
5.   G. Allon, "Concerning the History of Juridical Authorities in Palestine during the Talmudic Period," vol. 12.
6.   E.E. Urbach, "Political and Social Tendencies in Talmudic Concepts of Charity," vol. 16.
7.   E.E. Urbach, "Halakhot Regarding Slavery as a Source for the Social History of the Second Temple and the Talmudic Period," vol. 25.
8.   M. Beer, "The Exilarchs in Talmudic Times," vol. 28.
9.   B.Z. Dinur, "The Tractate Aboth (Sayings of the Fathers) as a Historical Source," vol. 35.
10.   J. Florsheim, "The Establishment and Early Development of the Babylonian Academies, Sura and Pumbeditha," vol. 39.
11.   J. Geiger, "The Ban on Circumcision and the Bar-Kochba Revolt," vol. 41.
12.   Moshe David Herr, "The Causes of the Bar-Kokhba War," vol. 43.
13.   S. Safrai, "Kiddush Ha-Shem in the Teachings of the Tannaim," vol. 44.
14.   M.D. Herr, "Continuum in the Chain of Torah Transmission," vol. 44.
15.   Z.W. Falk, "On the Historical Background of Talmudic Laws Regarding Gentiles," vol. 44.
16.   A. Wasserstein, "Rabban Gamaliel and Proclus the Philosopher (Mishna Aboda Zara 3.4)," vol. 45.
17.   D. Goodblatt, "New Developments in the Study of the Babylonian Yeshivot," vol. 46.

18.   I. Gafni, "On D. Goodblatt's Article," vol. 46.

19.   O. Irsai, "R. Abbahu said: If a man should say to you 'I am God' -- He is a Liar," vol. 47.

20.   B. Rosenfeld, "The Activity of Rabbai Simlai: A Chapter in the Relations Between Eretz Israel and the Diaspora in the Third Century, vol. 48.

21.   R. Kimelman, "The Conflict Between the Priestly Oligarchy and the Sages in the Talmudic Period (An Explanation of PT Shabbat 12:3, 13C = Horayot 3:5, 48C))," vol. 48.

II.   The Use of Rabbinic Literature for the Study of Second Temple Times

1.   G. Allon, "The Attitude of the Pharisees Toward Roman Rule and the Herodian Dynasty," vol. 3.

2.   I.F. Baer, "The Historical Foundations of the Halacha," vol. 17.

3.   I.F. Baer, "On the Problem of Eschatological Doctrine During the Period of the Second Temple," vol. 23-24.

4.   I.F. Baer, "The Historical Foundations of the Halakha," vol. 27.

5.   J. Amir, "Philo's Homilies on Fear and Love in Relation to Palestinian Midrashim," vol. 30.

6.   Y. Baer, "Jerusalem in the Times of the Great Revolt," vol. 36.

7.   I.F. Baer, "The Service of Sacrifice in Second Temple Times," vol. 40.

Zion began in 1935. This study begins with volume one and ends with number 3 of volume 48 (1983). The total number of articles in these volumes is 476.

[2]We note that no articles on the period from ca. 70 to ca. 640 deal with any topic outside of Talmudic history, as defined in Flesher's catalogue in n. 1. So Talmudic history is the only history of the Jews as a group in the period at hand on which Zion published articles as all.

[3]I omit reference to Sinai, which in no ways strikes me as a journal responsive to the critical agenda of modern scholarship. That is not to say a handful of articles of scholarly quality have not been printed there. But Sinai serves a learned constituency out of all relationship to academic learning as it is practiced in the West and may be ignored in the present context. Tarbiz presents a separate set of problems entirely and requires analysis in its own context.

[4]I return to this matter below.

[5]Development of a Legend. Studies on the Traditions Concerning Yohanan ben Zakkai (Leiden, 1970: E.J. Brill) and The Rabbinic Traditions about the Pharisees Before 70 (Leiden, 1971: E.J. Brill) I-III.

[6]Leiden, 1965-1970: E.J. Brill, I-V.

[7]Social Science History, 1983:7, 458.

[8]I call attention to the forthcoming Hebrew translation by Sifriat Poalim of my Judaism: The Evidence of the Mishnah (Chicago, 1981: University of Chicago Press).

[9]My student, Mrs. Judith Romney Wegner, made useful comments on this paper, for which I express thanks.

Part One
"JEWISH HISTORY"
IN THEORY

1. Michael A. Meyer
IDEAS OF JEWISH HISTORY
History and Theory 1975 14:212-226

IDEAS OF JEWISH HISTORY. Edited, with introduction and notes by Michael A. Meyer. New York: Behrman House, 1974. Pp. xiv, 360.

This anthology, compiled by Professor Michael Meyer of Hebrew Union College, presents various historical writings by Jews on events from the Maccabees to modern times. Half of the book deals with chronicles and histories of the last two pre-Christian centuries and the first eighteen centuries A.D., the other half with "philosophy of Jewish history" in the nineteenth and twentieth centuries. The selections in the first half are only episodically historical, e.g., II Maccabees and Josephus. More commonly, they present fables and stories, moralistic and pseudo-historical homilies, and other raw materials unrefined into historical writing. The second, modern half, by contrast, wholly shifts the focus to philosophical and theological reflections on the meaning of Jewish history, "the suffering of the Jews," "the soul of Israel," "the preservation of Judaism through an historical approach," "the interpretation of Judaism through its history," "the fate and survival of the Jews," and similar religious concerns. The book closes with Leo Baeck's "Theology and History," as if to underline the primarily theological character of modern and contemporary Jewish historiography. Meyer's selections are organized in the following units: Hellenism and Apocalypticism; The Medieval Jew and History; Jewish Historiography of the Sixteenth and Seventeenth Centuries; Scientific Study of the Jewish Past; Nahman Krochmal; Heinrich Graetz; Simon Dubnow; Elder Historians of the State of Israel; and Three Diaspora Conceptions.

Clearly, "history" here is used in at least three ways, to mean, first, historiography as the writing of history, second, chronicles, the telling of homiletical stories about things which have happened, and third, theologizing or philosophizing about things which have happened; the latter differs from the second primarily in the philosophical pretensions of the moderns, who preferred to call themselves historians, rather than philosophical rabbis or theologians, and for whom scholarship was a mask for learned homiletics. But the problem confronting the anthologist of "ideas of Jewish history" is not primarily the disparate sorts of materials which fall under that rubric. It is to explain, analyze, and, if necessary, to defend the very doing of "Jewish history."

Before turning to Meyer's solution of the problem, let us spell out the conceptual difficulties to be worked out. The fundamental question, which Meyer does ask in his Preface and then carefully ignores in the shank of the book, is whether the Jews from Abraham to the present constitute an entity capable of presenting a single, unitary history. By the criteria to be adduced from the data conceived to form a normal historical unit, they do not. For that long period of time, the Jews have not occupied a single geographical area, have not spoken a single language, have not formed a single society, have not produced a single harmonious culture. Jews in limited areas and in finite periods of time, e.g., in medieval Europe or in the Islamic commonwealth, by contrast, did exhibit the sorts of social and cultural unities which permit the uncomplicated description of a single historical continuum. But, in those limited areas and times, the non-Jewish setting, which serves to demarcate "Jewish history," also presents equivalent coherence. The historian can describe important commonalities in medieval Christendom, or in classical Islam. We should not be surprised that, within those finite historical entities, Jews likewise should present verifiable and definitive traits, capable of sustaining the larger but limited conception of a single, unitary "Jewish history": the history of the Jews in Medieval Europe, or in America, or in classical Islam, for example. In that context, moreover, the Jews not only form a sub-group or clearly delimited community, but are defined within, and against, a coherent context. To be a Jew was a mode or aspect of a larger social and cultural life.

In social, economic, and political terms, however, it is difficult even to compare those social, economic, political, and cultural traits regarded as quintessentially and distinctively "Jewish" in one delimited setting with those universally understood as "Jewish" in some other; what made a person or a group "Jewish" in medieval Christendom, for example, bears virtually nothing in common with what made a person or group "Jewish" in Nazi Germany.

In more general terms, the Jews simply do not form the object of a single history in the way in which Britain or America or China defines an area of viable and coherent historical inquiry. The reason is not, it is to be stressed, merely the technical difficulty of learning the requisite languages, literatures, and histories pertinent to Jews from the time of the Egyptians, Babylonians, and Assyrians, to the twentieth century, though that formidable difficulty cannot be ignored. After all, historians of the Balkans or of the Middle East in medieval and modern times do learn many languages and the histories of discrete cultural groups ("peoples"). The reason is that the Jews have not had a single, continuous unitary history in the way in which Britain or America or China or even the Balkan peninsula has had a history. Historians normally are able to proceed on the assumption, whether based upon geographical, or political, or sociological, or cultural grounds, that they deal with a single entity which has had a unitary history, a history which an objective outsider as much as a contemporary participant is able to discern. Can an observer discern the elements of a common history among groups, called, to be sure, by a common name, from China to Britain, from the United Monarchy of David and Solomon to the United Jewish Appeal of New York?

Clearly, the Jewish historian of the Jews, intending, for reasons which will become clear later, to solve certain Jewish problems, thinks one can. That is why he will present us with a one- or multi-volume "history of the Jewish people from Abraham to the present." It is not common in such histories to be told exactly what constitutes the unifying datum or structure. That is why I ask whether an observer, who stands wholly outside the presuppositions of the Jewish faith (whether of gentile or of Jewish origin), is able to perceive those same unities and continuities as are taken for granted by believers. The participant in contemporary Jewish affairs, when he comes to write history, simply takes for granted the obvious and simple propositions that the Jews constitute a people, that that people is one people, that it has had a single unitary history, and similar conceptions. The historian who comes to analyze matters without the prior assumption that the Jews are a "people" (let alone a nation or a religious-nation or whatever) must take as his first task the justification of his historical agendum. It is on that basis that I think we have to distinguish between the historical observer of, and the participant in, "Jewish history." What is a problem to the one is a datum and established structure for the other.

The complexity of the problem of verifying, in ordinary data serviceable for any historical study, the construct, "Jewish people," may have parallels in the study of other histories, but I cannot think of what they may be. (That is not to suggest that the "Jewish people" or "Jewish history" is "unique.") Part of the problem, of course, is the immense period of time covered by "Jewish history." The few equivalent groups presently surviving from ancient times and flourishing do not present equivalent complexities. Chinese history begins long before the formation of ancient Israel. But it took place in a single geographical area, for one thing, and finds coherence in other ways as well. The history of Iran and the Iranians is characterized by remarkably unified cultural, not to mention geographical, traits, beginning with a language exhibiting a unitary continuum, with important stages and expansions, to be sure. The geographical setting of Iranian history expands and contracts, but Persepolis has always been Iranian, while Jerusalem has not always been Jewish. Another ancient and still flourishing people, a continuous history of which can be and has been written, is the Armenians, only a little less ancient than the Israelites. The Armenians, however, cannot be adduced as contrary evidence. If we are able to perceive as a continuum the history of the Armenian people, it is because, throughout their history in the Middle East, whether in Ararat or at the Bosporus or the Gulf of Alexandretta, the Armenians did speak Armenian, did constitute an identifiable ethnic group with a single set of social, cultural, economic, religious, and political characteristics. For the Jews to present an appropriately continuous counterpart, they should have had to have spoken Hebrew as their domestic language throughout their history, for example. From the Babylonian exile in 586 B.C. onward, the Jews have never used a single language in common.

Judeo-German, Yiddish, Judeo-Aramaic, Judeo-Arabic, Judeo-Persian, Ladino -- these undeniably Jewish languages admirably illustrate the ambiguity of the notion of "Jewish history." Each is "Jewish" in the context of the discrete language-system in which it was formed. But only traits common to all of them will serve to tell us what is quintessentially, distinctively, and ubiquitously "Jewish." Those uniform traits add up to resort to some Hebrew words and the use of the Hebrew alphabet. That is hardly the same thing as the persistence of the Armenian language as the primary means of expression, both among the virtuosi and among the masses, for more than twenty-five hundred years. Since what is Jewish about Judeo-Persian and what is Jewish about Yiddish exhibit no common trait of any substance, certainly none which is not superficial, outside of Hebrew we can hardly speak of a "Jewish language" except in the context of the non-Jewish linguistic system which identifies a particular dialect as Jewish. I tend to think that in that fact the much larger and more difficult matter of "Jewish history" is exemplified. An observer, lacking prior religious or ethnic commitment -- for instance, the conviction that the Jews are indeed one people -- can therefore hardly be asked to take for granted, without analysis of a searching sort, elements of a common history among discrete and disparate groups, all of them called, each for reasons largely though not wholly endemic to its context, Jews.

A great many people, including the historians anthologized by Meyer, think, by contrast, that we can and should take for granted the facticity and givenness of "Jewish history" and "Jewish peoplehood." That too is a datum of history. But it is to be analyzed, not merely accepted. If the dispassionate observer does not perceive much that links the history of King David's time to the history of American Jewry, Jews from ancient times onward have perceived a continuum -- and much else. For they indeed possessed sacred writings which told them that they were "a people." Of greater consequence, they formed communities, speaking various languages and living in various places, which did exhibit important distinctive traits in common. Divided in many ways, they shared a common law. Speaking many languages, they communicated internationally and for sacred purposes in one, Hebrew. A single holy literature not only was possessed by all, but also shaped the values and the institutions -- religious, social, and economic -- of all the discrete groups called Jewish. To the degree that this is so, one indeed can conceive of a single, unitary "history of the Jews." But it is, in particular, the history of those aspects of the disparate populations characteristic of them all. For long periods of time, moreover, that history would cover virtually all of the affairs of the Jewish group. When the Jews were both separate from the societies in which they were located and characterized by distinctive and international, or intercultural, traits of substance and importance, then a unitary history was possible. True, there might be significant local variations. The political settings of French Jewry and that of German Jewry in the time of the Crusades, for example, were quite different. The latter suffered grievously, the former little, if at all. So in writing the history of European Jewry in the Middle Ages, we should have to take account of regional variations, just as in writing the history of France or Germany in medieval times, we routinely take account of variations in political events, and structures.

Yet having conceded that much, we have surrendered nothing of our original contention. European Jewry in medieval times indeed constitutes a unitary social and cultural entity. But how is it linked, except in point of presumed origin, to the Jews of Palestine in the time of the Maccabees, for one example, or to the Jews of modern Britain and America? If we agree that we must begin with origins, then the history of the United States cannot be written without telling about the histories of the various peoples who came to the United States. So we must begin not with the Anglo-Saxons, but with Adam and Eve. American history no more begins in the forests of Central Europe of the eighth century than does the history of medieval Jewry begin in the wastes of Sinai in the eleventh century B.C. (to be sure, no more, but also, no less). But it is that longer, more encompassing continuum which is perceived, indeed insisted upon, by Jewish historians of the Jews. No "history of the American people" begins with the Iron Age, but every "history of the Jewish people" begins at Sinai -- if not when Abraham left Chaldea (as if that were an historical event!). The Jewish historians of the Jews therefore claim far more than that for particular periods of time, however long, and over specific geographical areas, however large, the Jews did (and do) form distinctive groups, the events among which do add up to a coherent history. For that much larger claim, it is difficult to find much support.

For the mere fact of a common Scripture proves little. The vastly different ways in which the Scripture has been understood, interpreted, and applied, must be taken into account. A unitary culture, let alone a single social or political entity, has not been generated by Scripture -- either among Christians or among Jews. It is at this point in the argument that the proponents of "Jewish history" introduce a major variable, already alluded to: the viewpoint of the participant in that "Jewish history," wherever and whenever he lived. He knows he speaks a different language and thinks in a different way from that of his "forebears" or "ancestors." He concedes, moreover, that these ancestors do not come down to him through biological links of a verifiable order, though it is known that East European Jews do form a single genetic pool. But, looking backward, he claims to perceive or feel a commonality of faith, a community of interdependence, just as, looking outward from the local community of America, Britain, or Argentina, he perceives himself to be part of an international community of fate. For contemporary times, that surely is a secular, verifiable fact. One does not have to believe that Jews are a people to see that fact. Less than three decades ago, all Jews, wherever they lived, were thrown into a single, disastrous category: the doomed. And one third of them indeed were killed for sharing what for many was not a very important trait: a single Jewish grandparent.

But do links of sentiment or belief, defined in contemporary terms, bind together the discrete data of Jewish societies and cultures, past and present? Not, I think, if these data exhibit no congruence, no common traits of any sort, other than the adjective "Jewish," meaning remarkably different things to different people in different settings. If we restrict the definition of a historical entity to this-worldly traits perceived, by both the participant and the objective historian, to be present, important, and distinctive, then how shall we concede that there was, or is, a single Jewish "people" or history from Abraham onward? What is it that forms the subject of that integrated historical investigation? If it is a common "sentiment," then it is the history of that common sentiment -- I mean, religion -- which can be investigated, together with the effects of that single conviction, or set of convictions, over a remarkably long time and in exceptionally diverse settings. The history of a single verbal formula or set of formulae, of a continuous, if continuously changing, perception of reality, surely is legitimate by the accepted criteria which serve to define an entity capable of sustaining historical investigation.

To put it more simply, while there is no single, unitary "Jewish history," there is a single (but hardly unitary) history of Judaism. The history of Judaism itself is extraordinarily complex, involving, as it does, the construction of definitions of "Judaism" capable of both defining and linking data spread over a long continuum. On the other hand, if by "Judaism" we mean "rabbinic Judaism," that form of Judaism shaped in the aftermath of the destruction of the Second Temple, A.D. 70, out of elements of the religion of Palestine before that time in a quite novel rearrangement, we do find a significant, continuous religious phenomenon. For rabbinic Judaism, consisting of the Hebrew Scriptures and the writings of the talmudic and later rabbis based upon those Scriptures, was shared by nearly all Jews, wherever they lived, from late antiquity to modern and contemporary times. That form of Judaism, moreover, reveals an amazingly consistent set of symbols and persistent myth, everywhere operative and universally formative of Jews' perceptions of reality. It is difficult to locate Jewish communities not subject to talmudic law and theology or responsive to its myth, though there were some. For example, the Jews of China and of the mountains of Southern Morocco seem to have based their religious life upon Scripture without the intermediation of the Talmud. To be sure, rabbinic Judaism fully took over a vast antecedent heritage, but in a form so thoroughly revised that its claim to continue the heritage of the Hebrew Scriptures and the religion therein is, speaking descriptively, exactly as valid as is that of the New Testament to constitute the completion and fulfillment of the Old.

If these observations are accepted, then it will follow that discussions of the "meaning of Jewish history," or "the nature of Jewish peoplehood," of "why the Jews are hated and the causes of Jewish suffering," "the soul of Israel," not to mention "the preservation of Judaism," "the significance of Jewish history," and "the teachings of Jewish history," have to be understood as fundamentally theological, and not historical, essays. For their ultimate topic is none other than that hoary problem, "Who is 'Israel'?" And no answer to that question is possible outside the realm of theology. Indeed, one viable description of "the history of the Jews" which would unify the discrete data of histories of various groups called Jewish under differing circumstances in different places would be the history of definitions of "Israel." Since the concept of "Israel" or "the Jewish people" functions in Jewish theology in ways analogous to "the Church" or "the mystical body of Christ" in Christianity, discussions of Jewish identity, translated into Christian terms, would fall into the category of ecclesiology. In like manner, "the meaning of Jewish history" is a Judaic way of phrasing eschatological issues, analogously argued within Christianity in terms of philosophical or theological, rather than of historical data.

In Meyer's anthology, the essays devoted to these theological issues are of two sorts, and the difference between them is suggestive. On the one side we have the pre-nineteenth century writers, few of whom raise so large and abstract a question as "the miracle of Jewish survival." The pre-modern reflections on the meaning of "Jewish history," with the exception of Solomon ibn Verga and perhaps David Gans, follow lines laid out by biblical historians, from the writer of Deuteronomy onward. "History" -- that is, "things that happen and have meaning" -- teaches lessons. The historian's task is to report what happened in such a way that the meaning of what happened -- the lesson of history -- is clear. Before modern times, ideas of Jewish history are, in the main, undisguised sermons, and the historian is, with exceptions, primarily a preacher. Solomon ibn Verga and David Gans, by contrast, diverge from this pattern, because, as Meyer makes clear, they are characterized by intellectual traits we associate with the moderns.

When we come to the nineteenth century, what changes is not the theological and homiletical purpose of historians, but the modes of thought and argument employed in the service of the faith. Now the sermons are disguised as scholarship and presented as fact. The historicistic method in Protestant theology proved deeply congruent to the polemical, theological agendum of the Jewish historians of the Jews. No longer telling pious stories, the historians wrote about "the developing idea of Judaism" or "a history of spiritual achievements." When, for example, Immanuel Wolf writes (ca. 1820) about the "spiritual content, the idea of Judaism," which is "the idea of unlimited unity in the all... contained in the one word YHVH, which signifies indeed the living unity of all being in eternity, the absolute being outside defined time and space," then we have nothing other than a venture into historicistic theology. What made the claim to do history compelling to the nineteenth-century theologians? It clearly was the superficially secular, positivist discourse made possible by historicism. The new "science of Judaism" was meant to solve "the Jewish problem" and to meet "an essential need for the Jews themselves." Its messianic purpose could not be more clearly stated than it is by Wolf: "The Jews must once again show their mettle as doughty fellow workers in the common task of mankind. They must raise themselves and their principle to the level of science, for this is the attitude of the European world. This attitude must banish the relationship of strangeness in which Jews and Judaism have hitherto stood in relation to the outside world. And if one day a bond is to join the whole of humanity, then it is the bond of science, the bond of pure reason, the bond of truth."

It is hardly surprising that the nineteenth-century Jewish historians of the Jews should have adopted historical language for the discussion of theological problems. This was, after all, characteristic of other German theologians. Furthermore, historicistic theology did not wholly impede the writing of first-class history. Major progress was made by theologian-historians, e.g., Zunz, Geiger and Graetz, both in theology and in history. What is remarkable is the persistence of historicistic-theological thinking among twentieth-century Jewish historians of the Jews, long after Protestant theological methods transcended historicism and developed quite new issues and questions. When, by contrast, we come to Meyer's twentieth-century sample, we find ourselves among historians still asking theological questions in historical language. They continue to answer questions of faith with the claim to speak of facts. What changes is that nonreligious historians, Marxists and Zionists in particular, now join the discussion, phrasing in a secular way the old questions about the meaning of "Israel" and the message of "Jewish history." That is a predictable change.

Yehezkel Kaufmann, for example, while admitting that "the history of Israel is part of general history," insists that "from historical laws alone it is impossible to explain the history of a people... The singular history of the people of Israel consists of a unique combination of two basic factors: the national and the religious." Kaufmann wrote these words in the 1920s as a critique of the militant secularism of Palestinian and European Zionism of that period. It was natural to take for granted the viability of the category everyone assumed at the outset of discussion: the people of Israel. He therefore found it unexceptional to phrase matters so: "The basic problem for historical inquiry is the phenomenon itself, which previously was not a problem at all -- the very nature of Israel's national particularity in the diaspora: Why did it not cease being an ethnic group...? What, therefore, brought it about that the people of Israel should be a single people despite its being scattered and dispersed among the nations?" I do not think Second Isaiah could have asked the question more vividly. Ben Zion Dinur, writing in 1958, chooses to clarify the following "fundamental points: 1. The unity of the nation. 2. The nature of the nation's unity in exile. 3. The nation's power of independent action in the Diaspora. 4. The reciprocal relations existing among the Jewish communities in the Diaspora. 5. The place of the Land of Israel in the life of the exiled nation." Of these five questions, only the third and the fourth are susceptible of a totally secular and descriptive analysis.

Nor should we ignore religious rhetoric -- or something that seems meant as pious blather -- produced by contemporary historians. Salo Baron writes, "The preponderant instinct among the majority, in any case, still perceptibly tells them that the Jewish religion, buttressed by the Jewish nationality, supernationally rooted in the Jewish religion, will weather the forthcoming storms, too, and that together they will continue their historic march into the unfathomable future." If we substituted supernaturally for supernationally, we should have an undisguised, instead of a thinly veiled, statement of religious faith. Not surprisingly, Ellis Rivkin, presenting "a radical new interpretation" of Jewish history, draws upon Deuteronomistic theology for his interpretation of "Jewish history": "The problems of Jewish history can be understood by means of the unity concept. For most of Jewish history, this concept was the affirmation that God was one and omnipotent." It is exceedingly difficult to know precisely what "problems of Jewish history" are to interpreted, let alone solved, in the light of "the unity concept." If this is not sheer gibberish (as I suspect), then it is historicistic theology (written in gibberish). While the author announces a "radical new interpretation," in fact his "new" idea would not have surprised Immanuel Wolf, who said the same thing in nearly the same words a century and a half earlier. Nor should that fact seem remarkable, since both writers on Jewish history, like many before them, simply restate the viewpoint of the Deuteronomic historians, as I said. Finally Leo Baeck is allowed the third and last "diaspora conception" of the idea of Jewish history: "The problem, through and on account of which Judaism in all of its particularity has become universal -- this specifically Jewish problem of world history -- is that of the incursion of the Infinite, Eternal, the One and Unconditional, into the finite, temporal, manifold and limited, and of the spiritual and moral tensions of the human fiber which is its result." Baeck, unlike the others, properly presents himself as a theologian, however, and so speaks of "the universal idea of Judaism" rather than "ideas of Jewish history." But Baeck remains within the historicistic framework and so appeals, in the end, to historical research in connection with theological reflection: "But it will be theology of Judaism... only if it seeks to comprehend and to realize out of that which is its own and out of the historical whole of Judaism what are its universal idea and its particular tradition, what constitutes its individuality in world history." Accordingly, the discussion of theological issues is linked to the description of a historical problem, namely, the "individuality of Judaism" in world history.

Obviously, much good work is done in the study of the history of the Jews in various places and under various circumstances. The sort of theologizing in historical language and rhetoric done by modern and contemporary Jewish historians of the Jews by no means comes from all historians working on topics pertinent to the Jews. On the contrary, the analysis of specific problems in the discrete histories of Jews, as of Judaism, is characterized by the expected detachment and secularity of historical sciences in general. The grand-scale "philosophies of Jewish history" have virtually no impact upon historians working on medieval or modern Jewry in Europe, the history of Zionism and the State of Israel, let alone of the Jews and Judaism in antiquity, to name three well-developed themes of scientific inquiry. The issues important to the ideologists are quite properly excluded.

The "ideas of Jewish history" to which Meyer devotes the second half of his anthology are important components in the formation of such religious discourse as takes place, on the other hand, among those Jewish intellectuals who are neither theologians nor historians. They are, rather, unselfconscious ideologues of another order, ideologues hoping to produce a non-religious and non-supernatural religion, a historicistic theology in the service of a wholly contemporary, entirely unintellectual and unreflective cause. Since, however, Meyer quite properly avoids asking to whom are "ideas of Jewish history" important and by whom are they now taken seriously, we may refrain from commenting upon the shoddiness and triviality of contemporary intellectual endeavor of Western and Westernized Jews. Perhaps it is unfair to observe that rabbinical students seem to flourish in courses on "Jewish history," while university courses in Jewish studies tend to occur in departments of religious studies and Near Eastern studies, organized around the disciplines of history of religions or history of theology, on the one side, and philological and exegetical study of Hebrew texts, on the other. "Jewish history" would thus seem, in the main, an exercise in the education of believers.

Let us turn instead to Meyer's anthology and ask whether he has given us a well-formed and carefully crafted account of his problem. Fair criteria for assessing the worth of an anthology are clarity of purpose, readily discerned in each selection, and unity of conception, apparent throughout. That, in turn, depends upon an exceedingly careful statement of the problem or issue to which the anthology is devoted, on the one hand, and obvious connections between an introduction and the several selections.

To his credit, in his Preface Meyer carefully delineates the problem of his anthology, which is not the writing of history but philosophies of "Jewish history" formed by historians. He excludes Jewish theologians who have written on the meaning of Jewish history and limits himself "to the writings of individuals known principally for their work in Jewish history." This seems to me a wholly valid distinction. Further, Meyer stresses the religious or ideological setting of the historians' writing: "For modern Jews," he begins, "a conception of their past is no mere academic matter. It is vital to their self-definition. Contemporary forms of Jewish identity are all rooted in some view of Jewish history, which sustains them and serves as their legitimation." It would be difficult to improve upon this as a description and definition of the work of historicistic theology in Judaism. Meyer furthermore stresses the diversities of the data of the histories of the Jews: "The great diversity of their historical experience has enabled modern Jews, themselves representing a variety of Jewish identities, to choose particular strands as paradigmatic of their own form of Judaism or even to declare their Jewishness basic or normative for all ages past. But it has also raised serious questions regarding the totality of that past. How is it to be conceived as a whole?" Since this is an anthology, Meyer quite properly refrains from forming his own answer to that question. He prefers to focus attention on the question itself, which he presents as the organizing and unifying issue of the writings before us. "An understanding," he writes, "of Jewish ideas of history therefore requires nothing less than a history of those views beginning with the Bible and continuing down to contemporary historians. In my general introduction to the readings in this volume, I have attempted briefly to present such a history. It is intended to provide a survey of conceptual development over the course of time so that the major themes and problems -- those common to all ideas of history as well as those specific to the history of the Jews -- may be generally understood before they are examined within the context of individual writings." The Preface raises the central issue, therefore, and does so forthrightly. It promises the first major investigation of the central problem in the self-consciousness of modern Jewish intellectuals. It further tells us that everything will be made clear in the Introduction, then spelled out in the anthology itself. So much, so good.

All depends, therefore, upon Meyer's Introduction. Unfortunately, the excellent preface is henceforward forgotten. Now Meyer gives us, first, a superficial account of "basic issues" both common to all historians, and specific to Jewish historians. Epistemology is disposed of in one brief paragraph. Causality and "the goal of history" are given extended treatment. None of this has anything to do with the fundamental question of how one can conceive of "Jewish history" as a whole. Why to begin with should anyone have come to such a conception? The biblical historians, whose influence surely exceeds that of any others, receive two pages and are not anthologized. The main point is that they were religious: "They wanted to show from the experience of the past that God was faithful to his covenant..." Historians writing in Greek ("Hellenistic") do not fare much better. They too were bent on making religious points. From this point onward, Meyer passes his opinion on the work of each of the ancients. Josephus lacks "depth of insight" and does not know the difference between "a datum of major significance" and "one with little historical effect." But he improves on the biblical hitorians because "he draws causality into the sphere of the human and frees it from the religious drama of reward and punishment; he does not, however, display an awareness of causal complexity." So much for Josephus.

At this point we come to the work of the rabbis of the Talmud. Here I must flatly state that Meyer does not remotely understand their conception of, or response to, history. He recognizes that they possessed "a distinctly nonhistorical view of the past," but cannot explain it. Since little strictly historical writing is preserved in rabbinic literature, and nothing remotely resembling a history emerges, Meyer is simply unable to answer in their behalf the fundamental question, "How is it [Jewish history] to be conceived as whole?" Indeed, it is difficult to see that he has remembered he promised to ask that question. Medieval Rabbinic Jews, it goes without saying, continued the established pattern. That is to say, since they did not write histories, we are not told about their conceptions of history. To fill this immense (and deeply revealing) gap, Meyer turns to the writers of chronicles and genealogies. He tells us (12) that the rabbis of the Talmud did not write history (in part) because no one else did (which is false!): "The Sasanian and later Muslim civilizations were likewise basically uninterested in understanding the course of profane events (though the Muslims lavished much attention on genealogies), Jewish thinkers received no outside impetus to study their history beyond the biblical period." Meyer next (16) offers us as history Igeret Rav Sherira Gaon, a genealogy of the leadership of the Babylonian Jewish academies (!).

It should be clear that between the Preface and the Introduction, the focus of interest has shifted radically. The Preface, as I have shown, asks exactly the questions raised by the title of the book, namely, what are "ideas of Jewish history" and how are these spelled out and justified? The Introduction is primarily devoted, from the beginning to the sixteenth century, to the nature of historiography pertaining to the Jews -- an utterly different problem. As noted, Josephus is criticized as a working historian, and the medieval chronicles are analyzed as historiography, that is, in terms of how history was written. I think the reason is clear. Before Samuel Usque, Solomon ibn Verga, and other sixteenth- and seventeenth-century precursors of modern Jewish experience, there simply is no "idea of Jewish history" other than the one the Deuteronomic historians laid down in the seventh century B.C. All Meyer therefore examines is examples of how history was written.

To put it differently, the idea of "ideas of Jewish history" is peculiarly modern. Before the chronic crisis of identity generated in West European Jewry by political and social changes in the nineteenth century, and in East European, American, and Israeli Jewry by those same changes in the twentieth, few were sufficiently self-conscious to perceive something so abstract and philosophical as "Jewish history," and fewer still found it necessary to resort to an idea to confront the problem of "self-definition." So far as we find sixteenth- and seventeenth-century writers facing the problem of defining themselves though the mateials of history, we are apt to stand in the presence of people for whom the experience of modernization came sooner than was generally the case in northern, central, and eastern Europe.

Quite properly, therefore, Meyer returns to his original problem only when he reaches the nineteenth-century writers, for reasons which already are obvious. It is at that point that "history" becomes the arena for theological discussion, indeed, becomes the sole arena for those for whom the biblical-rabbinic framework of discourse is not open. Or, to put it differently, it is with the end of rabbinic Judaism as the sole formative construction of reality among Jews that we witness the beginning of another, self-conscious mode of thinking about history. All the more pity, therefore, that Meyer has not asked about the conception -- "idea" -- of Jewish history characteristic of rabbinic Judaism, ancient, medieval, and modern. He evidently assumes that because people do not write chronicles (or history, for that matter), they have no large notion of the meaning of events and do not care about "history." That is an apalling error in the understanding of rabbinic Judaism, but this is not the place to correct it.

Once Meyer does reach the nineteenth-century historicistic theologians, he is on firm ground indeed. Now the data present the requisite uniformity. The technical traits of historiography therefore fade away. But the issue inherent in the data is not the one stated in the Preface, namely, how can there be a single, unitary "Jewish history"? Rather a third range of questions, those of "philosophy of Jewish history," presupposing the viability of the structure, "Jewish history," emerges. For the last half of his Introduction, as for the last half of the anthology proper, Meyer is able to present a continuous and coherent account, everywhere discussing the same thing, as I said, philosophy of "Jewish history." In fact, the treatment of the nineteenth- and twentieth-century philosophers of "Jewish history" both in the Introduction and in the anthology proper leave nothing to be desired as an account of an interesting aspect of modern Jewish religious thought ("theology" is too limited in this context). Had Meyer given us this account of what I have called historicistic theologians and he calls philosophers of Jewish history (or simply historians), and had he in addition done so self-consciously and economically, rather than supplying a muddled discussion of theological conceptions of history, historiographical techniques and problems, and similar discrete topics, each with its own morphology, he would have edited a very good book indeed.

My sole major reservation in Meyer's Introduction to the nineteenth- and twentieth-century "historians" is his pretentious insistence on telling us what he thinks of each one, as though he has attempted to do what they have done. It is not very interesting to be told what Meyer thinks is "wrong" with Graetz, Dubnow, or Salo Baron. Further, his criticism invariably focuses upon historiographical issues, while the writings themselves are about philosophy of history. It is as if the editor wished to underline his own hopeless confusion.

In his defense, however, I point to the concluding paragraph of the Introduction, the only point in the entire book at which the first and most fundamental question about "Jewish history" is asked. Since I have stated my reasons for agreeing with what is to follow, I give him the last word:

> Finally, a word should be said about the difficulty of conceptualizing the Jewish history of our own time. The establishment of the State of Israel in 1948 has raised serious questions regarding the proper subject matter of Jewish history following that watershed event. Does Jewish history encompass all aspects of the history of the State of Israel, or only those which are also of significance to Jews outside its borders? Or does it henceforth limit itself to

Diaspora existence alone, declaring the history of the State of Israel "Israeli history"? Does an Israeli who feels no connection with Jews outside [the State of] Israel belong within the purview of Jewish history any more than a Jew who has converted to Christianity? These new questions relate themselves to the older one: What constitutes Jewish history in the Diaspora? Is it everything noteworthy done by Jews (sports, politics, etc.), or only what was done by Jews (or to Jews) because of their Jewishness? These questions have yet to be confronted seriously by Jewish historians. All that can be stated with certainty is that today Jewish existence stands bifurcated into the life of a political state with a large degree of cultural independence and the life of Diaspora communities for whom Jewishness constitutes only a portion of total identity. Any new comprehensive idea of Jewish history will have to encompass these two highly dissimilar forms of present-day Jewish life.

What Meyer states about the period after 1948 seems to me equally pertinent to long centuries before that date. Meyer thus ends his Introduction with the question with which he began his preface: "how is it to be conceived as a whole?" What he has not done, alas, is to center his attention on that one encompassing question, either in the Introduction or in the anthology itself. In all, therefore, confusing historiography and philosophy of history, he has not fully succeeded in working out a complex and subtle problem. He has botched the job.

Postscript (1984): In two successive academic years (1982-83, 1983-84) I gave a course, "The Idea of History in Judaism," in which we read Meyer's anthology. What I found on very close reading of the book is that it also is not a very good textbook, because the bulk of the materials (though by no means all of them) turned out to be inaccessible and dull. The literary quality proved wanting. The representation of Jewish historical writing in Talmudic times is incompetent; Meyer simply had no idea of what to select, so he presented nothing. The medieval writings are not of the same character or quality, but most of them were unreadable. They scarcely made important points. The two parts of the book that do work well turned out to be those on the biblical and on the modern periods in history-writing. That is hardly surprising, since those are the two points in the history of Judaism in which historical writing constituted an important vehicle of theological expression. But not grasping that at hand is nothing other than theological writing, Meyer could not explain, let alone unpack, the character of history-as-theology revealed in the texts he presented. So, in all, for teaching the work is hopeless. Confessedly, I am one of the very few readers and teachers to have taken the book at all seriously. My error was to ask so much of so little: "blessed are those who expect absolutely nothing, they shall not be disappointed."

2. Salo W. Baron
HISTORY AND HISTORIANS
Judaism 1966, 15:120-123

HISTORY AND HISTORIANS: ESSAYS AND ADDRESSES. By Salo W. Baron. Compiled and with a Foreword by Arthur Hertzberg and Leon A. Feldman. Philadelphia: Jewish Publication Society of America, 1964, 504 pp.

This volume contains thirteen essays by Salo W. Baron, professor emeritus of Jewish history at Columbia University, as follows: I. Essays in History, Who is a Jew; World Dimensions of Jewish History; Modern Capitalism and Jewish Fate; Emphases in Jewish History; Newer Emphases in Jewish History; II. The Historical Outlook of Maimonides; III. Jewish Historians and their Viewpoints, Azariah de'Rossi: A Biographical Sketch; Azariah de'Rossi's Attitude to Life; Azariah de'Rossi's Historical Method; I.M. Jost the Historian; Heinrich Graetz, 1817-1891, A Biographical Sketch; Graetz and Ranke, a Methodological Study; Moritz Steinschneider's Contributions to Jewish Historiography; Levi Herzfeld, the First Jewish Economic Historian. The book also contains very full notes and a useful index.

These essays are meant to exhibit Baron's thought on the craft of the Jewish historian and his ideas on the interpretation of Jewish history. That thought is of great importance, for Baron is the broadest and most productive Jewish historian since the beginning of the science of Judaism, and has far outclassed his predecessors, about whom he writes here. His magnum opus, The Social and Religious History of the Jews, exerts enormous influence among all academic Jewish historians, because in it Baron demonstrates how social scientific perspectives, if brought to bear upon the study of Jewish history, can widen the scope of its horizons and render it relevant, as the early, philologically oriented humanists were unable to do, to a comprehensive and serious audience. Baron holds, in both the History and in these essays, that the Jews have produced too varied and interesting a history to be studied in isolation from the cultures in which they found themselves. Having developed a hybrid culture under varied conditions, their affairs must be subjected to the broadest possible investigations. Without knowledge of the Gentile background, the Jewish historian produces little more than melancholy sermons. From the beginning of his scholarly career, Baron determined to do more than that.

In the second and third groups of essays, Baron traces the origins of a critical and dispassionate, non-theological approach to Jewish history. By drawing together Maimonides' incidental and casual remarks on history, he shows why he made no serious contribution to historical literature: Maimonides regarded history as a sheer waste of time. For him, the Jews were the center of creation, but the most interesting thing about them after the Bible was not their history, which bore no new lessons or imperatives, but their metaphysics and their law. Baron delineates a chain of historiographical tradition which extended from Azariah de'Rossi through I.M. Jost, Graetz, Steinschneider, to Herzfeld. De'Rossi laid the groundwork for critical history by subjecting sources, both Jewish and Gentile, to searching analysis. Three centuries later, Jost produced the first comprehensive treatment of Jewish history, believing that through historical research men might understand the processes of growth, life, and decay which underlie all reality. Applied to Judaism, this view meant that a new form of revelation will emerge in historical studies. Yet this same inquiry began with the renunciation of theological conviction. Imbued with faith in the omnipotence of the historian's method, Jost and his successors assumed that Jewish history, which would shape the future of Judaism, to warrant serious attention must share the historiographical naturalism and philosophical idealism of the general historians, without subjecting these presumptions to critical analysis. The result, for Graetz, was devotion to the doctrine of "historical ideas," which held that every period reveals dominant trends, determining the evolution of discrete stages. A single people might, therefore, be the valid subject for historical inquiry, and valid historical explanations could emerge from the study of internal factors alone. The Jews were treated not only as if they had spent forty centuries in antiseptic isolation from other cultures, but as if their fate alone proved consequential in any given age. Baron's essays reveal, therefore, that Maimonides' fundamentally anti-historical bias reemerged under historical colors. The alternative, represented by Steinschneider, was to lay such stress on the non-Jewish setting that the Jews cease to be seen as a distinct entity apart from the civilizations in which they participated.

While Baron, in his History and in the first group of essays here, lays great stress on the Gentile background, he insists that he writes about the history of one people's life under many circumstances. He has to find out what is different about the Jews to separate them from cultures in which their culture appears as a local nuance. Based upon classical paradigms, his answer is that the Jews possessed a "messianic religion of universal significance." This is a theological and not a naturalistic or social-scientific viewpoint. I am not certain that, given the peculiar character of Jewish history, a completely worldly answer is possible. In any case, since Baron does not, in the end, give one, it would be useful to examine his theological ideas, to see how he might systematically expound the religion which, he holds, provides the foundation for any conception of the Jews as one people. One will not find such an exposition in this book. If the essays exhibit a unity of conception, despite their varying styles and subject, the editors have not articulated it, and the reader is left to discover for himself the underlying structure of Baron's ideas, values, and methods. Baron says that Jewish history is important, and that it is a valid enterprise both as a science about a singular phenomenon and as a way of understanding, if tentatively, Jewish existence. He defends the historical enterprise against the criticism implicit in the neo-Orthodox reappropriation of the classical perspective, "What was, was" -- from which we are supposed to infer, "So what?" For him, history clearly possesses its own intrinsic interest and can yield, moreover, finite and provisional truths capable of illuminating the Jews' limited perception of their condition.

History need not yield theology nor claim to produce new revelation in a more than human dimension. This is implied, and occasionally aaserted, in these papers. It is nowhere fully articulated and defended through rigorous argument.

This book merely provides, therefore, a convenient collection of interesting and significant essays, by-products of the great productivity of their distinguished author. It does not help us to understand his assumptions and methods nor does the figure of Baron himself emerge by contrast to the subjects he studies. If he represents, as I suggested, a great turning point in the history of Jewish historiography, then a collection of essays on his predecessors ought to show explicitly how he has moved beyond the limits set by earlier generations, as he certainly has. We do not find out here. The compilers claim that these essays center on the "interpretation of Jewish history," but none of the papers, and certainly not the forewords, tell us what that interpretation consists of. They express the hope that these essays will further our understanding of Baron's method and conception of Jewish history. I do not see how they do, because nowhere are these made explicit. The essays are, as I said, intrinsically interesting and important; it is good to have them in a single volume, since they are thematically related to one another. But they do not constitute variations on a stated theme, nor have the editors greatly helped us to perceive just what it is about both Baron and Jewish history that we are supposed to learn here.

3. Ellis Rivkin
THE SHAPING OF JEWISH HISTORY
Conservative Judaism 1972, 26:87-90

THE SHAPING OF JEWISH HISTORY: A RADICAL NEW INTERPRETATION. By Ellis
Rivkin, New York: Charles Scribner's Sons, 256 pp.

Professor Ellis Rivkin, who teaches Jewish history at Hebrew Union College --
Jewish Institute of Religion, Cincinnati, here proposes a "philosophy of Jewish history" in
the grand manner. He does not present new facts, but claims to "rearrange, reallocate,
and restructure the data already known... to make intelligible the entire range and sweep
of Jewish history, and to expose all of its remarkable complexity as the working through
of a concept of the unity of all reality, which I call the unity concept." By this Rivkin
means the concept of "the affirmation that God was one and omnipotent." Admittedly,
the meaning of those words is diverse, but "all content and all forms, however diverse, fit
under the unity concept, which is simply the notion that reality, be it simple, complex, or
changing, is amenable to a unifying idea."

I do not understand why Rivkin calls "the unity-concept" a "radical, new interpretation," since that concept is a commonplace in Judaic theology. For example, a century
and a half ago, Immanuel Wolf wrote, "What is this idea that has existed throughout so
much of world history...? It is the idea of unlimited unity in all. It is contained in the one
word YHWH which signifies indeed the living unity of all being in eternity..." (Publications
of the Leo Baeck Institute, Year Book II, 1957, pp. 194ff.) Wolf wrote in 1822!

Rivkin treats the biblical period in a routine way, except that he sees the creation
of the Pentateuch as the result of "the revolution of the Aaronides." The "Pharisaic
Revolution" produced individualism, the concept of the twofold Law, as well as a scholar
class with authority over this twofold legislation. The Pharisees further developed new
concepts of God, "giving place to a yearning for intimacy long felt, but never... fully
realized." "Once this happens the external, empirical world ceases to be reality. It is a
temporary, transient, and unpredictable realm; callous, cruel, indifferent. How different
the reality within!" Rivkin sees the Babylonian gemara as a reflection of Sasanian society:

...Just as the intellectual world of the Sasanians was nonrational and disorderly
when compared with that of the Greeks and Romans, so the Babylonian
scholars appear nonrational and disorderly, when compared to the scholars of
the Mishnah. And just as disorder in the realm of ideas was compatible with
economic, social, and political order in the Sasanian world, it was compatible
with orderly reasoning in the world of Jewish law... The Babylonian Talmud is
characterized by disorder. Differentiated categories of law simply disinte-
grate... What I am maintaining is that if one wants to make intelligible the

reason why the Babylonian Talmud is so different in form and structure from the Mishnah, he must look at the form and structure of the Sasanian-Zoro-astrian world...

The medieval period is treated under the rubric "Medieval Ways to Salvation. Diversity in Unity." Here Rivkin rapidly surveys the rise of Islam, Karaism, the Golden Age in Spain; then the Christian side of things. Rashi is compared to Maimonides; the growth of Responsa is alluded to; then come remarks on the Zohar and Kabbalah, the Italian Jews in the Renaissance, the formation of Polish Jewry, and anti-Semitism. The rise of capitalism is traced in terms of the Marranos.

The last four chapters deal with Jewish emancipation in the context of modern and contemporary economic history. But the Jews scarcely appear in the last two chapters -- "The Road to Auschwitz: The Disintegration of Nation-State Capitalism," and "The Road from Auschwitz: The Emergence of Global Capitalism" -- which present a history of the cold war.

What are we to make of this strange book? First, it does not have a single note, a single reference to another scholarly work, a single effort either to place an argument in a scholarly context or to spell out an argument in terms of sources and contrary opinions. Since Rivkin claims to deal with data "already known," one may understand why he does not supply extensive argumentation, but then he ought to have told the reader how factual his facts are, and where they come from. In other words, this cannot be seen as a scholarly book at all, for the beginning of historical scholarship is discipline, exactness, respect for the achievements and opinions of others. I am dumbfounded by such self-indulgence as Rivkin's omission of all other scholars' ideas.

Secondly, the book cannot register as a really wide-ranging account of the history of the Jewish people, for its agenda is centered upon European Jewry, and upon the emancipated part of European Jewry at that. What is important, as in the old Wissen-schaft, is literature; the history of the Jews is dealt with in terms of the books they wrote (Bible, Talmud, Spanish poetry, mystical texts). But here the literature Rivkin cites is narrowly defined; again in nineteenth-century Wissenschaft terms. There is nothing about Apocryphal and Pseudepigraphic writings, except Ben Sira. The Dead Sea community is ignored (in deference to Solomon Zeitlin). One cannot call this "a radical new inter-pretation."

Third, while the book is written with great care, in my opinion more attention is paid to rhetorical sweep than to precise expression. We often come upon unnecessary verbosity and repetitiousness, as in the following: "The downtrodden trade off trust for the psychic reassurance of ideas saturated with fantasies of ultimate liberation. So it was with Christianity, again and again. So it was with Judaism, again and again. So it has been with Marxism, again and again..." etc. Rivkin competes with other inspiration "philosophers of Jewish history," such as Max Dimont and Charles Raddock, who aim at a religious response on the part of the reader.

Fourth, Rivkin promises to show how "the concept of the unity of all reality" makes Jewish history intelligible. But he (mercifully) ignores the concept through most of the book. It surfaces here and there, generally at the homiletical sections of the several chapters, but plays no important role in the actual analyses and narrative. I am left with the sense that "the unity of all reality" is merely a homiletical flourish.

But the real issue of this "radical new interpretation" is whether the facts it purports to interpret are factual. If they are, then one has to take seriously how they are interpreted. If the "facts" are half-truths, untrue, or confused, then the historical interpretation is of no interest at all.

Unfortunately, Rivkin provides a classic model of bad argument. He says, for example, that the Aaronides edited the Pentateuch, but he does not wish to debate the complexities of the matter or to argue with other scholars:

> In applying the unity concept to Israel's beginnings, I take a tack different from contemporary biblical scholars... unlike Wellhausen, Albright, Noth, Kaufman, and others, I do not take as my starting point J, D or P... I do not assume redactors. I do not take for granted that the Pentateuch is primarily a record of traditions, religious themes, or stories. These are assumptions for which there are good and persuasive grounds, but they are assumptions nevertheless... I therefore see no cogent argument against approaching the Pentateuch from a very different angle of vision.

What I get out of this argument is that since biblical scholars differ from one another, "I might as well say anything I want, for no one really knows the facts of the matter." I regard this as a cheap and self-serving argument, which not only dismisses two centuries of careful work, but also ignores every critical issue faced by specialists. What kind of history is this? History as nonsense-talk.

I cited in some detail Rivkin's discussion of Babylonian Jewry under the Persian (Sasanian) dynasty. Let us now consider some of the "facts" on which he relies. First, Rivkin's view that the "intellectual world of the Sasanians was nonrational" is contradicted by the strong scientific and philosophical interests of the Sasanian court, which sponsored medical schools and universities, saw to the translation of Indian and Greek scientific and philosophical texts into Pahlavi, and in other ways showed its commitment to disciplined, rational learning. Moreover, one man's "disorder" is another man's architectonics: I think the classical sugyot of the Babylonian gemara are anything but disorderly. To be sure, they are put together differently from the Mishnah, but that is a fact of literary history, not a datum in the study of a whole culture. And as a matter of fact, the equivalent Sasanian law code, the Matigan-i Hazar Datastan, or Digest of a Thousand Points of Law, is beautifully organized, much like the Mishnah of Judah the Patriarch. So if the Babylonian gemara were in any way influenced by Iranian legal forms, it ought to have been "rational and orderly," in Rivkin's terms.

To claim that the Babylonian Talmud in any way relates to Iranian culture should suggest that other minority groups exhibit a similar relationship. Yet Christian-Syriac and Christian-Armenian writings produced in the same period have absolutely nothing in common, formally or substantively, with the Babylonian Talmud -- which is, so far as I know, unique -- or with extant Sasanian writings.

I have further reservations which are beyond the scope of this review, and I am confident that specialists in other aspects of Jewish history will find even more reservations than I have. In all, I found the book wanting as scholarship, unsatisfactory as historiography, primitive in its argumentation, and only partially accurate in those few areas in which I have sought to achieve professional competence.

But it is an important book in its main purpose, which is to present the author's own ideas on the meaning of the history of the Jewish people. For the purpose of philosophizing or theologizing, one need not rely too heavily on facts, for they can neither prove nor disprove theological truth. He has attempted to say something about the whole of Judaic experience: that he sees a vision of unity in diversity; that capitalism is a good thing for the Jews; that the fate of the Jewish people and that of the democratic West are intertwined. Had he written in a mode other than history, he would be subject to different criteria of criticism, but the substance of his case would have not changed very much.

4. H.H. Ben Sasson, ed.
A HISTORY OF THE JEWISH PEOPLE
American Historical Review 1977, 82:1030-1031

A HISTORY OF THE JEWISH PEOPLE. H.H. Ben-Sasson, editor. Cambridge: Harvard University Press, 1976. Pp. xii, 1170.

This huge collection of essays by "leading scholars at the Hebrew University, Jerusalem" brings to ultimate expression the "peoplehood-and-history" theory of Jewish historiography. The theory presupposes that a single, clearly defined entity, "the Jewish people," has produced a unitary and linear history, "Jewish history," which extends back to the time of Abraham. It draws together into one cultural, economic, and social continuum all the doings of Jews everywhere at any one time. So, on pages 468-69, H.H. Ben-Sasson gives us "Jewish Participation in the Reconquista Colonization," "Jewish Commerce in the Indian Ocean," "Jewish Economic Activity in Christian Spain," "The Livelihoods of Jews in the Byzantine Empire," and "The Transition to Money-Lending in Ashkenaz" -- in five contiguous paragraphs! Moreover, the theory takes for granted that certain (unspecified) traits are everywhere and always definitive of what is "Jewish." This last view culminates in the following judgement: "It is not surprising that many people, both Jews and gentiles, friends and enemies, have continued in modern times to occupy themselves with the riddle of the endurance, survival, and renaissance of the Jews. They ask why larger groups and equally strong cultures and civilizations -- the Persians in Moslem culture and the Greeks in Roman-Byzantine culture -- have vanished or have been absorbed, while the Jews have remained Jews" (p. 728, italics mine). In fact, the distinctive history of Iran within Islam, set apart in both language and theology, has left the contemporary Iranian in far closer touch with pre-Islamic Iranian civilization than is the contemporary Jew of New York or Tel Aviv with the talmudic world of pre-Islamic Babylonia.

But more to the point, the linear history follows a highly conventional, even canonical, definition of which Jews at a given time were engaged in the making of "Jewish history," Jews in Islamic countries, for example, scarcely participate in "The Modern Period," and those in the Greco-Roman and Iranian diasporas of late antiquity appear for only perfunctory paragraphs. Moreover, the authors stress political and institutional history (and, for the first two millenia, military history), while religion and literature are deemed mere curiosities. After nearly two hundred pages of biblical history, after extended accounts of invasions, international politics, and court intrigues, the reader's obvious questions -- what has happened to the prophets? where is cult? did not the Old Testament come out of this period? -- are answered as follows: "Neither the history of the religion of Israel nor the history of biblical literature have [sic] been included, as they are subjects adequately treated by biblical scholarship" (p. 181).

- 49 -

Also excluded is the massive body of scholarship on the historical sources of the post-biblical period, down to Islam. The account of "The Period of the Second Temple" is essentially a paraphrase of Josephus, and "The Era of the Mishnah and Talmud," predictably, is described principally by innocent narration of talmudic fables about rabbis.

Since "a history of the Jewish people" from the perspective of Jerusalem culminates in the creation of the State of Israel, it is no wonder that the modern period (but only the modern period in Europe and in Palestine) predominates. Still, the disproportions are genuinely surprising. The 1300 years from 640 to 1973 occupy 64 percent of the book, and the 2300+ years from Abraham (supposedly about 1700 B.C.) to 640 get 36 percent. True, the disproportion is natural, once political and institutional history is placed at the center, for much more is known about this kind of history in the medieval and modern European settings than in the ancient Middle Eastern one.

Still, even the discussion of medieval and modern Europe is confused. Ben-Sasson decides to treat Jews in both Islam and Christendom together -- they are, after all, "one people" -- with the result that "The Economic and Social Crisis in Christian Spain" stands cheek by jowl with "Jewish Settlement in Eastern Europe and the Barrier of Muscovite Russia" (pp. 568-71). The utter chaos produced by the unitary and linear theory of "Jewish history" is perhaps the book's best demonstrated proposition. In fact, it is the only really clear and well-documented one, since Ben-Sasson has not provided an introduction, explaining the purposes and methods of the work. Nor does the book contain a single footnote! Here too, self-indulgence under distinguished auspices tells us that not only is the emperor naked, so is the whole imperial court.

The fact that the contributors are deemed to be leading scholars in their fields gives this work its peculiar importance as an exceptionally clear and detailed example of what the "peoplehood-and-history" theory makes of "the Jewish people" and of "Jewish history." But it also demonstrates the limitations of this approach. Viewed separately, some of the essays are valuable. Three of them, S. Ettinger's The Modern Period, A. Malamat's Origin's and Formative Period, and H. Tadmor's The Period of the First Temple, are superb.

Part Two

"JEWISH HISTORY" IN PRACTICE

BIBLICAL AND TALMUDIC STUDIES

5. Morris Silver
THE POLITICAL ECONOMY OF ANCIENT ISRAEL
This World, 1984

PROPHETS AND MARKETS. THE POLITICAL ECONOMY OF ANCIENT ISRAEL. By
Morris Silver. Kluwer-Nijhoff Publishing, Boston, The Hague, London, 1983. Social
Dimensions of Economics. City College of the City University of New York, 306 pp.

This book represents the incompetent execution of a very good idea. It is prolix,
confusing, disorganized. But its thesis presents an important and challenging view of a
critical component of the world-view of the West. Silver, who teaches economics at City
College of the City University of New York, wants to explain why the Old Testament
prophets of the eighth and seventh centuries said what they said. The reason the answer
matters is simple. Proof-texts for all sorts of liberal and radical social philosophies and
economic positions flow from the prophetic books. To Christianity and Judaism these
proof-texts bear authority. They shape attitudes -- hence, also, politics and economic
viewpoints. Consequently, Silver quite rightly questions whether the prophets knew what
they were talking about, and, since he argues that they did not, he assesses the long-term
consequences of their fundamental theses.

It would be difficult to undertake a more daunting task. Conventional wisdom
imputes to the prophets -- who after all spoke in the name of God -- exalted standing and
authority. Their statements, of necessity always taken out of context, define the thought
of theologians of synagogue and church alike. The bias towards the left characteristic of
many of these theologians, deriving from their place in the caste of intellectuals, then
finds reenforcement and validation.

So, when I was brought up in a Reform Jewish Temple in West Hartford, Connec-
ticut, I gained the strong impression that God wanted me to love Franklin Delano
Roosevelt. Among the residents of that exceptionally rich suburb, we Reform Jews, along
with our Polish and Irish Catholic friends and neighbors, were the only Democrats. But,
alone among the Democrats, we in particular knew that, in wearing our Roosevelt buttons
amid a forest of Willkie and Dewey ones, we bore the insignia of God and did the Lord's
work. Letting justice well up as waters and righteousness as a mighty stream meant, in
practical terms, pretty much the same thing as taxing and taxing, spending and spending,
electing and electing.

Professor Silver maintains that the prophets were wrong and, furthermore,
destroyed the nation and society of which they stood as critics. He sees them as a
guilt-ridden upper class intellectuals, out to wreck their world that supported them. With
access to the highest levels of government and religion, they succeeded. The downfall of
Judea in the sixth century came as the result. That stunning thesis comes to clear and

complete expression at only one point in the book. Since, as I shall point out, it is never systematically argued or even stated in appropriate contexts, we do well to listen to the complete thesis exactly as he expresses it (pp. 247-249):

> After the death of King Solomon (c. 922), the United Monarchy of the Israelites split into a northern kingdom, Israel, and a southern kingdom, Judah. During the tumultuous ninth century, while king strove with king for trade routes and priest with priest for a place at the royal table, the Israelite economy grew quietly but strongly. By the beginning of the eighth century, Israel and Judah had been projected into a glittering era of prosperity and power.
>
> During the eighth and seventh centuries, specialized production centers emerged and applied mass-production techniques, most notably in the areas of ceramics and residential housing. Israelite agriculture exported its products and displayed notable technical sophistication, including a rather remarkable adaptation to the desert environment of the Negeb. Testimony to a lively commerce is provided not only by specialized production, but also by the growing use of stone in building, by warehouse facilities, firms with complex managerial structures, brand names, land consolidation, and by the existence of significant population concentrations such as Samaria and Jerusalem. During this period Israel-Judah also expanded territorially gaining control over Bashan's great granary, parts of the fertile Philistine Plain, several ports, and the two major north-south highways, the Via Maris and the King's Highway.
>
> Neither the Bible, archaeology, nor economic theory demonstrates that income differentials widened or became very pronounced. Specifically, there is no reason to believe that the real income or even the relative share of labor had to fall in the eighth and later-seventh centuries.
>
> The new wealth that poured into Israel-Judah was consumed in a variety of forms. There was, first of all, a significant extension in the quantity and quality of housing and other consumer durables. Second, the average Israelite enjoyed a diet that was tastier as well as more varied and nutritious. The bread (raised or leavened bread) was substituted for hard-barley cakes and gruel and finely sifted whiter flour for the coarser varieties. The quantity of meat increased, as did its quality with the substitution of beef for mutton and fattened for unfattened animals. The affluent ancient Israelite being necessarily "poor" in terms of modern amenities chose his luxuries accordingly. He enjoyed his many children and participated in great feasts; he made lavish provision to memorialize his ancestors and gave large public donations; he enjoyed fine art, archaeological objects, gardens, song, and drama; he concerned himself with wisdom and questions of human character and duty; and, of course, he sought to improve the position of those less fortunate than himself.

Since an appreciable number of Israelites became men of means, it is not surprising that the eighth and seventh centuries reverberated with the call for social justice. This theme was most prominent in the prophetic writings but it also penetrated law, history, the literature of prayer (the psalms), and the secular-wisdom literature (the proverbs). The basic thrust of this "prophetic revolution" was the attempt to transform the national God of the Israelites into a God of universalism and social justice. The ordinary Israelite, however, could not be converted to the worship of social justice as long as the ancient religion provided peace of mind and a sense of belonging. Therefore, the prophets bitterly attacked Israel's most sacred religious observances, those honoring God and ancestors by means of sacrifices and teraphim.

Amos, Micah, and the other prophets were not poor peasants, hermits, or eccentrics outside the mainstream of Israelite life. Instead, they were educated members of the Establishment who quite possibly, had begun their careers as cultic priests of the second (or prophetic) order. As have all social voluntarists, ancient or modern, they argued that social injustice is neither a private matter nor inevitable. Motivated by idealism or personal ambition they sought with the support of the affluents, to commit the rulers to programs of social amelioration and regeneration. We must not be misled by "the rejection of the 'writing prophets' by their age and [by] the prophetic view of inevitable calamity, these are literary motifs derived from the [traditional Mesopotamian] epic rather than historical facts" (Staples 1966, p. 112). In fact, Isaiah became the "great advisor" or "teacher" of Uzziah and Hezekiah while Amos sought, and may well have secured, a similar position under Jeroboam II. Jeremiah was an associate of the most powerful in the land and probably campaigned for cultic centralization. Micah's social ideas were heeded by Hezekiah while Zephaniah, very likely, was a powerful priest and a relative of King Josiah. Deuteronomy, the basic document of social reform, not only attacks traditional Israelite religion and the market system as the prophets demanded, but also strongly reflects their central ideological tenet, "No social justice, no land of Israel." Indeed Deuteronomy, as the Psalms, is permeated by the very language and images and rhetorical style favored by Amos, Hosea, and Jeremiah. How could this be if the prophets were ineffective in their own time? Traditional historiography influenced, I believe, by Jewish ideas of theodicy in which destruction proves evil doing, Christian ideas of the coming replacement of "ethnic-nationalist religions by the universal faith," and a general intellectual climate of distaste or outright hostility toward markets holds that Israel and Judah fell because the prophetic counsel was ignored. However, as an economist and social scientist, I can testify that whatever is presumed moral virtues, the advice of the classical prophets was destructive from the standpoint of economic affluence and political strength.

Once the prophets and their allies had won the support of the state's armed might, concerted action was taken on two fronts. First, in the interests of an immediate improvement in the behavior of the Israelites economic reforms were implemented. Second, in order to teach them to think more righteously a program of indoctrination was instituted within the cult. Deuteronomy was designed to fulfill both programmatic objectives. Ancient Israel experienced no less than three such cultural revolutions under Jeroboam II (ca. 751), Hezekiah (ca. 716/5), and Josiah (ca. 621). In each instance the results were disastrous: innocent people were humiliated and murdered, civil war flared, the economy was damaged, and foreign nations took advantage of the opportunity to tear away chunks of Israel-Judah until nothing remained.

That is Silver's thesis.

At issue is not the political utility of the thesis at hand. Obviously, Silver proposes to overturn centuries of interpretation of the holy texts. To my knowledge no one has ever taken the position he outlines here. Since his thesis so obviously conforms to the widely-held view (which I share) that ridicules limousine liberals and radical chic, we must take care not to nod our heads in agreement merely because we want Silver to be right. We have rather to ask whether Silver has done two necessary tasks. First, has he established his facts? Second, has he composed a rigorous and lucid argument, so that we can move with him from radical proposition to ineluctable conclusion?

My sense is that while he has done a first rate piece of research, Silver has totally failed to present his ideas in a lucid and well-argued manner. The one really accessible and interesting statement of his views has already been cited. The reader will look in vain for anything else of equivalent clarity of expression and vigor of argument. That is not to suggest that he does not propose to prove what he asserts. It is to state quite simply that he has not written a book. He has published an enormous file of notes. It seems to me that his book has all of the virtues of bad academic writing. It is compendious, erudite, thorough in its reading of secondary literature, careful in its attention to textual detail. But it has the vice as well: Silver, like many professors, just does not know how to write a book.

The reason is that, he thinks, the facts speak for themselves. And that is so. But the facts do not, by themselves, speak to anybody about anything. For that purpose, the scholar must become an author. He must propose to speak to some particular audience about a well-defined and carefully executed proposition. Saying the whole at the end as he does, Silver wants the reader to write the book for him. If these judgments sound harsh, the character of the work at hand validates them.

Silver's basic approach to the topic is to organize a great many facts into para-graphs and chapters. Thus, the book unfolds in the following units: specialized produc-tion: industry and agriculture (pottery, woolen textiles, wine, olive oil, metalworking and mining, residential housing, agricultural practices); adaptations to spreading markets: brands, management, and warehouses (jar-handle stamps, brands and packaging, officer seals and hierarchic firms, the Samaria ostraca and warehouse facilities); transport: routes, costs, and monopoly power (highways, economic importance of land and water transport, Israelite expansion, Judah alone); the economies of Israel's neighbors; the market for factors of production: commercial loans, slavery, and land consolidation; living standards: consumer durables (private homes, possessions, dress); diet (bread consumption, meat consumption, wine and oil); luxury consumption (cultic luxury consumption, social status: genealogies and mortuary wealth, plastic arts, performing arts, gardens, large families, education and wisdom); income distribution; the call for social justice: priests, prophets, proverbs, and psalms (the prophets as social reformers, the political potency of the prophets, prophetic symbols and ambitions, the joint ministry of priests and prophets, songs and words of social justice) and, finally, the implementation of social reform: three cultural revolutions (the program of social reform, the northern origin of Deuteronomy, the assault on ritual and tradition; cultic reforms and consequences; socioeconomic reforms and consequences. There are two appendices: markets and entrepreneurs in the ancient Near East, and historical evidence on the relationship between economic growth and land consolidation.

Each of the units consists of a set of facts, a card file of them. Let me give two examples of how Silver has composed the book:

Pottery

The raw-material base for a pottery industry was provided by clay marl of the Jordan and coastal districts. According to Wright (1965, pp. 155-56) the first half of the eighth century saw Israel manufacturing the most beautiful pottery ever produced in Iron Age Palestine. This elegant pottery, called Samaria Ware, because great quantities were found there, seems to have been produced in the surrounding area. More important, Heaton (1968, p. 37) adds that the beginning of the eighth century saw a "minor revolution" in the techniques of pottery production. "In towns like Jericho, Megiddo, Gezer, Lachish, and Hazor, where potters' wheels have been excavated..., bowls and jars became standardized in shape and size [the vessels could be nested] for mass-production methods and the employment of unskilled labor." Wright (1962, p. 196) explains that most vessels continued to be made individually on the wheel but special speed-techniques were adopted. Two specialists in modern ceramics, Kelso and Thorley (quoted in Wright 1962, p. 194) concluded in 1943 that Israelite commercial pottery compares favorably in terms of craftsmanship, form, and shape with the corresponding wares of their own time.

Wine

Gibeon in Benjamin was the site of a very significant center for the production of wine (Pritchard 1959, p. 249; 1962, pp. 40, 99; Reed 1967, pp. 234-35). Here were found no less than 63 underground wine vats and cellars (some seven feet deep) capable of storing 25,000 gallons of wine maintained by the underground rock at 65 degrees. In addition, many jar handles with Hebrew inscriptions dating from the seventh (or sixth) century B.C.E. were recovered from the debris of a large rock-cut pool. These inscriptions, the excavator Pritchard suspects, may have been the labels of private firms producing wine for export. Pritchard's conclusion is that the three centuries following the division of the kingdom were a time of "unrivaled prosperity and expansion" for Gibeon "which reached a peak in the seventh century" (Pritchard 1962, pp. 161-63).

Olive Oil

In the ancient Near East, olive oil served a variety of important purposes. It was used for cooking and with many foods (Ezek. 16:13; 1 Kings 17:12-13; Lev. 2:4-7; Num. 6:15; 1 Chron. 12:40-41), for anointing the hair, for various cosmetic and medicinal purposes (Isa. 1:6) including cleansing and, perhaps, lubricating the skin to prevent sunburn (Mic. 6:15), and as a base for perfumes (Eccles. 10:1), and for light when burnt in a lamp (Exod. 25:6). Judging by the quantity of olive pits found there, Lachish, beginning in the ninth-eighth centuries, must have hosted a significant olive-oil industry. A Hebrew inscription incised on the base of a bowl from the ninth-eighth centuries seems to indicate that Israelite oil was exported. This ostracon found on the surface at Tell Qasile, a port founded by the Philistines and later destroyed by the Assyrians in ca. 732 B.C.E. is probably a bill or an invoice (no price is mentioned) concerning the shipment of "a thousand oil and a hundred" by one Hiyahu (an Israelite name). Avigad (1979, p. 24) suggests that "since oil was probably not imported into the country this must have been a shipment for export."

All of the rubrics I catalogued above are treated pretty much in the same manner. For him scholarship remains at the primitive level of hunting and gathering, collecting and arranging. That is why Silver mostly collects and arranges facts. These then he assumes argue for or at least illustrate his thesis. But where is the thesis in the cited paragraphs? I do not see it.

Now the reader will quite fairly object that, after all, a thesis so revolutionary as the one at hand has to rest upon thorough documentation. True enough. But I find it difficult to locate the bridges between the boring compilations of facts and the revolutionary thesis with which the book concludes. The simple criterion is whether, and how, the author makes use of the facts at hand in the spinning out of his larger thesis. Here is how Silver concludes the chapter from which I have drawn the paragraphs cited above:

The Israelite economy of the eighth-seventh centuries was by no means primitive. It was a living economy whose entrepreneurs, as we shall have further occasion to demonstrate in the next chapter, responded positively and rationally to market opportunities. But is it really appropriate to view markets and entrepreneurs as agents in ancient Near Eastern economic development? The answer, as is shown in Appendix A is certainly yes.

To pursue this line of thought briefly, it is sometimes assumed that while the ancient economy was familiar with circulating capital not directly involved in the production process (for example, ships and warehouses) and with the relatively inexpensive tools of the artisan, it did not, in any meaningful way, know fixed capital. However, this kind of rigid formulation clashes with the presence in ancient Israel of industrial installations such as those at Gibeon and, especially, at Debir, with the significant investments in oil-presses, metallurgical facilities, terracing, irrigation, and, no doubt, in tree and vine stock. Obviously there are significant differences between ancient and modern industry, characterized by an increase in the range and variety of the fixed capital goods in which investment is embodied (see Hicks 1969, p. 143). But economic historians should be careful not to exaggerate these differences beyond proper proportions and, consequently, not overlook the possibility, indeed the probability, that the ancient epoch experienced lengthy periods of sharply rising labor productivity and per capita income.

These concluding remarks are highly suggestive. But at no point do they refer back to the facts with which the chapter has been stuffed. The reader is supposed to assume that Silver has proved his point. The facts adduced earlier are imagined now to show that "the Israelite economy... was by no means primitive." But exactly how what we are told about wine, olive oil, and pottery has demonstrated, or even illustrated, that judgment in particular, I do not know. Silver does not even tell us what he means by "primitive." The facts do not speak for themselves; they are not asked to. They are just there, filling up page after dreary page of what should have been an extraordinarily vital and rigorously argued monograph.

That is not to suggest Silver has not made important observations here and there. Quite to the contrary, along the way as he takes up every possible topic, being a scholar of obvious intellect, he offers striking comments on all manner of subjects. I was most taken by the contrast between his account of the Israelite economy of the period at hand and that of Salo Baron, whom Silver meets head on in a stunning, and entirely one-sided confrontation. Having cited Silver at some length, let me allow him once more to speak for himself:

In spite of the very significant accomplishments thus far reviewed, modern assessments of the eighth-seventh centuries B.C.E. are almost uniformly unflattering, so much so indeed that in the social scientist they must strike a

note of unreality, that is, of being out of social character. This negativism
can be partially traced to religious presuppositions. Israel-Judah was
ultimately destroyed. In some Jewish circles where ideas related to theodicy
prevail, the fact of destruction is sufficient proof that "the Israelites did evil
in the eyes of the Lord," while in some intellectual Christian circles, the
destruction symbolizes the coming replacement of "ethnic-nationalist religions
by the true and only universal faith" (see Kaufmann 1960, p. 135).

But presumptions of a Marxist-Leninist character are also important.
The market economy is visualized as a zero-or negative-sum game in which
every gain to the rich is matched, or more than matched, by a loss to the
toiling masses (see, for example, Neufeld 1960, p. 52). In short, Marx's
concept of the absolute and relative impoverishment of the working class is
applied. This approach is clearly reflected in Salo Baron's (1952) writings on
ancient Israel:

> General economic decline was accompanied by a steady
> process of differentiation. Some of the rich grew richer at the
> expense of their fellows under the prevalent precapitalistic forms
> of exploitation.
>
> Once some families had secured more than their due share,
> the trend became irresistible for the poorer farmers sooner or later
> to lose their land, while a group of comparatively few rich
> landowners accumulated large estates. (p. 68)

Here we have in addition to relative and absolute pauperization, the increasing
concentration of wealth, and the operation of mysterious, but irresistible,
historical forces, the application of the Marxist-Leninist notion of general
economic crisis to an economy that was in fact enjoying significant growth.
Notice also that since capitalism according to the dogma, must begin only in
Europe after the overthrow of feudalism, the Israelite forms of exploitation
are carefully called "precapitalistic." Add next a pinch of imperialism:
"Situated in the midst of the most advanced industrial civilizations of the
time... this small country was flooded with foreign products, and because of
political weakness it often had to admit foreign merchants against its will"
(Baron 1952, p. 69). So the period of Israel-Judah's greatest political strength,
in which it won control over the key trade routes and established trading
enclaves in Syria, is pictured as one of political weakness and of economic
ruination, as if it were India in the nineteenth century. The next addition must
include the element of reserve army of the unemployed:

> The poorer peasants were often permanently ruined by their debts,
> since the income from their agricultural production could not long

stand the strain of high interest rates... [T]he number of free landless workers constantly grew. Inevitably they had to accept low wages and often could find no work at all... [T]he country seems not to have escaped the evil of permanent unemployment. For this among other reasons, the 'Hebrew' slave sometimes chose to remain with his master even after he had completed his six-year term. (Baron 952, pp. 69-70)

Readers who study chapter 6 will agree with Silver's thesis and reject Baron's.

The importance of Silver's book becomes clear when we realize how much others have taken for granted. When we follow his case, we come away with the impression that a great many theologians and historians have been making things up as they go along. The power of the book, however, lies not in its confrontation with the opinions and results of other scholars, but in its mode of argument in behalf of the author's thesis. That, as I said, leaves much to be desired.

But in the balance, the author deserves a larger measure of praise than negative criticism. True enough, he has published a scarcely-digested cardfiles, so that most of his book simply is essentially beside the point he wants to make. He has indeed failed to construct a logical argument, to which facts should contribute. Instead he has substituted a mindless exercise in show-and-tell.

On the positive side, he has announced a thesis that is both totally original and extraordinarily suggestive. He has assembled a mass of facts in behalf of his case. No one can claim that the work lacks scholarship or accuracy. All he has failed to do is write a book. But many great scholars express their important ideas in a private and idiosyncratic manner. In that worthy company, Silver is, at least, intelligible and more than routinely interesting.

It remains to observe that Silver correctly avoids the inescapable theological issue: how could God have given so much poor economic advice to the prophets? And if social justice is not really the purpose and point of the holy society, what are we and what is our life? These are not the questions distinctive to the left as it addresses the right. They seem to me the profound issues perenially confronting American society. They derive from the ethical heritage of Judaism and Christianity. In light of this important book, the issues of the prophetic call to justice become all the more acute.

6. John M. Allegro
THE CHOSEN PEOPLE. A STUDY OF JEWISH HISTORY
FROM THE TIME OF THE EXILE UNTIL THE REVOLT OF BAR KOCHEBA
<u>Midstream</u> 1972, 18:76-77

THE CHOSEN PEOPLE. A STUDY OF JEWISH HISTORY FROM THE TIME OF THE
EXILE UNTIL THE REVOLT OF BAR KOCHEBA. SIXTH CENTURY B.C., TO SECOND
CENTURY A.D. By John M. Allegro. Garden City: Doubleday & Co., Inc., 1971, 320 pp.

Allegro presents a perfectly routine, school-book account of the history of the Jews
in the specified time, to which he adds -- mercifully, only from time to time -- perfectly
routine commonplaces of learned anti-Semitism. For his history he stays close to sources;
for his anti-Semitism, he does not much diverge from what has been said by malevolent
people for centuries. The book seems to have been whipped together to exploit the
popular interest in the works of the author of <u>The Sacred Mushroom and the Cross</u> -- a
work this writer is not half clever enough to review properly -- because occasionally we
find rather explicit references to the resemblances between the circumcised penis and the
mushroom. Then, to make the work appear somehow new, the author alleges that
whatever ill fortunes the Jews have suffered were brought by themselves on their own
heads ("Our blood..."). The net effect is a trivial piece of history-cum-dogma, the sort of
book which wins its author the deserved reputation of publishing too much.

At the outset the author tells us his sermon-topic: "Religious emotionalism... is an
extremely dangerous and unpredictable force. Moral and patriotic idealism that springs
from a racialist religion is a perilous philosophy..." Instead Allegro favors "reason and
rationality." There are several villains in the piece. Chief among the racists is, of
course, Nehemiah, whom Allegro really dislikes:

> Some seven weeks after his arrival in Jerusalem, Nehemiah had managed to
> reconstruct a makeshift city wall. The first physical barriers between the
> post-exilic Jew and the gentile world had been erected. Nehemiah had begun
> to translate into tangible reality the separatist policies advocated by the
> prophets. In those lines of heaped stones and rubble around Jerusalem we
> might discern the foundations of the walls that bounded the ghettos of
> medieval Europe, the gas chambers of Auschwitz, and the battle lines of
> modern Palestine.

I am not clear about how those "heaped stones" were so inflated as to extend to medieval
and modern times. Allegro further condemns the creation in the time of Ezra-Nehemiah
of the Torah-book. He feels sorry — who wouldn't? -- for the intermarriages broken up by
Nehemiah. The "racism" discovered by Allegro in Nehemiah's policies is forthwith
attached to the whole of the history of Judaism. The biblical account of creation is

interpreted to mean that the Jews believed they should rule the whole world: "And all history was directed to their glorification. Here we have the core of the doctrine of the Chosen People, whose working out in practical politics was to wreak such havoc among the nations of the world and to bring successive disasters upon the Jews themselves." And further: "The history of the Jews as revealed in the Torah was thus in a sense coextensive with the story of mankind, and in Adam's supremacy over the beasts of the field could be seen figured from the Creation the eventual dominion by the Jew of the whole world."

Allegro does not support his interpretation of the meaning to Judaism of the Creation story with a single reference to a Jewish biblical commentator who understood things in such a way. I know of nothing in the far reaches of talmudic and midrashic literature which remotely parallels his megalomanic nightmare of Jewish world-rule. Any half-educated Jew will have at hand dozens of contrary viewpoints on the relationships between Israel and the world. Indeed, Allegro is remarkably selective in his interpretation of the idea of the Chosen People. The rich theological tradition, beginning with Amos, about the responsibilities of the covenant -- "Only you have I known among the families of mankind, therefore I shall visit upon you all your iniquities" -- is nowhere to be seen. The rabbinic understanding of the Suffering Servant, of Israel's role as prefigured by Isaiah 52-53, would seem to suggest some viewpoint other than the one attributed to Nehemiah coexisted and competed with allegedly racist notions.

Allegro's treatment of the sixty years between the fall of the Temple and the Bar Kochba War is equally selective. The reconstruction at Yavneh and the irenic teachings of Yohanan ben Zakkai, the reconciliation with Rome attempted by Gamaliel II, the development of a religion of deeds of lovingkindness, prayer, study of Torah, the nurture of a tradition of non-violence and of ethical intensity -- none of these achievements of Yavneh appears to be known to Allego. Had they been known, they might have given the meaning of Israel's chosenness a less frightening dimension. Instead of the rabbinic movement, Allegro posits a drug-cult. What the Jews did between the destruction in 70 and the rebellion in 132 was to eat mushrooms: "What had been planned there [in ancient Babylonia] by expatriate Jewry, dreaming dreams and seeing visions of a Jewish world empire, was now activated [after 70] by a sinister power that derived from the earliest origins of Yahwism. The madness that now drove the players in this awful tragedy to the final holocaust arrived from a drug-fungus whose worship was older than history."

Allegro's Chosen People is nothing more than a recrudescence of the Protocols of the Elders of Zion for the age of Aquarius. His vision of ancient Jewry and its religion indeed brings up to date the identical vision of the 19th century forgers. All that has changed is the use of fairly good sources instead of forged ones and the introduction of a more contemporary motif -- instead of conspiracy with the powers of evil, the Jews turned on. The net effect is not much different.

I do not think the unbelievers will be converted by Allegro's fantasies. We do not live in 1890, when the product of a sick imagination could be taken seriously by reasonable people, or in 1930, when somehow Hitler could be seen as a creature of the Jews themselves, or even in 1945, when Hitler could claim the Jews had wanted the war and brought it on their own heads. The problem is, how could Allegro have come to so fantastic a view of Judaism, a tradition known by and open to the whole world, as to represent it in such a perverted way? The answer must be that in his years in Jerusalem, Jordan, he probably assimilated a view of Judaism appropriate to the politics of the time and place. Now, we are told, he lives on the Isle of Man. Should the name be appropriate, we may hope for works of greater humanity, and even of scholarly integrity.

7. Alexander Guttman
RABBINIC JUDAISM IN THE MAKING. A CHAPTER IN THE
HISTORY OF THE HALAKHAH FROM EZRA TO JUDAH I
Journal of Jewish Studies 1972, 23:92-93

RABBINIC JUDAISM IN THE MAKING. A CHAPTER IN THE HISTORY OF THE
HALAKHAH FROM EZRA TO JUDAH I. By Alexander Guttmann. Detroit: Wayne State
University Press, 1970, 323 pp.

Professor Alexander Guttmann, of Hebrew Union College-Jewish Institute of
Religion, Cincinnati, here presents the fruit of many years of labor on the history of the
halakhah to the end of the Mishnaic period. The work is thorough and painstaking and
contains a careful and critical survey of modern Jewish scholarship on each point under
discussion. Thus the book provides a reliable and comprehensive account of both the
problem itself and of the solutions proposed over the past century and a half.

Guttmann's intention is "to demonstrate for the first time in English how the
development of Jewish legal tradition was directed and implemented by the Pharisaic and
rabbinic leadership from the earliest times to the end of the tannaitic period, ca. 220
C.E." Rabbinism "prevailed... due to the clear vision and effective guidance of its
leaders, the rabbis. These men possessed a deep understanding of the need for a warm and
practical religious expression, genuinely Jewish, and at the same time harmonious with
the spiritual and material life of the peoples surrounding them [the Jews]." The prophets
had demanded perfection, so "were doomed to failure." The rabbis were "pedagogues."
"In guiding their people they took the realities of life, among them the weakness of man,
into consideration." They succeeded because they were able "to maintain a harmonious
state between Judaism and a continuously changing life." These rabbis presumably serve
as models for the Reform ones Guttmann teaches.

Guttmann quite properly turns to the detailed record of the Tannaitic movement.
He concentrates not on general issues but on specific problems. His work is divided into
three parts: (1) the "Soferic Period" (Ezra, the Great Assembly, and the Gerousia); (2) the
"Pharisaic-Early Tannaitic Period" (the Sanhedrin, Eshkolot, Zugot, Hillel and Shammai
and their Houses, Pharisees, Sadducees, Essenes, Simeon, Gamaliel, and Simeon b.
Gamaliel; (3) the "Tannaitic Period" (Yohanan b. Zakkai, Gamaliel, Eleazar b. Azariah,
Aqiba, Simeon b. Gamaliel, and Judah). The excellence of Guttmann's treatment of each
of these subjects lies, as noted, in his careful analysis of the theories of earlier scholars.
He provides a veritable compendium of opinions advanced by the Wissenschaft des
Judentums with full bibliographies, for each point. He formulates his own theses in the
full light of those that have gone before, a model of scholarly virtue and industry.

The primary problem of his book is that of the <u>Wissenshaftliche</u> tradition in talmudic matters, namely, the uncritical assumption of the historical reliability of all sources, early and late. Guttmann takes for granted that whatever a source claims to have happened, actually took place. The sources, by and large, have no history; they only supply one. They represent no particular viewpoints, serve no particular party or group. They were conceived only by a desire to report critically and exactly what happened. The sources, moreover, present few, if any, literary problems. None is to be analysed with a view to discovering strata and complexities; none stands at the end of a process of tradition. All of this, of course, is scarcely tenable and history composed upon such presuppositions is bound to be highly problematical at best. This book marks the end of a century and a half of historical work pursued in isolation from the critical study of ancient history, biblical literature, and other methodologically sophisticated scholarly disciplines. But compared to his predecessors, Guttmann exhibits the noteworthy, and uncommon virtues of respect for differing opinions, keen attentiveness to every available source, and a responsible effort, within obvious limitations, to produce a viable historical account. A great deal was achieved by the chain of Talmudic historians which ends with Guttmann, and <u>Rabbinic Judaism in the Making</u> is a convenient and excellent guide to those accomplishments.

8. Wayne Sibley Towner
THE RABBINIC "ENUMERATION OF SCRIPTURAL EXAMPLES."
A STUDY OF A RABBINIC PATTERN OF DISCOURSE.
WITH SPECIAL REFERNCE TO MEKHILTA D'R. ISHMAEL
Journal of Jewish Studies 1976, 27:92-93

THE RABBINIC "ENUMERATION OF SCRIPTURAL EXAMPLES." A STUDY OF A RABBINIC PATTERN OF DISCOURSE. WITH SPECIAL REFERNCE TO MEKHILTA D'R. ISHMAEL. By Wayne Sibley Towner. Leiden: E.J. Brill, 1973, XII, 276 pp.

The form-historical study of rabbinical literature begins in this excellent book. Professor Towner, originally trained in Old Testament, has applied, with suitable adaptation, methods established for nearly a century and beyond serious dispute. He has done so with exceptional sensibility and imagination. The fact that what the book does is so new to its subject testifies to the retrograde and uninformed character of much that pretends to be scholarship in rabbinic studies. We may take for granted that it will not be read and examined in yeshivot, or in the equivalent departments of Talmud attached to Israeli universities. But no critical considerations and methods are ever understood in such obscurantist places. For those of us who seek to tackle rabbinic documents in the ways in which other ancient sources are presently investigated, Towner's work is a major event.

The author carries forward research on numerical sayings in Old Testament literature into rabbinic texts. He analyzes the growth and development of the form of the numerical sayings. And he further comments on the form and content of thirty-five pericopae of Mekhilta d'R. Ishmael. The work begins with a careful explanation of the method and concludes with another major methodological statement. In-between are two long chapters, "from observation to exegesis," and "the 'enumeration of Scriptural examples' in Tannaitic literature." In the latter are treated the following types of materials: commonsense analysis of an individual text, hermeneutical analysis, lexical analysis, syntactical analysis, legal analysis, and technical-exegetical analysis. In a most persuasive chapter, Towner then turns to enumerations of Scriptural examples in non-rabbinic literature, first, Pseudo-Philo and the Samaritan Memar Marqah, second early Christian writings. The book includes a rich bibliography and detailed indexes.

The major conclusions are divided into discussions of form and the function of the pattern, and conclusions drawn from the histories of the specific pericopae.

Among the former conclusions are: 1. the 'enumeration of Scriptural examples' has a simple 'normative' pattern: to an interpretative remark with a numerical element a list of proof-texts is appended, appropriate in number and content to the terms of the remark in question; 2. the form falls into six functional categories; 3. the form of the enumeration-pattern does not follow its function; 4. the pattern is usually associated with midrash haggadah and usually serves a homiletical, as well as a mnemonic, function. The main points of the second set conclusions are as follows: 1. the type of evolution exhibited by individual enumeration pericopae in the course of their transmission comes about only because that process was largely oral in character; 2. the appended proof-texts appear to be the secondary and changeable part of the enumeration-pattern; 3. knowledge of the normative pattern of the enumeration provides an effective means of detecting glosses, homiletic expansions, intrusions of other stereotyped patterns, and errors in particular recensions of individual traditions; 4. with the 'enumeration of Scriptural examples,' the general development of form which emerges over the course of oral transmission is toward a more 'normative,' terse, simplified, and stereotyped pattern; 5. in one respect the enumeration pattern consistently undergoes elaboration, that is in the supplying of scriptural examples to initially 'proverbial' but potentially exegetical enumeration traditions.

The conclusions regarding the oral character of the transmission (and, I assume, formulation) of the form seem well-argued. He therefore raises the difficult matter of a rather complex literary-tradental situation in rabbinical literature. For the criteria used by him, and by David Weiss-Halivni (Meqorot umesorot) to demonstrate that a tradition was orally formulated and orally transmitted also demonstrate that traditions not exhibiting the pertinent traits were not orally formulated and not orally transmitted. Tosefta's provision, for Mishnah, of a sizable literature of exegesis, including direct quotations, and dissenting perspectives and opinions, surely presupposes a written, not oral, literature, as do redactional traits of both compilations. If Tosefta did have an oral literature, one must suppose, a quite different mode of supplying that "Talmud" which is formed by nearly two-thirds of Tosefta will have been made necessary. One does not comment on an oral tradition. One revises it to suit one's opinion of the substance of the matter. This is one of Halivni's major conclusions. But Tosefta does not revise Mishnah; it comments on a fixed and formal text. Mishnah itself contains a fair number of pericopae which serve as internal gloss and commentary, as Avraham Weiss showed (e.g. "Leheqer hassifruti shel Mishnah." HUCA 16 (1941), pp. 1-34 [Hebrew side]). This is not to suggest that we now know, or even have a viable and comprehensive theory about, the way in which the earlier rabbinic literature was formulated and transmitted. It is only to propose that we shall have to reckon with a rather complex situation, in which, it would seem, both oral and written modes were utilized.

At one point only does Towner's form-history touch upon form-criticism as elaborated by the present reviewer in his books on the Pharisees, Eliezer ben Hyrcanus and the mishnaic laws of purities. The recognition of the primary and normative form, he notes, serves to point out glosses and other secondary and tertiary accretions. This I think is one of form-criticism's two primary uses in the study of Mishnah-Tosefta and cognate materials. The other is still more important. Form-criticism helps us to locate and isolate the primary and distinct units of thought, the smallest constructions of an idea, thus enabling us to treat each of these units separately. As a result, we are for the first time in a position to determine the primary "historical" meanings intended by the creators of these simplest units of thought. Until now pericopae have been interpreted solely in relationship with the larger constructions to which they belong. This may, at times, distort the meaning of a primary unit of thought, for the significance of the whole is imposed upon the part. A fresh exegesis of the rabbinical texts is thus made possible, which reveals the changes of meaning imposed on the constituents of a composite pericopa by various redactors. This final meaning is usually the one discerned by Mishnah's perceptive exegetes in the Talmuds and by the earlier and later medieval commentators. Their interpretative solutions are always interesting, but real meaning or meanings are best understood when the literary problems are presented in their evolutionary complexity.

Towner's contributions to form-history and form-criticism applied to rabbinic literature deserve high praise. His method and results have so enriched our understanding of the early history of talmudic Judaism that no scholar worthy of this name may ignore them. Those who do will have only themselves to blame. For after Copernicus, Ptolemaic astronomy ceased to be persuasive, and after the oxygen-theory, few chemists needed phlogiston.

9. Henry A. Fischel
RABBINIC LITERATURE AND GRECO-ROMAN PHILOSOPHY:
A STUDY OF EPICUREA AND RHETORICA IN EARLY MIDRASHIC WRITINGS
and
Wayne Sibley Towner
THE RABBINIC "ENUMERATION OF SCRIPTURAL EXAMPLES"
Journal of the American Academy of Religion 1975, 43:356-358

RABBINIC LITERATURE AND GRECO-ROMAN PHILOSOPHY: A STUDY OF EPICUREA
AND RHETORICA IN EARLY MIDRASHIC WRITINGS (Studia Post-Biblica, vol. 21). By
Henry A. Fischel. Leiden: E.J. Brill, 1973. xii+201 pages.

THE RABBINIC "ENUMERATION OF SCRIPTURAL EXAMPLES." A STUDY OF A
RABBINIC PATTERN OF DISCOURSE WITH SPECIAL REFERENCE TO MEKHILTA D'R
ISHMAEL (Study Post-Biblica, vol. 22). By Wayne Sibley Towner. Leiden: E.J. Brill,
1973. xii+275 pages.

These two excellent books greatly enrich and expand the nascent inquiry into the
literary- and form-critical study of earlier Rabbinic documents, thus into the foundations
of Rabbinic Judaism. Each in its own way is both brilliant and exemplary. It is a pleasure
to say so.

Fischel's work is both exegetical and form-critical. He undertakes the comparison
of literary forms in Greco-Roman orations and important rhetorical topoi, taken over
"basically intact as to structure and stylistic devices," in Rabbinic literature. Sometimes
"not only literary form, but also ethical and philosophical religious content," passes over
as well. Fischel's larger inquiry is into the character of the "sophos-sapiens-hakham, the
sage," whom he characterizes as a "special brand of scholar-believer-bureaucrat, who...
strove mightly to uphold rational and emotionally balanced positions in many aspects of
civilized life." The bulk of the present work, however, is limited to a handful of
comparative, literary, and exegetical studies, in particular, to the story of the "Four in
Paradise," the saying, "There is no justice and there is no judge," and several stories
about, and sayings attributed to, Ben Zoma.

Fischel's method is, first, to establish a sound text and translate it; then to amass
the data on themes similar to those in the rabbinic saying or story; third, to show specific
and important relationships, parallels, or other points of comparison, between Greco-Roman and Rabbinic conceptions; fourth, to examine the concrete literary formulations,
themes, forms, and keywords characteristic of, or associated with, those same conceptions in Greco-Roman literature; and finally to list, point by point, equivalent literary
traits in the Rabbinic story. It goes without saying that the work rests upon unsurpassed,

dazzling erudition. Fischel has done his homework exceedingly well. Students of Hellenistic and Greco-Roman literature will have to evaluate his mastery and use of that evidence. On the Rabbinic side it is without significant flaw.

Yet the results in some measure exhibit a significant fault indeed. First, Fischel occasionally lapses into what Samuel Sandmel characterizes as "parallelomania," drawing parallels where to another eye none is to be discerned, amassing weighty evidence either to make an entirely obvious point, or not to make any clearly discernible point at all. Second, I am inclined to think it is his enthusiasm for the method and larger thesis, rather than a slow, inductive inquiry into the evidence, which leads him to see the famous story of the "Four in Paradise" -- the longest chapter -- as an anti-Epicurean tale: "another piece of anti-Epicurean polemic, and, as to its literary form, [it] represents two popular typologies: the first referring to four types of Epicureans and the second to four types of fate destined for Epicureans." Some may find the interpretation far-fetched, even forced, despite the extraordinary erudition amassed in its support.

At the end, in an appendix, we have "Epicurea et Rhetorica of Ben Azzai? A Survey," notes for further studies, wholly consisting of references to talmudic stories on the one side, and to pertinent Greek and Latin materials on the other. These thirteen items, bare bones of further studies I suppose, strongly suggest the starting point for the developed studies. Half the book is given over to notes and indices, a model of scholarly industry.

What lies beyond, obviously, cannot be merely further exercises in the gathering of parallels, but a much larger, more historically oriented, better balanced, well organized, and comprehensive account, first, of all literary forms shared by the two bodies of literature, with attention to location and attribution of each; second, of all major conceptions preserved in these parallel forms. Having demonstrated the importance and suggestiveness of the work, Fischel now must surely do it. These preliminary studies certainly vindicate his thesis.

Towner's work may be called form-critical in the more conventional sense of the word, since he brings to the study of Rabbinic literature a first-class form-critical education in the Hebrew Scripture and New Testament. He asks, specifically, about numerical sayings, already studied in the Hebrew Scriptures, applying to their study established methods, yet revising them in accord with the material; finally, the comments on thirty-five pericopes in Mekhilta deR. Ishmael. The word is lucid, well organized, and methodologically highly sophisticated, a pleasure to follow.

What is especially praiseworthy is Towner's excursus on method (pp. 23-58), and his systematic attention to the methodological laws, the results of his discrete analyses of pericopes. Like Fischel, Towner has the merit of turning to non-Rabbinic Jewish sources as well as early Christian writings in search of enumerations of Scriptural examples.

In this same regard, his "Form-Criticisms of Rabbinic Literature," Journal of Jewish Studies 24 (1972), pp. 101-18, must be recommended for its clear statements on the "laws of transmission" and other regularities Towner discerns in the history of the literature. Here too, Towner provides an account of the forms and functions of the pattern under study (pp. 244-47), as well as a summary of the specific conclusions drawn from the histories of the several traditions actually analyzed.

That is not to suggest one can safely skip from the opening to the closing methodological statements. The detailed inquiries themselves are as sensitive and perceptive as the generalizations are lucid and well argued. In all, Towner has given us a model for the study of the history and function of a particular literary form in the Rabbinic literature. This is precisely how the work should be done.

Fischel and Towner in quite different ways therefore show the complexity and richness of the new inquiries into the Rabbinic literature. Materials, the meaning of which has long been taken for granted yet never investigated, in Fischel's hands look new and fresh. Questions never before brought to the Rabbinic documents, when asked by Towner, produce important information, highly suggestive answers, generative of a new conception entirely of the formation and transmission of the Rabbinic traditions. Work along more narrowly historical lines has progressed as well. In all, we enter a new and promising era in the study of earlier Rabbinic literature, therefore also of religion and history, in which the generation of facts replaces sterile generalities, and solid inquiries into hard data, carefully examined with an open mind, render obsolete not merely the axioms and conventions of the passing age, but even the agenda thought worth discussing. Fischel and Towner not only give shape to the new agendum but show why it is worth pursuing. Erudition and breadth of inquiry brought to bear upon specific pericopae, in Fischel's case, and extraordinarily clear and careful analysis of exempla of a particular form in Towner's, yield the first really new and persuasive work in -- literally -- ages.

Part Three

DESCRIBING "JUDAISM"

10. Joseph Bonsirven

PALESTINIAN JUDAISM IN THE TIME OF JESUS CHRIST

and

Robert M. Grant

GNOSTICISM AND EARLY CHRISTIANITY

Judaism 1966, 15:230-240

PALESTINIAN JUDAISM IN THE TIME OF JESUS CHRIST. By Joseph Bonsirven. Translated from the French by William Wolf. New York: Holt, Rinehart and Winston, 1964.

GNOSTICISM AND EARLY CHRISTIANITY. By Robert M. Grant. New York: Columbia University Press, 1964.

I

The history of scholarship, like the waves, moves in inexorable tides, advancing, receding, and, for a few moments, standing poised in seeming indecision or confusion. Studies on Judaism in late antiquity are presently so poised, for the old directions, methods, questions, and certainties no longer conform to the state of our knowledge, and yet it is not all clear what is to happen next. Scientific studies on "Talmudic Judaism," which began about a century ago, led eventually to the grand syntheses of Moore, Schechter, and in their path, Ginzberg, Kadushin, and Finkelstein -- syntheses which rested on the presupposition that talmudic literature might by itself yield a whole and accurate view of Judaism in the early centuries of the Common Era. Aware of the existence of sources which did not quite fit into the picture that emerged from talmudic literature as it was understood in those years or which did not serve the partly apologetic purposes of their studies, Moore and others posited the existence of "normative Judaism," which is to be described by reference to talmudic literature and distinguished from "heretical" or "sectarian" or simply "non-normative" Judaism of "fringe sects." Normative Judaism, exposited so systematically and with such certainty in Moore's Judaism, found no place in its structure for mysticism (except "normal mysticism"), magic, salvific or eschatological themes except within a rigidly reasonable and mainly ethical framework; nor did Judaism as these scholars understood it make use of the religious symbolism or ideas of the Hellenistic world, in which it existed essentially apart and at variance.

Today no sophisticated student of Judaism in late antiquity works within the framework of such a synthesis, for this old way is no longer open. It was closed by a number of scholars and by the infusion of new attitudes, the former working in isolation from one another, and the latter barely articulated and yet informing the thought of recent scholars.[1] That talmudic literature evolved in creative symbiosis in the

Hellenistic-Roman world was proved in a most masterful manner by Saul Lieberman who, following the early researches of S. Krauss and others, demonstrated in great detail and with astonishing erudition how deeply embedded in late Hellenism were the methods and vocabulary of the Rabbis. But Lieberman went much further. In an essay, "Pleasures and Fears,"[2] the full significance of which has not been widely appreciated, Lieberman stated:

> The wisdom of the East [in this context, astrology] could not be entirely ignored. A learned and cultured man of those times could not reject the science of Astrology, a science recognized and acknowledged by all the civilized ancient world. To deny at that time the efficacy of Astrology would mean to deny a well established fact, to discredit a "science" accepted by both Hellenes and Barbarians...

Lieberman goes on to trace the attitude of the Rabbis toward astrology, and to show how they mediated between it and Judaism, concluding: "The power of Astrology is not denied, but it is confined to the Gentiles only, having no influence on Israel." What is important here is Lieberman's willingness to take seriously the challenges of Hellenistic science, magic, and religion, not merely in the faith of "assimilated" Jews nor in the practices of the "ignorant masses" but in the bastions of the faith and their guardians. Here we find no effort to explain away embarrassing and irritating contradictions to the prevailing view of a rationalistic and antiseptic this-worldly faith but rather a realistic effort to take all evidence seriously.

Nor does Lieberman stand alone. Gershom Scholem's researches[3] on Jewish mysticism in late antiquity have demonstrated, again in erudite ways, how both talmudic and extra-talmudic literature point toward the existence of Hellenistic themes, motifs, and symbols deep within the circles of "pious" Jews. Furthermore, the late Erwin R. Goodenough,[4] studying archaeological remains and Hellenistic literature, but barely literate in Hebrew and Aramaic sources, came to very much the same conclusions on the nature of Judaism, at least among the circles in which the artifacts bearing pagan symbols, or symbols bearing Jewish values different from those associated with their original pagan setting, were used. Finally, one must point out the contribution of A.J. Heschel[5] to the radical reinterpretation of the theology within talmudic literature itself. Heschel demonstrates not merely the presence of theological attitudes at least as self-consistent and rigorous as the legal ones, but he shows, even though he never makes this explicit, that some of these motifs must be seen against the background of theological inquiries among contemporary Gentiles who thought about the questions of transcendentalism and immanentalism in ways not wholly unlike the Jews'.

It was Morton Smith, one of the very few scholars adequately trained not only in history and philology but, most important, in the history of religions in antiquity, who first pointed out the striking convergence of scholarly results, based upon disparate sources and produced by scholars who, though aware of one another's work, were laboring mainly alone. Smith stated:

... it is amazing how the evidence from quite diverse bodies of materials, studied independently by scholars of quite different backgrounds and temperaments, yields uniform conclusions which agree with the plain sense of these discredited passages. Scholem's study of the materials in the hekhalot tradition, for instance, has just led us to conclusions amazingly close to those reached by Goodenough from his study of the archaeological remains: to wit, the Hellenistic period saw the development of a Judaism profoundly shaped by Greco-Oriental thought, in which mystical and magical... elements were very important. From this common background such elements were derived independently by the magical papyri, Gnosticism, Christianity, and Hellenistic and Rabbinic Judaism....[6]

Most recently, M. Margoliot succeeded in piecing together the Sefer HaRazim, which constitutes still another example of a Jewish magical papyrus, this time in Hebrew, illustrating once again the kind of Judaism strikingly different from that which the earliest scholars had led us to expect.

Naturally, efforts continue to be made to retain the old one-dimensional and rationalistic synthesis, to explain new evidence in terms of old hypotheses. One cannot hope to convince the proponents of the old view that we must reconsider matters in a fundamental way. But such efforts to explain away the evidence will produce less and less insight. Among them is the strikingly unconvincing view of E.E. Urbach, who states:

These finds from Beth She'arim [of scenes from pagan mythology in the sarcophagi of the rabbis] put an end to all the theories based on making a clear distinction between the private world of the Sages, as reflected in the talmudic and mishnaic laws about idolatry, and the other world that existed outside theirs....[7]

Urbach prefers to "explain" the evidence in a way calculated to rule out any genuine confrontation with Hellenism. Jewish artisans, he says, were employed in making statues and images for pagans. They sometimes sold their products to Jews without making any change in their design of conventional patterns for idol-worshipping Gentile customers. Urbach never says why Jews bought them, or why rabbis let Jews do so. In any event, even the pagans, Urbach says, used idols and images for decorative purposes only. He does not tell us just what that means or how he knows. If these paintings and adornments were introduced into private houses for aesthetic reasons, it is not surprising that they should have found their way into synagogues and cemeteries,[8] so Urbach.

Why is it not surprising? It seems that, for all his ostentatious erudition, Urbach has not paid serious attention to how surprising such phenomena would have been in an earlier period (before A.D. 70), as the archaeological evidence reveals, and in the period after they were very rigidly excluded (in the 5th and 6th centuries A.D.). If Jewish craftsmen did not, as Urbach says, consider it a sin to make use of pagan motifs in their work, still how liberal must the rabbis of Beth She'arim have been to accept such artifacts into their burial caves! I cannot regard his explanation, in any case, as wholly congruent to the phenomena to be explained, as relevant to all situations in which they are found and to all issues posed by their form and explanation. A more intelligent way of approaching matters is provided by Morton Smith in his "Image of God: Notes on the Hellenization of Judaism, with Especial Reference to Goodenough's Work on Jewish Symbols,"[9] which needs to be carefully studied both for its content and for the methodology demonstrated within it.

These remarks are meant to place into context two recent books relevant to Judaism in late antiquity -- Palestinian Judaism in the Time of Jesus Christ, by Joseph Bonsirven and Gnosticism and Early Christianity, by R.M. Grant. The first embodies the inadequacies of the systematic-theological approach to a limited body of isolated evidence, the second bears some of the rich promise of new questions and new approaches which are at hand.

II

Joseph Bonsirven, S.J. was professor of New Testament at the Pontifical Biblical Institute in Rome until his death in 1958. His Palestinian Judaism was originally published in France in 1950, and the English translation was prepared on the basis of that edition. However, someone has brought his bibliography "up-to-date" by adding the names of a few books published since 1950, indeed since Bonsirven's death. But a bibliography which omits, on Philo for example, any reference to Goodenough, or on the history of the Jews in the Tannaitic period, a single reference to G. Alon, can hardly be regarded as a serious effort. Goodenough has been the object of a decades' long campaign of Todschweigen, in which Bonsirven took part. So Bonsirven is not much of a scholar. What is gained by adding a book list not wholly the author's I simply do not know. What is lost, obviously, is a clear notion of what the writer did and did not see. (Instead of "improving" the bibliography, someone should have provided the book with an index.)

The chief question I feel obliged to raise concerning the publication of this book, however, is why it was necessary to bring out a book which is out-of-date on the day it appears. Bonsirven made no use of the newly-discovered literature of the Jewish communes in the Dead Sea area and elsewhere, and any description of first-century Palestinian Judaism which does not do this is woefully incomplete. Some scholars have challenged the dating of these Scrolls, and perhaps Bonsirven agreed with them. But I do not find reference to the problem of the Scrolls anywhere. It may be argued that Bonsirven's chief interest was in Pharisaism, but if that were the case one wonders why he makes such extensive use of Philo, Apocryphal, and Pseudepigraphical books which reflect little or nothing of the Pharisaic part of Judaism. Thus the book is as useful as a chemistry text based on the phlogiston theory!

Bonsirven's book contributes little to the knowledge of its subject, and in no way can I find significant grounds for favorable comparison with Moore's Judaism or Schechter's Aspects of Rabbinic Theology. Its chief advantage over the former is brevity and over the latter (if any) its greater catholicity. Bonsirven treats the following subjects: God, angels, Israel and the nations, the Torah, man and general ethics, religious life, special ethics (justice, charity, relations with Gentiles, individual perfection), life after death,

Messianism, and general.eschatology. On each theme the author gives a brief synopsis of Jewish thought and quotes from some relevant talmudic sources.

While Bonsirven does find many virtues in "Palestinian Judaism," his interest in it is motivated by his existential concern as a Christian. This he never lets the reader forget. For example, in discussing ideas about God he writes:

> In Christianity the mystery of the Holy Trinity provides us at once and correlatively with two benefits, a more profound knowledge of God's nature and the most intimate possible divine presence and immanence... (p. 25).

I have no objection at all to the inclusion of such a statement (and it is one among many) in this book, but I do think it should be made clear that the reader is not confronted with a (mere) statement of scholarship but rather with a statement of faith operating through scholarship. It might have been possible for the author to put all his apologetical remarks in one chapter or in some other way to separate a straight-forward presentation of Judaism from the religious polemic, however nicely phrased, which is attached to it.

It would have been interesting, in fact, for Bonsirven to write a comparison of Judaism and Christianity, as have other scholars, both Jewish and Christian. These writings have offered considerable illumination for the understanding of both faiths, and one need only consult the essays of Leo Baeck, H.J. Schoeps, A.H. Silver, on the Jewish side, and (most recently) W.D. Davies on the Christian, to be aware of how much is to be gained in such an enterprise. But I fail to see how religions are "compared," how understanding is to be gained, by constant asides to reassure the reader, at appropriate intervals, of the superiority of Christianity, and, more specifically, of Roman Catholic Christianity, over all religions, even so elevated and noble ones as the one at hand. I should emphasize that my objection is not to Bonsirven's frequent, and generally fair-minded, criticism of Judaism. I object only to his having made a study of Judaism into the occasion for Christian apologetics.

Bonsirven offers numerous generalizations which may puzzle students of talmudic literature. For example, he states (p. 46) that the Rabbinical writings speak very rarely about the Covenant (berit). He might have found reason to change his opinion in Bab. Talmud Shabbat 130a-137b, among other places. His interpretation of the difficult passage (Bab. Talmud Bava Batra 10b) on the alms of the nations would have been more convincing if he had seen the parallel passages. His discussion of the lack of Jewish proselytism (by contrast with the apostle Paul) suffers from his disinterest in the mundane reason for the cessation of that effort, specifically the decrees of the first Christian emperors. His discussion of the limited Jewish success in this regard, compared with that of Christianity, disregards the tragic history of the Jewish people under Rome in the first and second centuries. His interpretation of the passage (Pesikta de Rav Kahana 40a-b) in which R. Yohanan ben Zakkai says, "The dead body does not render unclean nor does the water purify... but it is the decree of the Holy One...," is quite wrong; Bonsirven thinks that it opposes the rational tendency of Alexandrian Judaism to try to find reasons for the laws. R. Yohanan ben Zakkai was famed (at least among students of Rabbinic literature) for his homer-exegeses, which have exact parallels in Philonic writings. What we have here, rather, is a statement of acceptance despite the lack of rational explanation, and, underneath, a confession of skepticism. He is even more wrong when he says that Pharisaism "did not escape the conviction that one can satisfy one's duties to God by fulfilling external rituals, which may easily be emptied of all love," as has been made abundantly clear by many better-qualified scholars of Tannaitic Judaism than Bonsirven.

Bonsirven's concluding discussion raises the question of whether Israel's refusal to accept Jesus as Christ may have been the consequence of another "more secret and prolonged infidelity, an infidelity to the spirit, or even to the letter, of the revelation of which Israel was the trustee and the missionary." Bonsirven is kind enough to absolve Judaism of "fundamental disloyalty." Rather, he says, it was guilty of a "distortion which was gradual and not realized for a long time." The result was that the Pharisees "tightened the static elements," in defending the faith against Hellenism, "in a protective conservatism meant to slow down external dynamic factors." That this was simply not true cannot be argued here, but it can, at least, be said that Bonsirven offers no evidence that it was true.

I cannot recommend this book. It is neither thorough nor original, contains errors of interpretation of Jewish sources, and questionable conclusions about those same sources. The author ignored a great body of new evidence, and by no means exhausted the information available in the old. His piety is admirable, and his honest respect for Judaism may represent a position unusual in his circumstance. One need not, however, express admiration or happy astonishment just because a book on first-century Judaism refrains from the commonplace, out-and-out anti-Semitism of so many Christian scholars of that subject. Bonsirven's book ought, in fact, to be measured not by academic, objective scholarly standards but rather by its effectiveness as a tract on Christian sacred history written from the perspective of Christian, particularly Roman Catholic, theology.

III

In order fully to appreciate the religious alternative facing Jews in the Tannaitic period, one must enter the complicated subject of Gnostic religion. Grant's book renders that subject accessible. It is informative, lucid, and interesting. One comes away from it enriched by the author's vast fund of facts and enlightened by his perspective.

Grant's thesis is that Gnosticism grew up in the ruins of Jerusalem, a weed sprouting amid the shattered stones. It was the natural consequence of earlier apocalyptic thought, which had tried to interpret events in the light of the final destination of history. With the destruction of the Temple, disheartened Jews rejected the world and its Creator, both of which they regarded as demonic, in favor of an unknown God, represented in this world by a savior who, descending into the worldly hell, himself needed to be saved. The activities of this savior are recognized by those who "know," who possess saving knowledge (gnosis), which transcends mere belief.

Grant's definition of Gnosticism is based on one borrowed from the Valentinians: "Who we were and what we have become, where we were and where we have been made to fall, whether we are hastening, whence we are being redeemed, what birth is and what rebirth is...." He who knows the answers to these questions is a Gnostic, though he who asks them is not necessarily so. Gnostics know that they were "originally spiritual beings who have come to live in souls and bodies.... Now thanks to their self-knowledge, they are hastening back above, having been redeemed from this world below." Thus, Grant tells us, the Gnostic is a Gnostic because he knows by revelation who his true self is.

The central issue of Grant's study is, what is the origin of Gnosticism? In the past it has been traced to Hellenistic philosophy, Oriental religion (chiefly Iranian), Christianity, or heterodox Judaism, and Grant argues for the fourth. His argument is stated as follows (p. 34):

> Not only apocalyptic enthusiasts, but Jews in general must have had their faith shaken. The temple services had come to an end, what were priests and Levites to do? With the temple destroyed, how could pious Pharisees continue to obey the law of Moses? With the failure of the apocalyptic vision, how could it be maintained by either Essenes or Zealots? The law and the prophets remained, but how were they to be interpreted?

As to Grant's thesis, I find it wanting for four reasons.

First, his definition of Gnosticism is too broad and imprecise. By it, practically anyone in this period would be in some way "Gnostic," including Pharisaic Jews, who also possessed knowledge which they regarded as of transcendent value.

Second, while I find it entirely plausible that the impact of the events of 70 and 135 on Judaism was catastrophic, and may well have disheartened many Jews and led them by diverse paths out of this world, it is impossible to see how all these phenomena associated with the word "Gnostic" emerged, so rapidly and universally, uniquely from the Jewish situation. Simon Magus was a Gnostic. Yet he was alleged to have lived in the last century before the destruction of the Temple. Likewise, many sayings in Paul's letters have been regarded as Gnostic, or as said to Gnostics, such as the well-known passages in Corinthians and Colossians. These have nothing to do with the chronology Grant requires.

Third, whoever speaks of "knowledge" is not necessarily "Gnostic." Grant, and many others (most brilliantly, of course, Hans Jonas in The Gnostic Religion) speak of "Gnosticism" as a "religion." Yet where do we find it? Was there a "Gnostic church"? Was there a "Gnostic community"? Bultmann, Reitzenstein, Jonas and Grant speak as if Gnosticism were a concrete phenomenon, from which were derived not only many specific sets but also substantial elements in early Christianity. Yet if that were the case, where do we find it outside of Mandaean and Manichaean circles? I prefer to follow Arthur D. Nock, who in Early Gentile Christianity and Its Hellenistic Background says (p. xiv):

> I must continue to hold that in the environment of early Christianity there were materials which could be built in Gnostic systems, but no Gnostic system; that there was an appropriate mythopoeic faculty -- but no specific myth; that there was a "Gnostic" state of mind -- but no crystallized formulation of that state of mind and no community or communities clinging to that formulation.

Nock thus insists that as historians we must persevere as extreme nominalists, describing phenomena as they become clear, but avoiding the temptation to reify, to describe as real, a construction of all phenomena into one neat "system," however much we may be attracted by the theological possibilities inherent in such an orderly system.

Finally, I think Grant focuses on the wrong question to begin with. He wants to know the "origins" of Gnosticism, and, having asked the question, is willy-nilly faced with a limited number of possibilities and a circumscribed frame of investigation. Do we really need to know the origins of a phenomenon before we can begin to understand and analyze it? Is this not a question which may in some studies be usefully postponed? In the case of Gnosticism, a clear definition of the phenomenon ought to precede, by a great deal, an effort to uncover its origins. A definition should both include and exclude, and should permit the simplest common denominator to emerge and be rigorously applied. Since so much is called "Gnostic," from within the heartland of Judaism to most distant Gaul on the west and Iran on the east, we clearly have no very helpful definition before us. To debate the old issues is sterile, therefore, particularly because so much remains to be done in publishing semi-Gnostic texts (in particular the 1945 find at Nag-Hammadi).

We may find in Professor Carsten Colpe's Religionsgeschichtliche Schule (Göttingen 1961) a useful, more precise definition. Gnosticism, Colpe proposes, is a religion, or theology, characterized by a focus on a saved savior, salvator salvandus. It seems to me this narrow definition which is lucidly and brilliantly argued by Colpe in the final chapter of his book, is congruent to all the phenomena clearly identifiable as "Gnostic" according to all opinions and all sources. It would, moreover, exclude the possibility of speaking further of "Jewish Gnosticism," and I think that is a substantial step forward in history of religion. A theology which, like other kinds of Gnostic theology, condemns the Creator God and calls the Law an instrument of the demonic and a source of sin can hardly be regarded, by the broadest historical definition and the lowest common denominator, as at all Jewish. Or, to put it differently, if "Gnosticism" may find a place within "Judaism," then "Judaism" is emptied of any phenomenological meaning whatever.[10]

The issues I have raised here ought not to be construed as criticism of Grant's book. It is, as I said at the outset, informative and challenging, and should find an audience among all students of talmudic, particularly Tannaitic, Judaism.

IV

The contrast between the two books is illuminating. Bonsirven's anachronistic work ignores vast bodies of evidence, obscures important sources on the nature of first-century Judaism in Palestine, and in the end at best yields merely a repetition of what one can learn from Moore, with minor variations, and in a far less palatable context. Grant, on the other hand, has raised a major challenge by bringing to bear his very deep knowledge of Gnosticism upon the issue of the character of Palestine Judaism after 70. In doing so, he has enriched our own understanding of the problems facing Jews in that age, and of alternatives explored by some of them. If I have raised some doubts about Grant's thesis, I do not want to leave the impression that I find it in the end entirely unacceptable. It is clear, for one thing, that some specific historical circumstances require further eluci-dation; the exact meaning of the word "Gnosticism" demands more precise denotation after Nock. But such a precise definition will, in the end, not necessarily exclude the possibility that "Gnosticism in the Jewish idiom" was, as Grant argues, born in the crucible of the national disasters of 70 and 132-135, even though it is quite clear that Gnosticism quickly took forms which would not have proven compre- hensible within the great and varied world of the Judaism of this period.[11]

Grant's work offers still another thesis, which I think in the end we shall have to understand and evaluate in the light of Smith's judgment:

> Of all these four bodies of evidence -- the works of the Biblical tradition, the Jewish literature of pagan style, the testimonia concerning Jews, and the archaeological material -- no one is complete by itself. Each must be constantly supplemented by reference to all the others. And each carries with it a reminder that the preserved material... represents only a small part of what once existed.... Yet even this preserved material... testifies consistently to the hellenization of ancient Judaism.[12]

In such a light, Grant's thesis does not appear incomprehensible, even though in time it may be useful to refine it further.

In the end, the old way leads directly into apologetics -- whether for a "pure" and "un-Hellenized" Judaism among the Jewish scholars, or for a praeparatio evangelica of a particularly noble sort for the Christians. The former synthesis cannot illumine new evidence, but requires its distortion, or necessitates that it be explained away. As in the last epoch of Ptolemaic astronomy, the epicycles multiply with each new observation, and the time seems near when the system will collapse of its own weighty complexity. We must remember that Copernicus did not prove that the world was not stationary while the sun, moon and stars move humbly above and around it; he simply offered a new hypothesis, a new synthesis which explained existing knowledge in a manner more reasonable, more efficient, and more fruitful than the old way. We await the formation of such a new synthesis.

NOTES

[1]This is not the place to spell out all of the attitudes which characterize the historical researches of the recent scholars, though, for a beginning, one should study the late Renée Bloch's "Note Methodologique pour l'étude de la littérature rabbinique," Recherches de Science Religieuse, 43, 1955, pp. 194-225 -- see how G. Vermes spells out Bloch's methodological proposals in his superb Scripture and Tradition in Judaism (Leiden, 1961) -- and compare the profound remarks of Brevard S. Childs at the end of his "Interpretation in Faith," Interpretation, A Journal of Bible and Theology, XVIII, Oct., 1964, pp. 432-49. The issue is not merely a broadening of the focus of interpretation, however. A graver problem is whether we know as much as we think we know. The

former generation of historians working with talmudic literature, for example, treated that literature as if descriptions of events were written by a stenographer for the use of a newspaper reporter; as if, in other words, talmudic sources provide an adequate, critical description of events. The great issue was to establish an accurate text. If they had such a text, the former historians thought that all their problems were solved, and that they knew fairly well exactly what had happened, what had been said, what had been done, even though the interpretation of events might still have posed problems. When one realizes the fact that critical history is a modern conception, and that no one in late antiquity, least of all Jewish chroniclers, wrote without a very clear-cut didactic purpose, and that in any case the talmudic accounts we have of events pertaining to the Jews and Judaism are by no means word-for-word transcriptions of what, if anything, observers saw and heard, then matters become much more complicated. An example of the literalism, not to say historiographical fundamentalism, of the greatest of talmudic historians may be seen in G. Alon's discussions of R. Yohanan ben Zakkai's escape to Yavneh, cited and criticized in my Life of Rabban Yohanan ben Zakkai (Leiden, 1962), pp. 104-128, 147-171. Alon offers an exegesis of what R. Yohanan said and did not say in his encounter with Vespasian which, to my way of thinking, ignores the nature of the sources available for such exegesis. There are numerous lessons still to be learned by students of this period from New Testament scholarship, the very first of them being the need to take a hard-headed ("higher-critical") view of what in fact we know, and how we know it. I have tried to do so in my Life and History of the Jews in Babylonia. Y. Liver's Toledot Bet David (Jerusalem, 1959) and Y. Heinemann's HaTefila biTekufat HaTannaim veHaAmoraim (Jerusalem, 1964) are excellent examples of needed historical criticism and form criticism respectively. But much of the new research ignores the most fundamental critical problems and therefore is disappointing, if not completely useless. Liver and Heinemann are still exceptional.

[2] Greek in Jewish Palestine (N.Y., 1942), pp. 115-143. Passage cited is on pp. 98-9.

[3] Besides the well-known Major Trends in Jewish Mysticism, see Jewish Gnosticism, Merkabah Mysticism, and Talmudic Tradition (N.Y., 1960), and the relevant parts of On the Kabbalah and its Symbolism (N.Y., 1955).

[4] Jewish Symbols in the Greco-Roman Period (N.Y., 1953 et seq.), vols. I-XII.

[5] See his Theology of Ancient Judaism [Hebrew: Torah Min HaShamayim beAspaklaria shel HaDorot], (London and New York) I, 1962, and II, 1965 [reviewed below].

[6] "Observations on Hekhalot Rabbati," pp. 153-4, in Biblical and Other Studies, ed. Alexander Altmann (Cambridge, 1963), pp. 142-160.

[7]"The Rabbinical Laws of Idolatry in the Second and Third Centuries in the Light of Archaeological and Historical Facts," Israel Exploration Journal, 9, 3-4, 1959, pp. 149-165, 229-245. Passage cited p. 153.

[8]Ibid., p. 237.

[9]Bulletin of the John Rylands Library, XL, 2, March, 1958, pp. 473-512.

[10]In my History, II. The Early Sasanian Period, pp. 180-188, I have argued that Rav followed the Gnostic style of telling Creation myths, but that he resurrected monotheist-Jewish ones, based upon the Scriptures which preserved an ancient Israelite cosmogony. Rav's "theology in the Gnostic manner" produced not a rejection of law, nor, all the more so, of the Lawgiver. Thus for him, the Gnostic style characterized the rejection of Gnostic doctrine.

[11]And I confess that the criterion of comprehensibility is a highly subjective and imprecise one. We do not really know what Jews would or would not have understood to be "Jewishly comprehensible." It is wholly a value-judgment, and one I ought not to offer as a serious conceptual instrument. For history of religions, it is probably out of place. [But see Sanders, below.]

[12]"Image of God," pp. 486-7.

11. George Foot Moore
JUDAISM IN THE FIRST CENTURIES OF THE CHRISTIAN ERA.
THE AGE OF THE TANNAIM
Journal of Jewish Studies 1980. 31:141-156

JUDAISM IN THE FIRST CENTURIES OF THE CHRISTIAN ERA. THE AGE OF THE
TANNAIM. By George Foot Moore. Cambridge, 1927: Harvard University Press. I-III.

Slightly more than a half-century has passed since George Foot Moore's Judaism in
the First Centuries of the Christian Era: The Age of the Tannaim made its appearance.
The work was published in May 1927 and reprinted in November, had a third printing in
1932, a fourth in 1944, and a seventh in 1954, and remains in print and current. Not only
was it an immediate success in the marketplace but the earliest reviews accorded the
book a remarkably favorite reception.[1] Among those of 1927 only one, F.C. Porter's,
which I shall cite at length below, raised important critical questions alongside entirely
appropriate, adulatory comments. The warmest tribute, of course, is envy and imitation,
and the main outlines of Moore's argument and the principal definition of issues and
methods came to be imitated in accounts of exactly the same subject, constructed in
exactly the same way, yielding exactly the same results, for the following fifty years.[2]
So for one set of reasons, Jewish scholars of Judaism, and for another set of reasons,
Christian scholars of Judaism, reached the same positive conclusion.[3] Moore had said the
last word, which now needed only to be repeated by scholars proposing to say their own
last word.

Had Porter's criticism been taken to heart, Moore's work would have enjoyed a more
just and appropriate afterlife. That is, it would have been deemed to mark an important
step forward, but, more significant, to stimulate further and better work. For the mark
of great scholarship is that it rapidly is made obsolete, having precipitated fresh thought
and having raised fructifying challenges for a new generation. Moore closed many doors;
he opened none. His book marks a dead end, signified by the honeyed praise in which
historical theologians preserved and embalmed his ideas. Among the English-language
reviews of 1927-1928, Porter's stood by itself. His thoughtful observations, centering on
Moore's failure to take account of the halakhic evidence at all, his definition of norms,
and his highly idiosyncratic conception of what evidence enters into the description of
"Judaism" and what does not, were not appreciated. Nor is it unfair to expect that in a
time during which American scholarship approached the history of ideas in the way that
Moore did, another sort of criticism, of a social and economic sort, should have been
forthcoming. But, as I shall stress, there is no clear social foundation for that construct,
"Judaism," of which Moore speaks. Consequently, there also is no self-evident boundary
which includes some evidence and excludes other evidence. The confusion in the

definition of the canon of usable evidence, illustrated by Urbach's notorious caprice (below) in his inclusion of Philo and exclusion of the whole Dead Sea library, begins in the failure to specify that social group or class (apart from "the nation") whose "Judaism" comes under description.[4] The utter absence of interpretation from Moore's work and the resort to apologetics in place of rigorous asking of fructifying theoretical questions would be recognized only much later on.

I wish here to outline a program for resuming progress in that enterprise in which Moore's work stands as a landmark, but not at the end of the way. In so doing, I shall first define that thing which is under study, in the assumption that, after all, we do not all know and agree upon that about which we are talking. From that point the logical question is what is wrong with Moore's account of this "Judaism," and why it requires successors, not merely works of improvement and restatement in the light of new evidence. Finally, I shall offer some planks in a platform of what is to be done in this next stage in the on-going task of the history of ancient Judaism.

I

What We Study When We Study "Judaism"

The critical problem of definition is presented by the organizing category, "Judaism." Moore does not think definition is needed. But we now know that it is. Explaining what we propose to define when we speak about "Judaism" is the work of both contemporary philosophy of religion and history of religion. In general historians of religions have tended altogether too rapidly to articulate that phenomenon, the history of which they claimed to describe. Moore fails to tell us also of whom he wishes to speak. So his repertoire of sources for the description of "Judaism" in the "age of the Tannaim" is awry. He makes use of sources which speak of people assumed to have lived in the early centuries of the Common Era, even when said sources derive from a much later or a much earlier time. But his error, on the side of including too much, surely is matched by scholars for whom "Judaism" is fully described out of the resources of apocryphal and pseudepigraphic writings of the period before 70, without any attention at all to the social foundations and the historical limitations of the documents adduced in evidence. What generates this error is the problem of dealing with a category asymmetrical to the evidence. That is, an essentially philosophical construct, "Judaism," is imposed upon wildly diverse evidence deriving from many kinds of social groups and testifying to the state of mind and way of life of many sorts of Jews, who in their own day would scarcely have understood one another (for instance, Bar Kokhba and Josephus, or the teacher of righteousness and Aqiba). So for Moore, "Judaism" is a problem of ideas, and the history of Judaism is the history of ideas abstracted from the groups that held them and from the social perspectives of said groups. This seems to me a fundamental error, making the category "Judaism" a construct of a wholly fantastic realm of thought: a fantasy, I mean.

This now brings us to the definition of what we propose to describe and interpret through the evidence of those whom Moore calls "the Tannaim," I mean, their kind of "Judaism." The problem of defining what sort of thing we study when we describe and interpret "Judaism" is in two parts. First, what kind of an "ism" is in hand? Second, what sort of subspecies of that "ism," the "Juda" kind of "ism," do we treat?

If we declare that we study a religion, with special attention to the Judaistic version of religion, we advance our discussion only a little bit. For precisely what we study when we study a religion, and what sorts of evidence we should examine and what kinds we may ignore when we do so, are not entirely clear. Indeed, if we reflect on the extant answers to those questions -- what do we study when we study a religion, and what kinds of data do we adduce for analysis in that connection -- we move far out, towards the limits of imagination and the data of culture. People write the history of early Zoroastrianism on the basis of meanings of words not even in sentences, having no other, better evidence (Boyce, 1979: 1-16). A complete version of a Judaism of late antiquity is teased out of evidence lacking all verbal explanation, namely symbols used in synagogue-art and on gravestones.[5] So from stones and single words, on upward to wall-frescos and sentences, paragraphs and rooms, all manner of writing and all kinds of buildings, evidence is found suitable for the description and interpretation of a religion. The definition of religion, for its part, loses all promise of precision, when, in our own day, "Marxism" and "psychoanalysis" are termed "religions." At the same time religion becomes an expression of something quite other than convictions of a transcendental and supernatural content. For instance, "religion" is represented as a not-well-disguised social movement (Donatism) on the one side, or as a response to contextual dissonance of a structurally fundamental social order (a "cargo cult") on the other.

So if we can use any evidence of any kind to study any phenomenon of any sort, what we do when we study religion and how we do it are not readily discerned. In this regard matters are admirably summed up in Arthur Darby Nock's inquiry about the matter of "Gnosticism." He wanted to know where are the Gnostic churches, who are the Gnostic priests, and what are the Gnostic church's books and doctrines.[6] What he meant was to point out that what we have are rather specific evidences, e.g., of Manichaeism or Mandaism (and now, of Nag Hammadi). Out of the agglutination and conglomeration of these diverse social groups and their writings scholars (not Jonas alone) formed (I should say invented) that higher idea, that "the" — the Gnostic religion. From a philosophical viewpoint the intellectual construct, Gnosticism, may bear scrutiny. From an historical viewpoint, it does not. The reason is that history, rightly done, must err on the side of radical nominalism, as against the philosophical power for tolerance of something close to pure realism. In invoking these categories of medieval philosophy for analogical purposes, I mean only to explain why, for the present purpose, "Juda" + "ism" do not constitute definitive categories.

What then is under discussion, stated quite simply, is the world-view and way of life which speak of transcendent things and claim to work out in this world supernatural norms (hence the religion) of a very small group of Israelites in the later first and second century. Their first creation, Mishnah, is important because in time it came to define major elements of the world-view and way of life of nearly the whole Jewish people. The second-century Tannaim laid the foundation for the religion of the Jews through almost the whole of the history of the Jewish people from the time of the formation of the Mishnah until nearly our own time, thus: Judaism. It goes without saying that in describing the seed-time of one kind of Judaism, scholars in no way claim to report on the character of the Judaism -- the supernatural way of life and the transcendent world view -- of nearly the whole of the Jewish people who expected the Messiah soon and who fought against Rome twice. This was during the very time in which this (then) special kind of Judaism -- represented by Mishnah -- was aborning. That kind of normal Judaism is represented by IV Ezra and II Baruch.

II
What Is Wrong With Moore

It is the history of the formation of a principal part of that distinctive kind of "Judaism" beginning in the period somewhat before the destruction of the Second Temple of Jerusalem in 70 and concluding with the formation and closure of Mishnah itself, in about 200, which is the subject of any book called Judaism: The Age of the Tannaim. I have at the outset to explain why I propose a program to succeed George Foot Moore's Judaism in the First Centuries of the Christian Era. The Age of the Tannaim. There is no point in merely replacing a treatment of a topic done wrongly by another one, also done wrongly, i.e., one in which the same topic is once more defined improperly and therefore worked out inappropriately (compare Porter on Moore, cited below).

What has now to be accomplished by doing things aright is to show what should have been done to begin with. It is by that criterion that I wish this program to be judged. If it is deemed to have failed, it will have been a noble failure. Moore speaks for me: "The aim of these volumes is to represent Judaism in the centuries in which it assumed definitive form as it presents itself in the tradition which it has always regarded as authentic. These primary sources come to us as they were compiled and set in order in the second century of the Christian era..." So Moore begins his masterpiece, the intention of which I have made my own in my Judaism: The Evidence of the Mishnah (Chicago, 1981: The University of Chicago Press).

Contrary to Moore's and everyone else's view, Mishnah is the first relevant document for the representation of Judaism as it presents itself, in the tradition it regards as authentic. Whether we call this kind of Judaism "rabbinic," "talmudic," "normative," "classical," or even "mishnaic" hardly matters. Under study is the nascent stage as revealed in the first document of that expression of the religious world-view and way of life which, from its own day to ours, has shaped the consciousness and culture of the Jewish people and has defined what we mean when we speak of Judaism. To be sure, there are two other writings which both derive from Israelite hands and also inform us about Israelite thinking in the same period, from 70 to ca. 200. These are II Baruch and IV Ezra.[7] While some maintain that chapters in other pseudepigraphic documents may derive from the times under discussion, all agree that these two certainly come to full expression after 70 and provide a glimpse into the mind of some people of that day. There are, in addition, allusions among Christian writers to the state of mind of Jews whom they claim to have known but may have invented as in the case of Justin Martyr. But so far as Moore's criterion governs the work of presenting Judaism in the centuries in which it comes to its first full expression, Mishnah is the document which Judaism has always regarded as authentic. The history of that kind of religion expressed in Mishnah therefore is to be presented under Moore's title. We shall not have to speak of all kinds of Judaism in the age of the Tannaim who framed one of those kinds, as Moore's title suggests is his intention. We should address only that one kind of Judaism, and its history, to which the principal and constitutive document of the Tannaim, Mishnah, gives full expression and rich testimony.

What is to be done, specifically, is to take the strata of Mishnah's intellectual history, such as I already have explained and analyzed in my history of Mishnaic law, and to put the parts together into that new and whole structure demanded for the purpose of historical reconstruction and interpretation. When that task has been accomplished we shall have a picture of the beginnings and first major expression of the Judaism of which Mishnah is the original flowering. What makes this account distinctively historical, however, will be the sustained effort to relate the unfolding of the ideas of Mishnah to the historical setting of the philosophers of the document, to compare context and concept, to ask about the interplay between ideal and social, material reality. The historical program of this work, therefore, is identical to that of Moore's. This is so, even though, in the nature of things, the evidence deemed relevant and the way in which the evidence is analyzed and brought together to form a reconstruction of the several stages in the formation of Judaism scarcely intersect with Moore's procedures at a single point. The difference is for two reasons.

First of all, as indicated, Moore's book is much too long. That is to say, the evidence he adduces derives from, and therefore represents, altogether too wide a range of varieties of Judaism, over too long a period of time. Much of the evidence for "Judaism" in Moore comes from, and faithfully portrays, either the age long before 70 or the period four or five centuries after the formation of the Mishnah in 200. More important: a vast amount of material derives from circles which cannot be deemed at all concentric with the social and intellectual group behind Mishnah.[8] Thus Moore describes many kinds of "Judaism" as if they formed a single concept.

Second, Moore's work to begin with is not really a work in the history of religions at all -- in this instance, the developmental and formative history of a particular brand of Judaism. His research is in theology. It is organized in theological categories. Moore presents a synthetic account of diverse materials, (deriving from diverse sources, as I said) focused upon a given topic of theological interest. There is nothing even rhetorically historical in the picture of opinions on these topics, no pretense of systematically accounting for development and change. What is constructed as a static exercise in dogmatic theology, not an account of the history of religious ideas and -- still more urgent -- their unfolding in relationship to the society of the people who held those ideas. Moore in no way describes and interprets the religious world-view and way of life expressed, in part, through the ideas under study. He does not explore the interplay between that world-view and the historical and political context of the community envisioned by that construction of a world. So far as history attends to the material context of ideas and the class structure expressed by ideas and institutions alike, so far as ideas are deemed part of a larger social system and religious systems are held to be pertinent to the given political, social, and economic framework which contains them, Moore's account of dogmatic theology to begin with has nothing to do with religious history, that is the history of Judaism in the first two centuries of the Common Era.[9]

Let me amplify this point to explain why I believe a fresh program to account for the formation of Judaism, specifically beginning with the evidence of Mishnah, is necessary. The question formulated and answered has to be spelled out carefully. Moore's systematic and dogmatic theology draws upon a vast range of evidence, adducing testimony for the character of the Judaism he describes from documents deriving from diverse groups which, in their own day, as I said previously, will not have understood one another, let alone have accepted as part of the same social and cultic community. When "Judaism" is made to refer to the exegetical compilations of the rabbis of the fourth and fifth centuries -- and much later -- as well as the writings of the "sectaries at Damascus" (as Moore calls them), then the term "Judaism" stretches so far, covers so much diversity, as to lose all definitive use. Evidence from the fifth century of the Common Era and from the first or second century before it -- six hundred years -- serves no more naturally to describe a single relation (if also no less) than the poetry of the age of Beowulf and that of our own day serves to describe a single language (if also no less).

In proposing a completely different approach to the description of Judaism in the First Centuries of the Christian Era: The Age of the Tannaim, I wish now to take full account of the important and prophetic criticism of Frank C. Porter.[10] I believe that Porter's review should have led to a fruitful debate with Moore and to a fresh approach to the work done by Moore so elegantly, but with such crushing flaws. So far as I know, from the time of Porter's review of Moore to this date, there has been no effort to take seriously the problems pointed out by Porter, even though many independently may have been aware of them. Indeed, the two principal flaws, first, the claim that the "Judaism of the Tannaim" was normative, and second, the systematic aversion to discussion of the Judaism revealed by the legal texts, were self-evident from that start. Yet everyone who came after Moore continued the work of dogmatic theology, resorted to precisely the same undefined and undefended, formless canon to fill in the same categories, and pretended that the Tannaim created everything and anything but the Mishnah.

It is time, therefore, for Porter to have that hearing denied him for diverse reasons for so long. I quote the principal paragraphs in which Porter sets forth the problem which has not been solved but has been sidestepped for so long. First let us consider Porter's criticism of the matter of normativity:

> The Judaism which Professor Moore describes with such wealth of
> learning is that of the end of the second century of our era, and the sources
> which he uses are those that embody the interpretations and formulations of
> the law by the rabbis, chiefly from the fall of Jerusalem, 70 A.D., to the
> promulgation of the Mishnah of the Patriarch Judah, about 200 A.D. When

Moore speaks of the sources which Judaism has always regarded as authentic, he means "always" from the third century A.D. onward. It is a proper and needed task to exhibit the religious conceptions and moral principles, the observances, and the piety of the Judaism of the Tannaim. Perhaps it is the things that most needed to be done of all the many labors that must contribute to our knowledge of that age. But Professor Moore calls this Judaism "normative"; and means by this, not only authoritative for Jews after the work of the Tannaim had reached its completion in the Mishnah, but normal or authentic in the sense that it is the only direct and natural outcome of the Old Testament religion. It seems therefore, that the task here undertaken is not only, as it certainly is, a definite, single, and necessary one, but that other things hardly need doing, and do not signify much for the Judaism of the age of Christian beginnings. The book is not called, as it might have been, "The Judaism of the Tannaim," but Judaism in the First Centuries of the Christian Era: The Age of the Tannaim. Was there then no other type of Judaism in the time of Christ that may claim such names as "normative," "normal," "orthodox"? The time of Deuteronomy was also the time of Jeremiah. The religion of revelation in a divinely given written law stood over against the religion of revelation in the heart and living words of a prophet. The conviction was current after Ezra that the age of prophecy had ended; the Spirit of God had withdrawn itself from Israel (I, 237). But if prophecy should live again, could it not claim to be normal in Judaism? Where, in the centuries after Ezra, are we to look for the lines of development that go back, not to Ezra and Deuteronomy, but to Jeremiah and Isaiah? R.H. Charles claims the genuine succession for his Apocalypses. The Pharisees at least had the prophets in their canon, and it is claimed by many, and by Moore, that the rabbis were not less familiar with the prophets than with the Pentateuch, and even that they had "fully assimilated" the teaching of the prophets as to the value of the cultus (II, 13), and that their conception of revealed religion "resulted no less from the teaching of the prophets than from the possession of the Law" (I, 235). Christians see prophecy coming back to Judaism in John the Baptist and in Jesus, and find in Paul the new experience that revelation is giving in a person, not in a book, and inwardly to each one through the in-dwelling Spirit of God, as Jeremiah had hoped (31:31-34). And now, finally, liberal Judaism claims to be authentic and normal Judaism because it takes up the lines that Jeremiah laid down.

It would require more proof than Professor Moore has given in his section on "History" to justify his claim that the only movements that need to be traced as affecting religion are these that lead from Ezra to Hillel and Johanan ben Zakkai and Akiba and Judah the Prince. Great events happened during the three centuries from Antiochus IV to Hadrian, events which deeply

affected Judaism as a religion. But of these events and their influence Moore
has little to say. It is of course in connection with these events that the
Apocalypses were written.

It is to meet Porter's first point that I define the program as I do: Judaism as portrayed
within a specific, socially-circumscribed corpus of evidence. But we must go a step
beyond what Porter calls for. For we should claim to speak not merely about the Judaism
of the Tannaim, but, at the outset, the Judaism portrayed by a single document, the first
one produced by, and attributed to, those authorities conventionally called "Tannaim."
For reasons which I shall make clear below, we must make ample provision for the
probability that there is much more evidence about the Judaism shaped by the authorities
who stand behind Mishnah than is contained solely within the framework of Mishnah. That
is why the program of describing the Judaism of the ancient rabbis must begin in one
place and move on from there.

Porter's second criticism of Moore seems to me still more telling. He points out
that Moore almost wholly neglects the Tannaitic legal corpus -- Mishnah itself:

> In [Moore's] actual exposition of the normative, orthodox Judaism of the
> age of the Tannaim comparatively little place is given to Halakah. One of the
> seven parts of his exposition is on observances; and here cultus, circumcision,
> Sabbath, festivals, fasts, taxation, and interdictions are summarily dealt with;
> but the other six parts deal in detail with the religion and ethics, the piety and
> hopes, of Judaism, matters about which the Haggada supplies most of the
> material, and for which authority and finality are not claimed. The tannaite
> (halakic) Midrash (Mechilta, etc.) contains a good deal of Haggada together
> with its halakic exegesis, and these books Moore values as the most important
> of his sources (I, 135ff.; II, 80). The principles of religion and morals do indeed
> control the interpretation of certain laws, so that Halakah is sometimes a
> source for such teachings, and "is in many instances of the highest value as
> evidence of the way and measure in which great ethical principles have been
> tacitly impressed on whole fields of the traditional law" (I, 134). This sounds
> as if the ethical implications constituted the chief value of the Mishnah for
> Moore's purposes. But these are not its chief contents. It is made up, as a
> whole, of opinions or decisions about the minutiae of law observance. It
> constructs a hedge of definitions and restrictions meant to protect the letter
> of the law from violation, to make its observance possible and practicable
> under all circumstances, and to bring all of life under its rule.
>
> The Jewish scholar, Perles, in a pamphlet with which Moore is in
> sympathy, criticized Bousset, in Die Religion des Judentums, for using only
> books such as Bacher's, on the Haggada, and for expressing a preference for
> haggadic sources; whereas the Halakah in its unity, in its definitive and
> systematic form, and its deeper grasp upon life is much better fitted to supply
> the basis of the structures of a history of the Jewish religion. Moore agrees
> with Perles' criticism of Bousset's preference for the later, haggadic,

Midrashim; but it is not because they are halakic that he gives the first place
to the early Midrash. "It is this religious and moral element by the side of the
interpretation of the laws, and pervading it as a principle, that gives these
works [Mechilta, etc.] their chief value to us" (I, 135). Perles insists on the
primary importance of the Halakah, not only because it shows here and there
the influence of prophetic ethics, but because throughout as it stands, it is the
principal work of the rabbis, and the work which alone has the character of
authority, and because, concerned as it is with ritual, cultus, and the law
(Recht), it has decisive influence upon the whole of life. This applies
peculiarly to the religion of the Tannaim. The Haggada neither begins nor
ends with them, so that Bousset ought not, Perles thinks, to have used
exclusively Bacher's work on the Haggada of the Tannaim, but also his volumes
on the Haggada of the Amoraim, as well as the anonymous Haggada which
Bacher did not live to publish. It is only in the region of the Halakah that the
Tannaim have a distinctive place and epoch-making significance, since the
Mishnah, the fundamental text of the Talmud, was their creation.

Would Perles be satisfied, then, with Moore's procedure? Would he think
it enough that Halakah proper, observances, should occupy one part in seven in
an exposition of the Judaism of the Tannaim, considering that in their classical
and distinctive work Halakah practically fills sixty-two out of sixty-three
parts? Moore agrees with Perles that there is no essential distinction between
earlier and later Haggada (I, 163), and that the teachings of the Tannaim about
God and man, morals and piety, sin, repentance, and forgiveness are not only
also the teachings of the later Amoraim, but run backward, too, without
essential change into the Old Testament itself. There is no point at which
freedom and variety of opinion and belief, within the bounds, to be sure, of
certain fundamental principles, came to an end, and a proper orthodoxy of
dogma was set up. But orthodoxy of conduct, of observance, did reach this
stage of finality and authority in the Mishnah; and the tannaite rabbis were
those who brought this about. It is in accordance with Moore's chief interests
in haggadic teachings that he does not confine himself to sayings of the
Tannaim, but also quotes freely from the Amoraim; how freely may be seen by
the list that ends Index IV.

Professor Moore's emphasis upon his purpose to present normative
Judaism, definitive, authoritative, orthodox, would lead one to expect that he
would give the chief place to those "jurisdic definitions and decisions of the
Halakah" to which alone, as he himself sometimes says, these adjectives
strictly apply. We should look for more about the Mishnah itself, about its
systematic arrangement of the laws, its methods of argument and of bringing
custom and tradition into connection with the written law, and more of its
actual contents and total character, of those actual rules of life, that
"uniformity of observance" which constituted the distinction of the Judaism of
the rabbis.

How in my Judaism I corrected this second, and principal, failing of Moore hardly needs specification. Curiously, in correcting Moore's failure to take account of the evidence of the halakah, that is, of Mishnah, of the second-century authorities, I focus upon that other error of description which strikes me as critical. I mean the ignoring of the social context of a religious structure and system. For the law deals precisely with that -- the construction of society, the formation of a rational, public way of life.

The history of a religion should tell how a religion took shape and describe its concern for a relationship to the concrete historical context in which that religion comes to full expression. These simply are not topics which form part of the hermeneutical framework of Moore's book. The critical issue in my view is the relationship between a religion, i.e., the world-view and way of life of a coherent social group, and history, i.e., the material, economic, and political circumstance of that same social group. This history in Moore simply is not addressed.

True, the history of a religion and the dogmatics of that religion are going to relate to one another. But a description of dogmatics of seven centuries or more and an account of the contents thereof simply do not constitute a history of the religion which comes to formal ideological expression in dogmatic theology. So Moore did not do what the title of his book and of his professorship ("professor of the history of religion") promises, even though in his work he discusses numerous matters bearing historical implication. Since his aim, which is the right one for the description and interpretation of a religion, remains unmet, I address it in my Judaism.

The proposed account of the interplay between religious ideas and the social group that held those ideas should take its first step by asking about the sort of social group represented by the data we clearly have in hand. A further step is to propose a statement of the social and class perspective of that group whose viewpoint is before us. To extrapolate from the facts we have, i.e., the ideas people clearly held at diverse times, and thus to offer a picture of the questions people propose to confront through those facts and the social perspectives which generate those questions, is an exercise not attempted by Moore. His successors then took for granted that Moore had defined the work to be done, but merely had not done it adequately. So each went over the same ground of dogmatic theology and called the result history. In my judgment the history of a religion is the social relation of the world-view and way of life of that religion to the material reality of the people who held those ideas. Self-evidently, we have first to trace and distinguish the layers of ideas welded together into a single, intellectually-composite document. But merely telling which idea came first and which came later is not history; it is not even much of a narrative.

To be sure, there is a further social history which must come, the objective history of the society in which the particular social group at hand formed a part. It is only in that larger, quite objective context that we can assess the character of a particular social perspective, a fantasy made concrete, such as is before us. True, we shall tell the story of how the things people in our document were saying related to the perspective, framed by them in particular, upon the encompassing context in which they lived. But then we have said nothing about the facts of circumstance, economy, and society, only about the viewpoints, the fantasies, of a particular group in context. Describing the social perspective of a document does not carry us far outside the framework of the document. It surely does not permit us to state the social facts to which the document constitutes a particular response, upon which the thinkers of Mishnah express their judgments. But describing a viewpoint does permit us to claim to move beyond the limits of the document itself, by using the facts therein to address the world outside -- if only through an account of the social imagination of the people who made up those facts.

III
What Is To Be Done?

The program adumbrated here must begin with an account of "Judaism: The Evidence of the Tannaim as Contained in Mishnah." The shift is from "age" to "evidence" and from general reference to all of rabbinic literature to a single, central document. In moving from "age" to "evidence" we free ourselves from a premature confrontation with all of the evidence for the period under discussion, both that produced at the same time as Mishnah but by other groups than those behind Mishnah, such as IV Ezra and II Baruch; and also that literature produced later on by the same (rabbinic) groups as receive and venerate Mishnah itself, such as the Siddur and piyyut, the early Midrashim, the Targumim, the qabbalistic writings, as well as the Talmuds, and so on (of which more in a moment). By dealing only with the unfolding of a single document, we establish a firm place for further work, a fulcrum on which we may move many weighty sources. We must not exclude the fact that, in documents redacted later on, there is apt to be evidence deriving from, and pertinent to, the period under discussion and the group subject to description. We simply present one set of facts pertinent to Judaism in the age of the Tannaim, difficult of access, prior to approaching yet other sets of facts, much more difficult of access. The criticism that accounts of the Judaism of the first and second century ignore the materials in the Targumim which can be shown to have circulated in that early period is telling and must be taken into account. It is taken into account when we claim to do only what we do, and not much more than what we do. The program is to start with one document, and tell the social history of the ideas of that document, so far as we are able.

So what is to be done is to describe the unfolding of one important stream of materials flowing into the formation of the kind of Judaism which took shape in the first few centuries of the common era and predominated thereafter. Those materials are the ones collected and expressed in Mishnah attributed to Judah the Patriarch, ca. 200. In concentrating on that singular corpus of ideas and how it takes shape, I do not wish to suggest that there is no other important evidence about the shaping of the kind of Judaism represented all together by Mishnah and its successors and continuators. The contrary is the fact. There is a vast corpus of relevant documents; these documents include two Talmuds, the compilations of biblical exegeses -- Midrashim -- made by rabbis of the fourth, fifth, and later centuries, the synagogue liturgy (Siddur, Mahzor, earliest Piyyut), the translations of the principal biblical writings used in the synagogue and otherwise (the Targumim), and the mystical and magical writings represented in the extant Sefer harazim, let alone ideas held earlier but preserved only later in such collections as the Hekhalot writings.

Nor should I wish to give the slightest credence to the conviction, which I reject, that it is only Mishnah which contains ideas likely to have been in the minds of those first and second century Israelites who stand behind Mishnah and take part in the creation of the mode of Judaism expressed -- in what degree and measure we do not know -- within Mishnah. I wish to stress the conviction that important materials in the Targumim and later midrashic compilations demonstrably circulated earlier. To be sure, how they circulated we do not know. In what form, for what purpose, and among what social circles they were formed in the first century of the common era, and even earlier than that time, we cannot necessarily say for sure.

This extended statement of qualification must be taken as the opening proposition of this program, or the claim and purpose of the program simply will not be understood, and unhappily, once more the best will be made into the enemy of the good and useful. What I propose is one important task in the systematic description of the formation and earliest social context and intellectual history of a kind of Judaism known to us from a number of sources, all socially and intellectually cognate to one another, each presenting its distinctive perspectives (and, alas, methodological problems). The ultimate, encompassing description of the Judaism of which we speak in its earlier formation, in the first and second centuries, will take account of more than what Mishnah has to tell us. But Mishnah is the first document to be redacted in something very like the character in which it now reaches us. It is a vast and complex document. It deserves full and reverent attention. The results of this program, based on over ten years of analytical work, in some measure will have to be brought into juxtaposition with, and contrasted to, parallel analyses -- as yet not undertaken -- into other documents. Then we shall know what is to be learned from them too about the same period in which Mishnah speaks.

When, moreover, we claim to speak of one kind of Judaism at a given period, we must not be accused of neglecting other kinds of Judaism, the religious systems worked out by others, of the same time and place. These too claimed to be not merely a part of "Israel" but "the true Israel." The testimonies to these other kinds of Judaism are contained not only in the parts of the New Testament, for example, Matthew, produced in the later first century in the Holy Land. They also persist, as I have stressed, in those massive and important compilations under the names of Baruch and Ezra, prepared in the aftermath of the destruction of the Second Temple and in response to the crisis of the spirit precipitated by it. A picture of Judaism which took full account only of those materials later on utilized by the kind of Judaism which became normative, will be seriously inadequate for the description of the origins of that kind of Judaism in the period in which we speak. Even the effort merely to contrast in the descriptive exercise the people whose writings we do employ and those whose writings we do not requires attention to the character of that excluded group of Israelites and its concerns. Otherwise the points of comparison and contrast will hardly be amply charted.

Furthermore, since the evidence of Mishnah begins in the period before 70, a full account of the social and religious context in which the ideas ultimately brought to closure in Mishnah takes shape would have to pay attention to the literary legacy of the Essenes contained in the library of Qumran and other places; the immense system of Philo, with its curious points of parallelism and intersection with ideas contained in much later rabbinic writings; and the evidence on the state of Judaic consciousness, imagination, society, and institutions, preserved for his own purposes by Josephus. We may, indeed, not neglect the bulk of those vast and diverse writings produced in the last two or three centuries before the common era and preserved, in the main, among circles other than those which succeeded and carried forward the legacy of Mishnah and its cognate writings.

In speaking of the unfolding of the ideas of Mishnah, I stress at the very outset the simple fact that these ideas testify to the inner life and world-view of only one group among many which ultimately gave shape to that Judaism later called talmudic or rabbinic, normative or classical. There are other sources -- Targumim, Midrashim, Talmudim -- for what was happening in circles contemporary to Mishnah and also represented, later on, in that same kind of Judaism. But we do not yet know the relationship of those circles and their ideas to the circles of thinkers who stand behind Mishnah. We also do not know how or when the writings of the one group, those of the people behind Mishnah, came to intersect with the writings of another, for instance, the people behind the Targumim, the synagogue liturgy, or the folk who created the aggadic tales and midrashic interpretations of Scripture, many of them demonstrably available in the same time in which Mishnah was coming to full expression but only much later written in the way in which we now have them. Perhaps the Targumim and Midrashim, the various fables and scriptural twists and turns, originated in other circles than those behind Mishnah and only later on were taken over and deemed "rabbinic." Perhaps they came into being in the same groups as stand behind the earliest layers of Mishnaic thought. At this time we cannot be certain, having no controls or certain criteria. Not all problems are to be solved at once.

NOTES

[1]The following are English-language reviews printed at the time of the publication of Moore's work: Barnes, 1927-28: 60-65; Cohen, 1928: 403-4; Kallen, 1927: 479-86; Porter, 1928: 30-62; Schulman, 1927-28: 339-355.

[2]See my review of Urbach and Sanders (below) for a more complete account of what I find faulty in the work of Moore's followers and imitators.

[3]The Jewish scholars were astonished at Moore's positive evaluation of Judaism. I am not entirely clear why Christian scholars of the same period in general accorded

Moore so positive a reception, or why for so many decades afterward his work was subjected to so much trivial correction and so little fundamental rereading. Moore's rejection of the anti-Semitic attitudes of Christian scholars of Judaism was already familiar in his "Christian Writers on Judaism."

[4]Israeli scholarship on ancient Judaism tends to project backward the ideology of the national-religious parties and to take for granted that there was a single ("Orthodox") Judaism, maintained by the entire "nation," except for a few "fringe-groups." Whether or not this is the contemporary state of affairs, it seems unwise to take for granted that it also pertained at the time under discussion -- or indeed whether the fundamental categories of analysis apply. But if there were a single "orthodox," normal, normative Judaism shared by the population of the country, it would appear to be that apocalyptic Judaism expressed in the diverse visionary writings and messianic movements which provoked a fair part of the population to undertake two massive wars against Rome. The motive for undertaking such wars is hardly to be located within the program of the Temple priests, on the one side, or their lay-imitators in Pharisaism, on the other. These groups, joined to the scribes, stand behind the method and message of the earliest documents of Rabbinic Judaism, beginning in Mishnah itself.

[5]I refer to Erwin R. Goodenough, Jewish Symbols in the Greco-Roman Period (1953-69), but of course that is something of a caricature, since Philo tends for Goodenough to supply many suggestive ideas indeed.

[6]I paraphrase Nock's review (1972) of Jonas, Gnosis and spätantiker Geist.

[7]On Jewish pseudepigraphic writings after 70, Professor James H. Charlesworth (personal letter, October 29, 1970) writes:

> The major writings in the Pseudepigrapha in the period after 70 but before 200 are 4 Exra and 2 Baruch. Enoch and the Apocalypse are usually dated to this period. The problem in working with them is that they are extant in Old Church Slavonic and with Slavic material we are faced with an exceedingly difficult problem which is unparalleled in our work on the other documents. We know that the documents extant in Slavonic have been preserved because of the Bogomiles. The Bogomiles, however, created pseudepigrapha; they were both shaped and formed by older pseudepigrapha and also wrote new ones. The task is exceedingly difficult, therefore, to be certain what is prior to the Bogomiles and, of course, that is our only interest.

[8]This notion of circles, concentric and otherwise, is beautifully utlized in Nock's review of Jonas, cited above.

[9]I wish to emphasize here that at fault in Moore is not merely that he takes for granted (1) whatever is attributed to an ancient rabbi really was said by him at the time he is supposed to have lived; and (2) whatever is told about an ancient rabbi really was done by him; and (3) the ancient rabbis defined a single, ageless, ahistorical "normative Judaism" and the like. These are faults of much work of his day. But the notion that the history of ideas unfolds in tandem with the history of the social groups which held such ideas, and that ideas express the particular viewpoint of a distinctive social group, was commonplace. After all, Moore worked in the same time as, among many other American social and intellectual historians, Charles Beard. The study of ancient Christianity as a social phenomenon, moreover, had long since gotten under way. If we do not wish to invoke the great name of E. Troeltsch, we may refer only to Shirley Jackson Case's work of approximately the same age.

[10]Journal of Religion 1928, 8:30-62.

12. Abraham Joshua Heschel
THEOLOGY OF ANCIENT JUDAISM.
TORAH MIN HASHSHAMAYIM BEASPAKLARIA SHEL HADDOROT II
Conservative Judaism 1966, 20:66-73

THEOLOGY OF ANCIENT JUDAISM. TORAH MIN HASHSHAMAYIM BEASPAKLARIA
SHEL HADDOROT, VOLUME II. By Abraham Joshua Heschel. London and New York:
Soncino Press, 1965. 440 pp.

This monumental volume continues Abraham Heschel's study of the major trends of
thinking in rabbinic Judaism. Heschel has devoted most of his scholarly and theological
career to the problem of revelation and inspiration. Indeed, if that fact is understood, one
can penetrate into the heart of both Heschel's scholarship and his theology. His major
works (dealing with the prophets, rabbinic Judaism, Saadia, Ibn Gabirol, Maimonides,
Hassidism, modern philosophy of religion and philosophy of religion and philosophy of
Judaism) have centered upon the theme, narrowly defined, of religious knowledge, but
broadly viewed, of the encounter between man and God in real, as opposed to (merely)
intellectual life. Having grown up in a society in which the presence of God was
everywhere apprehended, Heschel came to a unique understanding of the problems for
religious philosophy set forth by Hume and Kant, when he met their thoughts in Berlin.
Hume had destroyed the usefulness for the philosophy of religion of all arguments from
design; and in meeting this challenge Kant had transformed the arena for religious
discourse by stressing the peculiar inner, almost intuitive quality of religious discourse,
thus distinguishing it from discourse concerning other kinds of truth. From the
perspective of Judaism, these were major events, but by the time Heschel came upon the
scene, argument had moved into very rigid and unbending channels; indeed, the
"perspective of Judaism" was lost upon the Jewish followers of Kant, and the Kantian
problem never really troubled the others. Like other religious Jews, Heschel had the
unique advantage of knowing God long before he thought about him. Like other
philosophical theologians, on the other hand, he sought to examine that knowledge and to
reflect upon it. From the Jewish perspective, however, religious knowledge is based upon
divine revelation. It became Heschel's lifelong task to investigate the meaning of
revelation within Judaism, and the broader issue of the ontological aspect of religious
existence. I believe this is the key to understanding how his scholarly and theological
works relate to one another. The great moments in the experience of revelation within
Judaism were, after Sinai, in prophecy, and in the transformation of prophecy (both
Mosaic and literary) into Torah by the second century rabbis, and in Hassidism. For
modern philosophy of religion, the issue Heschel therefore stresses is the "way to God,"

the nature of religious knowledge; and his philosophy of Judaism focuses, similarly, upon the way Jews know God, or more acurately, the ways in which God makes himself known.

As I have stressed, Heschel's is both a theological and a scholarly enterprise. If he had not chosen to pursue scholarly themes, such as the one before us, he could have made an extraordinary contribution to philosophical theology alone. Indeed, many of his readers are quite unaware of his scholarship in biblical, talmudic and hassidic themes. Similarly, if Heschel had chosen the way of systematic historical scholarship alone, he would have reached great heights. He has sought both to recover the historical theology of Israel, and to contribute to Judaism's philosophical theology.

Before turning to the volume at hand, let us review the main themes of the earlier one.

In order to appreciate what Heschel has achieved in this work, one must keep in mind that until now we have had no really adequate explanation of the thought, or theology, behind the numerous sayings of talmudic rabbis dealing with matters of faith. We have had a number of jerry-built structures, which impose upon talmudic Judaism alien categories borrowed from other traditions (as in the case of Moore, in the preceding essay). We have had some excellent anthologies. We have had rather confused and functionally almost useless "harmonies" of talmudic ideas which, speaking from a historical viewpoint, never in fact existed in the mind of any one man, or in any one time or place. These studies all assume that the literature of a period of five or six hundred years may be expounded as a whole, as if everyone who said anything used language and possessed ideas that remained constant over the whole period. If you can take seriously the proposition that from Chaucer to Joyce we can speak meaningfully of "the English literary mind," then you can work with such categories.

Until Heschel produced these volumes, therefore, we have been in the situation of medieval Ptolemaic astronomy. We have had a great deal of data, very accurately understood, and some obviously unsatisfactory, cumbersome theories for explaining them. The cycles and epicycles have multiplied beyond belief. We have had no simple realistic, historically verifiable and economical way of explaining our data. Like Copernicus, therefore, Heschel has set the world on its head. He has assumed, first of all, that certain central figures should be made the focus of a historical-theological study, to see whether in a tentative fashion we may come to an adequate principle underlying and unifying their sayings and disputes. He has therefore cited numerous teachers, but stayed (in Volume I) mainly within the framework of the issues commented on by Akiba and Ishmael. Secondly, he has allowed the disputes of Akiba and Ishmael to provide the substance of his discussion, and has not claimed to explain all of "talmudic Judaism." He looks behind and beyond the details of their immediate discussions, however, to discover general interpretive principles not only to explain one or another detail, but to illuminate the central underlying issues separating two seminal men.

Heschel has found such a hermeneutical principle, outwardly a deceptively simple one, but one which is most helpful. Heschel holds that the disputes between Rabbi Akiba and Rabbi Ishmael are based upon a fundamental disagreement on the nature of revelation and religion. Rabbi Ishmael held that religion comes from God to man, and therefore lays stress upon the realities of language known to man. Religion is a matter which man's reason can comprehend, and his life express. Its terms are the language of this world, and its vocabulary is the raw material of daily life. God is transcendent, beyond the world, and all that we can know of Him and His will is its this-worldly manifestation. Rabbi Akiba, on the other hand, held that God is immanent, and that this world, as much as the next, contains the Presence. Therefore, revelation may speak in a language not wholly human in origin or intention, and speak not only of the world as man commonly understands it, but also of mysteries, of realities beyond those we can see and touch. Religion is a matter not only for man's comprehension, but stands in some measure beyond his capacity to understand. The Torah speaks of a reality that may transcend the world. Thus immanental religion stands opposed to transcendental religion, mysticism to rationalism, neo-Platonism to Aristotelianism, and Rabbi Akiba to Rabbi Ishmael.

This brief description can mean nothing to the reader if he thinks that all Heschel has done is to impose upon two Tannaim some category other than any yet tried. What is extraordinary is that, working within these categories, Heschel is able to organize and to make sense out of the great mass of otherwise discrete and sometimes arcane material. He has not tried to impose an external and irrelevant heuristic principle, but demonstrate over and over again that in one concrete dispute after another there are to be located the abstract principles of immanentalism versus transcendentalism. What is astonishing is that after a while, the participating reader can easily and acurately predict the position on a specific question to be taken by Rabbi Akiba and Rabbi Ishmael and their followers, given merely a statement of the question.

In Volume I, Heschel treated the interpretation of revelation, the nature of miracles, sacrifices, the Presence, suffering, theological language, and so forth. At each point he examined not only the numerous relevant sayings of the two chief figures, but those of others in their respective schools. Some readers of Volume I may have found excessive the many quotations provided by the author, but in establishing his thesis, completeness, order and precision were essential. Without actually examining the evidence, one can hardly be aware of how intrinsically valid is Heschel's hermeneutical principle. Without seeing how thorough and well-disciplined has been his study of talmudic literature, one cannot fully appreciate his achievment in bringing some order and sense to it.

Some have argued that aggadah, meaning here religion and theology as these words are understood today, is irrelevant. Judaism has no dogma, only halakhah -- which means a law, a pattern of actions. However, Jews are not robots, contented with mindless, thoughtless repetition of meaningless action. They have always, even the most stupid among them, been thoughtful people, who acted because of a faith, however naive or primitive or uncritical, and not in a spiritual or intellectual vacuum. Hence the aggadic parts of the Talmud and cognate literature have been included in our tradition, not because ancient academicians could not find a better entertainment for their idle hours, as some exceptionally dull-souled expositors have maintained. Heschel has demonstrated in these volumes that the Rabbis were just as serious, just as penetrating, and just as self-consistent in theology as in law, for precisely the same reason, and in much the same manner. He has shown that just as the talmudic Rabbis were men of formidable consistency in their legal opinions, so were they rational and fully sensible in their theological ones. And he has shown this not by preaching or argument, but by a close and careful study of sources. Until now, therefore, we have had to accept the judgment that the Rabbis were not really interested in ideas, only in law. That their main interest was in law was shown by their lack of principled thought on other issues. We no longer need to take seriously such a shallow opinion, for we can see it demonstrated with truly halakhic precision that the Rabbis of the Talmud were at least as concerned with theology as they were with law.

Heschel writes in a pleasing, modified rabbinic style, richly and allusively, with a control and taste one misses in some of his English essays. A Hebraist may want to compare his style in these volumes with that of S.Y. Agnon.

In Volume II, Heschel concentrates upon the major issues of revelation as they emerge in rabbinic theology. Having established the existence of two great and contrary principles by which revelation could be conceived, those of Rabbi Akiba and of Rabbi Ishmael, he here traces how the Rabbis thought about revelation in concrete and mostly exegetical images, stressing the specific tests which embody their basic theses. In many places, moreover, he moves far beyond the central theses themselves, in order to provide a fuller and richer account of rabbinic ideas on revelation. He is not, therefore, bound by the limits of his original presupposition, however fruitful and penetrating it is. The major themes of this volume are first, the idea of Torah in heaven, its pre-existence, its form, how it was written. Second, he treats of Moses' ascent to heaven. Rabbi Akiba's view was that Moses actually went up to heaven, and Heschel treats not only his ascent but the ascents of Enoch and Elijah. Third, he examines the idea of the descent of the Kavod. He considers further the idea of "Torah from heaven," carefully analyzing rabbinic ideas on the substance of Torah, and on the Ten Commandments as the whole Torah. He shows how the concept of Torah was broadened and extended in the Akiban school. He considers the views which the Rabbis declared to be heretical, such as that Moses made it up himself, that less than the whole Pentateuch was revealed, and the like. He examines the two approaches to Mosaic Revelation. Rabbi Ishmael's school held that Moses often paraphrased His will in his own words. In the Akiban school everything was believed to be in the precise form spoken by the Divinity, without exception.

Heschel turns to a very elaborate analysis of the figure of Moses, including attention to what he himself, by contrast to the Lawgiver, was believed to have said, the school of Ishmael tending to delimit, and that of Akiba to extend, the role of the divinity in revelation. He shows that the two schools differed fairly consistently on whether the prophet was a partner in, or merely an inert vessel of, revelation, with the Akibans holding the latter view. The greatness, prophecy and literary achievements of Moses produced varying schools of thought, which are traced, in general, to the underlying principles elucidated in Volume I. Heschel discusses the prophetic foundations of other books, such as Job; prophecies which were lost or suppressed, and the like. This is clearly a work of gigantic proportions, for Heschel has not merely demonstrated that the Rabbis were as serious about and as consistent in theological as in legal issues, but he has recovered from the vast literature of ancient and medieval Judaism just how those issues were shaped concretely in their exegetical and heuristic setting. Sometimes the reader may feel that in trying to prove that the Rabbis were "talmudic" even about aggadah, Heschel himself has composed a highly "talmudic" account, but mostly he does not.

However, I found a number of difficulties in studying this volume. First, it is positively deplorable that the publisher has not seen fit to prepare an index, a list of sources quoted or cited (of which there are hundreds), a survey of sages mentioned and a complete bibliography. The absence of these normally commonplace aids greatly diminishes the usefulness of the volume for future reference and research. However carefully one may study it, he cannot remember every place where Heschel treats a given text or idea, and since this work will remain absolutely essential for all future studies of rabbinic theology, many future students are going to regret the failure to provide these basic tools. (The same indifference to the daily usefulness of major scholarly works characterizes the publication of the writings of J.N. Epstein, among others.) One hopes that those who take the trouble to publish such magnificent books will take the slight additional trouble of making them constantly, daily accessible.

Second, I think Heschel has here quoted in full far too many sources. While they are not all easily available, that is no reason to quote each and every one verbatim. Some could have been summarized; some paraphrased briefly; some merely cited. Many sources make the same point. Indeed, whole chapters or sections merely provide new illustrations of an idea already quite adequately set forth and abundantly demonstrated. Since this is a relatively long book, one might have expected that it would seek to treat tangential or minor points with some brevity. This unfortunately is not the case. In many places the narrative simply stands still; no new ideas emerge, and one merely reconsiders what the author has already made quite clear. On the other hand, I wish Heschel had provided a more extensive abstract presentation of the basic issues and ideas of Volume II. He very frequently assumes that the main idea comes across quite clearly from the text he is quoting and briefly commenting on. This is not the case. The felicitous presentation of the basic theses of Volume I is not duplicated here. Much is quoted; little is spelled out in thoughtful, one might say theological detail. The introduction, by contrast to the fifty-nine pages in Volume I, is only six pages long, and consists mainly of a polemic on the importance of theology. No one who doubts that is going to study this book.

These technical problems trouble me far less than the more fundamental methodological issues unresolved in Volume II. Volume I is both a theological and a historical work. Heschel is interested both in exposing the inner elements of a major complex of ideas, and in finding their historical settings in the great academies. On the whole, the line between theology and history is clearly drawn and almost never violated. Here, by contrast, I found a frequent confusion of historical and theological language. Heschel rightly treats the medieval and early modern exemplars of the basic principles under study, showing how the issues elicited continuing attention and hermeneutical dispute in later times. This is a thoroughly valid, historical-theological investigation. He also pays some attention to discussions of these same problems in late antiquity, but here I found the treatment most inadequate. He discusses Philo, but I could find slight evidence that he had made a close and careful study of Philonic scholarship. A major concern is the figure of Moses, yet how Moses was described in contemporary Christian thought, which had to confront the same theological issues concerning revelation as did the Rabbis, is never considered. The figure of Moses in the Fourth Gospel, for example, presents a most complex and subtle problem. One should imagine that men practically contemporaneous with the Rabbis and living in the same country, touched upon themes which concerned the "philosophers" of Judaism as well. The Samaritans, who were certainly a major element in Jewish Palestine in this period, actually centered their religious thought upon the figure of Moses. Indeed, Heschel's stress on the Mosaic figure recalls more than anything else that of the fourth century Samaritan teacher Marqah. When discussing the state of theological ideas in a given period, one must, I think, pay close attention to how kindred groups treated these same ideas. Here one ought to consider whether the Rabbis were influenced by the conceptions of those living close at hand, such as, in this instance, the Samaritans and the Christians.

Heschel treats a great mélange of medieval philosophical and Kabbalistic works in the very context of his historical and theological investigation, but never makes explicit the relations between them. He seems to suppose that the _theological_ issue is what makes it possible to compare the Zohar and the Talmud, and this may well be so; but I do not see how the Zohar (or Maimonides for that matter) can be used _historically_ to illuminate the theology of late antiquity.

Within talmudic materials, moreover, he mostly ignores serious historical issues, accepting as completely factual accounts about the Rabbis which by no means reveal what was happening, but only what later figures thought had happened earlier. I was disappointed to learn, for example, that Heschel regards as quite historical the accounts of Rabban Yohanan ben Zakkai's disputes with the Sadducees, which are almost certainly very late and imaginative at best. If one is elucidating an _idea_, he need not pay much attention to the historical setting in which the idea was manifested. However, if, like Heschel, he wants to trace the development of that idea by specific schools and teachers, he cannot very well ignore major historical issues inherent in the sources. Using historical language requires adherence to the canons of historical inquiry.

A pioneering work such as this is bound to reveal not only new information but also new methodological issues. In noting the chief of these, namely the unsatisfactory state of Heschel's thought on the relationship between historical and theological research, I do not wish to leave a false impression. Volume I required a sequel such as this, in which the great issues would be not merely set forth, but spelled out. If Heschel had only isolated the exegetical issues in which major theological principles could be discerned, as he does here, Volume II would have been an exceptionally important book. Having seen that the two great theologies of revelation held by rabbinic schools would yield numerous concrete problems, he has provided an exemplary demonstration of painstaking research concerning precisely what was said and why. I do not think he has overstated his case, nor has he transformed a very fine insight into a blunt axe, with which to chop apart and mechanically rearrange the sources. The richness of this volume testifies to the subtlety and sensitivity of his mind.

13. Ephraim E. Urbach

THE SAGES. THEIR CONCEPTS AND BELIEFS

Journal of Jewish Studies 1976, 27:23-35

THE SAGES. THEIR CONCEPTS AND BELIEFS. By Ephraim E. Urbach. Translated from the Hebrew by Israel Abrahams. Jerusalem: The Magnes Press, The Hebrew University, 1975. Two volumes -- I. Text: pp. xxii and 692. II. Notes: pp. 383.

Ephraim E. Urbach, professor of Talmud at the Hebrew University and author of numerous articles and books on the Talmud and later rabbinic literature, here presents a compendious work intended "to describe the concepts and beliefs of the Tannaim and Amoraim and to elucidate them against the background of their actual life and environment." When published in Hebrew, in 1969, the work enjoyed immediate success, going into a second edition within two years. Urbach is an imposing figure in Israeli scholarly and religious-political circles, serving as president of the Israel Academy of Sciences and Humanities and running for the presidency of the State of Israel as candidate of the right-wing and "religious" political parties. Within Orthodox Judaism Urbach derives from the German stream, which proposes to combine piety with academic learning.

The work before us has been accurately described by M.D. Heer (Encyclopaedia Judaica 16:4): "He [Urbach] outlines the views of the rabbis on the important theological issues such as creation, providence, and the nature of man. In this work Urbach synthesizes the voluminous literature on these subjects and presents the views of the talmudic authorities." The topics are as follows: belief in one God; the presence of God in the world; "nearness and distance -- Omnipresent and heaven;" the power of God; magic and miracle; the power of the divine name; the celestial retinue; creation; man; providence; written law and oral law; the commandments; acceptance of the yoke of the kingdom of heaven; sin, reward, punishment, suffering, etc.; the people of Israel and its sages, a chapter which encompasses the election of Israel, the status of the sages in the days of the Hasmoneans, Hillel, the regime of the sages after the destruction of the Temple, and so on; and redemption. The second volume contains footnotes, a fairly brief and highly selective bibliography, and alas, a merely perfunctory index. The several chapters, like the work as a whole, are organized systematically, consisting of sayings and stories relevant to the theme under discussion, together with Urbach's episodic observations and comments on them.

In the context of earlier work on talmudic theology and religion. Urbach's contribution is, as I said, a distinct improvement in every way. Compared to a similar, earlier compendium of talmudic sayings on theological subjects, A. Hyman's Osar divré hakhamin ufitgamehem (1934), a collection of sayings laid out alphabetically, according to catchword, Urbach's volumes have the advantage of supplying not merely sayings but cogent discussions of the various sayings and a more fluent, coherent presentation of them in essay form. Solomon Schechter's Some Aspects of Rabbinic Theology (1909, based on essays in the Jewish Quarterly Review printed in 1894-1896) covers exactly what it says, some aspects, by contrast to the much more ambitious dimension of the present work. The comparision to George Foot Moore's Judaism in the First Centuries of the Christian Era: The Age of the Tannaim (1927-1930) is somewhat more complex. Moore certainly has the advantage of elegant presentation. Urbach's prose, in I. Abraham's English translation, comes through as turgid and stodgy, while Moore's is the opposite. Morton Smith comments on Moore's work, "Although it too much neglects the mystical, magical and apocalyptic sides of Judaism, its apology for tannaitic teaching as a reasonable, humane, and pious working out of biblical tradition is con- clusive..." (Encyclopaedia Judaica 12:293-4; compare Harvard Library Bulletin 15, 1967, pp. 169-179). By contrast to Moore, Urbach introduces sayings of Amoraim into the discussion of each category, and since both Urbach and Moore aim to present a large selection of sayings on the several topics, Urbach's work is on the face of it a more comprehensive collection.

Urbach's own comments on his predecessors (I, pp.5-18) underline the theological bias present in most, though not all, former studies. Wilhelm Bousset and Hugo Gress-mann, Die Religion des Judentums im späthellenistischen Zeitalter (1926) is wanting because rabbinic sources are used sparingly and not wholly accurately and because it relies on "external sources," meaning apocryphal literature and Hellenistic Jewish writings. Urbach's own criticism of Moore, that "he did not always go deeply enough into the essence of the problems that he discussed," certainly cannot be leveled against Urbach himself. His further reservation is that Moore "failed to give an account of the origin of the beliefs and concepts, of their struggles and evolution, of their entire chequered course till their crystallization, of the immense dynamism and vitality of the spiritual life of the Second Temple period, of the tension in the relations between the parties and sects and between the various sections of the Sages themselves." This view underlines the historical ambition of Urbach's approach and emphasizes his view of his own contribution, cited at the outset: to elucidate the concepts and beliefs of the Tannaim and Amoraim against the background of their actual life and environment. Since that is Urbach's fundamental claim, the work must be considered not only in the context of what has gone before, in which, as I said, it emerges as a substantial step forward, but also in the setting of its own definition and understanding of the historical task, its own theory of how talmudic materials are to be used for historical knowledge. In this regard it is not satisfactory.

There are some fairly obvious problems, on which we need not dwell at length. Urbach's selection of sources for analysis is both narrowly canonical and somewhat confusing. We often hear from Philo, but seldom from the Essene Library of Qumran, still more rarely from the diverse works assembled by R.H. Charles as the apocrypha and pseudepigrapha of the Old Testament, and the like. If we seek to describe the talmudic rabbis, surely we cannot ask Philo to testify to their opinions. If we listen to Philo, surely we ought to hear -- at least for the purpose of comparison and contrast -- from books written by Palestinian Jews of various kinds. The Targumim are allowed no place at all because they are deemed "late." (The work of historians of traditions, e.g. Joseph Heinemann, and of comparative midrash, e.g. Renée Bloch and Geza Vermes, plays no role at all in this history!) But documents which came to redaction much later than the several Targumim (by any estimate of the date of the latter) make rich and constant contributions to the discussion. Within a given chapter, the portrayal of the sources will move rapidly from biblical to Tannaitic to Amoraic sources, as though the line of development were single, unitary, and harmonious, and as though there were no intervening developments which shaped later conceptions. Differentiation among the stages of Tannaitic and Amoraic sayings tends to be episodic. Commonly, slight sustained effort is made to treat them in their several sequences, let alone to differentiate among schools and circles within a given period. Urbach takes with utmost seriousness his title, the sages, their concepts and beliefs, and his "history," topic by topic, reveals remarkably little variation, development, or even movement. It would not be fair to Urbach to suggest that all he has done is publish his card-files. But I think his skill at organization and arrangement of materials tends to outrun his interest in differentiation and comparison within and among them, let alone in the larger, sequential history of major ideas and their growth and coherent development over the centuries. One looks in vain for Urbach's effort to justify treating "the sages" as essentially a coherent and timeless group.

Let us turn, rather, to the more fundamental difficulties presented by the work, because, as I said, it is to be received as the definitve and (probably) final product of a long-established approach to the study of talmudic religion and history. Urbach has certainly brought to their ultimate realization the methods and concepts of his predecessors.

First, let us ask, does the world-view of the talmudic sages emerge in a way which the ancient sages themselves would have recognized? From the viewpoint of their organization and description of reality, their world-view, it is certain that the sages would have organized their card-files quite differently. We know that is the case because we do not have, among the chapters before us, a single one which focuses upon the theme of one of the orders, let alone tractates, within which the rabbis divided and presented their various statements on reality, e.g., Seeds, the material basis of life; Seasons, the organization and differentiation of time; Women, the status of the individual; Damages, the conduct of civil life including government; Holy Things, the material service of God; and Purities, the immaterial base of divine reality in this world. The matter concerns not merely the superficial problem of organizing vast quantities of data. The talmudic rabbis left a large and exceedingly complex, well-integrated legacy of law. Clearly, it is through that legacy that they intended to make their fundamental statements upon the organization and meaning of reality. An account of their concepts and beliefs which ignores nearly the whole of the halakhah surely is slightly awry.

In fairness to Urbach, I must stress that he shows himself well-aware of the centrality of halakhah in the expression of the world-view of the talmudic rabbis. He correctly criticizes his predecessors for neglecting the subject and observes, "The Halakha does not openly concern itself with beliefs and concepts; it determines, in practice, the way in which one should walk... Nevertheless beliefs and concepts lie at the core of many Halakhot; only their detection requires exhaustive study of the history of the Halakha combined with care to avoid fanciful conjectures and unfounded explanations." Urbach occasionally does introduce halakhic materials. But, as is clear, the fundamental structure of his account of talmudic theology is formed in accord not with the equivalent structure of the Talmud -- the halakhah -- but with the topics and organizing rubrics treated by all nineteenth- and twentieth-century Protestant historical studies of theology: God, ethics, revelation, and the like. That those studies are never far from mind is illustrated by Urbach's extensive discussion of whether talmudic ethics was theonomous or autonomous (I, pp. 320ff.), an issue important only from the viewpoint of nineteenth-century Jewish ethical thought and its response to Kant. But Urbach's discussion on that matter is completely persuasive, stating what is certainly the last word on the subject. He can hardly be blamed for criticizing widely-held and wrong opinions.

Second, has Urbach taken account of methodological issues important in the study of the literary and historical character of the sources? In particular, does he deal with the fundamental questions of how these particular sources are to be used for historical purposes? The answer is a qualified negative. On many specific points, he contributes sporadic philological observations, interesting opinions and judgments as to the lateness of one saying as against the antiquity of another, subjective opinions on what is more representative or reliable than something else. If these opinions are not systematic and if they reveal no uniform criterion, sustainedly applied to all sources, they nonetheless derive from a mind of immense learning. Not all judgment must be critical, and not all expression of personal taste systematic. The dogmatic opinions of a man of such self-evident mastery of the tradition, one who, in addition, clearly is an exemplar of the tradition for his own setting, are important evidence for the study and interpretation of the tradition itself, particulary in its modern phase.

Yet we must ask, if a saying is assigned to an ancient authority, how do we know that he really said it? If a story is told, how do we know that the events the story purports to describe actually took place? And if not, just what are we to make of said story and saying for historical purposes? Further, if we have a saying attributed to a first-century authority in a document generally believed to have been redacted five hundred or a thousand years later, how do we know that the attribution of the saying is valid, and that the saying informs us of the state of opinion in the first century, not only in the sixth or eleventh in which it was written down and obviously believed true and authoritative? Do we still hold, as an axiom of historical scholarship, ein muqdam ume-uhar ["temporal considerations do not apply"] -- in the Talmud?! And again, do not the sayings assigned to a first-century authority, redacted in documents deriving from the early third century, possess greater credibility than those first appearing in documents redacted in the fifth, tenth, or even fifteenth centuries? Should we not, on the face of it, distinguish between more and less reliable materials? The well-known tendency of medieval writers to put their opinions into the mouths of the ancients, as in the case of the Zohar, surely warns us to be cautious about using documents redacted, even formulated, five hundred or a thousand or more years after the events of which they speak. Urbach ignores all of these questions and the work of those who ask them.

There is yet a further, equally simple problem. The corpus of evidence is simply huge. Selectivity characterizes even the most thorough and compendious accounts, and I cannot imagine one more comprehensive than Urbach's. But should we not devise means for the filtering downward of some fundamental, widely- and well-attested opinions, out of the mass of evidence, rather than capriciously selecting what we like and find interesting? We have few really comprehensive accounts of the history of a single idea or concept. Urbach himself has produced some of the better studies which we do have. It seems somewhat premature to describe so vast a world in the absence of a far more substantial corpus of Vorstudien of specific ideas and the men who held them than is available. Inevitably, one must characterize Urbach's treatment of one topic after another as unhistorical and superficial, and this is despite the author's impressive efforts to do history and to do it thoroughly and in depth. He is not merely selective. He is downright capricious.

After all, Urbach has done this great work without the advantage of studies of the history of the traditions assigned over the centuries to one authority or another. He has at hand scarcely any critical work comparing various versions of a story appearing in succesive compilations. He has no possibility of recourse to comprehensive inquiries into the Talmud's forms and literary traits, redactional tendencies, even definitve accounts of the date of the redaction of most of the literature used for historical purposes. He cannot consult work on the thought of any of the individual Amoraim or on the traits of schools and circles among them, for there is none of critical substance. Most collections which pass as biographies even of Tannaim effect no differentiation among layers and strata of the stories and sayings, let alone attempting to describe the history of the traditions on the basis of which historical biography is be recovered. The laws assigned, even in Mishnah-Tosefta, to a given Tanna have not been investigated as to their underlying presuppositions and unifying convictions, even their gross thematic agendum. If Urbach speaks of "the rabbis" and differentiates only episodically among the layers and divisions of sayings, in accord either with differing opinions on a given question or with the historical development of evidently uniformly-held opinions, he is no better than anyone else. The episodic contributions he himself makes in large measure constitute such history of ideas as presently is in hand. And, as I said, even that history is remarkable for the pre-critical methods and uncritical presuppositions upon which it is based.

Nor have I alluded to the intractable problems of internal, philosophico-theological analysis of ideas and their inner structures, once their evident historical, or sequential, development, among various circles and schools of a given generation and over a period of hundreds of years, has been elucidated. That quite separate investigation and analysis of the logic and meaning of the concepts and beliefs of the sages requires definition in its own terms, not in accord with the limited and simple criteria of working historians. If Urbach does not attempt it, no one else has entirely succeeded either. In this regard, Urbach's cavalier dismissal of the work of Marmorstein, Heschel, and Kadushin, among others, is pure quackery. While they may not have "persuaded" Urbach of the correctness of their theses, while they may have been wrong in some of their conclusions, and while their methods may have been unrefined, they at least have attempted the task which Urbach refuses even to undertake. One of the less fortunate aspects of Urbach's book, which makes for unpleasant reading, is the way in which he treats the work of other scholars. In the case of the above-named, this is not only disgraceful, it also is disastrous for Urbach's own undertaking. And since the whole opinion on works of considerable scholarship is the single word "worthless" or "unpersuasive," it may be observed that there is certain subjectivity which seems to preclude Urbach's reasoned discussion of what he likes and does not like in the work of many others and to prevent any sort of rational exchange of ideas. That is what I mean by quackery.

Urbach's work, as I said, in the balance brings to their full realization the methods and suppositions of the past hundred years. I cannot imagine that anyone again will want, from these perspectives, to approach the task of describing all of "the concepts and beliefs of the Tannaim and Amoraim," of elucidating all of them "against the background of their actual life and environment." So far as the work can be done in accord with established methods, here it has been done very competently indeed. Accordingly, we may well forgive the learned author for the sustained homiletical character of his inquiry and its blatantly apologetic purposes:

> The aim of our work is to give an epitome of the beliefs and concepts of the Sages as the history of a struggle to instill religious and ethical ideals into the everyday life of the community and the individual, while preserving at the same time the integrity and unity of the nation and directing its way in this world as a preparation for another world that is wholly perfect... Their eyes and their hearts were turned Heavenward, yet one type was not to be found among them... namely the mystic who seeks to liberate himself from his ego and in doing so is preoccupied with himself alone. They saw their mission in work here in the world below. There were Sages who inclined to extremism in their thoughts and deeds, and there were those who preached the way of compromise, which they did not, however, determine on the basis of convenience. Some were severe and exacting, while others demonstrated an extreme love of humanity and altruism. The vast majority of them recognized the complexities of life with its travail and joy, its happiness and tragedy, and this life served them also as a touchstone for their beliefs and concepts.

All of this may well be so, but it remains to be demonstrated <u>as historical fact</u> in the way in which contemporary critical historians generally demonstrate matters of fact. It requires analysis and argument in the undogmatic and unapologetic spirit characteristic of contemporary studies in the history of ideas and of religions. But in the context in which these words of Urbach are written, among the people who will read them, this statement of purpose puts forth a noble ideal, one which might well be emulated by the "sages" -- exemplars and politicians of Orthodox Judaism -- to whom, I believe, Urbach speaks most directly and persuasively, and by whom (alone) his results certainly will be taken as historical fact. The publishing success of the book and the recognition accorded its learned author are hopeful signs that the ideal of the sage of old indeed has not been lost upon their most recent avatars. It is by no means a reduction of learning to its sociological and political relevance to say that, if it were only for his advocacy of the humane and constructive position just now quoted. Urbach has made a truly formidable contribution to the contemporary theological life of Orthodox Judaism.

To respond to a work of such importance as Urbach's, it will not suffice to outline what is wrong with his book. Having stressed, for example, the importance of beginning the inquiry into the world-view of the talmudic rabbis with the study of the law, in particular of the earliest stratum, faithfully represented by Mishnah-Tosefta, I have now to propose the sorts of work to be done. Since I have raised the question of how we know what is assigned to a person was really said by him, and since by implication I have suggested that we cannot affirmatively answer that question, what sort of inquiry do I conceive to be possible, and upon what historical-epistemological basis? Let me here present very briefly an alternative conception of how to define and approach the formidable task accomplished by Urbach in accord with the prevailing methods and within established suppositions about the detailed and concrete historicity of talmudic evidences: the description of the world-view of "our sages." What happens when Fundamentalism dies, as it will even in Orthodox Jerusalem?

The problems that lie ahead and the line of research leading to their solution are now to be specified. Let us begin with the matter generally regarded as settled: the meaning of the texts. While philological research by Semitists and archaeological discoveries self-evidently will clarify the meanings of words and the identification of objects mentioned in the rabbinical literature, there is yet another task, the fresh exegesis of the whole of rabbinical literature within the discipline of contemporary hermeneutical conceptions. The established exegesis takes for granted an axiom which is simply false: that all texts are to be interpreted in the light of all other texts. Talmudic discussion of Mishnah and its meanings invariably shapes the received interpretation of Mishnah, for example. If Tosefta -- itself a commentary -- supplies a conception of Mishnah's principle or rule, then Tosefta places the imprint of its interpretation upon the meaning of Mishnah.

Now no one would imagine that the original meaning of Tanakh is regularly to be uncovered in the pages of Midrash or in the medieval commentaries to the Scriptures. On the contrary, everyone understands that Tanakh has been subjected to a long history of interpretation, and that history, while interesting, is germane to the original meaning of Tanakh only when, on objective and critical grounds, we are able to affirm it by historical criteria. By contrast, discussion of Mishnaic pericopae in Talmud and medieval commentaries and codes invariably exhausts the analysis of the meaning of Mishnaic pericopae. It is to the credit of H. Albeck (a better scholar than Urbach) that his excellent commentary to Mishnah makes the effort at many points deliberately to exclude considerations introduced only later on. This is done not merely to facilitate a simple and popular interpretation, though Albeck admirably succeeds in doing just that, but also to present what Albeck considers to be the primary and original meaning of the law. It is no criticism of Albeck, limited as he was by his form, a commentary of the most abbreviated sort, to say that the discussion of the primary meaning of Mishnah has to begin.

What is meant is simply, What did these words convey to the people who made them up, in the late first and second century? What issues can have been in their minds? True, much is to be learned from the answers to these questions supplied by the exegetes from the third to the twentieth century. But since, in the main, the supposition of the established exegetical tradition is non-historical and therefore uninterested in what pericopae meant at the outset, the established tradition, without re-evaluation, will not serve any longer. That is not to suggest it cannot be drawn upon. The contrary is the case. I know no other road into the heart of a pericope. At the same time, the established agendum -- the set of issues, problems, and questions deemed worth consideration -- is to be drastically reshaped, even while much that we have received will be reaffirmed, if on grounds quite different from those which motivated the great exegetes.

The classical exegetes faced the task of showing the profound interrelationships, in logic and meaning, of one law to the next, developing and expanding the subtleties and complexities of law, in the supposition that in hand is a timeless and harmonious, wholly integrated and unitary structure of law and logic. In other words, the established exegetical tradition properly and correctly ignores questions of beginnings and development, regarding these questions as irrelevant to the true meaning of the law under the aspect of eternity. And that is indeed the case -- except when we claim to speak about specific, historical personalities, at some one time, who spoke the language of their own day and addressed the issues of their own epoch. Urbach claims to tell us not about "talmudic Judaism" in general -- organized, as is clear, around various specific topics -- but to describe the history and development of talmudic Judaism. Yet, if that is the case, then the sources adduced in evidence have to be examined with the question in mind, What did the person who made up or formulated this saying mean to tell us? And the answer to that question is not to be located either by repeating the essentially eisegetical results already in hand, or by pretending that everything is obvious.

We have to distinguish between the primary issue, present to begin with in a pericope, and secondary problems or considerations only later on attached to the pericope. How do we confidently distinguish between the primary message of a pericope and the secondary eisegesis found in the great commentaries? We have to ask, What does the narrator, legislator, or redactor propose to tell us in a particular, distinct pericope? That is to say, through the routine form-analytical and literary-critical techniques already available, we have to isolate the smallest units of tradition, and, removing them from their redactional as well as their exegetical-eisegetical framework, ask about their meaning and original intent. Modes of emphasis and stress, for example, are readily discerned. Important materials will commonly be placed at the beginning of a pericope, or underlined through balanced, contrary allegations. But stylistic considerations and formal traits are helpful primarily in isolating pericopae and establishing their primary units for analysis. What is decisive is the discernment of what the narrator includes or omits, what seem to be his obvious concerns and what he ignores.

Once the importance of a fresh exegesis of rabbinical texts is established, the next problem is to select the documents on which the work should begin. Here Urbach's work illustrates the fateful error of assuming that rabbinical literature is essentially timeless, so that there is "neither early nor late in Torah." Applied to the present work, it results in the notion that whatever is attributed to anyone was really said by the person to whom the saying is attributed, therefore tells us about the period in which he lived -- and this without regard to the date at which the document in which the said saying occurs was redacted, as I have stressed. Thus side by side in Urbach's compilation are sayings in Mishnah and in late Amoraic and even medieval compilations of materials. In a fresh approach to the problem of the history of talmudic Judaism, we should, I believe, establish guidelines by which we evaluate materials first occurring in late compilations. Mishnah-Tosefta assuredly comes to redaction by ca. A.D. 200. On the face of it, Mishnah-Tosefta therefore constitutes a more reliable testimony to the mind of second-century rabbis than does Yalqut Shimeoni or Yalqut Reuveni. If that is obvious, then it follows that we have to begin our work with the analysis of the main ideas attributed to authorities in Mishnah-Tosefta. These have clearly to be worked out, and the materials occurring in later compilations, of Amoraic and medieval origin, are to be tested for conceptual and even thematic congruence against the materials occurring in earlier documents.

The question remains, If it is assumed that Mishnah-Tosefta testifies to the time in which the document was finally redacted, then how shall we know what layers of thought come before the time of the redaction of the document itself? How shall we know, furthermore, whether a person to whom a saying is attributed really said it? To deal with the latter question, I do not believe we have any way of verifying whether a person to whom a saying is attributed actually said it. Our history of talmudic Judaism will unfold by periods, may even produce significant differentiation among named authorities within the several periods, but it will, so far as I can see, not supply a definitive answer to the question of whether Aqiba really said what he is claimed to have said. While that question -- whether we have ipsissima verba of a particular historical figure -- is deemed terribly pressing in the study of the founder of Christianity, the importance of the question is for theological, not historical reasons. We do not know everything we might like to know; that does not mean what we do know is not worth knowing. Yet the other matter -- how we can find out whether anything in Mishnah-Tosefta antedates the redaction of Mishnah-Tosefta -- requires more considerable attention. Here we must begin with a working hypothesis and test that hypothesis against the results attained in its application.

The simplest possible hypothesis is that the attributions of sayings to named authorities may be relied upon in assigning those sayings to the period, broadly defined, in which said authorities flourished. We do not and cannot know, for example, whether Aqiba actually said what is attributed to him. Are we able to establish criteria by which we may conclude that what is assigned to Aqiba likely belongs in the period in which he lived, e.g., to his school or associates or even to the man himself? This proposition can indeed be tested. We have laws which interrelate in theme and conception and which also bear attributions to successive authorities, e.g., to a Yavnean, to an Ushan, and to an authority of the time of Rabbi. If we are able to demonstrate that what is assigned to a Yavnean is conceptually earlier than, and not dependent upon, what is assigned to an Ushan, then, on the face of it, the former indeed is an earlier tradition, the latter a later one. The unfolding of the rabbis' ideas on legal and other questions may be shown to take place through sequences of logic, with what is assigned to later masters often depending upon and generated by what is assigned to the earlier ones. When we find a correlation between such logical (not merely thematic) sequences and temporal ones, that is, if what is assigned to a later master does depend in theme, conception, principle, and inner logic upon what is attributed to an ealier master, then we have history: we know what comes earlier, what comes later. We are able therefore to describe ideas probably characteristic of authorities between the disaster of 70 and the Bar Kokhba debacle, and from that time to the period of Rabbi, and in the time of Rabbi. Doubtless work on Amoraic materials will yield the same series of disciplined sequences of correlated attributions and logical developments, showing the general reliability of the attributions by periods and making possible a description of ideas held in a given period by various authorities. On that basis, indeed, we can describe the ideas really characteristic of one period in the historical unfolding of talmudic Judaism and relate them to ideas characteristic of earlier and later periods. That sort of historical inquiry is virtually not attempted by Urbach, simply because he takes for granted, as I said, that what is assigned to a given authority really was stated by that authority. Having no problems, he obviously is unable to propose solutions and then to test them.

A further descriptive historical task is to be undertaken. When we concentrate attention on the most reliable witnesses to the mind of the earlier rabbis, those of the first and second century, we find ourselves engaged primarily in the analysis of legal texts. Mishnah-Tosefta and related literature focus attention on halakhic problems. Are there underlying unities of conception or definitions of fundamental principles to be discerned within the halakhah? No one familiar with the literature and its classical exegesis is in doubt that there are. These are to be spelled out with some care, also correlated and compared to conceptions revealed in writings of other Jews, not solely rabbinic Jews, as well as Christians and "pagans." When, for example, we describe primary concerns and perennial issues inherent in laws attributed to Ushans, we find that, in much acute detail, rather fundamental issues of physics are worked out, e.g., the nature of mixtures, which will not have surprised Stoic, natural philosophers. Again, an enduring interest of Yavnean pericopae is in the relationship between intention and action, an issue both of interest to Paul and those who told stories about Jesus, on the one side, and of concern to philosophers of disaster and rebuilding in the earlier destruction, for instance,

Jeremiah. The thought of Yavneh in any event has to be brought into relationship with the context in which the rabbis did their work, the aftermath of the loss of the Temple, just as the work of the Ushans, following the much greater this-worldly catastrophe brought on by Bar Kokhba, must always be seen against the background of crisis. Indeed, the formation of earlier rabbinic Judaism, from its primitive beginnings after 70 to its full and complete expression by the end of Ushan times in 170, is the product of an age of many painful events, events deemed at the time to bear the most profound theological weight. Much of the halakhah both can and should be interpreted in this particular context, and many of its issues, not to be reduced to economic or social concerns, express profound thought on the issues and inner meanings of the age itself. It follows that once the exegetical work is complete (if provisionally) and the historical sequences of individual units of law fairly well established, the larger issues emergent in underlying unities of conception and definitions of fundamental principles are to be uncovered, so that the legal materials may produce a history of major ideas and themes, not merely sets of two or three logical-temporal sequences of minor details.

That is how we must answer the question, If Mishnah was redacted in ca. A.D. 200, then how do we know that anything in Mishnah derives from before A.D. 200? Traditionalists in Jewish scholarly circles have different answers. They posit transmission in exact words said by a given authority through oral means. They further hold what is not assigned to a given authority goes "way way back." But materials not given in the name of a particular master share not only the literary, but also the conceptual, traits of materials assigned to a great many named masters, in particular in the period from 130 to 170. The traditional view in this matter is simply wrong.

In time, when the work sketched here is done, we shall see the outlines of the much larger history of legal, therefore religious, ideas, the unfolding of the world-view of the rabbis who created rabbinic Judaism. These outlines will emerge not merely from discrete sayings, chosen more or less at random, about topics of interest chiefly to us, e.g., was rabbinical ethics theonomous or autonomous? what did 'the rabbis' believe about life after death, the Messiah, eschaton? and so on. Rather, the morphology of the rabbinic world-view will emerge inductively, differentiated as to its historical stages and as to the distinctive viewpoints and conceptions held by individual authorities or circles within which that larger world-view originated.

Second, a new approach to the description and interpretation of the world-view of the earlier rabbis should emerge. This proceeds along critical-historical lines, taking account of the problems of dating sayings, of the diversity of the documents which purport to preserve opinions of the earlier masters, and the like. That is important, to be sure. But there are more important aspects of this work.

People do not seem to realize the immense dimensions of the evidence in our hands. We have much more than just a few sayings on this and that. We have a vast law-code, a huge exegetical corpus in respect to the Hebrew Scriptures and their translation, collections of stories about authorities, various kinds of sayings assigned to them -- an extraordinarily large mass of materials. Our approach, for the first time, must encompass the totality of the evidence, cope with, take account of, sources of exceptional density and richness. The law, as I said, is the definitive source of the world-view of the earlier rabbis. What is earliest and best attested is Mishnah-Tosefta. Therefore, if we want to know what people were thinking in the first and second centuries, we have to turn, to begin with, to that document, which must serve as criterion in the assessment of whatever first appears in the later compilations of rabbinical sayings and stories. Books on rabbinic Judaism which focus upon non-legal sayings (without regard, even, to the time at which the documents containing those sayings were redacted) simply miss the point of rabbinic Judaism.

But the legal sayings deal with picayune and inconsequential matters. The major problem is to derive, from arcane and trivial details of laws of various sorts, the world-view which forms the foundations of, and is expressed by, these detailed rules. That work must be done in a systematic and comprehensive way. And, in consequence, the definition of the agendum of scholarship is to be revised, not merely in terms of the adaptation and systematic application of methods of literary-, form-, and redactional-criticism, hitherto unknown in this field, nor in terms of the introduction of historical-critical considerations, hitherto neglected or introduced in an episodic way and with a lack of historical sophistication, but in terms of its very shape and structure. The total failure of all prior approaches finds definitive illustration in Urbach's disastrous work. Critics of the old approaches could not have provided a better satire of the intellectual bankruptcy of the age that has gone before than does Urbach himself.

14. E.P. Sanders

PAUL AND PALESTINIAN JUDAISM:

History of Religions 1978, 18:177-191

PAUL AND PALESTINIAN JUDAISM: A COMPARISON OF PATTERNS OF RELIGION.
By E.P. Sanders. London: SCM Press, 1977. Pp. xviii+627.

"Palestinian Judaism" is described through three bodies of evidence: Tannaitic
literature, the Dead Sea Scrolls, and Apocrypha and Pseudepigrapha, in that order. I shall
deal only with the first. To each set of sources, Sanders addresses questions of systematic
theology: election and covenant, obedience and disobedience, reward and punishment and
the world to come, salvation by membership in the covenant and atonement, proper
religious behavior (so for Tannaitic sources); covenant and the covenant people, election
and predestination, the commandments, fulfillment and transgression, atonement (Dead
Sea Scrolls); election and covenant, the fate of the individual Israelite, atonement,
commandments, the basis of salvation, the gentiles, repentance and atonement, the
righteousness of God (Apocrypha and Pseudepigrapha, meaning, specifically: Ben Sira, I
Enoch, Jubilees, Psalms of Solomon, IV Ezra). There follows a brief concluding chapter
(pp. 419-28, summarizing pp. 1-418), and then the second part, on Paul, takes up about a
fifth of the book. Sanders provides a very competent bibliography (pp. 557-82) and
thorough indexes. So far as the book has a polemical charge, it is to demonstrate (pp.
420-21) that "the fundamental nature of the covenant conception... largely accounts for
the relative scarcity of appearances of the term 'covenant' in Rabbinic literature. The
covenant was presupposed, and the Rabbinic discussions were largely directed toward the
question of how to fulfill the covenantal obligations." This proposition is then meant to
disprove the conviction ("all but universally held") that Judaism is a degeneration of the
Old Testament view: "The once noble idea of covenant as offered by God's grace and
obedience as the consequence of that gracious gift degenerated into the idea of petty
legalism, according to which one had to earn the mercy of God by minute observance of
irrelevant ordinances."[1]

Sanders' search for patterns yields a common pattern in "covenantal nomism,"
which, in general, emerges as follows (p. 422):

The "pattern" or "structure" of covenantal nomism is this: (1) God has chosen
Israel and (2) given the law. The law implies both (3) God's promise to
maintain the election and (4) the requirement to obey. (5) God rewards
obedience and punishes transgression. (6) The law provides for means of
atonement, and atonement results in (7) maintenance or re-establishment of
the covenantal relationship. (8) All those who are maintained in the covenant
by obedience, atonement, and God's mercy belong to the group which will be

saved. An important interpretation of the first and last points is that election and ultimately salvation are considered to be by God's mercy rather than human achievement.

Anyone familiar with Jewish liturgy will be at home in that statement. Even though the evidence on the character of Palestinian Judaism derives from diverse groups and reaches us through various means, Sanders argues that covenantal nomism was "the basic type of religion known by Jesus and presumably by Paul..." And again, "covenantal nomism must have been the general type of religion prevalent in Palestine before the destruction of the Temple."[2]

The stated purposes require attention. Sanders states at the outset (p. xii) that he has six aims: (1) to consider methodologically how to compare two (or more) related but different religions; (2) to destroy the view of Rabbinic Judaism which is still prevalent in much, perhaps most, New Testament scholarship; (3) to establish a different view of Rabbinic Judaism; (4) to argue a case concerning Palestinian Judaism (that is, Judaism as reflected in material of Palestinian provenance) as a whole; (5) to argue for a certain understanding of Paul; and (6) to carry out a comparison of Paul and Palestinian Judaism. Numbers (4) and (6), he immediately adds, "constitute the general aim of the book, while I hope to accomplish the others along the way." Since more than a third of the work is devoted to Rabbinic Judaism, Sanders certainly cannot be accused of treating his second goal casually.

Having described the overall shape of the work, let me make explicit the point at which I think historians of religion should join the discussion, since, it is self-evident, the long agendum of this book touches only occasionally upon issues of history, history of religions, and history of ideas. In fact, this is a work of historical theology: wissen-schaftliche Theologie. But Sanders' very good intention deserves the attention of students of religions who are not theologians, because what he wanted to achieve is in my view worthwhile. This intention is the proper comparison of religions (or of diverse expressions of one larger religion): "I am of the view... that the history of the comparison of Paul and Judaism is a particularly clear instance of the general need for methodolo- gical improvement in the comparative study of religion. What is difficult is to focus on what is to be compared. We have already seen that most comparisons are of reduced essences... or of individual motifs..." This sort of comparison Sanders rejects. Here I wish to give Sanders' words, because I believe what he wants to do is precisely what he should have done but, as I shall explain, has not succeeded in doing:

> What is clearly desirable, then, is to compare an entire religion, parts and all, with an entire religion, parts and all; to use the analogy of a building to compare two buildings, not leaving out of account their individual bricks. The problem is how to discover two wholes, both of which are considered and defined on their own merits and in their own terms, to be compared with each other.

Now let us ask ourselves whether or not Sanders has compared an entire religion, parts and all, with other such entire religions.

On the basis of my description of the contents of the book, we must conclude that he has not. For the issues of election and covenant, obedience and disobedience, and the like, while demonstrably present and taken for granted in the diverse "Judaisms" of late antiquity, do not necessarily define the generative problematic of any of the Judaisms before us. To put matters in more general terms: Systemic description must begin with the system to be described. Comparative description follows. And to describe a system, we commence with the principal documents which can be shown to form the center of a system. Our task then is to uncover the exegetical processes, the dynamics of the system, through which those documents serve to shape a conception, and to make sense, of reality. We then must locate the critical tensions and inner problematic of the system thereby revealed: What is it about? What are its points of insistence? The comparison of systems begins in their exegesis and interpretation.

But Sanders does not come to Rabbinic Judaism (to focus upon what clearly is his principal polemical charge) to uncover the issues of Rabbinic Judaism. He brings to the Rabbinic sources the issues of Pauline scholarship and Paul.[3] This blatant trait of his work, which begins, after all, with a long account of Christian anti-Judaism ("The persistence of the view of Rabbinic religion as one of legalistic works-righteousness," pp. 33-58), hardly requires amplification. In fact, Sanders does not really undertake the systemic description of earlier Rabbinic Judaism in terms of its critical tension. True, he isolates those documents he thinks may testify to the state of opinion in the late first and second centuries. But Sanders does not describe Rabbinic Judaism through the systemic categories yielded by its principal documents. His chief purpose is to demonstrate that Rabbinism constitutes a system of "covenantal nomism." While I think he is wholly correct in maintaining the importance of the conceptions of covenant and of grace, the polemic in behalf of Rabbinic legalism as covenantal does not bring to the fore what Rabbinic sources themselves wish to take as their principal theme and generative problem. For them, as he says, covenantal nomism is a datum. So far as Sanders proposes to demonstrate the importance to all the kinds of ancient Judaism of covenantal nomism, election, atonement, and the like, his work must be pronounced a success but trivial. So far as he claims to effect systemic description of Rabbinic Judaism ("a comparison of patterns of religion"), we have to evaluate that claim in its own terms.

Since in a moment I shall turn to the impact, upon Sanders' topic, of work completed since his book was written in 1973 or 1974, I wish to stress that my criticism at this point concerns how Sanders does what he has chosen to do: systemic comparison. His notion of comparing patterns of religion is, I believe, promising. But what he has done, instead, is to impose the pattern of one religious expression, Paul's, upon the description of another, that of the Tannaitic-Rabbinical sources.[4] He therefore ignores the context of the sayings adduced in the service of comparison, paying little attention to the larger context in which those sayings find meaning. In this connection I point to the observation of Mary Boyce (A History of Zoroastrianism [Leiden, 1975], p. 246):

Zoroaster's eschatological teachings, with the individual judgment, the resurrection of the body, the Last Judgment, and life everlasting, became profoundly familiar, through borrowings, to Jews, Christians, and Muslims, and have exerted enormous influence on the lives and thoughts of men in many lands. Yet it was in the framework of his own faith that they attained their fullest logical coherence....

What Boyce stresses is that, taken out of the Zoroastrian context, these familiar teachings lose their "fullest logical coherence." Sanders, for his part, has not asked what is important and central in the system of Tannaitic-Rabbinic writtings. All he wants to know is what, in those writings, addresses questions of interest to Paul. In my judgment, even in 1973 he would have been better served by paying close attention to his own statement of purpose.

But since 1973 the state of the art has shifted its focus, from the mass of writings in which authorities of the first and second centuries (Tannaim, hence Tannaitic literature) are cited, to the character of the documents, one by one, which contain and express Rabbinic Judaism. Future work of comparison, then, will have to take up the results of something less encompassing than "the Tannaitic view of...," all the more so, "the rabbinic idea of...." The work of description, first for its own purposes, then for systemic comparison, begins with Mishnah.

Mishnah certainly is the first document of Rabbinic Judaism. Formally, it stands at the center of the system, since the principal subsequent Rabbinic documents, the Talmuds, lay themselves out as if they were exegeses of Mishnah (or, more accurately, of Mishnah-Tosefta).[5] It follows that an account of what Mishnah is about, of the system expressed by Mishnah and of the world-view created and sustained therein, should be required for systemic comparison such as Sanders proposes. Now if we come to Mishnah with questions of Pauline-Lutheran theology, important to Sanders and New Testament scholarship, we find ourselves on the peripheries of Mishnaic literature and its chief foci. True, Mishnah contains a very few relevant, accessible sayings, for example, on election and covenant. But on our hands is a huge document which does not wish to tell us much about election and covenant and which does wish to speak about other things.

Description of the Mishnaic system is not easy. It has taken me twenty-two volumes to deal with the sixth of Mishnah's six divisions,[6] and while I think I can describe the Mishnaic system of uncleanness, I still have no clear notion about the relationship between that Mishnaic subsystem and the other five divisions of Mishnah and their, as yet undescribed, subsystems.[7] We cannot therefore blame Sanders for not doing what has only just now been undertaken. But we have to wonder whether Sanders has asked of himself the generative and unifying questions of the core of Mishnah at all: Has he actually sat down and studied (not merely "read") one document, even one tractate, beginning to end, and analyzed its inner structure, heart, and center? By this question I do not mean to ask whether Sanders has mastered Rabbinic writings. The evidence in his book is that he can look things up, presumably with Billerbeck's help. He knows Hebrew and is competent, if no expert (!). The question is, Does Sanders so grasp the problematic of a Rabbinic compilation that he can accurately state what it is that said compilation wishes to express -- its generative problematic? Or does he come to the Rabbinic literature with a quite separate and distinct set of questions, issues in no way natural to, and originating in, the Rabbinic writings themselves? Just now we noticed that Sanders' theological agendum accords quite felicitously with the issues of Pauline theology. To show that that agendum has not been shaped out of the issues of Rabbinic theology, I shall now adduce negative evidence on whether Sanders with equal care analyzes the inner structure of a document of Rabbinic Judaism.

First, throughout his "constructive" discussions of Rabbinic ideas about theology, Sanders quotes all documents equally with no effort at differentiation among them. He seems to have culled sayings from the diverse sources he has chosen and written them down on cards, which he proceeded to organize around his critical categories. Then he has constructed his paragraphs and sections by flipping through those cards and commenting on this and that. So there is no context in which a given saying is important in its own setting, in its own document. This is Billerbeck-scholarship.

Of greater importance, the diverse documents of Rabbinism are accorded no attention on their own. Let me expain what I mean. Anyone who sits down and studies Sifra, in a large unit of its materials, for example, can hardly miss what the redactor of the document wants to say. The reason is that the polemic of that document is so powerfully stated and so interminably repeated as to be inescapable. What Sifra wishes to say is this: Mishnah requires an exegetical foundation. But Mishnah notoriously avoids scriptural proof-texts. To Sifra none of Mishnah's major propositions is acceptable solely upon the basis of reason or logic. All of them require proper grounding in exegesis -- of a peculiarly formal sort -- of Scripture. One stratum of the Talmuds, moreover, addresses the same devastating critique to Mishnah. For once a Mishnaic proposition will be cited at the head of a talmudic pericope, a recurrent question is, What is the source of this statement? And the natural and right answer (from the perspective of the redactor of this sort of pericope) will be, As it is said..., followed by a citation of Scripture.

Now if it is so that Sifra and at least one stratum of Talmud so shape their materials as to make a powerful polemical point against Mishnah's autonomous authority ("logic"), indifferent as Mishnah is to scriptural authority for its laws, then we must ask how we can ignore or neglect that polemic. Surely we cannot cite isolated pericopae of these documents with no attention whatsoever to the intention of the documents which provide said pericopae. Even the most primitive New Testament scholars will concur that we must pay attention to the larger purposes of the several evangelists in citing sayings assigned to Jesus in the various Gospels. Everyone knows that if we ignore Matthew's theory of the law and simply extract Matthew's versions of Jesus' sayings about the law and set them up side by side with the sayings about the law given to Jesus by other of the evangelists and attitudes imputed to him by Paul, we create a mess of contradictions. Why then should the context of diverse Rabbinic sayings, for example, on the law, be ignored? In this setting it is gratuitous to ask for an explanation of Sanders' constant reference to "the Rabbis," as though the century and a half which he claims to discuss produced no evidence of individuals' and ideas' having distinct histories. This is ignorant.

Still more telling evidence that Sanders does not succeed in his systemic description comes when he gives one concrete example (in the entire 238 pages of discussion of "Tannaitic" Judaism) of what a document wishes to tell us. I shall focus on the matter because Sanders raises it. He states (p. 71):

> Rabbinic discussions are often at the third remove from central questions of religious importance. Thus the tractate Mikwaoth, "immersion pools," does not consider the religious value of immersion or the general reason for purity, much less such a large topic as why the law should be observed. It simply begins with the classification of the grades among pools of water. This does not mean that there were no religious principles behind the discussion; simply that they (a) were so well understood that they did not need to be specified and (b) did not fall into the realm of halakah.

Now on the basis of this statemant we must conclude that Sanders has looked at M. Miqvaot 1:1, perhaps even the entire first chapter of the document. It is true that tractate Miqvaot does begin with classification of the grades among pools of water. But a study of the tractate as a whole reveals that it certainly has its own issues, its own critical concerns, indeed, its own generative problematic.

In fact the shank of the tractate -- M. Miq. 2:4-5:6 -- asks about collections of diverse sorts of water and how they effect purification. A secondary development of the same theme follows: the union of pools to form a valid collection of water, and yet a tertiary development, mixtures of water with other liquids (wine, mud). Therefore the primary interest of the tractate is in water for the immersion pool: What sort of water purifies? Now anyone interested in the document must wonder, Why is it that, of all the possible topics for a tractate on purification, the one point of interest should be the definition of effective water? And the first observation one might make is that Scripture, for its part, would be surprised by the datum of Mishnah-tractate Miqvaot.[8] For, in the opinion of the priestly authorities of Leviticus and Numbers, still water by itself -- not spring water, not standing water mixed with blood or ashes, for example -- does not effect purification. Water may remove uncleanness, but the process of purification further requires the setting of the sun. Water mixed with blood may purify the leper; water mixed with the ashes of a red cow may purify one made unclean by a corpse. But water by itself is inadequate to complete purification. At best, Scripture knows running water as a means of purification. But Mishnah-tractate Miqvaot stresses the purificatory properties of still water, and explicitly excludes spring water from the center of its discussion.[9]

My own conception of what it is that Mishnah wishes to say in this tractate is at best a guess,[10] but it is worth repeating so that the full character of Sanders' "defense" of this particular tractate may become clear:

> What is the fundamental achievement of our tractate? The Oral Torah [Mishnah] provides a mode of purification different from that specified in the Written Torah for the Temple, but analogous to that suitable for the Temple. Still water serves for the table, living water [approved by Scripture] cleans the

Zab, and, when mixed with blood or ashes, the leper and the person unclean by reason of touching a corpse. All those other things cleaned by the setting of the sun, the passage of time, in the Oral Torah [Mishnah-tractate Miqvaot] are cleaned in the still water [of the immersion pool, which, Mishnah makes clear, must be] gathered in the ground, in the rains which know no time, but only the eternal seasons.[11]

Now it may be that that is the whole story. What follows is my own obiter dictum on the matter, my conception of the world-constructing meaning of the laws just now summarized:

In an age in which men and women immersed themselves in spring-fed lakes and rushing rivers, in moving water washing away their sins in preparation for the end of days, the Pharisees observed the passing of the seasons, which go onward through time, immersing in the still, collected water which falls from heaven. They bathe not in running water, in the anticipation of the end of days and for the sake of eschatological purity, but in still water, to attain the cleanness appropriate to the eternal Temple and the perpetual sacrifice [of the very real, physical Temple of Jerusalem]. They remove the uncleanness defined by the Written Torah for the holy altar, because of the conviction of the Oral Torah [Mishnah] that the hearth and home, table and bed, going onward through ages without end, also must be and can be cleaned, in particular, through the rain: the living water from heaven, falling in its perpetual seasons, trickling down the hills and naturally gathering in ponds, ditches, and caverns, for time immemorial. As sun sets, bringing purification for the Temple, so rain falls, bringing purification for the table.[12]

Now I cite this passage to juxtapose it to Sanders' judgment that Miqvaot "does not consider the religious value of immersion or the general reason for purity." I think it does exactly that -- in its own way.

In my view, Sanders finds in Miqvaot no answers to questions of religious value because he has not asked how Miqvaot asks its questions to begin with. And that is because he has not allowed the tractate to speak for itself, out of its own deepest stratum of conceptions. He has brought to the tractate an alien set of questions and, finding nothing in the tractate to deal with those questions -- that is, no sayings explicitly addressed to them -- he has gone his way. It is true that the tractate does not consider "the religious value of immersion," and that is because it has quite separate, and, if I am right, more profound, issues in mind.[13] To say, "This does not mean that there were no religious principles behind the discussion" is not only patronizing, it also is ignorant. To claim that the "principles were so well understood that they did not need to be specified" is true but beside the point, if Sanders cannot accurately tell us what these principles were. Granted that we deal with a system of "convenantal nomism," what is it that that covenant was meant to express? And how did the ancient rabbis interpret that covenant and its requirements for their own trying times? Answering these questions requires Sanders to take Judaism seriously in its own terms. But this he does not do.

Now I must repeat that I do not propose to criticize Sanders on the basis of his not having read a book which appeared two or three years after his own work was completed (which I believe, on the basis of his discussion and bibliography, to have been in 1973 or 1974). It is to point out, on the basis of an example of his own selection and what he has to say about that example, that the promised systemic description simply does not take place. The claim, in this very context, that religious principles cannot be discussed in the Mishnah because of the character of Mishnah, would be more persuasive if there were substantial evidence that Mishnah to begin with has been studied in its own framework. Sanders says (p. 71):

> We should at least briefly refer to another characteristic of the literature which makes a small-scale analysis of basic religious principles impossible: they are not discussed as such. Rabbinic discussions are often at the third remove from central questions of religious importance.

There follows the treatment of Miqvaot cited above. I contend that it begs the question to say "basic religious principles" are not "discussed as such."[14]

The diverse Rabbinic documents require study in their own terms. The systems of each — so far as there are systems -- have to be uncovered and described. The way the several systems relate and the values common to all of them have to be spelled out. The notion that we may cite promiscuously everything in every document (within the defined canon of "permitted" documents) and then claim to have presented an account of "the Rabbis" and their opinions is not demonstrated and not even very well argued. We hardly need dwell on the still more telling fact that Sanders has not shown how systemic comparison is possible when, in point of fact, the issues of one document, or of one system of which a document is a part, are simply not the same as the issues of some other document or system. That is, he has succeeded in finding Rabbinic sayings on topics of central importance to Paul (or Pauline theology). He has not even asked whether these sayings form the center and core of the Rabbinic system or even of a given Rabbinic document. To state matters simply, How do we know that "the Rabbis" and Paul are talking about the same thing, so that we may compare what they have to say? And if it should turn out that "the Rabbis" and Paul are not talking about the same thing, then what is it that we have to compare?

Even by 1973 it was clear that the issue of historical dependability of attributions of sayings to particular rabbis had to be faced, even though, admittedly, it had not been faced in most of the work on which Sanders was able to draw. I do not wish to dwell upon the problem of why we should believe that a given rabbi really said what is attributed to him, because I have already discussed that matter at some length.[15] Still, it seems to me that the issues of historical evidence should enter into the notion of the comparison of systems. If it should turn out that "the Rabbis'" ideas about a given theological topic respond to a historical situation subject to fairly precise description, then the work of comparison becomes still more subtle and precarious. For if "the Rabbis" address their thought -- for example, about the right motive for the right deed -- to a world in which, in the aftermath of a terrible catastrophe, the issue of what it is that human beings still control is central, the comparison of their thought to that of Paul requires us to imagine what Paul might have said if confronted by the situation facing "the Rabbis."

A powerful motif in sayings assigned to authorities who lived after the Bar Kokhba war is the issue of attitude: the surpassing power of human intention in defining a situation and judging it. In many ways diverse tractates of Mishnah seem to want to say that there are yet important powers left in the hands of defeated, despairing Israelites. The message of much of Mishnaic halakhah is that there is an unseen world, a metaphysical world, subject to the will of Israel. Given the condition of defeat, the despair and helplessness of those who survived the end of time, we may hardly be surprised at the message of authorities who wish to specify important decisions yet to be made by people totally subjugated to the will of their conquerors. Now if we ignore that historical setting, the dissonances of theology and politics, in which the message concerning attitude and intention is given, how are we properly to interpret and compare "the Rabbis'" teachings on the effects of the human will with those of Paul, or those assigned to Jesus, for that matter? If they say the same thing, it may be for quite divergent reasons. If they say different things, it may be that they say different things because they speak of different problems to different people.

Now these observations seem to me to be obvious and banal.[16] But they are necessary to establish the urgency of facing those simple historical questions Sanders wishes to finesse (by quoting me, of all people!).[17] If we have a saying assigned to Aqiba how do we know it really was said by him, belonging to the late first and early second century? If we cannot show that it does go back to A.D. 100, then we are not justified in adducing such sayings as evidence of the state of mind of one late-first- and early-second-century authority, let alone of all the late-first- and early-second-century authorities -- and let alone of "the Rabbis" of the later first and whole of the second centuries. I cannot concede that Sanders' notion of systemic description, even if it were wholly effected, has removed from the critical agendum these simple questions of historical study we have yet to answer.

Nor should we ignore the importance in the work, not only of comparison, but also of interpreting a given saying, of establishing the historical context in which the saying was said (or at least in which it was important to be quoted). Sanders many times cites the famous saying attributed to Yohanan b. Zakkai that the corpse does not contaminate, nor does purification water purify, but the whole thing is hocus-pocus. That saying first occurs in a later, probably fourth-century, Midrashic compilation. Surely we might wonder whether, at the time of the making of that compilation, issues of magic were not central in Rabbinic discourse.[18] The denial of efficacy, ex opere operato, of a scriptural purification rite, addressed to a world in which magic, including Torah magic, was deemed to work ex opere operato, may be interpreted as a powerful polemic against a strong current of the fourth-century Palestinian and Babylonian Jews' life, a time at which Rabbinical circles, among others, were deeply interested in the magical powers inherent in Torah. Now I do not mean to suggest that the proper interpretation of the saying is in accord with this hypothesis,[19] nor do I even propose the stated hypothesis for serious consideration here. I only offer it as an example of one context in which the saying is credibly to be interpreted and, more important, as evidence of the centrality of context in the interpretation of each and every saying. If we do not know where and when a saying was said, how are we to interpret the saying and explain its meaning?

In my view the meaning of a saying is defined, at the outset, by the context in which it is meaningful. To be sure, the saying may remain meaningful later on, so that, cited for other purposes, the saying takes on new meanings. No one denies that obvious proposition, which, after all, is illustrated best of all by the history of the interpretation, but, of greater systemic consequence, the deliberate misinterpretation, of the Old Testament in Judaism and Christianity. If that is so, then we surely should not reduce to a fundamentalistic and childish hermeneutical framework the interpretation by sayings attributed to rabbis in Rabbinic documents of diverse periods, put together, as I said earlier, for diverse purposes and therefore addressed, it seems to me self-evident, to historically diverse circumstances.

Since this is one of the most ambitious works in Pauline scholarship in twenty-five years and since, as I just said, it does adumbrate initiatives of considerable methodological promise, we must ask ourselves what has gone wrong with Sanders' immense project. I think the important faults are on the surface.

First, his book should have been subjected to the reading of two kinds of editors, a good editor for style and a critical editor for the planning and revision of the book. As a whole, it simply does not hang together. Sanders writes in a self-indulgent way.

Second, I think Sanders pays too much attention to the anti-Judaism of New Testament scholars. It is true, I suppose, that there is a built-in bias on the part of some of Christian scholarship on Rabbinic Judaism, leading to negative judgments based upon fake scholarship (Sanders' attack on Billerbeck is precise and elegant). But the motive for a major scholarly project must be constructive. One must love one's subject, that is, one's sources and scholarly setting.

Third, if, as I believe, Sanders has given us a good proposal on "the holistic comparison of patterns of religion" (pp. 12-24), then he should have tried to allow his book to unfold as an exposition and instantiation of his program of systemic comparison. This he does not do.

Fourth, his approach to the Rabbinic literature covers too much or too little (I am not sure which). That is, he begins with a sizable description of methodological problems. But when he comes to the substantive exposition of the Rabbinic theology important for his larger project, Sanders seems to me to have forgotten pretty much everything he said on method. There are acres and acres of paragraphs which in sum and substance could have been lifted straightaway from Schechter, Moore, or Urbach,[20] to name three other efforts at systematic dogmatics in early Rabbinic religion. I found the systematic theology of the Dead Sea Scrolls equally tedious but know too little of the problems of working on those sources to suggest how things might have been done differently and better. But to produce Sanders' substantive results of the theological discussions, from election and covenant to the nature of religious life and experience (pp. 84-232), we simply do not need to be told about critical problems ("the use of Rabbinic material, the nature of Tannaitic literature") laid out earlier (pp. 59-83). In all, it seems to me a bit pretentious, measured against the result.

Still, in Sanders' behalf it must be repeated: He has defined the work to be done in terms which I think are valid and fructifying. He has done his scholarly homework with more than routine ambition. He has laid forth an apologetic for Rabbinic Judaism and a powerful critique of ignorant or malicious or out-and-out anti-Semitic reports of, and judgments on, Rabbinic Judaism (or simply "Judaism"). Even though that theological enterprise cannot be deemed consequential for the study of the history of the religious world of ancient Judaism, it surely is not irrelevant to the context in which that history is written. The book is more than a mere compendium of this and that. It is based upon a carefully thought-through program. Sanders' insistence that when Judaism is studied by Christian scholars, it must be considered without the endemic anti-Judaism characteristic of earlier work, is important for both social and academic reasons. The sort of people who believed that Judaism was depraved also maintained, like Kittel in 1933, that the best solution (if inexpedient) to the Jewish problem was to exterminate the Jews. In its apologetic aspect, Sanders' book addresses itself to a considerable social problem of our age. But, alas, it also is a service to scholarship in the history of religions to insist, as Sanders does, that religions, including Judaism, be studied sine ire et studio. So as it is a document of the times, Sanders' book is on the side of life and learning.

That is all the more reason to insist that, in regard to Rabbinic Judaism, Sanders' book also is so profoundly flawed as to be hopeless and, I regret to say it, useless in accomplishing its stated goals of systemic description and comparison. No, systems which have not been accurately described cannot be compared. And the work of description surely involves critical intiatives in selection and interpretation. But to take up the work of interpretation, to design a project of comparison and carry it through, to reckon with the complexities of diverse documents and systems -- these are essentially the tasks of our own exegesis of these ancient texts and systems. To effect the comparison of patterns of ancient Judaism, what is needed is our self-conscious exegesis of their unself-conscious exegesis. For the history of religions is the exegesis of exegesis.

NOTES

[1] The polemic against New Testament scholarship on Judaism is a powerful theme which runs through the book and takes many forms. It is difficult to locate a major unit of thought which is not in some way affected by Sanders' apologetic interest. This example should not be thought to exhaust the matter, but shows how, at the very center of the book, issues are defined in contemporary theological terms. As we shall see in a moment, the very work of description itself becomes flawed on this account.

[2] So far as I can see, Sanders is reticent about the meaning of "religion" in this context, and other "types of religion" which are not to be found in Palestine before A.D. 70, but which might have been present there, also are not defined or discussed. I find a

general lack of precision in terminology. But Sanders' purpose is not to contribute to the theoretical literature of religious studies.

[3]See above, n. 1.

[4]Try to imagine the scholarly agendum if Christianity were the minority religion, Judaism the majority one. Books on "the Christian background of Judaism" and "what Paul teaches us about the world of Mishnah" surely would distort the interpretation of Paul. After all, "Paul and the dietary laws" would not focus upon an issue at the center of Paul's thought, though it might be a principal point of interest to theological faculties. Proof that Jesus made important contributions to Judaism through his disciple, Hillel, or that Jesus was a Pharisee, would seem still more ridiculous, except that, the apologetic mind being what it is, they are written even here and now.

[5]In fact, all descriptions of the Talmuds tell us that the Talmud consists of the Mishnah and the Talmud (or Gemara, the terms are interchangeable), the latter being an exegesis of the Mishnah. I believed that view with perfect faith until I began work on Mishnah-tractates for which we have Talmud and found that, after a certain limited point, the Talmud really is not much interested in Mishnah and does not pretend to be. Still, the Talmud is so put together as to constitute a kind of "commentary" to the Mishnah, and this formal trait, so predominant in the sight of literary theorists, has to be taken seriously.

[6]A History of the Mishnaic Law of Purities (Leiden, 1974-77), vols. 1-22.

[7]Why a doctoral program, such as Brown's, calling itself "History of Religions: Judaism," should find its principal intellectual challenges to be those of exegesis, and how participants in that program conceive the purposes of history of religions to be served by their work, are not questions to be dealt with here, although the answers are suggested at the end of this paper. A general statement of our program is in William Scott Green, Approaches to Ancient Judaism (Missoula, Mont.: Scholars Press for Brown Judaic Studies, 1978), with special reference to the papers by William Scott Green, Jonathan Z. Smith, and this writer.

[8]This is worked out in my History of the Mishnaic Law of Purities, vols. 13, Miqvaot. Commentary, and 14, Miqvaot. Literary and Historical Problems (Leiden, 1976). One of the most complex problems of Mishnah-study is the relationship of the diverse tractates of Mishnah to Scripture. I have dealt with this problem in "From Scripture to Mishnah: The Origins of Mishnah-tractate Niddah," Journal of Jewish Studies; "From Scripture to Mishnah: The Exegetical Origins of Maddaf," Festschrift for the Fiftieth Anniversary of the American Academy for Jewish Research; "From Scripture to Mishnah: The Case of Mishnah's Fifth Division," Journal of Biblical Literature (March

1979); "The Meaning of Torah shebe al peh, with Special Reference to Kelim and Ohalot," AJS Review I (1976): 151-70; and in the various volumes of Purities, Holy Things, and Women. I do not understand why Sanders does not begin his work of description with an account of the Old Testament legacy available to all the groups under discussion as well as with an account of how, in his view, each group receives and reshapes that legacy. Everyone claimed, after all, to build upon the foundations of Mosaic revelation ("covenantal nomism"), indeed, merely to restate what Moses or the prophets had originally said. It seems to me natural to give the Old Testament a central place in the description of any system resting upon an antecedent corpus of such authority as the Mosaic revelation and the prophetic writings. Systemic comparison on diverse relationsips to, and readings of, Scripture certainly is invited. In this context I must reject Sanders' critique of Vermes (pp. 25-29). His omission of reference to the Targumim because they are "generally late" is self-serving. The Targumim are diverse and hard to use; not all are in English. Sanders chokes on the gnat of the Targums and swallows the camel of the Midrashim. Sanders says, "Even if generally late, the Targums may, to be sure, contain early traditions. But these must now be sought out one by one." True indeed. And the same is so for the whole of Tannaitic literature! By "Tannaitic literature," Sanders means literature containing sayings attributed to Tannaim, or authorities who are assumed to have flourished before A.D. 200. As I shall suggest in a moment, such "early traditions" as occur in the name of first- and second-century authorities in documents of the third and later centuries also must be sought out, one by one. Sanders' more honest reason follows: "In general, the present state of Targumic studies does not permit the Targums to be used for our purposes." That is, I suppose, they are hard to use as he wants to use them. My argument is that the same is self-evidently true of the earlier Rabbinic documents. But Sanders successfully answers his own objection, with his stress on systemic -- therefore diachronic -- as against merely synchronic, comparison. Omission of the Targums is less damaging than failure to exploit the sizable legacy of the Old Testament, which surely is available, all parties concur, by the first century B.C. That omission is incomprehensible.

[9]That is the point of the redactor's beginning with the chapter of Miqvaot which Sanders does cite.

[10]It is a tribute to the kindness of the reviewers of my Purities that the theory now laid forth has been received with a certain patience. Louis Jacobs, writing in Bulletin of the School of Oriental and African Studies, vol. 40, no. 2 (1977), very correcty states, "Here, too, there is a fascinating theory about Pharisaic notions of purification, but one which does not necessarily follow from the acute analysis Neusner has given us of the Mishnaic sources." Jacobs then cites the passage before us. Jacobs is surely right that this theory does not necessarily follow from the sources. It is my guess at what the sources mean.

[11]Purities, 14:204-5.

[12]Ibid., p. 205.

[13]I must concede that it is asking much of scholars to sit patiently to master the details of the Mishnaic (and other Rabbinic) law and only then to raise the questions of the deeper range of meanings of that law. But the work of interpretation begins in exegesis and only ends in the formation and history of ideas. If people find too arduous, or merely dull, the work of patient exegesis, then of the recombinant history of small ideas, let them write on some subject other than earlier Rabbinic Judaism. The legal materials are not easy to understand. They are still more difficult to interpret as statements of philosophical or metaphysical conceptions. My message is that only in the work of exegesis is that task of interpretation to be undertaken, and it is only through interpretation that the meaning of the law is to be attained. Nobody begged Sanders to come and defend the Jews.

[14]Anyhow, why should "the religious value" of immersion be spelled out by the second-century rabbis in terms immediately accessible to a twentieth-century theologian? Mishnah's audience is second-century rabbis. How can we expect people to explain to outsiders ("why the law should be kept" indeed!) answers to questions which do not trouble insiders to begin with. The whole statement of the question is topsy-turvy. I find deplorable Sanders' failure to object to the notion of "central questions of religious importance" and "religious principles." Taken for granted is the conception that what are central questions to us are central questions to all "worthwhile" religious literature. It follows that if we cannot locate what to us are "religious principles," then we have either to condemn or to apologize for the documents which lack them. Stated in this way, the implicit position takes for granted "we all know" the meaning of "religion," "religious importance," "religious principles." In the case of the vast halakhic literature, we do not find readily accessible and immediately obvious "religious principles." When, moreover, we do find those conceptions, subject to generalization and analysis, which do address issues of common, even contemporary concern, we sometimes discover a range of topics under analysis more really philosophical than religious (in the contemporary sense of these words). An apology for Rabbinic Judaism bypassing the whole of the halakhic corpus which constitutes its earliest stratum is cosmically irrelevant to the interpretation of Rabbinic Judaism, therefore to the comparison of that system to others in its own culture. Is this a defense of Judaism at all? Who needs such friends!

[15]"The History of Earlier Rabbinic Judaism: Some New Approaches," History of Religions 16 (1977): 216-36.

[16]Only people wholly ignorant of the way in which context, both literary and social, affects interpretation of ideas will even imagine that I here commit reductionism. I need hardly point out that I do not claim the context exhausts the meaning or even definitively establishes the parameters of meaning. That is why I insist these observations are obvious and banal.

[17]See pp. 63-64, 70.

[18]I assemble the evidence on rabbinical wonder-working (magic) in the period under discussion in my History of the Jews in Babylonia, vol. 3, From Shapur I to Shapur II (Leiden, 1968), pp. 102-30; vol. 4, The Age of Shapur II (Leiden, 1969), pp. 330-63; and vol. 5, Later Sasanian Times (Leiden, 1970), pp. 174-93. There is some indication that more wonder-working or magical stories are told about third- and fourth-century rabbis than about second-century ones, and this corresponds to a general rise in magical activity.

[19]That is, the story is meant as an antimagical polemic or an effort to claim that the Torah's ritual laws have magical power, a claim very widely advanced in Rabbinical circles and also in regard to Jews or Jewish magicians.

[20]Solomon Schecter, Some Aspects of Rabbinic Theology (beginning in essays in Jewish Quarterly Review, 1894); George Foot Moore, Judaism in the First Centuries of the Christian Era: The Age of the Tannaim (Cambridge, 1927); and Ephraim E. Urbach, The Sages: Their Concepts and Beliefs (Jerusalem, 1975). I cannot imagine how Urbach, fifty years after Moore, has advanced the discussion, except in some matters of detail. Indeed methodologically it is a giant step backward, excluding evidence Moore included and adding an explicit apologetic layer to the discussion left by Moore with a (merely subterranean) apologetic implication.

Part Four

INTERPRETING "JUDAISM"

15. Erwin R. Goodenough

JEWISH SYMBOLS IN THE GRECO-ROMAN PERIOD I-VIII

Conservative Judaism 1963, 17:77-92

JEWISH SYMBOLS IN THE GRECO-ROMAN PERIOD. By Erwin R. Goodenough. New York, 1953 et seq.: Pantheon. I-VIII.

A work of such vast erudition as this should properly be reviewed by scholars whose skills and competence equal the author's. There are not many so qualified. Furthermore, fully to understand Professor Erwin Goodenough's work one must not only share his erudition, but also his spiritual capacity, and such are even rarer. Hence the essay that follows is not in any sense a "review," but rather, an effort to do the following: first, to indicate why these volumes are important and should be read; second, to offer some extended comments on specific and, from the viewpoint of the volumes themselves, relatively tangential questions, based on my perspective as a student of the history of Judaism in the classical age; and, finally, briefly to suggest what I believe to be the scholarly contribution made by Goodenough up to this point.

I

In every generation, a few scholars emerge, whose work exemplifies for students and colleagues alike the purpose of the scholarly enterprise. Concerning such work one does not decide whether it is "right" or "wrong," any more than the passengers of an ocean liner assure the helmsman who chooses a course in the unknown ocean, "You direct us rightly." They ask only, "Is this the course to the distant shore?" and hopefully examine the signs and omens of the voyage.

From the perspective of the history of Judaism, Goodenough's work stands on that same elevated plateau as that of Ezekiel Kaufman, Gershom Scholem, and their equals. Indeed, truly to understand the challenge of Goodenough, one must have in mind Kaufman's great and utterly contrary thesis. Kaufman's History of Israelite Faith attempts to demonstrate historically the essential uniqueness of Israelite monotheism, its final and irrevocable singularity in ancient civilization. For Kaufman, Israelite faith represents the uncompromising rejection of ancient paganism. It is the effort to transform the common raw material of ancient culture in the crucible of the Israelite world view. Kaufman claims that the Israelite segment of the human enterprise of the age was utterly different from its setting, so wholly other that the world about it can neither explain it nor be explained by it. Goodenough's view is that Israel was, in the epoch he studied, profoundly integrated into its age and setting, and that it consistently appropriated the advanced and sophisticated elements of that age for its own specific, but not existentially-unique, purposes. Goodenough's thesis is that Israel formed a part of the cultural continuum of its environment.

Ideology must follow, not precede scholarship. It would, therefore, be of no value to say that "the truth lies somewhere in between," for as much as some contemporary Jews would like to agree, perhaps not at the same instant, with both Kaufman and Goodenough, the claim of each is to a proposition diametrically opposite to the other's. Rather one must examine the evidence brought and interpreted by each scholar, and come to conclusions founded on the most detached critical canons at one's disposal. The basis of conclusion must be history, evidence, sound and broad understanding, especially, evaluation of method and not a priori predilection.

We must regret the fact that while among learned Jews Kaufman is widely discussed, the work of Goodenough and its implications for the age it discusses are almost ignored. Goodenough's vast volumes have been praised but not read, mentioned but not studied. Those who are disciples of Kaufman complain about the offhand, inadequate and superficial "reviews" of Moshe Greenberg's fine condensation of his books. But it is regrettable that they themselves have given such little attention to Goodenough's suggestive studies. The reason for this lamentable situation is twofold. First, Goodenough's work has appeared only relatively recently, and it takes time for novel ideas to find a willing audience, particularly when these ideas contradict widespread assumptions upon which not a few rest their faith. Second, the sheer volume of Goodenough's publications tends to discourage the more casual reader.

I should say at the outset that my brief comments upon a few salient ideas will convey next to nothing of the impression that Jewish Symbols must make. A personal reference may be in order. I was at first deeply shocked by the artifacts Goodenough discusses, so much so that I wished we could bury them again, for good. As the weight of evidence piled up, however, I began to realize that my former image of an aniconic and opaque faith represented nothing more than a superficial and unreal view of what must have been a very widespread and profound use of religious symbolism by ancient Jewry. As an historian, I became impelled to take seriously the relics and antiquities of ancient Jewry and to try to envisage them and the realities that lie behind the arcane shards and remnants of the talmudic age. At the end, I understood and shared the evocative thought of Goodenough: "As I worked out the historic associations of these symbolic forms... they gradually came to register their wordless beauty and power within me. Ultimately I have written rather to convey that power and beauty than to explain it or prove it" (VIII, p. 220). When I began, Goodenough's main thesis on the existence of a former Judaism quite different from that represented by the extant literature of the period seemed utterly preposterous; but at the end of months of reading, such a thesis has come to appear entirely conservative and sound to me, the only issues remaining being how to revise the historical consensus to reckon with it.

II

JEWISH SYMBOLS IN THE GRECO-ROMAN PERIOD: THE ARCHAEOLOGICAL EVIDENCE FROM PALESTINE. Vol. I. New York: Pantheon, 1953.

JEWISH SYMBOLS IN THE GRECO-ROMAN PERIOD: THE ARCHAEOLOGICAL EVIDENCE FROM THE DIASPORA. Vol. II. New York: Pantheon, 1953.

JEWISH SYMBOLS IN THE GRECO-ROMAN PERIOD: ILLUSTRATIONS. Vol. III. New York: Pantheon, 1953.

The first three volumes collect the Jewish realia uncovered in the past by archaeologists working in various parts of the Mediterranean basin. Goodenough's interest in these artifacts began, he reports, with the question of how it was possible, within so brief a span as fifty years, that the teachings of Jesus could have been accommodated so completely to the Hellenistic world. Not only central ideas, but even widespread symbols of early Christianity appear in retrospect to have been appropriated from an environment alien to Jewish Palestine. "For Judaism and Christianity to keep their integrity, any appropriations from paganism had to be very gradual" (I, p. 4). Yet within half a century of Jesus' death, Christian churches were well established in Hellenistic cities, and Christian teachings were within the realm of discourse of their citizens. If the "fusion" with Hellenistic culture occurred as quickly as it did, then it seems best explained by reference to an antecedent and concurrent form of Hellenistic Judaism that had successfully and naturally achieved a comfortable accommodation with Hellenism.

Was there such a Jewish appropriation of Hellenism that remained at the same moment part of Judaism? The writings of Philo indicate that a few highly educated and advanced Judaists did attempt such a fusion. (One need not enter into the question of whether Philo's Hellenism was a mere veneer covering ideas essentially identical with those of rabbinic Judaism, or was, as Goodenough contends in By Light Light, rather a Judaic formulation of a mystic gospel comprehensible to any who spoke the idiom of Hellenistic religions. In either instance, none disagree that Philo does represent an effort to talk about Judaism in the Hellenistic idiom, and that is all that matters for the present.) But Goodenough argues Philo was not unique, for we have access to a larger group of writings addressed to Hellenized Judaists, such as the Wisdom of Solomon, the Letter of Aristeas, the Jewish Sybilline Books, and so forth. What was the extent of these groups? This question cannot be answered definitively, for we do not know how many readers these books had and where they were. The failure of later, allegedly "normative" Jewish literature to preserve evidences of such groups proves nothing but that the editors of this literature did not choose to perpetuate writings with which they disagreed or regarded as "inauthentic."

The allegedly widespread authority of the Tannaitic sages and their doctrines cannot be demonstrated convincingly from the extant sources, Goodenough points out. However great the moral influence of the sages and the Nasi may have been, there is little to show "that in practice, except in problems of the calendar, this extended to actual supervision of Jewish thought" (I, p. 12). (The well-known "institution" of the apostolate could not have exercised widespread supervision, unless the institution was far more elaborate than the evidence suggests.) In any case, Goodenough concludes, "We cannot a priori fill with rabbinism the silence of the Judaism of the Roman diaspora in this period" (I, p. 13). Goodenough considers the rabbis, therefore, as a group who "aspired to much power in regulating the lives of Jews, and eventually got it, but who for centuries even in Palestine fought a hard battle for popular prestige and support" (I, p. 16).

Unfortunately, Goodenough's hardheadedness and strict adherence to sources do not sustain him when he attempts a description of "normative Judaism." He writes sympathetically but non-developmentally, and repeats the propositions about Pharisaic-Rabbinic-talmudic Judaism that, in the pages of Moore and others, imply a temporal and intellectual unity not found in the sources themselves. These propositions have become part of a linear and monolithic Heilsgeschichte, which in itself makes them suspect. Following expositions of "Tannaitic/Rabbinic/Talmudic Judaism," Goodenough says, "Believing actively in a God who made men that they might live a certain type of life... the business of a devotee was to study the tradition in which that way of life had been revealed, and to try... to live according to it" (I, p. 18). But one asks two questions, not of Goodenough but of the authorities he cites. First, what was the inner quality of the way of life so achieved? Was it so opaque and one-dimensional that mere performance of the requisite action, and study about it, rendered the devotee oblivious to further meaning or reference? Every group in ancient Judaism had its halakhah, as Goodenough points out in volume VIII. Was the halakhah recorded in talmudic literature unique in containing within and beyond itself no vital spiritual experience? Yet Goodenough would look in vain for a statement of the inner quality of the "life according to the law" prevailing in this period, unless he turns, as he does, to the writings of Scholem and others, expounding a very different body of theology (and law). This is not to suggest that the "halakhic" Jews were also in some sense "mystics" (I, p. 19); they were also not automatons.

Second, is the so-called "normative Judaism" to be derived from study of talmudic literature so wholly divorced from historical development that one may cite, as equally representative and authoritative, anyone who himself is cited in this vast literature, without regard for when he lived, or where, or how? Did the rabbinical literature of this age represent a consensus so all-embracing and authoritative that the attributes of growth, change, controversy, and dialectic are ultimately irrelevant? Did the tumultuous age from Ezra to Rav Ashi affect nothing and change nothing? If so, one may discuss the "classical" ideas about God or revelation or the Torah, and Goodenough's sense that a dichotomy existed between "rabbis" and the "Hellenistic Jews" conforms to historical reality. If not, however, the division between the normative Jews represented in talmudic literature and those represented by the monuments becomes a mirage. One may one day, therefore, hope to move between the one and the other, and look for the religious and cultural continuum within which both, apparently, thrived. This is in no sense a criticism of the Judaism of the age (I, p. 19), but rather an effort to illuminate aspects of it.

Goodenough's main point, however, stands: "While rabbinical Judaism can adjust itself to mystic rites... it would never have originated them." We should look vainly for the origins of the various symbols and ideas of Hellenistic Judaism in the circles among whom talmudic literature developed. Hence Goodenough's view of "normative Judaism" is correct so far as it needs to be: if we should uncover -- as we shall -- evidences of the use of the pagan inheritance of ancient civilization for specifically Jewish purposes, we shall most likely be confronted by Jews whose legacy is not recorded in the pages of the Talmud.

E.E. Urbach's paper, "The Rabbinical Laws of Idolatry in the Second and Third Centuries in the Light of Archaeological and Historical Facts," (Israel Exploration Journal, IX, 3, 1959, pp. 149-165; 229-245) attempts to reconcile the existence of various pagan motifs in Jewish venues with the prohibition of graven images. Urbach denies that such non-rabbinic groups existed, because in the burial ground of the sages at Beth Shearim, marble fragments of reliefs portraying scenes from pagan mythology have been uncovered. From this Urbach concludes, "These finds from Beth Shearim put an end to all the theories based on making a clear distinction between the private world of the Sages, as reflected in the talmudic and mishnaic laws about idolatry, and the other real world that existed outside theirs." Urbach holds (p. 165) that the sarcophagi at Beth Shearim also appear to have come from Jewish workshops, and "it is possible that some of them were originally made after conventional patterns for idol-worshipping gentile customers and subsequently sold to Jews without any change being made in their design." This taxes one's credulity far more than the thesis that there were several kinds of Jews and Judaism in second and third century Galilee. Urbach is apparently prepared to assume that these symbols were of mere ornamental value (and in this he is not alone). Be that as it may, is it conceivable that the Jews were so utterly indifferent to their coffins and to ornaments inscribed on them that they thoughtlessly made use of pagan sarcophagi? If so, one can only conclude that all of the laws on the subject of idolatry were indeed irrelevant, a point Urbach repeatedly denies. One does not have to conclude that symbols were more than ornamental to stand in astonishment before allegedly Jewish use of unmodified and purely pagan images anywhere, let alone on sarcophagi and synagogues. Thus the choice is apparently between admitting that some Jews were not responsive to some aspects of Jewish laws, in particular, about not rendering images or formal symbols of any kind, and that all Jews were indifferent to these same laws, at least as they apply to proper vessels for burial. Unless it can be demonstrated that the halakhah of the Galilean sages would permit such images to be engraved on sarcophagi for Jewish use, whether de novo or de facto, the very finds at Beth Shearim prove that there must have been several under-standings of what is a permissible symbol in Judaism. Boaz Cohen's article, "Art in Jewish Law," (Judaism, vol. III, 1954, pp. 165-176; see also Goodenough's "The Rabbis and Jewish Art in the Greco-Roman Period, "Hebrew Union College Annual, XXXII, 1961, pp. 269-279) suggests that such a halakhah as is needed to harmonize the various coffins in Beth Shearim with extant laws will not, in truth, be found; one looks forward to Cohen's longer study of the same question.

The above digression was intended to illustrate a representative criticism leveled at Goodenough's thesis about non-rabbinic Jews and Judaism throughout the Greco-Roman world, including Palestine, and to indicate the necessary next step in Goodenough's argument. If, as he contends, not all Jews (perhaps, not even many Jews) were under the hegemony of the aniconic rabbis of the Talmud, then what shall we think if we discover substantial, identifiably Jewish, and fully representational remains? What, in addition, shall we think if these remains indicate the use by Jews and for apparently Jewish purposes (whatever that might mean) of forms we should expect to uncover not in a Jewish but rather in a pagan setting? To these two questions the eight volumes are devoted, for very substantial, identifiably Jewish iconic remains have been uncovered from Tunisia to Dura, from Rome to the Galilee, and at many places in between, and these remains are, form the viewpoint of talmudic law, shocking!

One conclusion would render these finds insignificant and irrelevant: that while illegal, symbolic representations of lions, eagles, masks, and so forth were made for merely ornamental purposes, "the rabbis" may not have approved of them, but had to "reckon with reality" and "accepted" them. Goodenough repeats litanously, symbol by symbol and volume by volume, (see I, p. 108) that it is difficult to agree that the handful of symbolic objects so carefully chosen from a great variety of available symbols, so frequently repeated at Dura, Randanini, Bet Alpha, Hammam Lif and elsewhere to the exclusion of many other symbols, and so sloppily drawn that no ornamental artist could have done them, was merely decoration. Furthermore, it begs the question to say that these symbols were "merely" ornamental: why specifically these symbols and no others? Why in these settings? One need not hold that a "symbol" is perpetually symbolic, retaining its emotive value forever and everywhere, in order to deny that symbols (in this sense, representations of parts of reality) are in a given context never more than "mere" ornament. I should add, moreover, that it would be illuminating to know precisely what is meant by "mere ornament," in the historical context; and to know what other instances may be cited of wholly meaningless decoration attached to other places of worship and burial, which in antiquity were normally adorned, with meaningful and evocative designs.

Goodenough attempts, therefore, to uncover the meaning of various symbols discovered in substantial quantities throughout the Jewish world of antiquity. His procedure is, first, to present the finds in situ, second (and quite briefly), to expound a method capable of making sense out of them, and, third, to study each extant symbol with the guidance of this method.

Goodenough begins (I, ch. 2) by citing the literary evidence for the religion of the Jews in the Roman world, drawn from pagan, Christian, and various categories of Jewish sources (rabbinic, apocalyptic, and Hellenistic), presenting mainly the testimony of the pagans and Christians. While his hesitation in presenting the Jewish sources is entirely comprehensible (it would have entailed at least eight more volumes), I do think it regrettable that he has not taken sufficient note of the deeply Hellenized character of Palestinian Pharisaic Judaism before and in the period at hand, not because such a study would have materially altered his conclusions, but because he might have shed considerable light on Pharisaism itself; and might also have read the talmudic sources he does cite from a rather less monistic perspective. Seeing the Pharisees and their heirs as themselves the product of a long process of Hellenization, Goodenough might have found it less surprising to confront equally Hellenized but quite different Jews; and his contrast between the talmudic and the mystic groups would have been far subtler than it is. The issue was not, I think, Hellenization, but rather how to appropriate and accommodate oneself to Hellenizations; this was a very ancient issue indeed, certainly faced from the time of Simeon the Righteous, if not long before. Thus Goodenough might have seen both the mystic groups and the rabbinic groups as modulations of Jewish Hellenism, as they may, after further research, appear to have been; and the nuances of this Jewish Hellenism will become clearer. In any case, I looked in vain for references to the work of Yohanan Levi, E. Bickerman, I. Levi (La Legende Grec de Pythagore en Palestine, Paris, 1924), and others. I do not know what, if anything, the evidence brought by these scholars might have suggested to Goodenough, but I cannot believe that they are entirely irrelevant to his work.

Goodenough presents a majestic array of photographs and discussion, presenting in one place for the first time a portrait of Jewish art in antiquity which is perhaps as magnificent as will ever appear. One must never underestimate either the effort or the achievement involved in the first three volumes. He begins with the art of the Jewish tombs in Palestine and of their contents, studying the remains by chronological periods, and thus indicating the great changes in funerary art that developed after 70 A.D. He is consistently cautious in dating and discussion; if an item is possibly attributable to pagans, he does not accept it as evidence. Further, while his reviewers who specialize in classics and history of art have advanced a number of specific technical criticisms, none has cared to demonstrate a general technical "incompetence." Rather, the numerous points of difference advanced by some reviewers serve to reassure the outsider of a very broad area of agreement with Goodenough's treatment of the artifacts.

Goodenough proceeds (I, ch. 5) to the synagogues of Palestine, their inscriptions and contents, describing (sometimes briefly) more than four dozen sites. He concludes (I, p. 264):

> In these synagogues certainly was a type of ornament, using animals, human figures, and even pagan deities, in the round, in deep relief, or in mosaic, which was in sharp distinction to what was proper for Judaism... The ornament we are studying is an interim ornament, used only after the fall of Jerusalem and before the completion or reception of the Talmud. The return to the old standards, apparently a return to the halakhic Judaism that the rabbis advocated, is dramatically attested by the destruction, obviously by Jews themselves, of the decorative abominations, and only of the abominations, in these synagogues. Only when a synagogue was abandoned as at Dura... are the original effects preserved or the devastations indiscriminate.

I may note, parenthetically, that the decoration in these synagogues must have seemed more than merely decorative to those who destroyed them so discriminatingly.

Goodenough turns (II, chs. 1-5) to the archaeological evidence from the diaspora. Here he presents the remains of the Roman Jewish catacombs, as well as symbols used with burials outside Rome, synagogues of the diaspora, small objects such as lamps and glass remnants, the evidence of the inscriptions, and charms and amulets. Every student of the Talmud is aware, of course, that amulets and charms were part of the setting of rabbinic Judaism as well, but most are prepared to dismiss such matters as evidence of the "superstition" of the "ignorant masses." Kaufman consistently treats references in the prophetic literature to such syncretistic practices as examples of the folk fetishism of the masses, which do not give evidence that the masses themselves fully accepted these same fetishes as they were understood by pagans. Goodenough argues that the distinction between fetishistic magic and religion is generally subjective, and imposed from without by the embarrassed investigator. He points out (II, p. 156) that magical characteristics, such as the effort to achieve material benefits by fundamentally coercive devices are common (whether we recognize them as such or not) in the "higher" religions. It is certainly difficult to point to any religious group before the present time that did not quite openly expect religion to produce some beneficial consequence, and if that consequence was to take place after death, it was no less real. Hence Goodenough concludes that "magic is a term of judgment," and thus the relevance of charms and amulets is secured. Goodenough summarizes the consequences of his evidence as follows (II, p. 295):

> The picture we have got of this Judaism is that of a group still intensely loyal to Yao Sabaoth, a group which buried its dead and built its synagogues with a marked sense that it was a peculiar people in the eyes of God, but which accepted the best of paganism (including its most potent charms) as focusing in, finding its meaning in, the supreme Yao Sabaoth. In contrast to this, the Judaism of the rabbis was a Judaism which rejected all of the pagan religious world (all that it could)... Theirs was the method of exclusion, not inclusion...

The problem is then how to establish a methodology by which material amassed in the first three volumes may be studied and interpreted.

III

JEWISH SYMBOLS IN THE GRECO-ROMAN PERIOD: THE PROBLEM OF METHOD. Vol. IV. Part 1. New York: Pantheon, 1954.

The simplest method Goodenough might have used would have been to interpret the archaeological evidence on the basis of written documents of the period, but it is obvious that the written documents, particularly the talmudic ones, will hardly suffice to interpret symbols so utterly alien to their spirit, and in any case, so rarely discussed in them. Furthermore, even where some of the same symbols are mentioned in the Bible or Talmud and inscribed on graves or synagogues, it is not always obvious that the biblical antecedents or talmudic references engage the mind of the artist, particularly when it is so clear that he is following the conventions of Hellenistic art, and not only Hellenistic art, but the conventions of the artists who decorated cultic objects and places. Goodenough reviews other efforts to interpret this material, for he is not the first to see it.

Reading the summaries of the interpretation of those scholars who are willing to take the material seriously, I wondered why no one had used the old fundamentalist argument that some malevolent angel had scattered these objects about to challenge our faith in the ubiquity and normative character of talmudic Judaism, indeed, in the monolithic and linear character of Jewish religion. Watzinger, for instance, suggested that the synagogues may have been gifts to the Jews from the Roman governors, and had to be accepted "ready-made." Goodenough asks, however, for a general theory to make sense of all the evidence, something no one gives, and asks (IV, p. 10), "Where are we to find the moving cause in the taking over of images, and with what objective were they taken over? It seems to me that the motive for borrowing pagan art and integrating it into Judaism throughout the Roman world can be discovered only by analyzing the art itself." And for this, an interpretive method needs to be devised.

Goodenough succinctly defines this method:

The first step... must be to assemble... the great body of evidence available... which, when viewed as a whole, demands interpretation as a whole since it is so amazingly homogeneous for all parts of the Empire. The second step is to recognize that we must first determine what this art means in itself, before we begin to apply to it as proof texts any possible unrelated statements of the Bible or the Talmud. That these artifacts are unrelated to proof texts is a statement which one can no more make at the outset than one can begin with the assumption of most of my predecessors, that if the symbols had meaning for Jews, that meaning must be found by correlating them with Talmudic and biblical phrases... The art has rarely, and then only in details, been studied for its possible meaning in itself: this is the task of these volumes.

I should want to add a possible way to consider the relationship of this body of evidence to biblical literature.

While Goodenough does pay close attention to the possible biblical antecedents of many of the symbols he discusses, it would have been interesting if he had discussed, also, the great corpus of biblical images (in words or from the relics of the period) from which the Hellenistic Jews might have borrowed, comparing that group to the much smaller body of images that they did in fact borrow. Such a procedure might reveal at least as convincingly a reference to the pagan understandings, in various periods, of these same images, a clear-cut and integrated criterion for selection of a few particularly relevant and meaningful syumbols from a great body of available symbols. Thus he might demonstrate further the existence of a precise and well-defined myth which underlay the various manifestations in the remains. Of a given collection of biblical symbols, only a few survive in the Hellenistic Jewish remains. Why these few? Goodenough argues case by case that these images preserved or conveyed particular meanings or values held in common, but understood quite differently, by pagans, Jews and Christians, respectively. Hence, if a given image does appear in Scripture as well as in paganism, Goodenough frequently interprets it by reference to its pagan and mystic, rather than its (more opaque) Scriptural value. This method could, as I have said, be further substantiated by showing the symbols, equally available, that were not appropriated from biblical literature for Hellenistic Jewish purposes, for one would be led to conclude that an exclusion represented a choice, and that grounds of this choice might be delineated by uncovering the common quality of all such choices and exclusions. The common quality of the choice would probably emerge as their usage in mystery cults (possibly, as well as in the Temple), and the common quality of those excluded may very likely be that in Hellenistic times, none appears in paganism, in particular, in the pagan art of the mystery cults, and hence was useless for the purposeful appropriation of the Jewish mystics.

Conversely, it would be interesting to consider those symbols available to the Jews from the world of pagan religions which never appear in Jewish remains, a second possible indication that those that do appear were quite consciously appropriated for Jewish purposes. In general such symbols that do not appear relate to the actual worship of pagan gods revered at that time; such would obviously have been unacceptable in Jewish art. If future discoveries should add to the wealth of information on symbols used by Jews, it seems unlikely that the fundamental principles of selection manifested up to now would be greatly modified. Since biblical images presently not extant from the Greco-Roman period, or pagan images which according to our present thesis on the religion of these mystic groups would have been useless to them may turn up in identifiably Jewish settings, Goodenough hesitates to pursue this line of argument. After all, according to all earlier understanding of Judaism in the classical age, we should not have found a synagogue like that at Dura-Europos! Nonetheless, this is a means of testing the thesis and proving its soundness which is available, if only temporarily.

Goodenough does consider the relevance of rabbinic evidence, and concludes, "Even if some rabbis tolerated such an image, the implication is that they were far from taking the initiative in introducing anything of this kind," (IV, p. 15), a point that must be kept in mind throughout. At best it can be shown that a few rabbis "did not forbid" or "did not hinder" such art as is under consideration; there may indeed have been some pressure to accept this or that item. But the materials at hand were used widely and evidently intentionally; they apparently reflect a creative purpose, and not mere "compromise" with an alien, attractive culture.

Goodenough's method, presented in volume IV, ch. 2, is clearly articulated in advance, and used throughout. He always comes to a conclusion through explicit statement of his reasoning, a quality of real courage considering how easily one may then quibble at this point or that. His method is never obscure, though the consequences occasionally represent thinking other than fully rational; and if the succeeding volumes exhibit a monotonous quality, as one symbol after another come under discussion and produces an interpretation very close to that to follow, the reason is neither Goodenough's lack of ingenuity (on the contrary, some of his reviewers think he is too ingenious) or of scholarly imagination, but rather his tenacious use of a method clearly thought through, clearly articulated and clearly applied throughout.

What is this "method"? Above I have quoted its steps. The problem here is to explain step two, namely, how Goodenough determines what this art means in itself, a very difficult undertaking for him at the outset, and for me now.

Goodenough begins by asking (IV, p. 27):

> Admitting that the Jews would not have remained Jews if they had used these images in pagan ways and with pagan explanations, do the remains indicate a symbolic adaptation of pagan figures to Judaism or merely an urge to decoration?

He defines a symbol as "an image or design with a significance to one who uses it quite beyond its manifest content... an object or a pattern which, whatever the reason may be, operates upon men and causes effect in the viewer beyond mere recognition of what is literally presented in the given form." Recent philosophy, in particular that represented by the name of Suzanne Langer, has suggested that "to project feelings into outer objects is the first way of symbolizing and thus of conceiving those feelings," and hence, before conception, may well come "pure feeling." Goodenough emphasizes that most important thought is in "this world of the suggestive connotative meaning of words, objects, sounds, and forms..." He adds (IV, p. 33) that in religion, a symbol conveys not only meaning, but also "power or value." Further, some symbols move from religion to religion, preserving the same "value" while acquiring a new explanation. Here we may note that for the Jewish reader, this is an entirely comprehensible process, for we are witnesses to the capacity of religious "symbols" in the form of actions or prohibitions to endure through many, varied settings, acquiring new explanations and discarding old ones, and all the time retaining religious "force" or value or (in more modern terms) "meaning." A cursory examination, for instance, of I. Heinemann's Taamei HaMitzvot beSifrut Yisrael will suggest, first, for how many varied reasons Jews have kept "the commandments," and yet, second, how abiding are the values that may be discerned through each intellectual age and nuance. Hence, the Jewish reader will understand what Goodenough refers to when he writes (IV, p. 36):

> Indeed when the religious symbols borrowed by Jews in those years are put together, it becomes clear that the ensemble is not merely a 'picture book without text,' but reflect a lingua franca that had been taken into most of the religions of the day, for the same symbols were used in association with Dionysius, Mithra, Osiris, the Etruscan gods, Sabazius, Attis, and a host of others, as well as by Christianity later. It was a symbolic language, a direct language of values, however, not a language of denotation.

Goodenough is far from suggesting the presence of a pervasive syncretism, but rather, of pervasive religious values applied quite parochially by various groups, including some Jews, to the worship of their particular "Most High God." These values, while connotative and not denotative, may, nonetheless, be recovered and articulated in some measure by the historian who makes use of the insights of recent students of psychology and symbolism:

The hypothesis on which I am working... is that in taking over the
symbols, while discarding the myths and explanations of the pagans, Jews and
Christians admitted, indeed confirmed, a continuity of religious experience
which it is most important to be able to identify... for an understanding of
man, the phenomenon of a continuity of religious experience or values would
have much more significance than that of discontinuous explanations (IV, p. 42).

At this point Goodenough argues that the symbols under consideration were more than
merely space-fillers; first, because they were all living symbols in surrounding cultures;
second, because the vocabulary of symbols is extremely limited, on all the artifacts not
more than a score of designs appearing in sum, and thus highly selected; third, the reason
alluded to above, namely, that the symbols were frequently not the work of an ornamental
art at all; fourth, that the Jewish and "pagan" symbols are mixed on the same graves, so
that if the menorah is accepted as "having value" then the peacock or wreath of victory
ought also to have "had value"; and finally, that the symbols are found in highly public
places, such as synagogues and cemeteries, and not merely on the private and personal
possessions of individuals, such as amulets or charms.

From here, Goodenough's method becomes clear and irrevocable: he must state
carefully where and how each symbol occurs, thus establishing its commonplace quality;
he must then show the meaning that the symbol may have had universally, indicating its
specific denotative value in the respective cultures which used it. He considers its
broader connotative value, as it recurs in each culture, because a symbol evokes in man,
not only among specific groups of men, a broader, psychologically oriented meaning.
Naturally, this last step will be difficult for many to take, particularly because some
religious people are loathe to consider the sexual aspect of evocative religious symbolism
as psychologists have expounded it. Others will not be prepared to accept the psycholo-
gical unity of mankind, or at least, of that part of mankind that responds to religion.
Goodenough cannot ever convince such people that he is right, nor they him that he is
wrong; these are categories that, as I said at the outset, cannot apply here. Interpretation
of symbols is not at a sufficiently sophisticated stage that one can "prove" the rightness
or wrongness of an interpretation. Furthermore, Goodenough's statement on the nature of
religious psychology will appeal to a specific kind of religious mind, that prepared to
contemplate the unity of the human spirit with the divine being, while the more prosaic
will insist that it is all beyond proof, if not, indeed, beyond relevance.

Goodenough's psychology of religion recognizes "a profound urge to life, to the
realization, expansion and perpetuation of life," and holds that man attempts to escape
the inevitability of personal annihilation through death by achieving a union with the
enduring life-force, represented frequently by sexually grounded symbols:

This psychology of religion... centers upon the phenomenon of a great
life urge, a drive to self-fulfillment which may express itself in a desire for
mystic union with the Mother-Father or for security through obedience to the
Father.

The basic value of the religious symbols in pagan -- and Jewish Hellenistic -- antiquity was erotic.

The alternate way in religion, the way of obedience (in the case of Judaism) to Torah and commandments is "the way of the Father," which alleviates the sense of guilt while it still "accentuates the duality of Father and devotee. It is in religions centering not in obedience but in the birth and death and resurrection of the god or his son that mystical assimilation of the devotee with the Mother, or Father-Mother, is the objective..." (IV, p. 59). Further, Goodenough adds, the formal state religions of Athens, Rome, and Jerusalem, had a quite different basis, and had little (if any) use for the symbols at hand. These symbols, he holds, were of use "only in religions that engendered deep emotion, ecstasy, religions directly and consciously centered in the renewing of life and the granting of immortality, in the giving to the devotee of a portion of the divine spirit or life substance." So he states:

> At the end we shall see that these symbols appear to indicate a type of Judaism in which, as in Philonic Judaism, the basic elements of 'mystery' were superimposed upon Jewish legalism. The Judaism of the rabbis has always offered essentially a path through this present life, the Father's code of instructions as to how we may please him while we are alive. To this, the symbols seem to say, was now added from the mystery religions, or from Gnosticism, the burning desire to leave this life altogether, to renounce the flesh and go up into the richness of divine existence, to appropriate God's life to oneself.

> These ideas have as little place in normative, rabbinic Judaism as do the pictures and symbols and gods that Jews borrowed to suggest them... That such ideas were borrowed by Jews was no surprise to me after years of studying Philo... What is perplexing is the problem of how Jews fitted such conceptions into, or harmonized them with, the teachings of the Bible.

IV

JEWISH SYMBOLS IN THE GRECO-ROMAN PERIOD: SYMBOLS FROM THE JEWISH CULT. Vol. IV, Part II. New York: Pantheon, 1954.

JEWISH SYMBOLS IN THE GRECO-ROMAN PERIOD: FISH, BREAD, AND WINE. Vols. V and VI. New York: Pantheon, 1956.

JEWISH SYMBOLS IN THE GRECO-ROMAN PERIOD: PAGAN SYMBOLS IN JUDAISM. Vols. VII and VIII. New York: Pantheon, 1958.

In these volumes, Goodenough turns back to the symbols whose existence he reported in Volumes I-III, and attempts a systematic interpretation of them according to the method outlined in Volume IV, part I. I shall merely summarize the items discussed, because, as I noted earlier, and as Goodenough himself notes in Volume IV, part I, the conclusions are astonishingly uniform throughout.

In his discussion of symbols from the Jewish cult, Goodenough attempts to explain what these symbols may have meant when reproduced in the noncultic settings of synagogue and grave, specifically, the Menorah, the Torah shrine, lulab and etrog, shofar, and incense shovel. These symbols are, of course, definitely Jewish, and yet seem to have been transformed into symbols (IV, p. 67), "used in devotion, to have taken on personal, direct value," to mean not simply that the deceased was a Jew but to express a "meaning in connection with the death and life of those buried behind them." It would be simple to assign the meaning of these symbols to their biblical or cultic origins, except for the fact that they are often represented with less obviously Jewish, or biblical symbols, such as birds eating grapes and the like. Rather, Goodenough holds that these devices may be of some direct help in achieving immortality for the deceased, specifically "the menorah seems to have become a symbol of God, of his streaming light and Law... the astral path to God. The lulab and ethrog carried on the association of Tabernacles as a festival of rain and light, but took on mystical overtones, to become a eucharist to escape from evil and of the passing into justice as the immaterial Light comes to man...." He concludes:

> They could take a host of pagan symbols which appeared to them to have
> in paganism the values they wanted from their Judaism and blend them with
> Jewish symbols as freely as Philo blended the language of Greek metaphysics
> with the language of the Bible...

In Fish, Bread and Wine, Goodenough begins by discussing the Jewish and pagan representations of creatures of the sea, in the latter section reviewing these usages in Egypt, Mesopotamia, Syria, Greece, and Rome (a recurrent inquiry), then turns to the symbolic value of the fish in Judaism, and finally, to bread. The representations of "bread" often look merely like "round objects" however, and if it were not for the occasional representation of baskets of bread, one should be scarcely convinced that these "round objects" signify anything in particular. The section on wine is the high point of these volumes, both for its daring and for its comprehensive treatment of the "divine fluid" and all sorts of effulgences from the godhead, from Babylonia and Assyria, Egypt (in various periods), Greece, Dionysiac cults in Syria and Egypt, as well as in the late syncretistic religions. Goodenough finds considerable evidence in Jewish cult and observance, but insists that fish, bread and wine rites came into Jewish practice during and not before the Hellenistic period, and hence must be explained by contemporary ideas. Wine, in particular, was widely regarded as a source of fertility, but its mystic value was as an expression of the "craving for sacramental access to Life."

Pagan symbols used in Jewish contexts include the bull, lion, tree, crown, various rosettes and other wheels (demonstrably not used in paganism for purely decorative purposes), masks, the gorgoneum, cupids, birds, sheep, hares, shells, cornucopias, centaurs, psychopomps, and astronomical symbols. Goodenough treats this body of symbols last because, while some may have had biblical referents, the symbolic value of all these forms seems to him to be discovered in the later period. Of the collection, Goodenough writes (VIII, p. 220):

They have all turned into life symbols, and could have been, as I believe they were, interpreted in a great many ways. For those who believed in immortality they could point to immortality, give man specific hopes. To those who found the larger life in a mysticism that looked, through death, to a final dissolution of the individual into the All... these symbols could have given great power and a vivid sense of appropriation... The invasion of pagan symbols into either Judaism or Christianity... involved a modification of the original faith but by no means its abandonment. Symbolism is itself a language, and affected the original faith much as does adopting a new language in which to express its tenets. Both Christians and Jews in these years read their Scriptures, and prayed in words that had been consecrated to pagan deities. The very idea of a God, discussion of the values of the Christian or Jewish God, could be conveyed only by using the old pagan theos; salvation by the word soteria; immortality by athanasia. The eagle, the crown, the zodiac, and the like spoke just as direct, just as complicated a language. The Christian or Jew had by no means the same conception of heaven or immortality as the pagan, but all had enough in common to make the same symbols, as well as the same words, expressive and meaningful. Yet the words and the symbols borrowed did bring in something new...

Goodenough continues (VIII, p. 224):

When Jews adopted the same lingua franca of symbols they must... have taken over the constant values in the symbols.

not of "Jewish pagans" but rather Hellenized Jews. Otherwise, Goodenough repeatedly argues, the Jews would have lost their connection with Judaism; but the Hellenized Jews bore as great a scorn for "paganism" as the rabbis or the church fathers. That is surely not to argue that Philo is the one literary source able to bring meaning to these artifacts, however, but only that Philo, Paul, John and others all addressed themselves, in varying ways, to a Hellenized audience in a Hellenized idiom. Thus Jewish Hellenism represented a conglomerate of "Hellenistic Judaisms" to be distinguished carefully and systematically:

The uniformity of Jewish symbolism... seems to me to reflect not a basic document of mysticism or metaphysics, like the writings of Philo, but a body of common hopes -- hopes that found better expression in Greek figures of speech (for Philo) or in Greek plastic forms (for the groups under considera-tion) than in traditional Jewish formulations because these hopes had come into Judaism from paganism... (VIII, p. 226).

Finally, Goodenough reviews the lessons of the evidence. From the cultic objects we learn that the Jews used images of their cultic objects in a new way, in the pagan manner, for just as the pagans were putting the mythological and cultic emblems of their religions on their tombs to show their hope in the world to come, so too did the Jews. From fish, bread and wine, we learn that the Jews were thus partaking of immortal nature. In reference to the symbols that had no cultic origins (VII and VIII) and, on the face of it, slight Jewish origins (apart from the bull, tree, lion, and possibly crown, which served in biblical times) Goodenough proposes that the value of these objects, though not their verbal explanations, were borrowed because some Jews found in them "new depths for his ideas of... his own Jewish deity, and his hope of salvation or immortality...."

V

Goodenough's work has thus far been discussed from somewhat tangential viewpoints. In the extended commentary above, the books have been necessarily misrepresented, for the emphases of my discussion are not the emphases of Goodenough, and the questions and suggestions advanced above touch points of far more interest to students of Judaism in this period than to students of Jewish symbolism and mysticism, chief among them, of course, Goodenough himself.

Hence, the question should be answered: What is the essential contribution made by Jewish Symbols in the Greco-Roman Period? Why are these books so important? And why should they be studied carefully?

First, a great deficiency in earlier scholarship on the archaeology of this period has been the failure of most investigators to reckon open-mindedly with the implications for classical Judaism of the relics of a supposedly aniconic faith, consistently using plastic symbols of all shapes, sizes and significations. Whether one holds that decoration is "mere ornament" or not, one cannot lightly and unconcernedly dismiss the astonishing appearance of pagan ornament in Jewish settings, as many have done. Such offhand dismissal represents an act of faith in prevailing presuppositions that no scholar can afford to make. The eagle, the vine, the human and divine figures, including the head of Zeus, the wreath, etc., all warrant serious consideration in the context of the art in which they generally were found, namely pagan art, as well as in the unexpected places in which they turned up, on Jewish synagogues and ossuaries. By simply reviewing the finds in such a way, Goodenough has forced a reconsideration of their meaning. By proposing an explanation of them, he has forced the scholarly world to reconsider its consensus and to come to a thoughtful reappraisal of its earlier position: and he has rightly insisted that if his theses are rejected, others must be proposed in their place. In all this, a deficiency in earlier treatment of Jewish symbols in the Greco-Roman period has been removed.

Second, Goodenough's essential contribution is, in my opinion, to be measured by evaluating not his "proof" of any of his theses, but rather his method and its cumulative consequences. Goodenough does not claim to "prove" anything, for if by proof one means certain and final establishment of a fact, there can be no proof in the context of evidence such as this. The stones are silent; Goodenough has tried to listen to what they say. He reports what he understands about them, attempting to accomplish what the evidence as it now stands permits; the gradual accumulation of likely and recurrent explanations derived from systematic study of a mass of evidence, and the growing awareness that these explanations point to a highly probable conclusion. That is not a "demonstration" in the sense that a geometrical proposition can be demonstrated, and for good reason are the strictly literal (and, therefore, philological) scholars uncomfortable at Goodenough's results. But all who have worked as historians even with literary evidence must share

Goodenough's underlying assumption, that nothing in the endeavor to record historical truth is in the end truly demonstrable or positive, but nonetheless significant statements about history may be made.

Third, Goodenough has clearly indicated a substantial probability that recurrently emerges from this mass of evidence. If the cumulative evidence is inspected as cautiously as possible, it can hardly yield a statement other than the following: At the period between the first and sixth centuries, the manifestations of the Jewish religion were varied and complex, far more varied, indeed, than the extant talmudic literature would have led us to believe. Besides the groups known from this literature, we have evidence that "there were widespread groups of loyal Jews who built synagogues and buried their dead in a manner strikingly different from that which the men represented by extant literature would have probably approved, and, in a manner motivated by myths other than those held by these men." The content of these myths may never be known with any great precision, but comprehended a Hellenistic-Jewish mystic mythology far closer to the Kabbalah than to talmudic Judaism. In a fairly limited time before the advent of Islam, these groups dissolved. This is the plain sense of the evidence brought by Goodenough, not a summary in any sense of his discoveries, hypotheses, suggestions, or reconstruction of the evidence into an historical statement.

Such a summary would not be possible since Goodenough's central interest is the material and the method by which it may be dealt with, grave by grave, and symbol by symbol. But such a summary does indicate, I think, a very substantial contribution to scholarship indeed, the great significance of which should impel many readers to turn to the evidence itself for closer study.

Goodenough certainly describes a religion that does not conform to positivist conceptions of what Judaism should be, and I may add, it is likely that talmudic Judaism (and early Christianity) conformed just as little to the antiseptic vision of the eighteenth and nineteenth century Maskilim, philosophers and founders of Jewish Science. If he offers an explanation of the artifacts and a general theory to account for them, this is a demonstration not only of imaginative scholarship and learning, but also of courage and character, courage to question both prevailing assumptions and widespread indifference, and character to persist for so many, many years at a task now only half-completed.

16. Carl H. Kraeling

THE SYNAGOGUE

and

Erwin R. Goodenough

JEWISH SYMBOLS IN THE GRECO-ROMAN PERIOD IX-XI

History of Religions 1964, 4:81-102

THE EXCAVATIONS AT DURA EUROPOS CONDUCTED BY YALE UNIVERSITY AND THE FRENCH ACADEMY OF INSCRIPTIONS AND LETTERS, FINAL REPORT, VIII, PT. I: THE SYNAGOGUE by Carl H. Kraeling, with contributions by C.C. Torrey, C.B. Welles, and B. Geiger, A.R. Bellinger, F.E. Brown, A. Perkins, and C.B. Welles (eds.) (New Haven, 1956).

JEWISH SYMBOLS IN THE GRECO-ROMAN PERIOD (N.Y., 1963) IX-XI. Symbolism in the Dura Synagogue, By Erwin R. Goodenough.

When the painted walls of the synagogue at Dura-Europos emerged into the light of day in November, 1932, the modern perspective on the character of Judaism in Greco-Roman times had to be radically refocused. Until that time, it was possible to ignore the growing evidence, turned up for decades by archaeologists, of a kind of Judaism substantially different from that described in Jewish literary remains of the period. Those remains specifically contained in the Talmud and Midrash were understood to describe an aniconic, ethically, and socially oriented religion, in which the ideas of Hellenistic religions, particularly mystery religions, played little or no part. Talmudic Judaism had, by then, been authoritatively described in such works as George Foot Moore's Judaism, and no one had reason to expect that within what was called "normative Judaism" one would uncover phenomena he might, in other settings, have interpreted as "gnostic" or mystical or eschatological in orientation. It is true that archaeological discoveries had long before revealed in the synagogues and graves of Jews in the Hellenistic worlds substantial evidences of religious syncretism, and of the use of pagan symbols in identifiably Jewish settings. But before the Dura synagogue these evidences remained discrete and made slight impact. They were not explained; they were explained away.

After the preliminary report, the Dura synagogue was widely discussed, and a considerable literature, mostly on specific problems of art but partly on the interpretation of the art, developed; in the main, the Dura synagogue was studied by art historians, and not, with notable exceptions, by historians of religion or of Judaism. When, in 1956, Carl H. Kraeling published The Synagogue, it seemed that no substantial revision of earlier ideas on Judaism at this period would be required. Kraeling argued that the paintings might be interpreted for the most part by reference to the so-called rabbinic literature of the period, and impressively used the talmudic, midrashic, and targumic writings for that purpose. He writes (pp. 353, 354):

> The Haggadic tradition embodied in the Dura synagogue paintings was, broadly speaking, distinct from the one that was normative for Philo and for that part of the ancient Jewish world that he represents... This particular cycle [of paintings] as it is known to us at Dura moves within a definable orbit of the Haggadic tradition,... this orbit has Palestinian-Babylonian rather than Egyptian relations.

Kraeling's method and conclusions are re-examined, and a wholly different method, leading to quite other conclusions, is proposed by Erwin R. Goodenough in the newest volumes of Jewish Symbols in the Greco-Roman Period, which have just appeared. My purpose here is, first, to contrast the findings of Kraeling and Goodenough on a number of specific, suggestive problems; second, to summarize the general picture of Dura Judaism described by each; and, finally, to offer a historian's judgment on the issues at hand.

II

THE PROBLEM OF METHOD

While an argument in abstract terms can yield at best only imprecise insights, Kraeling and Goodenough disagree so diametrically on the basic issue of how to interpret the art that at the outset one may usefully articulate their differences.

Kraeling argues that the biblical references of the Dura paintings are so obvious that one may begin by reading the Bible, and proceed by reading the paintings in the light of the Bible and its Midrashic interpretation in the talmudic period. He says (p. 351):

> Any community decorating its House of Assembly with material so chosen and so orientated cannot be said to have regarded itself... remote from religious life and observance of the Judaism that we know from the Bible and the Mishnah... It would appear [p. 352] that there is a considerable number of instances in which Targum and Midrash have influenced the pictures.

Kraeling provides numerous examples of such influence. He qualifies his argument, however, by saying that the use of Midrashic and Targumic material is "illustrative rather than definitive." While he makes reference, from time to time, to comparative materials, Kraeling does not in the main feel it necessary to examine the broad iconographic traditions operating in Dura in general, and most manifestly in the synagogue art, for he holds that whatever conventions of pagan art may appear, the meaning of the synagogue art is wholly separated from such conventions and can best, probably only, be understood within the context of the Judaism known to us from literary sources.

Goodenough's argument, repeated in the newest volumes from the earlier ones, is that literary traditions would not have led us to expect any such art as this. We may find statements in talmudic literature which are relevant to the art, but we must in any case after assembling the material determine what this art means in itself, before we begin to apply to it as proof texts any possible unrelated statements of the Bible or the Talmud. That these artifacts are unrelated to proof texts is a statement which one can no more make at the outset than one can begin with the assumption of most of my predecessors that if the symbols had meaning for Jews, that meaning must be found by correlating them with Talmudic and biblical phrases [IV, 10].

Goodenough argues, therefore, that talmudic literature would not lead us to expect the appearance of this kind of art at all. We should search in vain in its pages for the origin of creative exploitation of the kinds of pagan imagery widespread in Jewish synagogues and sarcophagi and, now, additionally, in the Dura synagogue. The rabbis of the Talmud may have tolerated certain limited exemplars of pagan art; but they would not have initiated its use, and in their literature, one may, therefore, hardly find the interpretive principles which illumined the mind of those Jews who did use it. On the other hand, archaeological remains from other places, if carefully examined, would most certainly have led us to less astonishment than exhibited when Dura was uncovered, and than has continually been displayed wherever and whenever archaeologists unfamiliar with the great corpus of Jewish use of pagan conventions have uncovered pagan art in Jewish settings. Goodenough therefore denies at the outset that literary explanations may be attached to this, or any other, Jewish art in antiquity, unless those explanations take into account what the particular symbols meant within the context of other cultures from which they were obviously borrowed.

Goodenough's argument against the use of "proof texts" is supported by Morton Smith in "The Image of God."[1] Smith points out,

> Discussions of the hellenization of ancient Judaism often take for granted that any material for which precedent can be found in the Old Testament is therefore independent of Hellenistic influence. This supposition neglects the fact that rabbinic literature is almost entirely homiletic and legal. Preachers and lawyers must find proof-texts in certain books which are authoritative for their purposes. But they do not necessarily get their ideas from those books to which they must go for their proof-texts... Of course, proof-texts sometimes do happen to contain the ideas attributed to them. But even when they do, the taking up and development of ideas by later writers may be evidence of outside influence... In such instances as these, the preacher who comes to the Bible looking for a proof-text happens to find a good one, one which really says what he wants said. But this does not alter the fact that he finds it because he looks for it, and he looks for it because of the practices or ideas which have become important in the world around him. Therefore when we discuss the influences at work on a religion we must look first of all to the world around it, its immediate environment [pp. 473, 474, 481].

Thus, even though the art of the Dura synagogue may at the first glance seem to be related to the Midrashic ideas, even found in a few cases to reflect Midrashic accounts of biblical events, nonetheless one is still not freed from the obligation to consider what that art meant to a contemporary Jew, pagan, or Christian who was familiar with other art of the age. Since both the architectural and the artistic conventions of the Dura synagogue are demonstrably those of the place and age, and not in any way borrowed from pre-existent "rabbinic" artistic conventions -- because there weren't any! -- one must give serious thought to the meaning and value, or the contest, of those conventions elsewhere and assess, so far as one can, how nearly that value and meaning were preserved in the Jewish setting.

Both Kraeling and Goodenough agree that there was a plan to the art of the synagogue, and that biblical scenes are portrayed not only as mere ornament or decoration but as a means of conveying important religious ideas, so that the walls of the sanctuary might, in truth, yield sermons. Before considering the content of those "sermons," we may usefully turn to specific points of disagreement in interpretation so that we may, in the whole, recognize the more concrete role of the interpretation of the parts.

III

SPECIFIC POINTS OF DIFFERENCE

The methodological difference between Goodenough and Kraeling on how to interpret the art may be best illustrated by considering specific cases. Here we shall consider three examples. What will become clear, it seems to me, is that Goodenough demands explanation for a far greater number and variety of details; he sees more in the art and asks more about it. Kraeling uses, in the main, a single body of literature, while Goodenough ranges far and wide in his search for ideas and artistic conventions relevant to Dura synagogue art. Whether or not we are better off on that account may only be decided on the basis of the results. My purpose here is to summarize a very small part of their respective treatments. The reader will need to turn to the works of the two scholars and, most of all, to the art itself.

IV

ORPHEUS/DAVID

Across the middle of the reredos on the west wall of the synagogue is painted a figure of Orpheus playing to the animals. Both Goodenough and Kraeling call the figure "David," although the kinds of animals surrounding him are in dispute.

Goodenough (IX, 93-94) turns, therefore, to the figure of Orpheus, and asks what it was about the pagan Orpheus which prompted Jews (and Christians) to borrow the figure. The figure of Orpheus represented the power of divine song to quiet human savagery. Kraeling (224-25) agrees;

> There can be no doubt that Orpheus has served the artist in part at least
> as the model of the representation... The question whether an allusion to
> Orpheus charming the beasts was intended... can be answered properly only in
> the light of the purpose the artist had in mind introducing the figure of the

musician... The lyre-player must be David, the classic historical representative of the "kings... in the house of Judah."... In view of the uncertainties
about many of the details of the area, the only inference that can safely be
drawn from the upper part of the Lower Center Panel about the influence of
the Orpheus tradition upon the Synagogue paintings is that the artist fell back
upon the best-known and most appropriate of the many clichés for musicians
as a happy device for portraying David in the role assigned to him by II Sam.
22.
Goodenough goes on, however, to raise questions Kraeling does not raise (IX, 94):
> Primarily why did the artist want to put David as the tamer just here?
> We have seen that the original vine or tree growing from a vase was changed
> to make more explicit the symbolic and ritualistic implications of the vase...
> Granted that Orpheus was thought to be David, what did David mean to the
> congregation that with his animals he could have been put thus in the center of
> the tree?
To answer this question, Goodenough turns, as he does frequently in Volumes IX-X, to the
writings of Hellenistic Judaism, and to Philo in particular. He finds that Philo regarded
David as a thespios man, which means "one who is superhuman to the point of being
divine." Goodenough, however, holds that the figure of the mystic musician was primary
and his identification with David secondary. He points out that the design as a whole
denotes nothing historically or biblically objective. David alone could have been
designated very clearly, as other figures such as Aaron are, by writing his name by the
drawing. This was not done, and it is reasonable to suggest that David the singer in this
setting and according to these conventions may be illuminated by references from other
besides Jewish literature. Goodenough cites Hellenistic Jewish writings in which Orpheus
was regarded as having drawn his mystery entirely from Moses and shows that Orphic
material was prized among Jews. He alludes also to the merkavah mysticism (which, we
shall see, was probably a characteristic of Babylonion Judaism at this period) and holds
that the reredos painting represents (IX, 103) an adumbration of the merkavah vision:
> David, who as Orpheus, plays his music and tames birds and beasts in the
> great tree-vine that leads up to the Throne of the Three...
It must be obvious to the reader that we cannot decide, on the basis of this brief
summary, "who is right." But it must be equally obvious that two wholly different
perspectives have come to bear on the figure of David-Orpheus, one unwilling to pursue
the meaning, if any, behind the use of the conventions of pagan art, and the other eager to
do so.

V

MOSES, APHRODITE, AND THE NYMPHS/PHARAOH AND THE INFANCY OF MOSES

In register C of the west wall, numbered by Kraeling WC4, is a painting of the
discovery of the infant Moses. Goodenough's and Kraeling's descriptive titles of the panel
are given above.

The female figures in this panel are identified by Kraeling (p. 173) with the two midwives of the Exodus narrative, and the third woman represents Jochebed, the mother of Moses (p. 174) depositing her infant son in the ark. If correct

> it implies that the artist has acted quite drastically and fearlessly in placing in two planes two consecutive scenes whose actions clash so violently with each other; the one showing the Pharaoh issuing the orders for the destruction of the Hebrew infants, the other showing Moses' mother saving her child from Pharaoh's anger... the resultant composition is not without an element of irony in exhibiting futility of the king's efforts.

The upper portion of the scene portrays the princess' attendants, three in number. They carry the princess' toilet accessories, a small gold jug, a bowl, and a paneled ivory casket. In the foreground the scene shows the "daughter of Pharoah" finding the child Moses in the ark. She stands up to her thighs in the water. Princess and child are both nude. Of course, Kraeling points out (p. 177) that it was the handmaid of Pharaoh's daughter who fetched the child, but, he says,

> It can be explained... by assuming that the artist depended upon the Targumic version for his inspiration, for in the Targum Onkelos the statement "she sent her handmaid to fetch it" it rendered "she stretched out her arm and seized it."

In the panel, however, the daughter of Pharaoh, actually standing in the water, does not appear to have "stretched out her arm"; she is actually holding the baby while standing in the water, the baby being "cradled" in her outstretched arm. The intent of the Targum would seem to me to be that the woman, kneeling on the bank, stretched out her arm to receive the child so as not to get into the water; in any case, the Targum does not imply that she got into the water. Here, one is struck first by the fact that she is standing in the water and that her position there is not accounted for by desire to fetch the child, whom she holds.

Goodenough's discussion (I, 198-226) of the discovery of Moses begins with the assertion that the "princess" of Kraeling is in fact a divine figure, and that the representations of the goddess Anahita with her female attendants are so similar that one may clearly identify the woman who finds and extracts the baby with that divinity. This assertion is in no way tendentious; Goodenough cites numerous instances of paintings of Anahita in which important details of the painting before us are found. Anahita was, Goodenough adds, no mere iconographic cliché, but one of the most popular deities of the period in Iran. She was associated by the Greeks with the Great Mother and Aphrodite; further, Goodenough points out, the female in the Nile is very much the Aphrodite type:

> Not only in general Sasanian tradition... but in a house practically adjacent to the synagogue we have a figure of Aphrodite-Anahita who in general outline, hair, and the position of her hands startlingly resembles the figure who takes the baby from the ark.

The baby himself "just as startlingly resembles the Eros beside Aphrodite in the position of his hands." Goodenough argues, therefore, that a contemporary observer could not have missed the resemblance. The three maids, moreover, are in fact nymphs, and "present so striking an invasion of a pagan element into the biblical scene that we must stop to go thoroughly into the matter to demonstrate that these actually are the nymphs, and to ascertain what their presence would have implied for the interpretation of the biblical incident."

As always, Goodenough then amasses a majestic array of comparative materials and shows that the nymphs who wash a baby, in both pagan and Christian usage, "indicate that the baby was a god in the pagan sense." On this basis, Goodenough concludes:

> the master designer at Dura introduced the Nymphs deliberately and skilfully into the scene of the infant Moses and did so in order to intensify the notion that Anahita-Aphrodite was drawing from the water a Wunderkind with royal nature at least "hedged" with divinity.

Goodenough says, in this instance as in numerous others, that what we have before us is an example of the adoption of Greek and Iranian conventions "only to show that Judaism, when properly understood, presents all religious values, even the pagan values, better than the pagans themselves." Goodenough then expounds the view of Moses held by Hellenistic Judaism, as exemplified by Philo in particular and shows that, in Philo, Moses emerges as a supreme, royal character and, at birth, was a divine child:

> The evidence seems to lead to the following conclusion: In Hellenized Jewish tradition the great biblical heroes began as Wunderkinder, extraor- dinary in their conception, effulgence, beauty, and precocity. These perquisites of the Wunderkinder were given them by the Nymphs or Graces, the flowing Grace of God... In Hellenistic tradition a Wunderkind becomes normally a god or king or both, and the symbolic tradition for representing this was by having him washed by the spirit-filled water of the Nymphs. The tradition went over into the Hellenized Jewish art, where it was used for both Moses and David, and later adopted by Christians for the births of Mary and Christ. The same tradition explicitly appears in the Dura painting of the infancy of Moses, though adopted more skillfully to the biblical narrative than in the Octateuchs.

Thus the painting portrays a Hellenized Jewish idea, that Moses was a Wunderkind, of royal nature, and as such he could go to Sinai, get the Law, and give it to the people. "Nothing in pictorial design could have proclaimed his character more specifically than to have him drawn from water by Aphrodite and presented by her to the mymphs, and finally, held up for adoration in his own right."

There can be no more concrete example of the contrast between Goodenough's and Kraeling's approaches. If Kraeling had considered and refuted the kinds of evidences Goodenough regards as relevant, one might be in a clearer position to evaluate his explanation. But where Goodenough provides an abundance of comparative material, both artistic and literary, on the basis of which to evaluate his interpretations, Kraeling provides only a single verse of the Targum, and that, to my way of reading it, by no means conclusive. One may continually say that the use of pagan art is wholly conventional, just as the critics of Goodenough's earlier interpretations repeat that the symbols from graves and synagogues were "mere ornament" and imply nothing more than a desire to decorate (none surely can say this of Dura, and no one has, for the meaningful character of Dura synagogue art is so self-evident as to obviate the need to argue it). But having asserted that pagan art has lost its value and become, in a Jewish setting, wholly conventional, is one better off? Does one therefore understand <u>why</u> pagan conventions were useful for decoration? Is the matter to be reduced to a mere accident of taste? If so, one would have to take far less seriously than Kraeling does the phenomena of Dura synagogue art.

VI

THE STAFF OF MOSES/CLUB OF HERACLES

When Moses led Israel out of Egypt, he carried, as everyone knows, a staff. In Dura, however, the staff is portrayed as no shepherd's staff ever was; it was a club. This is on the west wall, Kraeling's listing as Panel WA3. That this <u>is</u> Moses is indicated by a <u>titulus</u> between the legs of the first figure of Moses, "Moses when he went out from Egypt and cleft the sea."

The figure of Moses standing ready to strike the sea Goodenough (X, 119-25) associates with Heracles, and he examines the value of the figure Heracles in contemporary religion and provides an interpretation of what that figure, identified with Moses, would have meant to Dura Jewry. The identification of Moses' "rod" with the club of Heracles is established by Goodenough first, by pointing out that it is not a wand, as it is portrayed elsewhere, but a club, and second, by showing that only two characters, Theseus and Heracles, ever carry a club:

> There can be no doubt... that this identification of Moses' rod with the club of Theseus and Heracles was intentional, and so strange an identification seems to indicate that Moses was the Jewish Theseus-Heracles... The knobby club especially marked these heroes, and since they alone of all mythological figures carry or use it, the artist could have put it into Moses' hands only because of its immediately symbolic reference to their special characters and to his.

Actually, the "club" appears in other Jewish remains. Heracles, for his part, was very popular in the East, being worshipped widely and associated with numerous other hero-gods. Moses, Goodenough holds, was the Ares-Heracles of Judaism, and his function and nature "were properly characterized by showing him with the club in this setting." Further, Philo's interpretation of the migration, which harmonizes with the painting, is as a "renunciation of the flesh and pleasure... the <u>agon</u> with their own lower natures... It is interesting to see that Philo knew also the appropriateness of Heracles to symbolize this struggle."

I am unable to find that Kraeling says more about the rod/club than (p. 81) that Moses carries a "long, knobby staff."

The second and third cases which we have considered suggest to Goodenough that Moses was more than a merely human figure to the Jews of Dura-Europos. If one begins

with the widespread assumption that "Jewish artists... reveal themselves as immune to all
instrusions of Hellenistic god-man ideas, although the Jews were willing to thank the kings
as protectors in a charismatic sense,"[2] then one must reject out of hand the kind of
conclusions to which Goodenough comes. However, it seems to me that this statement is
based not on a close, detailed, and careful reading of the Jewish artifacts, but on a
philosophical, and anachronistic view of what "normative" and monolithic Judaism seemed
to its examiners in much later ages to have been. If the Jews represented some of their
heroes in garb normally reserved, conventionally, to pagan gods when in pagan settings,
one must at least be open to the possibility that the Jewish heroes were believed, by the
Jews, to have divine qualities. No one has argued, least of all Goodenough, that the Jews
were pagans in a Jewish idiom. But it seems reasonable to accept the possibility that the
Jews learned something from pagans and that, when they borrowed the artistic and
religious conventions of their neighbors, the value, though obviously not the verbal
explanation, these conventions bore for the pagan continued to retain meaning for Jews.
It is true in the case of Moses that in talmudic literature Moses is belittled. But it is
equally true, as Smith showed in "Images of God," that the divine-human idea was most
certainly found in Jewish art and in talmudic literature; for example, that "the saint (the
perfect man) is the image of God, and that the cosmos, also perfect, is the image of God,
and that the Menorah, the image of God, was also the image of both saint and cosmos" (p.
508). We know that in the burial place of some rabbis, Bet Shearim, the figure of a man
with a menorah on his head is found, and one can hardly interpret such iconographic
evidence rightly if one assumes at the very outset that the divine-human man, or a symbol
that the divinity may rest on man, will never be found in Jewish remains "because the
Jews were 'immune' to all such intrusions of Hellenistic god-man ideas"! If one is open to
the possibility that Moses may appear in a more than human dimension, then Goodenough's
interpretations of the birth scene and the club do not greatly contradict other information
we have; are based, in fact, upon widespread and well-attested conventions; and from the
evidence of the general plausibility of a Jewish man-god figure uncovered by Smith in
talmudic literary evidences, appear to be at least as plausible explanations as we are
likely to come by. All this, moreover, ignores the facts of Hellenistic Jewish literature,
in which, Goodenough shows, Moses does appear as a god-man figure.

VII

JUDAISM AT DURA: GENERAL POINTS OF DIFFERENCE

If we had begun with a statement of Kraeling's and Goodenough's view of Dura
Judaism, without a preliminary examination of some specific problems of interpretation, it
seems to me wholly likely that Kraeling's view, and not Goodenough's, would have
prevailed. Having seen in three specific instances, however, adumbrations of the very
solid basis upon which Goodenough bases his general assertions (in fact, the specific
analysis of the art far outweighs the generalizations in both Kraeling's and Goodenough's
studies), the reader will be more likely to take seriously a radical reinterpretation of the
whole.

Here I shall let the scholars speak for themselves, first, on the general meaning which emerges from the paintings as a whole and, second, on the nature of Judaism at Dura.

While both scholars interpret the pictures in detail, each provides a summary of the meaning of the art as a whole. Kraeling's is as follows (pp. 350-51):

A closer examination of the treatment of Israel's sacred history as presented in the Synagogue painting leads to a number of inferences that will help to appraise the community's religious outlook... These include the following:

a. There is a very real sense in which the paintings testify to an interest in the actual continuity of the historical process to which the sacred record testifies. This is evidenced by the fact that they do not illustrate interest in the Covenant relationship by a combination of scenes chosen from some one segment of sacred history, but provide instead a well-organized progression of scenes from the period of the Patriarchs and Moses and Aaron, from the early days of the monarchy, through the prophetic period, the exile, the post-exile period, to the expected Messianic age as visualized by prophecy...

b. There is a very real sense in which the history portrayed in the paintings involves not only certain individuals, but concretely the nation as a whole, and in which the course of events in time and space are for the individuals and the nation a full and completely satisfactory expression of their religious aspirations and ideals...

c. There is a very real sense in which the piety exhibited in, and inculcated by, the paintings finds a full expression in the literal observance of the Law. This comes to light in the effort to provide the historical documentation for the origin of the religious festivals... in the attention paid to the cult and its sacra, including the sacrifices: and in the opposition to idolatry.

d. Because they have this interest in the historical process, in the people of Israel, and in the literal observance of the Law, the paintings can and do properly include scenes showing how those nations and individuals that oppose God's purposes and His people are set at naught or destroyed...

In other words, the religious problem which the synagogue paintings reflect is not that of the individual's search for participation in true being by the escape of the rational soul from the irrational desires to a higher level of mystical experience, but rather that of faithful participation in the nation's inherited Covenant responsibilities as a means of meriting the fulfillment of the divine promises and of making explicit in history its divinely determined purpose.

Goodenough's interpretation of the whole west wall follows (X, 137-38):

The west wall of the synagogue as a whole is indeed coming to express a profoundly consistent Judaism. On the left side a miraculous baby is given by Elijah, but he ties in with the temporal hopes of Israel, exemplified when

Persian rulership was humiliated by Esther and Mordecai. Divine intervention brings this about, but here brought only this. Above is the cosmic interpretation of the Temple sacrifice of Aaron, and Moses making the twelve tribes into the zodiac itself.

On the right, just as consistently, the immaterial, metaphysical values of Judaism are presented. Moses is the divine baby here, with the three nymphs and Anahita-Aphrodite. Kingship, as shown in the anointing of David by Samuel, is not temporal royalty, but initiation into the hieratic seven. Above these, the gods of local paganism collapse before the Ark of the Covenant, the symbol of metaphysical reality in Judaism, which the three men beside the ark also represented, while that reality is presented in a temple with seven walls and closed inner sanctuary, and with symbols from the Creation myth of Iran. At the top, Moses leads the people out to true spiritual victory.

In the four portraits, an incident from the life of Moses is made the culmination of each of these progressions. He goes out as the cosmic leader to the heavenly bodies alongside the cosmic worship of Aaron, the menorah, and the zodiac. He reads the mystic law like the priest of Isis alongside the closed Temple and the all-conquering Ark. He receives the Law from God on Sinai beside a Solomon scene which we cannot reconstruct: but he stands at the Burning Bush, receiving the supreme revelation of God as Being, beside the migrating Israelites, who move... to a comparable, if not the same, goal.

The reader must be struck by the obvious fact that, in the main, both scholars agree on the substance of the paintings, though they disagree on both their interpretation and their implications for the kind of religion characteristic of this particular synagogue.

Concerning Dura Judaism, Kraeling argues that the Jews of Dura had fallen back "visibly" upon the biblical sources of religious life (p. 351). Kraeling says throughout that the Jews in Dura were, for the most past, good, "normative," rabbinic Jews:

If our understanding of the pictures is correct, they reveal on the part of those who commissioned them an intense, well-informed devotion to the established traditions of Judaism, close contact with both the Palestinian and the Babylonian centers of Jewish religious thought, and a very real understanding of the peculiar problems and needs of a community living in a strongly competitive religious environment, and in an exposed political position [p. 335].

Goodenough, in his description of Judaism at Dura (X, 196-209), holds that these were not participants in the "established traditions of Judaism," and that they did not have close contact with Babylonian or Palestinian Judaism (he follows the general view of Babylonian Judaism as "rabbinic," which I shall question below). The walls of the synagogue are not, he argues, representations of biblical scenes, but allegorizations of them (as in the specific instances cited above). The biblical scenes show an acceptance of mystic ideas which the symbolic vocabulary of Jews elsewhere in the Greco-Roman world, studied in the first eight volumes, suggested. He says (p. 205):

While the theme of the synagogue as a whole might be called the celebration of the glory and power of Judaism and its God, and was conceived and planned by men intensely loyal to the Torah, those people who designed it did not understand the Torah as did the rabbis in general. Scraps stand here which also appear in rabbinic haggadah, to be sure... But in general the artist seems to have chosen biblical scenes not to represent them but, by allegorizing them, to make them say much not remotely implicit in the texts... On the other hand, the paintings can by no means be spelled out from the pages of Philo's allegories, for especially in glorifying temporal Israel they often depart from him altogether. Kraeling astutely indicated... that we have no trace of the creation stories, or indeed of any biblical passages before the sacrifice of Isaac, sections of the Bible to which Philo paid almost major attention. This must not blind us, however, to the fact that the artist, like Philo, presumed that the Old Testament text is to be understood not only through its Greek translation, but through its reevaluation in terms of Greek philosophy and religion. Again, unlike Philo in detail but like him in spirit, the artists have interpreted biblical tradition by using Iranian costumes and such scenes as the duel between the white and black horsemen... The Jews here, while utterly devoted to their traditions and Torah, had to express what this meant to them in a building designed to copy the inner shrine of a pagan temple, filled with images of human beings and Greek and Iranian divinities, and carefully designed to interpret the Torah in a way profoundly mystical.

VIII

JUDAISM IN PARTHIAN BABYLONIA

I have mostly refrained from offering an opinion on either the technical or the interpretive issues at hand. I am not qualified to do so. However, having given considerable attention to the Jews in Parthian Babylonia, I am qualified to describe what we know -- which is very little -- of their religious life and to suggest, in the light of this, why I believe that this evidence lends greater support to the approach of Goodenough that to that of Kraeling.

Both Goodenough and Kraeling accept the conventional view of Babylonian Judaism. It is normally portrayed as a wholly isolated legalistic and law-abiding religion, deeply engaged by its own interests and traditional concerns, and wholly divorced from the surrounding culture. Goodenough describes Babylonian Jewry as an island, a cultural ghetto (IX, 8-10), where the Jews occupied themselves in the study of the law in its most halakhic sense, while the Dura community, "engulfed" by the pagan world, was far more deeply influenced by pagan culture. Kraeling, likewise, views Babylonian Jewry as living in towns predominantly Jewish (p. 325) and generally loyal to the halakhah as it was later recorded.

The conventional view is based on a conflation of all information, early or late, into a static and one-dimensional portrait. What we know about the Jews in Babylonia before

226 does not support this view. It contradicts it. The evidence is, to the contrary, that the Jews in Babylonia lived in relatively close contact, both physical and cultural, with their neighbors. Their main center, Nehardea, was not far from the great Hellenistic city, Seleucia on the Tigris; and in any case, Greeks, Babylonians, Pagan Semites, Jews, and Parthians all inhabited the narrow strip of fertile land around the Royal Canal which later historians so generously assigned to the Jews alone. We know, for example, that in the first century, when the Jewish barony of Anileus and Asineus was established, the local Greeks and Babylonians opposed it and eventually succeeded in gaining Parthian support to destroy it, but that, for a time, the two brothers ruled <u>both</u> Jewish <u>and</u> Hellenistic and Babylonian populations, all in a relatively small area around, but apparently not including, Nehardea itself. And there were Greeks in Nehardea. It should be emphasized, therefore, that the Jews were only one minority in the region, and, so far as one may guess, they were not the most numerous. Furthermore, the Greek city of Seleucia contained a Hellenized Jewish population.

Not only were Babylonian Jews in the Parthian period <u>not</u> physically isolated from others in the region, but there is evidence that some Jews significantly participated in Parthian political and economic life. For example, in the first century B.C., Zamaris, a Jew from Babylonia who had mastered the Parthian shot, fled to the west and settled in Palestine. According to Josephus' account, Zamaris was a feudal lord in Parthia and fled on account of an unhappy turn in local politics. He was, moreover, not the only Jew to master Parthian military tactics. A century and a half later, we have some evidence that Jews took Parthian names, one, Arta/Arda, being a good Parthian translation of the Hebrew Zadoq, the other Pylybarys, meaning possibly "elephant rider"; they wore Parthian noble garb; and exerted influence with the government and were probably, therefore, also familiar with the language of the court. Moreover, we know that at least one Tanna from Babylonia, R. Hiyya, visited the Parthian court; and that a Parthian governmental title, PHTY, meaning satrap, was applied by him, at the very least as a term of endearment (though I think more) to his nephew Rav. We may, moreover, be fairly certain that good "normative" Jews, in particular Hiyya, participated in the international silk trade, which was closely supervised by the Parthian government and hence must have had commercial dealings with that government. We know that a Jewish civil authority, the exilarch, was recognized by the Parthian government and exerted <u>de jure</u> authority over Jews in the second century, if not before; and we know that he was given, as an insignia of office, the right to wear the <u>kamara</u>, a belt which signified governmental recognition. Thus the evidence, very briefly summarized here, points to extensive Jewish participation in Parthian affairs. Participation in political, commercial, and possibly military affairs could not have been carried on by people "wholly isolated" from the culture of the government. One should expect to find among them substantial marks of knowledge of surrounding culture. Not the least of the contacts of the Jewish masses with that culture would have been through the coinage, which certainly yielded some information on the pagan religion of the Iranian Empire, and on the local Semitic and Hellenistic cults as well. It is too much to conclude that political, commercial, and military contacts had led to the utter assimilation of Babylonian Jewry into Parthian culture; and I do not for one instant believe that Babylonian Jewry in the mass had done so. But one ought not to be surprised to find traces of Parthian (and hence Parthian-Hellenistic) influence on Babylonian Jewry. I should expect to see similar influences in Dura, a town held by Parthia until circa 160 A.D. and should be astonished to find no knowledge of Iranian culture half a century later in such a place.

It is frequently asserted, moreover, that Babylonian Jewry was dominated at this period by Palestinian Judaism. This cannot be demonstrated. The evidence is this. Before the Bar Kokhba war, there were two or three Tannaim in all of Mesopotamia, one Judah b. Bathyra in Nisibis, another Hananiah, the nephew of R. Joshua in the south, in Nehardea. This same Hananiah, moreover, engaged in an action which, if successful, would have resulted in the freedom of Babylonian Jews from Palestinian domination of the sacred calendar, one of the chief means by which the Palestinian patriarch exerted influence in the diaspora. If "normative" Tannaitic Judaism was otherwise represented in the east, we have absolutely no record of it. (We shall see below evidences of something quite different.) At the time, and as a direct consequence of the Bar Kokhba war, some Palestinian Tannaim fled to Mesopotamia. The students of Aqiba settled in the north, in Nisibis, while those of Ishmael settled in Huzal, so far as I can tell a town near Nehardea, in the south. The former returned to Palestine, probably by 145 A.D., but the latter remained in Babylonia and trained students such as R. Ahai, Issi b. Judah, Hiyya and Rav, who later achieved distinction in the Palestinian academies. Thus only in 135 at the very earliest do we have a well-established Tannaitic academy across the Euphrates; and before that time there was, so far as we can tell, no means by which Pharisaic-Tannaitic traditions might be transmitted in the east in a systematic, orderly, continuing way. I have contended that the basis of certain sections of the Mekhilta was laid in Huzal between 135 and 150; but this is the only record we have, if that, indeed, is accepted, of production of Tannaitic literature in Babylonia. I fail utterly, therefore, to see how Babylonian or Mesopotamian Judaism was under Palestinian religious and cultural hegemony. So far as we know, Babylonian Jewry was not dominated by Pharisaic Judaism.

In fact, we have some reason to believe that Babylonian Jewry had an indigenous tradition of its own. We know very little about pre-Amoraic Babylonian Judaism. But what we know points to a kind of Judaism deeply affected by Ezekiel and probably also engaged (at least in the sophisticated centers) by the merkavah tradition. These points cannot be overemphasized. The bottom register of the north wall of the Dura synagogue was covered by an Ezekiel cycle. Goodenough has argued, moreover, that elements of merkavah mysticism may be discerned in the reredos and elsewhere (see X, 70-71, 87, 178 [on the Ezekiel cycle]). It seems to me entirely natural that Ezekiel, and the kind of mysticism based upon his prophecies, should have been well represented through Babylonia, where he allegedly prophesied, and where his traditions were, in any case, probably cultivated from the earliest times as those of a local and indigenous prophet. The evidence that Ezekiel studies, including the merkavah aspect of them, were important in the Babylonian academies is, like every other kind of evidence on Babylonian Judaism in

Parthian times, very slender. Yet the fact is that most of what we know about the kinds of midrash agadah pursued in these academies concerns the book of Ezekiel, merkavah mysticism, or verses from other books which were related to merkavah mysticism. We do not, as I said, know very much; but all that we do know relates to this single prophet, except for the evidences in Mekhilta, and the sayings of men such as Nathan and the Ishmaelites, who were trained in Palestine as well as in Babylonia. For example, we have one teaching of Hammuna the Scribe of Babylonia. A student of his, Hanina b. Hama, corrected the reading of Judah, the prince, of Ezekiel 7:16, and that particular verse had eschatological significance in the midrashic tradition. By itself this proves nothing. But we also know that when Levi b. Sisi preached in Babylonia, he preached on Ezekiel. When Hiyya, a Babylonian, was in Palestine, he pursued esoteric lore based on Ezekiel I, the merkavah vision. A saying of Levi relates, also, to the Shiur Qoma tradition (to which Goodenough makes reference, if only tentatively). Furthermore, Scholem[3] cites a saying of the above-mentioned Hananiah, the nephew of R. Joshua, which indicates familiarity with Jewish mystical tradition. Finally, it is well known that the first-century Tanna, Hillel, a Babylonian, transmitted a mystical tradition in his academy. (His disciple, R. Yohanan ben Zakkai, was a leading exponent of the merkavah tradition in the decades before and after the destruction of Jerusalem.) When Rav came to Babylonia at the beginning of the third century, he brought further elements of Jewish mystical tradition. When the father of Samuel and Levi experienced the Shekhinah in the synagogue in Nehardea, that experience was described in terms used by Ezekiel. This much is therefore beyond question: In the light of the findings of Scholem and others, on the existence of a mystical tradition as evidenced by Hillel the Babylonian, and in the early second century by Hananiah, the nephew of R. Joshua (and possible Yosé of Huzal, but this involves variant readings in the Mishnah), and in the light of the later second- and early third-century evidence alluded to above, there can be no doubt that the curriculum of Babylonian Jewish academies at the beginning of the third century included some kind of mystical tradition, and that speculation, specifically, on Ezekiel's vision was carried on.

With this in mind, I find it very difficult to question the importance ascribed by Goodenough to mysticism in Dura. I do not argue that his interpretations are, in detail, correct, for I am not competent to make a judgment on that question. But I do think that the importance of Ezekiel in Dura, and the details, if correctly discerned, of various kinds of traditional mystical speculation, which Goodenough finds on the walls of Dura synagogue, are both wholly congruent to what we know of Babylonian Judaism before circa 220 A.D. One should not be surprised to find some kind of syncretistic, mystical tradition in Jewish Dura. Considering the situation of the Jews there, and considering what we know of the religious culture of the Jews in Babylonia, who probably exerted some influence there, and who may have, in the beginning, provided the first Jewish settlers in Dura, one should have expected to find something approximating the Judaism discerned by Goodenough, specifically a kind of Judaism in which Ezekiel plays a very important role and in which the mystical speculations associated in part with his writings are represented, just as they were in the academies to the south.

Goodenough and Namenyi (IX, 9) hold that "Dura would have represented Babylonian Judaism before the halakhic reform." I cannot doubt that Dura largely as interpreted by Goodenough would be at least a fair approximation of Babylonian Judaism before the great expansion of Pharisaic-Tannaitic-Amoraic Judaism in the period after Rav's coming. What, exactly, happened after Rav's coming I cannot say. But since Rav was a mystic, I am fairly certain that it did not involve the suppression of earlier mystical traditions but, more likely, their refinement and cultivation. Rav brought with him from Palestine (assuming that his mystical sayings were not acquired before his migration to Judah's court) a considerable body of mysticism.

Even if Rav had wanted to suppress mysticism, moreover, whether he could have done so in Dura-Europos before the time of the paintings in the middle of the fifth decade may be questioned. He allegedly came circa 226. When he came, he found observance of the law abysmal and founded an academy to stand alongside of Samuel's as an exemplar of how the law should be observed, and to send forth teachers of the law to effect a reform throughout Babylonian and (one assumes) Mesopotamian Jewry. It is difficult to believe that in two decades his influence would have reached Dura, or that if it had, it would have worked to destroy mysticism there! It is difficult, therefore, to follow Kraeling in believing that a wholly ethically centered, and wholly "biblically and historically" centered Judaism prevailed in Dura.

One must, in any event, wonder how much influence the "anti-mystical Pharisaic-Tannaitic-Amoraic" attitude actually had in Dura. So far as we know, that community would have been influenced by it, if at all, only through the sermons of itinerant apostles of the patriarchate. Yet, as we noted above, one of the few sermons we know about was Levi ben Sisi's, and this concerned mysticism. If the Palestinian "antimystical tradition" was to influence Dura Judaism, that influence could only have been exerted after circa 160 A.D., when the city fell into Roman hands. Before that time, Dura was under Parthian rule. The Parthians did not allow Roman government officials, such as the Palestinian patriarch, to govern their minority groups. They were, on the contrary, careful to establish their own minority representatives where needed, as in the case of the exilarchate. One is reduced, therefore, to the necessity of arguing that between 160 and 240, the antecedent Judaism of Mesopotamia was obliterated at Dura and that in its place a one-dimensional, opaque religion was substituted. I should not be convinced by such an argument, because it explains none of the facts at hand.

How then may we understand the great redecoration of the Dura synagogue, which took place circa A.D. 245? In my opinion, one must see it in the context of the state of religions generally in early Sasanian Iran. The redecoration of the synagogue represents, according to both Kraeling and Goodenough, an act of tremendous religious creativity as the response of an extraordinary mind to the Jewish tradition, whether (Kraeling) to the rabbinic tradition alone or (Goodenough) to the tradition as modulated by current ideas and attitudes. No era in the history of religions was more diverse or creative than the early middle third century, and no place ever exhibited greater variety or vitality than Mesopotamia. When we consider the maelstrom of religious activity in this brief period, we may see extraordinary signs of creativity and vitality. In the small region, a parallelogram of no more than 200 miles in length and 50 in breadth, we find the following: first, and most important, the resurgence of a conquering, proselytizing Mazdeism, propagated by the state under Ardashir, and established (if in a tolerant manner) as the state religion under Shahpuhr with its exponent, Kartir; second, the development of an Iranian gnostic syncretism by the prophet Mani, who, at the time of the redecoration of the Dura synagogue, proclaimed a new religion and in the next decades attracted a wide following in Iran and in the Roman Empire as well; third, the advance of Christianity (Mani's father was probably a Christian, and Jesus played a part in his theology) into the Mesopotamian valley from Edessa, where, by 201, it had become well established; fourth, the great expansion of cults within the Iranian idiom, in particular Mithraism, in both Iran and the Roman Empire, to the point where Mithraism was perhaps the single most popular religion on the Roman side of the frontier; fifth, and by no means least, the beginnings of a revolution in Babylonian Judaism, which transformed the earlier indigenous religion into a fair representation of the ideas of the Palestinian Tannaim (this much we may say, but obviously no more), and which must have created a tremendous upheaval in Babylonian Jewry. These events, each of them of lasting importance in the religious life of Mesopotamia, took place within a brief period; one may say that from circa 220 to circa 250, in Babylonia, Manichaeism, Rabbinic Judaism and Mazdeism were all taking form. To such events, Dura's Jewish philosopher might well have responded, as Goodenough says he did, by a series of symbolic comments on the religions of the day and on Judaism's superiority to all of them.

NOTES

[1] "The Image of God: Notes on the Hellenization of Judaism, with Especial Reference to Goodenough's Work on Jewish Symbols," Bulletin of the John Rylands Library, XL, No. 2 (1958), pp. 473-512.

[2]F. Taeger, Charisma (Stuttgart, 1953), I, 304.

[3]See G. Scholem, Jewish Gnosticism, Mevkahah Mysticism, and Talmudic Tradition (N.Y., 1960), p. 56.

Part Five

THE PHARISEES, JESUS, PAUL
CHRISTIANITY AND JUDAISM LATER ON

17. Ellis Rivkin

A HIDDEN REVOLUTION

American Historical Review 1980. 85:863-864

A HIDDEN REVOLUTION. By Ellis Rivkin. Nashville: Abington. 1978. Pp. 336.

This deeply personal and religious statement of the definition and meaning of the Pharisees, a sect in ancient Judaism, emerges from nearly four decades of reflection, including two of active research. The Pharisees are presented as "a class of audacious revolutionaries." Their principal doctrine concerned a two-fold revelation of God to Moses at Mount Sinai, part in writing, part orally formulated and transmitted, and, later on, taught by the Pharisees themselves.

This thesis is worked out through a study of the three principal sources that refer to the Pharisees: passages of the Gospels, allusions in the historical writings on Josephus, and sayings, tales, and fables in the latter rabbinic literature about sages who lived before the destruction of the Temple of Jerusalem in A.D. 70. Rivkin analyzes the information in these several sources and then undertakes a historical reconstruction. The third part of the work is his synthesis of the results of the thoroughgoing analysis of the sources. The Pharisees were "a scholar class, championing the twofold Law (Torah) and enjoying great power and prestige" -- that is the sum and substance of the matter. From this definition, Rivkin proceeds to ask when the Pharisees came into existence. It was in 280 or 180 B.C., and the book of Ben Sira, which represents a "pre-Pharisaic and pre-twofold Law society" indicates the date must be the later of the two. The chief result of this Pharisaic revolution was to incorporate within Judaism "major structural components and major conceptual notions prevalent in the Greco-Roman world." The book is written vividly, but with control and taste. It is a model of first-class historical argumentation and exposition. The author's personal conviction of the authority for his own religious life of the facts he relates in no way intervenes in his lucid mode of thought. What is advocated is a historical position, and, only secondarily, a pious evaluation of that position. But the outcome is merely religious.

The principal difficulty is that the allegations of all the sources constitute the starting point for argument and analysis. The literary problems to be solved before the sources are to be believed as fact simply are not taken up. The fact, for example, that the Mishnah and the later rabbinic writings come four or more centuries after the events of which they speak and the men to whom they attribute sayings, does not stop Rivkin from using them any way he wants. True, Rivkin recognizes that the Mishnah comes long after the Pharisaic "revolution" has run its course. But the character of the Mishnah's evidence for that "revolution" nonetheless is taken to be definitive. Josephus is cited as a totally accurate reporter of events. The same is so for the other sources assembled to form the book's thesis. It would not be fair to call the work wholly gullible and credulous, let alone fundamentalist. Rivkin takes a position quite independent of his sources. But the position is built out of essentially unanalyzed and uncriticized sources. The problems of using those sources for historical reconstruction are not systematically and rigorously confronted. So for Rivkin, the sources present facts, and the facts define the problem. In my view, the sources themselves constitute the first and prncipal problem. Still, this fundamental difference of opinion on method in no way prevents recognizing Rivkin's imaginative and often profound contribution to the interpretation of Pharisaism as a religious movement, even though that interpretation deals with what, in historical fact, never existed: as with Elisha, no bears, no forest.

18. John Bowker
JESUS AND THE PHARISEES
Journal of Jewish Studies 1974, 25:454-456

JESUS AND THE PHARISEES. By John Bowker. Cambridge: Cambridge University Press, 1973. 192 pp.

This curious book does not contain a single idea that one may confidently assign as original to its author. Neither does it offer a careful account of the state of scholarship about its subject. And, while it proposes to provide a repertoire of sources pertinent to the topic, the compiler of the sources tells us so little about them that we can hardly be sure why he thinks they are important, or what we are to learn from them. The book is filled with portentous generalizations, some of them bordering on the meaningless, e.g. "But the critical point is that the substance, or purpose, of the narrative may well persist unchanged, even though the circumstantial details, or the names, are insecure. This does not mean that the substance of a narrative can automatically be assumed to go back to the original moment; it does mean that once a narrative emerged to exemplify a particular point, or points, it is likely to have persisted for as long as those points needed exemplifying in that particular way -- which may, in fact, be down to the present day." What all these words add up to, the reader must figure out for himself.

Let me now describe what Mr. Bowker has actually done. He begins with an introduction of 52 pages, followed by 24 pages of sources on "controversies against Sadducees and/or Boethusians" (filled with long citations from biblical and rabbinic literature), and 103 pages of translations (the bulk of them not his own). In other words, somewhat less than a third of the book is contributed by the author. The translation of Josephus comes from Loeb, that of Mishnah from Danby, the Babylonian Talmud from Soncino, which leaves Tosefta and a sparing selection of Yerushalmi. To compile his additional note on the Sadducees, he quotes biblical passages easily accessible in anyone's library, then summarizes Finkelstein's equally available opinions.

Josephus's accounts of the Pharisees follow. Bowker gives the later references (those contained in Antiquities) before the earlier ones (found in War), thus obscuring the development from War to Antiquities in Josephus's picture of the Pharisees. The author does not appear to be acquainted with Morton Smith's "Palestinian Judaism in the First Century" in Israel, Its Role in Civilization, ed. Moshe Davis (N.Y., 1956), pp. 67-81, where the relationship between the quite distinctive pictures of the Pharisees given first in War and then in Antiquities is explained. Another bibliographical curiosity is the absence in a book on "Jesus and the Pharisees" of any mention of recent books bearing almost the same title, e.g. Wolfgang Beilner, Christus und die Pharisäer (Vienna, 1959) or Asher Finkel, The Pharisees and the Teacher of Nazareth (Leiden, 1964).

The repertoire of sources from the Mishnah and other rabbinic writings is not accompanied by a single critical or explanatory comment other than cross-references to further unexplained passages. The reader will frequently wonder why some of the texts have been included in this volume, e.g. mPes. 4:4, "Where the custom is to eat flesh roast on the nights of Passover, they eat it so; where it is not... they may not do so..." What in the world, we may ask, has this to do with either Jesus or the Pharisees? Lest it may be thought that this is an exception, I will point to the inclusion of mKet. 13:1, mSot. 3:4, mSanh. 7:2, etc., within a span of three pages, none of which contains a reference to Pharisees or hakhamim or even claims to speak about matters of the period prior to 70.

In the first fifty pages, Bowker struggles manfully with the identity of the Pharisees, their origins and divisions. Then follow "Jesus and the Pharisaioi" (sic!), and the offence and trial of Jesus. I leave to N.T. scholars the task of evaluating Bowker's views on the last two subjects. As to the first three, he reproduces the suggestive ideas of Ellis Rivkin, particularly from "Defining the Pharisees", HUCA 40, 1969, pp. 205-49. Bowker's main contention is that Pharisaioi in Greek sources and Perushim in "Semitic" ones do not seem wholly to correlate with one another. Solomon Zeitlin's excellent remark that Perushim are to be distinguished from hakhamim is repeated. Various passages are cited, all demonstrating that Bowker has difficulty with the simplest kind of source analysis of historical and literary criticism. He is unwilling to concede either the historical usefulness or the historical uselessness of the evidence he offers, and, in the absence of a method capable of producing reasonable hypotheses, he generally prefers -- irrespective of the number of words used -- to say as little as possible. For example, his Hakamic movement sought to insure "that the definitions of Torah should be both intelligible and applicable." This required attention to the application of Scripture to new situations: "The circumstances were often those which actually occurred, but, equally, attention was given to circumstances which might occur -- hence the juxtaposition of both actual and theoretical considerations in rabbinic works. Eventually, highly detailed methods of exegesis were developed, but these only gradually emerged." In writing this, Bowker manages to fill up about a third of a page, without actually stating anything. Having quoted, on p. 18, n. 1., Leo Baeck's meaningless assertion: "The Pharisees were not a party... or yet a school or sect... but a movement within the Jewish people," three pages later Bowker advances it in his own name: "The movement was not intended to be a party within Israel. It was intended to be Israel itself." Now, however, a note refers to Allon's Researches, which points out that the Pharisees were concerned with "the proper ordering of the whole of society." Predictably, the author does not tell us how a "movement" differs from a "party," "school," or "sect," or why these differences might be important.

Bowker claims that his book is intended "to be introductory" and a few lines later apologizes for giving us merely "the structure of a possible argument, rather than the full argument itself... But that kind of elaboration would probably prove confusing to those who are not already familiar with the field." "Even if these suggestions [made in the Introduction] seem unconvincing, the Introduction may nevertheless still help to make clear what the problems are." His purpose is to persuade N.T. scholars that they should

not "talk (as some undoubtedly have) of the Pharisees as though they were an undifferentiated group without a history of their own." Having first promised an elementary
textbook, he then tells us that we must know "the history of the period in question, even if
only in narrative or outline form. It also presupposes my earlier book, The Targums and
Rabbinic Literature." I am not sure what he will have thought his readers were then to
do. An author who is unable to provide critical guidance to his assembled sources; who
does not given a responsible account of the historical problems pertaining to those
sources; who fails to survey in full former scholarly efforts on the subject; who cannot
even produce a reliable bibliography, is unlikely to supply a clear picture of the problems,
the minimum we may expect from an "introduction."

19. GEZA VERMES
JESUS THE JEW. A HISTORIAN'S READING OF THE GOSPELS
and
GEZA VERMES and FERGUS MILLAR
THE HISTORY OF THE JEWISH PEOPLE IN THE AGE OF JESUS CHRIST
Midstream 1974, 20:70-73

JESUS THE JEW. A HISTORIAN'S READING OF THE GOSPELS. By Geza Vermes. London: Collins, 1973. 286 pp.

THE HISTORY OF THE JEWISH PEOPLE IN THE AGE OF JESUS CHRIST (175 B.C.-A.D. 135). By Emil Schürer. A New English Version Revised and Edited by Geza Vermes and Fergus Millar. Literary Editor: Pamela Vermes. Volume I. Edinburgh: T. & T. Clark, 1973. 613 pp.

These two magnificent volumes bring into focus the central issues of the historical study of the beginnings of Christianity and rabbinic Judaism in the centuries before and after the beginning of the Common Era. Geza Vermes, Reader of Jewish Studies at the University of Oxford, has devoted himself for more than a quarter-century to the study of Midrashic and Targumic literature, the Dead Sea scrolls, and the other literary sources for the study of Jewish history and of Judaism in late antiquity. In his Jesus the Jew and in the corresponding revision and up-dating of Schürer's standard work, he, along with his associates in the latter project, has taken the position that considerable historical information is to be derived from those sources.

The central issue, clearly, is going to be those two intractable and complex corpera of sources, the Synoptic Gospels, on the one side, and the earlier rabbinic compilations, the Mishnah-Tosefta in particular, on the other. In general, much New Testament scholarship takes a severely skeptical position on both bodies of evidence. To his credit, Vermes (Jesus, p. 235, n. 1) faces that skepticism head-on: "My guarded optimism concerning a possible recovery of the genuine features of Jesus is in sharp contrast with Rudolf Bultmann's historical agnosticism: 'I do indeed think,' he [Bultmann] writes, 'that we can now know almost nothing concerning the life and personality of Jesus, since the early Christian sources show no interest in either, are moreover fragmentary and often legendary....' The real question is this: how much history can be extracted from sources which are not primarily historical?"

In answer to this question -- which is the right one -- Vermes maintains we can gain a clear picture of Jesus. He is understood as utterly unrelated to the messianic claims associated with him by his followers. Vermes describes the Messianic claim as "the strange creation of the modern myth-makers." Jesus rather is understood as part of "the

- 189 -

venerable company of the Devout, the ancient Hasidim." In particular, he is to be compared to Hanina ben Dosa and Honi HaMe'aggel (the Circler). Vermes admits that not a great deal can be historically authenticated. But "the positive and constant testimony of the earliest Gospel tradition, considered against its natural background of first-century Galilean charismatic religion, leads not to a Jesus as unrecognizable within the framework of Judaism as by the standard of his own verifiable words and intentions, but to another figure: Jesus the just man, the zaddik, Jesus the helper and healer, Jesus the teacher and leader...." These results are argued in two pellucid sections, first, the setting, which treats Jesus the Jew, Jesus and Galilee, and Jesus and Charismatic Judaism (certainly the most important chapter), and second, the titles of Jesus: prophet, lord, Messiah, son of man, son of God.

Vermes's claim is carefully phrased. He does not suppose that the stories about and sayings attributed to Jesus are in every detail exact records of what really was done and said on a specific occasion. He stresses that we stand at one remove; we do not know so much as the Gospels claim to tell us. On the other hand, we do have a fairly firm tradition. I may add that that tradition was worked out in an astonishingly brief period. Within less than half a century after the death of Jesus, the Gospels had come to their present state. Granted that what we have are the stories and sayings the early Church chose to preserve out of a great mass of material, and granted that much of the material is disharmonious, nonetheless, the corpus as a whole is, for its setting, a first-rate body of historical evidence. What it tells us, further, is more than the state of the early Church's convictions. The stories and sayings -- many of them remarkably firm, despite their several versions, as to their primary assertions about Jesus's teachings -- derive from many sources, not from one small circle, and were subject to the correction and criticism of various parties, not all of them remote from the events depicted in the traditions, and many of them in first-hand relationship with the earliest followers.

Now if we ask, Did Jesus really say and do these things? we should have to answer, with Bultmann, that we cannot be certain. But if we ask the correct question, which is, what is the relative status as historical evidence of these materials, the answer is quite different. By every criterion established in the study of the world of late antiquity, the materials are excellent. But, I stress, what they are good for is this: the establishment not of a detailed biographical narrative, but of a reasonably reliable historical account of traditions about an unrecoverable life. That is, we know a good bit about Jesus as he is portrayed by others, thus as a cultural and historical figure, even though, as I stressed, we know less than the Gospels suggest about the details of his actual life and death (let alone what happened then). To put it differently, while biography is not possible, a historical inquiry about the growth of tradition is entirely feasible.

That is why Vermes is on strong ground indeed in asking not, what did Jesus really say or do, but rather, in what aspect of the religious and social setting of his day would a man alleged to have said and done these things have found a congenial place? The comparison of the figure of Jesus represented fairly consistently in the Gospels to have done wonders and signs (magic in the eye of the outsider) with Honi or Hanina, men of grace, seems to me apt and accurate. The claim, at the end, that the titles later assigned to Jesus in general were remote from his conception of himself, as evidenced in the more reliable sayings, is well founded. The argument is a sound one, carefully worked out, with full and requisite attention to the varieties of Judaism, the strata of the rabbinic literature, the entire range of critical problems important in contemporary New Testament and rabbinic scholarship.

Any historian would be satisfied, given the state of the evidence and of the art of interpreting it, with these results. But the New Testament scholars have a second, entirely unhistorical agendum, and that is a search, with a historical map, for theological truths not to begin with included in the cartography of historical studies. For them, merely interpreting the evidence along the lines followed by Vermes is unsatisfying. Their aspiration is to recover what really happened, because, if they can persuade themselves of the detailed veracity of at least some elements of the Gospels' account, then they will have solved through critical history the insoluble problems of faith. Standing on the fringes of the Christian community, the theologian of historicistic persuasion does not enjoy the theological certainty of the believers and has lost touch with the "Christ of faith." On that account, either he will find a verifiable saying -- to which, "merely as a historian," he may then pay obeisance -- or he will pass out of the circle of the faith entirely. That accounts, I think, for the remarkable intensity of the question, Did he really say it? As if about anyone in this period an answer to such a question is possible! I think Bultmann is entirely right in holding that we shall never know what the sources, to begin with, do not contain. These are not letters written by Jesus himself, nor are they stories composed by witnesses to the events for the purposes of a newspaper account or achival record. But I think Vermes is correct in maintaining that historical studies are nonetheless feasible: "How much history can be extracted...?"

It remains to query the exact meaning of the phrase in which the religious signi- ficance of Jesus is assessed, "Second to none in profundity of insight and grandeur of character, he is in particular an unsurpassed master of the art of laying bare the inmost core of spiritual truth and of bringing every issue back to the essence of religion, the existential relationship of man and man, and man and God." In its context, the author contrasts Jesus with charismatic leaders of his age, for instance, Hanina ben Dosa or Honi HaMe'aggel. But if an absolute evaluation of Jesus is intended within the framework of Jewish spirituality at large, then, in the absence of comparative evidence, it cannot command the same degree of intellectual assent as the rest of the work.

But, for the moment, let us pretend to be faced with the task of comparison -- Vermes's work aside -- and ask, viewed as a single man, without regard to the religious movement inspired by him, how does Jesus compare to any other rabbi of the day (assuming there were other rabbis before 70)? If sayings attributed to Hillel were really said by him, then I think profundity of insight and access to spiritual truth characterize the man who, after all, is alleged to have taught pretty much the same ethical and moral message as Jesus. If, of greater weight, we take the collective spiritual achievements of the early rabbis, the masters of Yavneh and Usha, then I think the contrast between their massive work and the paltry sayings attributed to Jesus is striking. The rabbis took as their task the creation of law and theology to define in everyday terms not "the essence of religion" but the requirement of the hour, not the "existential relationship" in the abstract, but the ordinary, workaday relationships experienced by real people. The contrast between that work and the few, to be sure worthy and noble, sayings assigned with some confidence to Jesus, in my judgment favors the achievements of the rabbis, or any one of them. The richness of their ethical and moral insight, the profundity of their conception of man and society, the genius of their articulation of that conception for the benefit of ordinary folk -- these mark the rabbis as men of insight and character, but also of social responsibility and moral dignity, of surpassing sublimity.

Let us now turn to the second book, the problems of which are quite different from those of research into the Gospels and related sources.

Schürer's Geschichte des jüdischen Volkes is nearly a century old, having begun as Lehrbuch der neutestamentlichen Zeitgeschichte in 1874, and reached its definitive version in 1901-1909. The reason for its enduring value was the author's comprehensive account of the state of learning, his thorough mastery of all primary sources and important bibliography, his taste, judgment, and impressive intelligence, and his effort at a critical and objective presentation, rather than at justifying a personal synthesis.

Alas, Schürer has been out of date for many years, for the advance of learning, because of both major archaeological discoveries and of significant scholarly advances, has made his work obsolete. Yet no work of historical synthesis ever took the place of Schürer. What has long been required was either a new synthesis or a revision of the old. Vermes and Millar took upon themselves the exacting task of bringing Schürer up to date, so preserving all that was good in the old, while adding what is of enduring importance in the new. It is a work not solely of scholarship and amazing erudition, but also of cultural responsibility and supreme commitment to learning.

The result must be pronounced simply the most important work on the history of the Jewish people from the Maccabees to Bar Kokhba published in the 20th century. We now are given, in one handsome volume [to be complete in three], judicious and careful accounts of everything known about the times, together with comprehensive biblio-graphies, thoughtful judgments -- an utterly comprehensive and complete picture of the formative period in the history of Judaism and Christianity.

The literary quality, for one thing, is an immeasurable improvement. The 1890 translation begins, "In the fulness of time the Christian religion sprang out of Judaism; as a fact, indeed, of divine revelation, but also inseparably joined by innumerable threads with the previous thousand years of Israel's history." Mrs. Pamela Vermes now gives us, "Since it was from Judaism that Christianity emerged in the first century A.D., nothing in the Gospel account is understandable apart from its setting in Jewish history, no work of Jesus meaningful unless inserted into its natural context of contemporary Jewish thought." This sort of literary elegance characterizes the whole work, which makes the new Schürer a contribution to the literature of history, written with elegance and spirit, for which British historians are everywhere admired.

The scope and purpose of the work are vastly increased. It goes without saying that the Dead Sea discoveries are introduced, but not alone. The section on the Targumim, to take one example, includes the best bibliography on that subject known to me. The account of the sources brings up to date the information on each and every subject, even though the study of many of the sources has developed into a field of scholarly specialization by itself. Yet, modestly, Vermes and Millar take pains to submerge their contribution into the text, simply introducing their changes, unmarked, into the text and notes. They delete out of date items of bibliography and polemics (Schürer's notorious anti-Semitic remarks, for example), revise and bring up to date not only the bibliographies, but also the references to literary texts, papyri, inscriptions, and coins.

The editors tell us the work remains Schürer's -- yet it is they who have given Schürer a well-deserved second century of life. And a sign of the meaning of this new century, and of the spirit of the editors, is not to be missed. The old Schürer (I, ii, p. 320-1) ends with a description by Jerome of how the Jews on the 9th of Av would "gather in mournful companies, to utter forth their grievous complaints," concluding with the words, "Ululant super cineres sanctuarii et super altare destructum et super civitates quondam munitas et super excelsos angulos templi, de quibus quondam Jacobum fratrem Domini praecipitaverunt." [They wail over the ashes of the sanctuary, and over the destroyed altar, and over the city which once was fortified, and over the high walls of the temple, from which they had once pushed down James, the brother of the Lord.] The new Schürer then adds, as _its_ concluding word: "Yet the tears of mourning concealed hope, and hope refused to die."

20. E.P. SANDERS
PAUL, THE LAW, AND THE JEWISH PEOPLE

PAUL, THE LAW, AND THE JEWISH PEOPLE. By E.P. Sanders. Philadelphia: Fortress Press, 1983.

Sanders presents himself as an expert on Palestinian Judaism. In the work at hand, on the basis of that knowledge he provides a wide-ranging interpretation of passages in the Pauline corpus dealing with "the law," (sometimes nomos, sometimes Scripture), and Israel. In my review of Sanders' Paul and Palestinian Judaism: A Comparison of Patterns of Religion (Philadelphia, 1977: Fortress Press), published in History of Religions 1978 18:177-191 and reprinted in W. S. Green, ed., Approaches to Ancient Judaism (Chico, 1980: Scholars Press for Brown Judaic Studies) 2:43-64, I raised a set of questions about Sanders' results and method. These questions, left unanswered, render the new work a mere curiosity. My questions were of two kinds, first, conceptual, second, epistemological. The former set, on which, mistakenly, I laid emphasis, raised the issue of the asymmetry of Sanders' categories of description -- sin, atonement, and "covenantal nomism," for instance -- to the documents of the form of Judaism under study, for which the stated categories play no substantial role at all. The latter, expressed very briefly (since it seemed to me self-evident), asked how Sanders knows so much about "Judaism," so that all of the sayings and stories he cites actually do testify to the state of opinion in the period in which Paul lived.

In my review I said this very simply: "Nor should we ignore the importance... of establishing the historical context in which the saying was said... If we do not know where and when a saying was said, how are we to interpret the saying and explain its meaning?" (Green, op. cit., p. 58). Reviewing the same book, A. J. Saldarini (Journal of Biblical Literature 1979, 98:299-303) raised a similar range of questions.

The work at hand chooses to ignore these questions. The names of Neusner and Saldarini do not appear even in the bibliography. Yet Sanders everywhere builds his book upon the results of his Paul and Palestinian Judaism, as though those results had sustained the vigorous criticism of his colleagues. I find it puzzling that Sanders has chosen in his new book simply not to answer critics of the old. Ignoring important issues they raised suggests he has no answer. Pretending that criticism simply does not exist, however, serves no good purpose. The result is a work more deeply flawed, if possible, than the one on which it is based.

To state the reason Sanders' original picture of "Judaism," repeated here, is worthless is very easy. He does not explain what (he thinks) we know about the first century and how (we think) we know it.

First, he simply takes for granted that whatever is said by any rabbi or other authority within the canon (the authoritative books) Sanders chooses as his "Judaism" testifies to the character of "Judaism" characteristic of most Jews in the first century.

Second, he takes for granted that if a saying is attributed to a rabbi or a story told about him, that saying or story tells us about things really said and done not only at the time of the rabbi in question, but also (mutatis mutandis) in the first century.

Finally, he ignores every difficulty in harmonizing the diverse rabbinic documents, which derive from more than half a millenium and two different countries, and treats all of them as homogeneous -- hence, "Judaism" -- in Paul's time.

In other words, Sanders ignores the critical program of biblical studies of more than two hundred years, as that program has addressed the problems of the documents of the rabbinic canon. I cannot blame him for ignoring me (among others), since, had he paid attention, he could not have written the book he wanted to write. He supposes the people for whom he writes -- Roman Catholic and Protestant theologians -- do not know the difference.

Let me now describe the book and explain, first, why the methodological failure renders useless everything it says about Judaism, and, second, why that matters and does make a difference.

This sequel to Paul and Palestinian Judaism: A Comparison of Patterns of Religion takes up two problems, the first at length, the second briefly. In part one Sanders deals with Paul and the Law. He treats the topics and theses that follow: the law is not an entrance requirement; the purpose of the law; the law should be fulfilled; the old dispensation and the new. At the conclusion, on Paul and the law, he treats the origin of Paul's thought about the law, Paul's critique of Judaism and of legalism in general, and law and Scripture.

In the second, briefer part, Sanders discusses Paul and the Jewish people, with attention to the problem of "Paul as apostle of Christ and member of Israel." The subjects here are "the third race;" Paul's missionary practice; conflicts with his own people; the salvation of Israel. Sanders concludes with a brief essay on "Paul and the break with Judaism."

This brief description of the contents conveys a false impression. The book looks to be a sustained essay on the topics I have listed. In fact it is a sequence of protracted exegetical footnotes, themselves heavily footnoted, with little effort invested in a clear and sustained argument in behalf of (or against) a well-presented proposition. The book is discursive without being encompassing, argumentative without being purposeful, protracted without producing rigorous analysis and argument. Sanders resorts to a rather pedestrian and verbose style; he cannot be said to take pride in elegant or even lucid presentation of his ideas. Without the first person singular pronoun, he would be speechless. In all, what we have is not a sequel, but merely an appendix, to his Paul and Palestinian Judaism, a long, rambling letter to some (but not all) of the critics of that work, now turned into a book.

While the definition of "Judaism," and analysis of problems dealing with Judaic sources play scarcely any role in Sanders' argument, as I shall show, the work rests upon the results of such a definition and the solution of those problems. Over and over again, Sanders appeals to "Judaism," which he repeatedly indicates he can define with little difficulty. Quite fairly, he assumes that in his earlier work he has done so. That is why, in the present one, he thinks he can concentrate on the exegesis of Pauline writings, secure in the knowledge of their Judaic context. Time and again, therefore, Sanders argues that "Paul was Jewish, therefore..." (e.g., p. 66, 96) or speaks of "the standard Jewish way" (p. 105). The content of Judaism and the substance of "the standard Jewish way" in Sanders' mind derive from the rabbinic literature, or the Hebrew Scriptures read through the prism of the rabbinic literature. The literature testifies everywhere and with equal force -- always to the condition of "Judaism" in the mid-first century, in which Paul lived, and everywhere Paul went. In this regard Sanders carries forward the traditions inaugurated first by (Strack-)Billerbeck, who treats Judaism in all its literary evidences as monolithic and homogeneous, and second by George Foot Moore, who describes "Judaism" within categories of Protestant dogmatic theology.

The result of the method at hand may be seen in a single example, which Sanders himself designates "an example:"

> One of the factors which makes Paul's statements about the law hard to
> unravel is the general difficulty of distinguishing between the reason for which
> he held a view and the arguments which he adduces in favor of it. To take an
> example: It is clear in 1 Corinthians 11 that Paul thinks that men should pray
> with heads uncovered and that women should pray with heads covered. In
> favor of this view he says that for a woman to pray with head uncovered is the
> same as if her head were shaved (1 Cor.: 11:5). He also says that she should
> pray with her head covered "because of the angels" (11:10). He then asserts
> that nature itself teaches that men should have short hair and women long hair
> (11:14f.; although how this supports his main point is not quite clear). Finally
> he says to those still unconvinced that "we recognize no other practice," nor
> do the other churches (11:16). In this particular case he may never state the
> real reason for his position: he was Jewish. Nevertheless, we see how he can
> mingle all sorts of arguments. This fact, as we shall see, helps to explain why
> scholars disagree about why he said what he said about the law: reason and
> argument are not always easy to distinguish.

The simple statement, "He was Jewish," leads to the one footnote (no. 6) on the Jewish origin of the practice at hand. It is to Sifré Num. 11 (on Num. 5:18). I should be surprised if many of Sanders' readers turn to the passage at hand. The verse states that the priest shall "unbind the hair of the woman's head..." I assume that, among the several sayings grouped in the paragraph at hand, Sanders alludes to this one: "This teaches that Israelite women cover their head, and even though there is no clear proof for that fact, there is at least some hint of it: 'And Tamar put ashes on her head' (2 Sam. 13:19)." In context, in fact, this head-covering is a sign of mourning and humiliation, as with the sotah (accused wife).

Now even a Talmudist proving that Jewish women usually covered their heads surely requires more than a single proof-text. If such were Sanders' serious interest, he might have looked for evidence in portraits of Jewish women, e.g., in mosaics, on synagogue murals, and the like. There are diverse sayings on the question, which indicate that a mark of unusual modesty and piety for a woman was to keep her head covered. To some that might suggest that ordinarily, women did not do so. There are lists of women's duties and obligations, many of which know nothing of the particular mark of modesty at hand. In all, Sanders' "real reason", namely, that "Paul was Jewish," is gross. And that, alas, is a minor instance of a major mode of argument.

So we see that Sanders' is the kind of argument built upon a homogenization of all sources deriving from all sorts of Judaisms, or all layers and groups within the rabbinic type of Judaism. All sources speak of one Judaism. That Judaism prevailed everywhere not only in the seventh but even in the first century. Every source may be asked to supply its quota of proof-texts for whatever Sanders requires. Since Sanders addresses New Testament scholars, who, he assumes, know even less about "Judaism" than does the author of Paul and Palestinian Judaism, he can play pretty fast and loose with the Judaic sources and ignore the criticism of those who know them. These critics, as I said, will not be heard by his real and intended audience.

Sanders takes for granted, also, that what Paul meant by being a Pharisee is self-evident. That is why he can declare "It would... be extraordinarily un-Pharisaic and even un-Jewish of Paul to insist that obedience of the law, once undertaken, must be perfect." But what sources of Pharisaism, in particular, deal with that question? Sanders does not tell us. If we ask whether, in some particular context, Pharisaic law does demand perfection, and how, in that context, it deals with lapses, we can find answers. One of the marks of Pharisaism was to concern oneself with the cultic purity of food one ate outside of the Temple. Pharisaic expectation in this regard was that, when they ate meals at home, ordinary folk would imitate the priests of the Temple as the latter ate their priestly rations. Now what would happen if a person deliberately contracted uncleanness and then ate food requiring observance of the rules of cultic purity? Such a person would certainly cease to be regarded as "reliable," within the framework of the law at hand. Now exactly what Sanders means when he says that it would be "unPharisaic" to exact perfect obedience to the law I do not know. But I do know that, in the typical context of cultic cleanness, the Pharisaic law most certainly did demand "perfection" in this detail. How so? Deliberate violation of the law indeed would produce important practical consequences within the Pharisaic framework (as much as within that of the Essenes at Qumran).

Sanders adduces in evidence of the prevailing opinion in "Judaism" stories that, he himself states, may or may not have been told in the first century and have represented broad circles of Jewish opinion at that time. So p. 55, n. 42: "Sanhedrin 101a. For the present purpose it does not matter whether or not the story is apocryphal." I am not clear why it does not matter. I am certain that, if we wish to speak of the time of Paul in particular, we should know whether or not the story at hand circulated in Paul's period and represented broadly held opinion then. Again, Sanders wishes to argue that "Paul's injunctions are not to be considered binding as law; the law does not function as law in the standard Jewish way." If the reader wishes to know what Sanders means by "the standard Jewish way," look at p. 118, n. 36. Here he refers to diverse important scholars of Paul, but not to a single pertinent scholarly work on the law in Judaism (of any sort).

The reader may well ask how critical a flaw the problem at hand constitutes for Sanders' larger argument. For, after all, this is not Sanders' book on Palestinian Judaism. As we know, he already has published that one. Here we have his exegesis of Pauline texts on the stated topics.

In my judgment, the characterization of "Judaism" forms the foundation for everything else, even though, as I indicated at the outset, most of the book talks about other things. Why so? The reason is that, time and again, at the critical turning in the argument, Sanders appeals to "Judaism" -- pure and simple. Let us consider, once more, a turning (p. 111) in Sanders' assessment of the thesis that "the law should be fulfilled:"

> Before considering the implication of this discussion of deeds for understanding Paul's view of the law, we should first note how thoroughly at home all of Paul's positions are in Judaism. The passages which we have considered are in and of themselves not detailed or precise enough to allow us to make firm statements about Paul's views of transgression, obedience, reward, punishment, atonement, exclusion, and condemnation. Yet they make such good sense when seen against more or less contemporary Jewish views that some conclusions may be drawn. As did his contemporaries in Judaism, Paul thought that salvation basically depends on membership in the in-group, but that within that context deeds still count. Transgressions must be repented of or they will deserve God's punishment.[68] Punishment itself, however, provides atonement. Both punishment and reward take place within the in-group, whether here or hereafter. Loss and commendation (1 Cor. 3:15; 4:5) are both earned in the sense of "deserved," but salvation itself is not earned by enumerating deeds or balancing them against one another.[69] While there is a firm belief in rewards and punishments which are appropriate to deeds, there is understandable reluctance to say precisely what the reward or punishment will be, especially when recompense is reserved for the final judgment.[70]

To the paragraph at hand, Sanders appends three footnotes (p. 122). I reproduce these as they appear:

> 68. One may note the prominence of punishment in the DDS, especially in 1QS, and the relative lack of emphasis on repentance, as well as the overwhelming rabbinic stress on repentance. Paul mentions repentance to God only once and punishment or chastisement more often. The view of punishment as atoning is widely attested in rabbinic and other sources (Ps. Sol.), however, and Paul's view is in any case too undeveloped to allow one to say that it is especially connected to any one movement in Judaism.

> 69. PPJ, e.g., p. 126.

> 70. PPJ, pp. 125-28.

Now, as we note, "the contemporaries in Judaism" to whom n. 68 makes reference are not specified; we do not know whom Paul means. But now they are Essenes of Qumran. That means they are not talmudic rabbis, whose sayings elsewhere speak for this same "Judaism." The other two notes are to his other book.

Now, as I said, when we turn to Paul and Palestinian Judaism, we find the same methods yielding the same results. These methods -- the ones of Billerbeck and Moore -- produce a picture of Judaism pretty much as full and complete, as homogeneous and neatly theological, as the results of Moore and his continuators. What is difficult to understand is why Sanders has chosen to ignore blatant problems inhering in those methods. To go over only a few, simple questions:

First, if we describe how matters stood in the first century, on what basis do we cite stories that first occur in documents closed a hundred or two hundred or even five hundred and a thousand years later?

Second, if we cannot demonstrate that a given rabbi made a saying attributed to him or did a deed told about him, then how can we cite such a story as evidence of things said and done in the time that rabbi lived?

Third, if documents came to closure over a period of half a millennium, as they did, how can we treat them all as essentially homogeneous and representative of a single "Judaism" -- and forthwith assign the provenance of that "Judaism" to the first century and to the Land of Israel?

Finally, how do we know that the documents at hand represent a broad range of national belief, practice, and opinion, so that we may impute to Jewry at large both in the Land of Israel and everywhere overseas (and so, to Paul in particular) a given set of convictions and practices? These formidable obstacles to the use of the rabbinic sources in the way that Sanders wishes to use them surely stand in the way of facile movement to the conclusions he proposes.

To this list of problems that seem to me to prevent Sanders from working as he does, let me append yet another list. For, in fairness to Sanders, one may wish to argue that in his field -- which is New Testament, not the study of ancient Judaism -- matters are worked out differently. Hence, one might propose, Sanders ignores problems particular to the rabbinical canon because in the New Testament canon they do not matter. But the contrary is the case. The entire critical program for the rabbinical canon of ancient Judaism corresponds to that devised in biblical studies in general, and in the study of the New Testament in particular. Sanders therefore works on rabbinical documents in ways in which he would not imagine dealing with New Testament ones. Philip S. Alexander, in his "Rabbinic Judaism and the New Testament," Zeitschrift fuer die neutestamentliche Wissenschaft 1983, 74:237-246, addresses New Testament scholars with exactly that argument, namely, critical considerations they take for granted in their own studies belong also in the study of Judaic sources.

The importance of his catalogue of problems, quite distinct from the one I have just now offered, justifies a full precis of his statements, which follows:

1. The State of the Texts. Most New Testament scholars ignore the fact that many early Rabbinic texts are not available in critical editions provided with a proper critical apparatus....

2. The Understanding of the Texts. There is also a basic problem relating to our understanding of the content of early Rabbinic literature. In many crucial cases New Testament scholars are still reading the Rabbinic texts through the spectacles of the classic mediaeval commentators....

3. Dating the Texts. New Testament scholars still largely accept the dates assigned to the early Rabbinic texts by the great 19th century Jüdische Wissenschaft scholars like Zunz. Often these dates are highly questionable and reached on very subjective grounds. Rabbinic literature is made up of school texts containing the deposit of a tradition which grew up over many centuries. As such they are extremely hard to date. In many cases we could be dealing with margins of error of up to 200 years....

4. Accuracy of Attributions. New Testament scholars are still much too credulous as to the accuracy of attributions in rabbinic literature. If the Talmud says Rabbi X said "such and such", then for all practical purposes they accept that he said it. I find it astonishing that Gospel scholars should fall into this trap. Critics who would not for a moment accept without question that any given dominical saying in the Gospels is a genuine logion of Jesus, seem happy to accept as genuine a logion attributed to Hillel in a text edited 500 years after Hillel's death.... critical prudence dictates that we should be as suspicious of the accuracy of attributions in Rabbinic texts as in any comparable ancient document, and our suspicion and uncertainty should increase in ratio to the distance of the document from the time of the master whose saying is quoted. A number of the facts are beyond dispute:

    (a)   Some attributes are uncertain. The same saying is attributed to different masters, sometimes in the text itself, sometimes in different manuscripts of the text.

    (b)   The content of the traditions did not remain stable during transmission but altered substantially. This is conclusively proved by those instances where we can compare synoptically different transmissions of the same tradition.

    (c)   It is unlikely that we can ever recover the ipsissima verba of any individual Rabbi. Unless we are prepared to believe that the Rabbis in real life actually spoke in the clipped, formulaic, anonymous style of Mishnah and Midrash, then we must acknowledge that the external form of the early Rabbinic traditions has been largely determined by the transmitters and editors. We can only hope that this editorial recasting of the original utterances into the standard patterns has preserved their substance unchanged.

   5. <u>Literary and Form Criticism</u>. New Testament scholars generally fail to carry out the <u>necessary literary and form-critical analysis</u> of the rabbinic texts which they utilize, and, because of the comparatively primitive state of Rabbinics, do not often find such analysis ready to hand. They treat the material which they extract as though its meaning can be determined without reference to the literary context in which it is found. Once again I am astonished to see Gospel critics -- so sophisticated in the application of literary-critical procedures in their own field -- behaving in this way. Many of the most significant advances in the study of Rabbinic literature have resulted from extrapolating the analytical methods of Biblical scholarship....

   6. <u>Anachronism</u>. Many New Testament scholars are still guilty of massive and sustained anachronism in their use of Rabbinic sources. Time and again we find them quoting <u>texts from the 3rd, 4th or 5th centuries AD, or even later, to illustrate Jewish teaching in the 1st century</u>. It must surely be a basic assumption in the historical study of any religion that religions change and develop through time. We may still be a long way from writing the definitive account of the history of early Judaism, but academic caution demands that we regard it as a priori unlikely that the Judaism of Hillel in the 1st century AD was identical to the Judaism of Hoshaiah in the 3rd....

   7. <u>Parallelomania</u>. Many New Testament scholars are still afflicted by the scourge of "<u>parallelomania</u>". They crudely juxtapose elements of early Judaism and Christianity, detect similarities, and on the basis of these supposed similarities conclude that Christianity has "borrowed from", or "been influenced by" Judaism. The fallacy of this procedure was exposed long ago. Parallelomania involves a failure to see the implications of the diversity of early Judaism.

It is important to pay attention to Alexander's detailed address to New Testament scholarship, because Sanders has chosen to ignore every consideration important to Alexander's argument, as much as to mine. The citations given above show how Sanders prefers to refer to, and utilize, the rabbinic sources.

   But what my earlier citations do not indicate is that in his earlier book, Sanders pursued the same methods, yielding precisely the results on which he builds in the present work. As we noted, time and again his basis for making a statement about "Judaism" consists of a reference to <u>PPJ</u>, that is, his earlier work.

   Since I have devoted this review to methodological issues, let me close with attention to substantive problems in Sanders' book. Paul describes himself as a Pharisee, and Acts has him as a disciple of Gamaliel. Hence we should have a clear picture of what Pharisaism meant for Paul and to Paul. It is not merely that Sanders does not provide such a picture. The problem is that what we know about Pharisaism itself presents a fair number of puzzles on its own. Let me list only two.

   First, if Paul grew up outside of the Holy Land, what could being-a-Pharisee have meant, if, as the sources surely indicate, included in the definition of Pharisaism was the requirement to eat food in a state of cultic cleanness? By definition all land outside of the Holy Land was not profane but unclean with corpse-uncleanness. So, also by definition, one could not keep the laws of cultic cleanness outside of the Land. Then what did being-a-Pharisee involve for Paul in Asia Minor? Did he become a Pharisee only when he came to Jerusalem to study with Gamaliel? Then why did he come in the first place?

Second, just what did Paul mean by "the law," and what did he not mean by it? Here, Sanders does make episodic remarks, some of them quite suggestive. He distinguishes a number of meanings and contexts in which "the law" plays a part, as either (1) law/halakhah, or (2) law/Torah, or even (3) law/Scripture ("the Old Testament"). My sense is that Sanders finds the issue troubling. But nowhere in his book do I find a systematic account of the problem.

This is not really a book about "Paul, the Law, and the Jewish people." It is a set of Sanders' comments in response to his critics and observations on this and that -- a research report, now waiting to be written into a sustained and rigorous, well-argued and thoughtfully presented book. If, nonetheless, I take seriously Paul and Palestinian Judaism and Paul, The Law, and the Jewish People, it is because I want to see Sanders succeed in his work. He has taken as his task the refutation of negative judgments on Judaism put forward by New Testament scholars, particularly specialists on Paul. As a Jew I recognize the this-worldly importance of his scholarly aspiration. But as a scholar I can offer a critical judgment based only on criteria of substantive learning, argument, reflection. By those criteria the book and its predecessor prove hopeless. But, it must be said, because of the books' widespread reception as a reliable account of Judaism. I have taken both works very seriously indeed. I shall continue to follow Sanders' writings on Judaism and, where appropriate, criticize, and, when possible, learn from them. I hope that the latter exercise proves more common than the former. But, as I said, to date, the work has been intellectually rather vulgar.

JEWS, PAGANS, AND CHRISTIANS IN CONFLICT
Jewish Quarterly Review (in press)

JEWS, PAGANS, AND CHRISTIANS IN CONFLICT. By David Rokeah. Jerusalem and
Leiden: The Magnes Press of the Hebrew University and E.J. Brill, 1982. Studia
Post-biblica vol. 33.

This erudite book spends a great deal of effort at proving a proposition without
interest or consequence, namely, that between pagans and Christians there was a polemic,
but between Jews and Christians, only a dispute. While the author is surely wrong, he
reviews a great many interesting passages and contributes diverse apercus of no little
value. So, on the good side, Rokeah amasses a great deal of evidence and comments on
it. But on the bad side, the evidence is meant to prove an insubstantial and trivial point --
and in the end fails to do so. Let me explain.

Rokeah presents us with a model of how not to write a book. His book is unreadable,
because it follows no clear argument or program but consists in the main of a mass of
disjointed observations. The thesis is announced, but never analyzed. The author
constantly loses his way in a mass of undifferentiated detail. Yet these traits do not
constitute the important failure of the book. What Rokeah does is ignore nearly the
entirety of scholarly work in the past century -- and that on a variety of subjects. Among
these, two stand out. First, Rokeah utilizes categories that homogenize highly differentiated phenomena. Second, he treats as fact every allegation in the rabbinic sources
that a given authority made a given statement or carried out a specified action.
Consequently, his categories of analysis make no sense, and his use of evidence is based on
false premises concerning the character of the evidence. Since he provides no bibliography, furthermore, we know what he has read only from footnotes. These consist
mainly, though not exclusively, of references to sources. He further has read a handful of
scholars, most of them in Jerusalem or in communication with Jerusalem.

What he does not do is deal with that rather substantial corpus of scholarship in the
West in which such categories as "Judaism," "Christianity," and "paganism" raise more
questions than they answer. For Rokeah, by contrast, there really was a "Judaism,"
defined by harmonizing pretty much all sources written by Jews, so too a "Christianity"
and a "paganism." These gross categories serve no useful purpose.

The method of the book is truly bizarre. Indeed, I doubt that in half a century
anyone has written a book on early Christianity like this. Since Rokeah wishes to write
about "paganism" and "Christianity," he constructs his little canon of pagan philosophers
and theologians of Christianity. (I shall enumerate the entries in a moment.) These he
then approaches with his several topics. He collects what each of his Christian and pagan

theologians has to say about said topics, and voilà! "Christianity" and "paganism" on that topic. The work is mechanical, the result pathetic. Here is the sequence of topics and authorities in his principal chapters (Two, Three, Four):

Chapter Two: Recognition of God, revelation, religious myth. 1. Recognition: Philo (Jew), Julian (Christian, pagan), Arnobius (Christian). 2. Religious myth: Stoics, Philo, Aristides, Justin, Clement, Tertullian, Arnobius (at length), Celsus/Origen (at length), Porphyry, Eusebius, Julian (at great length), talmudic sources, Josephus.

Chapter Three: Divine providence, demons, election of Israel. 1. Providence: Philo, Josephus, Clement, Eusebius, Arnobius (at length), Porphyry (at length), Julian. 2. Demons: Justin, Eusebius, Celsus/Origen (at length), Julian (at length). 3. Election of Israel: Origen, Eusebius, Julian (at length).

Chapter Four: Culture and enslavement; the religious inference of human history. 1. Israel's "enslavement": Apion/Josephus, Philo (at length), Celsus/Origen, Justin/Tatian, Minucius Felix, Tertullian, Arnobius, Porphyry (at length), Eusebius (at length), Julian (at great length), talmudic references to Israel's history and its meaning, categorized by proposition.

It now is fairly easy to see how Rokeah composed the book. He divided up his card-file into six main topics. The categories are post-Reformation in origin. Then he worked his way through the authors cited. He copied out what they had to say about the various topics. He then split up the materials among his files and was ready to write. He took up each file, organized the sayings by theme (not chronologically, as is clear), tacked on some rabbinic items, and wrote up his results.

So the work emerges from a considerable labor of collecting and arranging, being fixated at the primitive stage of hunting and gathering rather than of intensive cultivation. The notion that Philo, Josephus, and the Talmud and related literature then constitute "Judaism" is exactly as defensible as its counterpart. Does anyone any longer write books that give us a "Christianity" based on collections of sayings on standard themes deriving from diverse Church fathers? I can think of very few. Since books on "Judaism" from Schechter and Moore to Urbach and Sanders collect and arrange sayings and so purport to give us a "Judaism" on one topic or another, Rokeah cannot be said to stand all by himself. But he is within a diminishing circle.

The various Christian authorities, of course, wrote individual books. The problem of homogenizing appropriate sayings in these books into a single picture of the view of Christianity on a given topic therefore proves blatant. The Judaic writings exhibit exactly the opposite characteristics. So they present Rokeah with a different set of problems. Those writings homogenize to begin with, drawing together sayings attributed to diverse authorities on a given topic and proposing a homogeneous doctrine on that topic. What Rokeah has done for "Christianity," the Talmud has done for Rokeah.

But then Rokeah has to take for granted that what in the rabbinical canon is attributed to a given authority really was said by him. That is assured without the slightest interest in how the framer of a given text knew what that authority had said.

Since the texts at hand derive from diverse periods, from the late second century for the earliest through the late medieval times for the latest, Rokeah might have wondered on what basis (other than the claim that "our holy rabbis would not lie") we are supposed to take at face value the allegations of the texts at hand. Accordingly, we must ask why, merely because a saying is attributed to a second century figure, that saying belongs to that figure and testifies to the state of opinion among "the Jews" at a given time in the second century and so defines "Judaism." We must ask on what basis we ignore the entire critical program of historical studies from the eighteenth century onward. That program has insisted that, before we accept the allegation of an ancient text about a fact of history or a hero of the faith, we must adduce sound reasons, based on systematic and thorough examination of all cases, for doing so. Nothing is taken for granted. In Rokeah's hands, everything is taken for granted.

Because Rokeah so sedulously ignores the simple considerations just now outlined, I think ample instances of the result should come before the reader. Otherwise the full extent of his fundamentalism in reading the rabbinic canon will not be grasped. The catastrophic results for his book then will be missed. For that purpose, I present two sizable extracts. The first (pp. 53-56, text only), shows how Rokeah not only takes for granted that what is attributed to an authority really was said by him. It also proves that he further believes that what that authority said was the case really was so. Hence it is a kind of double-gullibility, one concerning attribution, the other, the story or saying that is attributed. What we now see is how Rokeah creates a pastiche of sayings deriving from all rabbinic texts, whether the Babylonian Talmud, of the sixth or seventh century, or Genesis Rabbah and Leviticus Rabbah, of the fourth or fifth century, or the Mishnah, of the late second century, or of Song of Songs Rabbah, a date for which we do not have, but which cannot come early in the period at hand, or even Deuteronomy Rabbah, which most authorities place in post-talmudic times altogether. All texts equally testify to the period at hand -- a century beyond the date of the earliest document cited, over a millenium beyond the date of the latest. Further, as I stressed, everything cited authorities say represents "Judaism," which furthermore recorded popular opinion among all Jews. We then proceed to read in that same manner and context the pagan literature, as though we had solid evidence of the Judaic side to matters. Now Rokeah:

> In order to avert criticism, and to confirm my hypothesis that the Jews were not an active party to the polemic, I will now present some indications of the atmosphere in the Jewish community then, as it is reflected in the Talmudic sources. I will also examine whether or not one may perceive the beginning of a change in thinking in the second century C.E., a change that became more solidly based in the third and fourth centuries. In order to do this, I will now present some explicit sayings in Talmudic literature which convey the dilemma posed by the existence of the Roman Empire, of which Judaea was one of the smaller provinces and subject to its jurisdiction and good will. These sayings indicated the position taken by the Sages towards the government and its methods.

The famous baraita in the BT (Shabbath, 33b) betrays the esteem felt by R. Yehuda ben Ilai for Rome's colonizing activity: "How fine are the works of this people [= the Romans]!. They have made streets [for 'market-places'], they have built bridges, they have erected baths," as well as the denigration expressed by R. Simeon ben Yohai: "All what they made they made for themselves. They built market-places to set harlots in them; baths, to rejuvenate themselves; bridges to levy tolls for them." Similarly the opinions of Resh Lakish (= Rabbi Simeon ben Lakish) and Rabbi Simon were divided about the character of the law and justice instituted by Rome in the world: "R. Simeon b. Lakish said: 'Behold, it was very good.' [this refers] to the earthly kingdom [= Rome]. Is then the earthly kingdom very good? How strange! (It earns that title) because it exacts justice [= dikiot = dikai] for men...." And on the other hand: R. Pinehas and R. Hilkia, in the name of R. Simon.... Why is it [i.e. Edom or Rome] compared to a 'hazir' (swine or boar)? -- To tell you this: Just as the swine when reclining puts forth its hooves as if to say: See that I am clean, so too does the empire of Edom [Rome] boast as it commits violence and robbery, under the guise of establishing a judicial tribunal" [= bêma].

The opposition and hostility to Rome, oppressor of the nation and destroyer of the Temple, probably brought about a stricter attitude towards idolatrous objects that had any connection with emperor-worship: "... only that is forbidden which bears in its hand a staff or a bird or a sphere." The same held true for collaboration in any form with the authorities. The Sages viewed it unfavourably, chastized and even initiated sanctions against those subservient to the Romans. This animosity found its passive expression in the hope that "Rome is designed to fall into the hands of Persia."

But the dominant voices advocated moderation towards the authorities and objected to uprisings and sedition. Thus, for example, R. Yehuda the Patriarch ordered his sons in his testament: "... And do not seek to evade toll tax...." (BT Pesahim 112b) contrary to the position of his predecessors R. Akiva and Rabbi Ishmael (BT Baba Kama, 113a; JT Nedarim, chap. 3,38b). Other Sages of the second to fourth centuries C.E. spoke unequivocally: "What does it mean 'Turn you northward' (Deut., 2:3)? R. Hiyya said: He said unto them: if you see that it wishes to provoke you, do not stand up against it but hide yourselves from it until the time of its rule will pass" (MR Deuteronomy, 1:17); "But the bird divided he not (Gen., 15:10). R. Abba b. Kahana said in R. Levi's name: The Holy One, Blessed be He, intimated to him that he who attempts to resist the wave is swept away by it" (MR Genesis, 44:15); "... That text is required for (an exposition) like that of R. Yosé son of R. Hanina who said: 'What was the purpose of those three adjurations? [Song of Songs, 2:7; 3:5, 5:8] -- One, that Israel shall not go up (all together as if surrounded) by a wall; the second, that whereby the Holy One, Blessed be He, adjured idolators

[v.l. "The nations of the world"] that they shall not oppress Israel too much'"
(BT Ketuboth, 111a), and, finally "R. Helbo said: Four adjurations are
mentioned here. [= Song of Songs, 2:7; 3:5; 5:8; 8:4] God adjured Israel that
they should not rebel against the Governments, that they should not seek to
hasten the end, that they should not reveal their mysteries [= mysteirin =
mystêria] to the other nations and that they should not attempt to go up from
the diaspora as a wall... R. Onia said: He addressed to them four adjurations
corresponding to the four generations who tried to hasten the end and came to
grief, namely, once in the days of Amram, once in the days of Dinai, once in
the days of Ben Coziba, and once in the days of Shuthelah the son of
Ephraim." The Sages wished to prevent rash and dangerous acts, and tended to
attempt to allay tension in the relations of the Jews with the government; a
similar tendency was conspicuous in the attitude of the Roman authorities
towards the Jews after the Bar-Cochba revolt. It is reasonable to expect that
signs of this change may be found in pagan literature, too, which I will now
examine.

It may be fairly argued that Rokeah here proposes to establish a broadly held view, so that
whether or not a given authority really said what is assigned to him does not matter all
that much. He does not, after all, subject any of the cited sayings to considerable
analysis. So, it may be thought, he does not build a substantial case on the sayings at hand.

Rokeah shows, quite to the contrary, that he takes at face value every detail of a
story. My claim that we deal with total credulity of a simple-minded sort does not
overstate matters. Here is an example of how Rokeah not only indicates that he believes
each detail but even proposes to interpret the motives of the hero of the tale (not of the
story-teller!). He can even tell us what the hero was thinking. The tale at hand appears
in a very late compilation of exegeses of Qohelet (Ecclesiastes), composed many centuries
after the time at which the hero is supposed to have lived. But Rokeah will now show us
how to read these stories as though they came from people present on the very day -- and
also conversant with what was in the hero's mind that day.

In the later period, the purely disputative character of the exchanges was
prominent. This may be shown from a few examples. In Kohelet Rabba, 1:25,
we read about Rabbi Yehuda ben Nakossa (flourished in the beginning of the
third century C.E.): "... the minim had been dealing with him: they were
asking him questions and he answered them, asking him and he answered. He
said to them: your retorts are useless; come, let us agree among us that each
man who will achieve victory over his competitor will strike his competitor on
the head with a mallet. And he defeated them and wounded their heads till
they were full of wounds. When he returned, his disciples said to him: Rabbi,
you were helped by heaven and you were victorious. He said to them: and was
it for nothing? Go and pray for that man and for that bag which was full of
precious stones and pearls, but now is full of coals." From the story of Rabbi

Yehuda ben Nakossa, one realizes that he was thoroughly tired of the
unproductive character of the dispute with the <u>minim</u> and, in order to bring
about its intensification, he made his drastic suggestion. However, when it
was over, he was very upset by the result. It might be argued that this
tradition should not be accepted as something that really happened, but rather
that it was invented to prove that the Jewish Sages had the upper hand in their
debate with the <u>minim</u>. Such a conclusion would not endanger my deductions,
since I am interested in the atmosphere of general indifference, before its
artificial intensification by Rabbi Yehuda, which is revealed in this story.

Lest the reader once more imagine that I exaggerate, let us now hear how Rokeah
concludes the discussion of which the cited extract constitutes a high point:

I have tried to show that, following the middle of the second century
C.E., there was a radical change in the relations among Jews, pagans, and
Christians. The polemic which had dealt with problems of existence and
conflict was now replaced by a barren, colourless dispute. The main argument
of the scholars who insist on the continuance of the polemic during the two
hundred years after the Bar-Cochba revolt is based on the existence of Jewish
religious propaganda directed towards pagans and Christians a potential
converts to Judaism. This assumption must be rejected because of the lack of
sufficient and decisive proof; with this assumption there also falls the
designation of the Jews as an autonomous party to the polemic. The <u>Adversus</u>
<u>Iudaeos</u> literature too can be interpreted plausibly as not contradicting the
hypothesis that the Jews were a sort of "middlemen" in the polemic between
the pagans and the Christians. Other sources -- pagan and Christian alike --
confirm this hypothesis.

So far as we must read the rabbinical sources as Rokeah does in order to reach the
conclusion he reaches, I think we must reject his thesis out of hand. It is not because the
thesis is not plausible. It is because it rests upon suppositions about the character of the
evidence that, in the case of the rabbinical writings, have long ago ceased to be tenable.
So his arguments based upon "Judaism" are senseless -- and that on methodological
grounds.

But that hardly disposes of the thesis itself. What in fact does Rokeah wish to
argue, and why is it important to him?

First, Rokeah makes the distinction between "polemic" and "dispute." The former
indicates "a campaign or conflict having the aim of changing an opponent's views or his
religion." The latter involves merely "an interchange of words aiming at the clarification
of various matters" (p. 9).

The distinction is important, because, second, Rokeah thinks that Jews had no
important role in the pagan-Christian polemic. "Jews were no party to it," he says.

He qualifies forthwith: "However, without the Jews' existence and independent
attitude towards Christians and pagans alike, and without their holy scriptures and the
writings of Hellenistic Jewry, the pagan-Christian polemic could not have taken the

course and shape it did." This somewhat murky allegation is less portentous than it sounds. Rokeah seems to mean that without Jewish writings, Christianity would not be what it was, and hence would not have engaged paganism in the way that it did. That may be news in Jerusalem, but nowhere else. Exactly how the Jews' "existence and independent attitude towards Christians and pagans" shaped the "polemic" between paganism and Christianity Rokeah cannot say. He hastens to observe, "Both Christians and pagans made extensive use of all facets of Judaism..." So what else is new? In all, "antagonism between the pagans and Christians falls into the category of polemic, whereas the Jewish-Christian and the Jewish-pagan confrontation was no more than a dispute." He refers, specifically to the period from the second to the fifth century.

Since Rokeah frames his thesis in these simple terms, it is easy enough to adduce important Christian evidence contradicting it. He does not appear to read Syriac or to know much about the existence of Christianity in Syriac-speaking countries. If he did, he would not find it possible to allege that Jews and Christians did not conduct polemics against one another. Aphrahat, the Persian sage, did just that. From his writings there can be no doubt that Jewish opponents replied in kind. Yet Rokeah does read Greek, and I looked in his book in vain for substantial attention to the Antiochene Christians, typified by John of the Golden Tongue, who surely did conduct with the Jews something more heated than a little "dispute" about this and that. Still more astonishing, Rokeah never takes up the question of what surely must be regarded as a polemic -- not merely a "dispute" — against the Jews in the Fourth Gospel, to mention only one minor but puzzling omission in his deeply flawed case. And surely John is close enough to the second century to count.

Yet if Rokeah had been able to prove his case, how should we have a deeper understanding of matters? The distinction at hand, while surely valid, seems to me not to make much of a difference. It leads to no further insight. If Rokeah proposes to demonstrate that Judaism and Christianity really did not engage in a bitter struggle in the centuries under discussion, he runs contrary to the results of the vast preponderance of scholarly opinion. And yet, at no point does he tell us what broader implications he suggests, what deeper understanding of the age at hand we gain, in consequence of his thesis.

The exercise in the end proves not only incompetent, but arid. If he were right, so what? Here is his answer:

> The religious and, to a certain extent, the intellectual background of the parties to the polemic provided the polemic with a common base. Nevertheless, the polemic might have degenerated into one of abuses and insults, of casting aspersions on and of concocting unfounded and malicious libels about one's opponents, were it not for the Jewish factor. The influence of the Jews was instrumental in raising the level of the polemic, and in intensifying the consideration of problems of essential importance as being worthy of historical-theological-philosophical contemplation in their own right. It is true that, since we are dealing with a polemic, the parties to it were not very strict

about pursuing truth for its own sake -- as they repeatedly claimed -- but endeavoured to derive the maximum benefit for their cause, as well as to frame arguments, from that which was considered and presented as the factual truth. Although we did not gain much, in this sense, we did profit immensely by the unique preservation of fragments of various works, Jewish-Hellenistic and pagan, as the result of their use in the polemic. The way in which people of later antiquity viewed their past is an instructive lesson for us, a lesson to which we should pay attention, when we approach the task of summing up the inheritance of the ancient world, which has cast its stamp on Western society and culture to this very day.

Whether or not scholars in the broad ranges of patristic literature will concede that the Jews of antiquity raised "the level of the polemic" I cannot say. I do know the writings of Aphrahat backward and forward, and there Rokeah is simply wrong. Just how Jews helped Ephrem or Chrysostom to phrase their polemic against paganism in a more civilized manner than they otherwise would have done even Rokeah will find difficult to show. How all this is relevant to the preservation of "fragments of various works" I cannot say; that sentence seems to me simply parachuted down. And the rest is mere verbiage. It remains to make articulate what the reader may already have noted, which is that Rokeah also does not write very well.

In all we have a childish apologetic about the enlightened Jews and the benighted Christians and pagans, who, but for the Jews, would have lacked all civilized manners of good argument. The polemic in favor of the restrained, enlightened Jews calls to mind similar claims laid down in the writings of the Wissenschaft des Judentums in the nineteenth century. I do not know who is interested in apologetics anymore. Rokeah has given us little more than a curiosity, witless and provincial, a fine example, as I said, of exactly how not to write a book.

Part Six

THREE BIBLIOGRAPHICAL ESSAYS

22. THE HISTORICAL STUDY OF TALMUDIC LITERATURE

[The Allan Bronfman Lecture, Shaar Hashomayim Synagogue, Montreal, November 8, 1978, The Hill Professor's Lecture, University of Minnesota, Minneapolis and St. Paul, November 15, 1978, and a Plenary Lecture in honor of the tenth anniversary of the founding of the Association for Jewish Studies, Boston, December 17, 1978. Printed in Method and Meaning in Ancient Judaism (Missoula, 1979: Scholars Press for Brown Judaic Studies) 1:41-58.]

I

Enduring works of the intellect last because they speak to minds beyond limits of space and boundaries of time. The mark of greatness is the vision and will to transcend all frontiers and address an age one can scarcely imagine. But what is heard beyond the bounds of space and time is not always, and perhaps not ever, what the original mind meant to say. Like a diamond, which reveals a different light to the eyes of each of those who see it, these lasting works of mind, whether in art or music, philosophy or literature, religion or science, enjoy a diverse reception. People hear what they are capable of perceiving. One generation reads Shakespeare in light of one set of issues and another, in light of a different set. The history of the reception of the thought of Socrates is shaped by Plato and of that of Plato, by Aristotle. As Harold Cherniss points out, Aristotle's criticism of pre-Socratic philosophy, of Plato, and of the Academy is complicated by Aristotle. For he attributes to Plato a theory which is not in Plato's writings (1935, 1944, 1945). On this basis, Cherniss (1934:ix) accepts the possibility that "Aristotle was capable of setting down something other than the objective truth when he had occasion to write about his predecessors."[1] The discovery of that possibility, however, had to await the coming of Harold Cherniss, twenty-three hundred years after Aristotle. The reason for the delay explains much about the consciousness and culture of the West in the intervening centuries. So it is self-evident that the great intellectual accomplishments of humanity, the ones which endure for centuries, not only transcend the limits of time and space,[2] they also overcome the barriers of their own composition: the mind of the maker, the world to which the maker spoke and which, to begin with, received the work and accepted (or rejected) it. This is so for the diverse collections of the Hebrew Scriptures, for Plato, for the traditions of Chinese and Indian philosophy and Christian theology, and for that document distinctive to the inner life of the Jewish people for nearly two millenia, the Talmud.

A history of the study of the Talmud, from the Talmud's formative period in the first and second centuries of the common era down to the present day would provide insight into the intellectual history of Judaism, of which the Talmud is the principal component. It also would give us important facts about the sociology of the Jewish people, the character of its religious life in diverse dimensions, the nature of the educational and cultural institutions which express and shape that life. The reason is that the conditions of society define the things society wants to know. The shape of the program of study of the inherited monuments of culture is governed by the people who propose to carry out that program and the interests of the people who are supposed to contemplate the results of the work.

To take one very current example, Christopher Lasch explains the reason that The University of Chicago became the great center for sociology which it did -- the place in which, for a long time, the issues of sociology were defined -- and also the reason that sociology done in Chicago took up the very questions asked:

> The presence in other departments of the university of such important thinkers as Veblen, John Dewey, and Mead; the enterprise of Jane Addams... and other settlement workers in accumulating empirical data on urban life and insights into its pathology; the many-sided intellectual awakening known as the "Chicago renaissance"; the existence of the city itself as a laboratory of industrial conditions -- all these made Chicago almost inevitably a center of sociological studies. Nor is it surprising that those studies addressed themselves especially to the sociology of urban life. From the perspective of Chicago, which had grown from a frontier settlement to a huge industrial metropolis in less than a century, completely rebuilding itself after the fire of 1871, rapid urbanization loomed as the central fact of modern society.... Accordingly, the city should be studied as a total environment that gave rise to a distinctive way of life (1977:33-34).

I quote Lasch at length because he provides a model for two propositions. First of all, he shows that the conditions of society generate the data to be examined by the intellectuals. Second, he indicates that the character of the studies carried out by them is defined by those same conditions. Sociology took up the questions of society and family, in the place in which the work was done, by the people by whom the work was done, specifically because the context defined both what was to be studied and who should do the work.

If then we ask how the Talmud was studied, we transform a question of intellectual method, superficially a formal question about traits of logic and inquiry. We find ourselves asking about the world in which Jews lived, the values they brought to the Talmud, and the reasons that moved them to open its pages to begin with. So, as I said, when we contemplate the study of the Talmud, we find ourselves examining the history of the inner life of the Jewish people and, self-evidently, the intellectual history of Judaism.

I argue this proposition with some care so that my basic perspective on historical interest in the Talmud will be clearly defined. The questions I wish to answer are these:

First, why was the Talmud studied as a historical document?

Second, what was the intellectual program of the people who originally decided that the Talmud should be studied as a historical document?

Third, why is the Talmud studied today, in a very considerable measure, as a historical document?

Fourth, what is the intellectual program of the people who today do the work?

Persuasive answers to these four questions will give us a clearer notion of the work we do and a firmer definition of the work to be done in the future. So when we speak of the Talmud as history, we address ourselves to questions of acutely contemporary character and cultural consequence.

II

The beginnings of the study of the Talmud as history, like the beginnings of nearly all of the methods and ideas of the "Jewish humanities," lie in nineteenth-century Germany. Ismar Schorsch (1974:48) points out that the definition of the modern debate about the Talmud, in mostly historical terms, was supplied in a single decade, the 1850s. Four books were published in less than ten years, which defined the way the work would be done for the next one hundred years. These are Leopold Zunz's publication of Nahman Krochmal's Moreh nebukhe hazzeman ("guide to the perplexed of our times"), 1851; Heinrich Graetz's fourth volume of his History of the Jews from the Earliest Times to the Present, which is devoted to the talmudic period, 1853; Geiger's Urschrift und Uebersetzungen der Bibel, 1857; and Zechariah Frankel's Darkhe hammishnah ("ways of the Mishnah"), 1859.[3] These four volumes place the Talmud into the very center of the debates on the reform of Judaism and address the critical issues of the debate: the divine mandate of Rabbinic Judaism (Schorsch, 1975:48).[4]

The talmudic period defines the arena of the struggle over reform because the Reform theologians made it so. They had proposed that by exposing the historical origins of the Talmud and of the Rabbinic form of Judaism, they might "undermine the divine mandate of rabbinic Judaism" (Schorsch, 1975:48). As Schorsch points out, Geiger's work indicates the highwater mark of the attack on Rabbinic Judaism through historical study.[5] Krochmal, Graetz, and Frankel present a sympathetic and favorable assessment. In so doing, however, they adopt the fundamental supposition of the Reformers: the Talmud can and should be studied historically. They concede that there is a history to the period in which the Talmud comes forth. The Talmud itself is a work of men in history.

The method of Graetz and of Frankel, therefore, is essentially biographical. One third of Frankel's book is devoted to biographies of personalities mentioned in the Talmud. What he does is collect the laws given in the name of a particular man and states that he appears in such and such tractates, and the like. His card file is neatly divided but yields no more than what is filed in it (Gereboff, 1973:59-75).[6] What is important is not what he proves but, as I said, what he implicitly concedes, which is that the Mishnah and the rest of the rabbinic literature are the work of men. Graetz likewise stresses the matter of great men. As Schorsch characterizes his work:

Graetz tried valiantly to portray the disembodied rabbis of the Mishnah and Talmud as vibrant men, each with his own style and philosophy and personal frailties, who collectively resisted the disintegrating forces of their age.... In the wake of national disaster, creative leadership forged new religious institutions to preserve and invigorate the bonds of unity.... He defended talmudic literature as a a great national achievement of untold importance to the subsequent survival of the Jews (1975:48).

Now why, in the doing of history, the biographies of great men should be deemed the principal work is clear: the historians of the day in general wrote biographies. History was collective biography. Their conception of what made things happen is tied to the theory of the great man in history, the great man as the maker of history. The associated theory was of history as the story of politics, thus of what great men did. Whether or not the Jewish historians of the "talmudic period" do well, moderately well, or poorly, the sort of history people did in general I cannot say. The important point is that the beginnings of the approach to the Talmud as history meant biography.

What was unimportant to Graetz, Frankel, and Krochmal, was a range of questions of historical method already thoroughly defined and worked out elsewhere. So the work of talmudic history was methodologically obsolete by the standards of its own age. These questions had to do with the reliability of sources. Specifically, in both classical and biblical studies, long before the mid-nineteenth century a thorough-going skepticism had replaced the gullibility of earlier centuries. Alongside the historicistic frame of mind shaped in the aftermath of the Romantic movement, there was an enduring critical spirit, formed in the Enlightenment and not to be eradicated later on. This critical spirit approached the historical allegations of ancient texts with a measure of skepticism. So for biblical studies, in particular, the history of ancient Israel no longer followed the paths of the biblical narrative, from Abraham onward. In the work of writing lives of Jesus, the contradictions among the several gospels, the duplications of materials, the changes from one gospel to the next between one saying and story and another version of the same saying and story, the difficulty in establishing a biographical framework for the life of Jesus -- all of these and similar, devastating problems had attracted attention. The result was a close analysis of the character of the sources as literature, for example, the recognition -- before the nineteenth century -- that the Pentateuch consists of at least three main strands: JE, D, and P. It was well known that behind the synoptic Gospels is a source (called Q, for Quelle) containing materials assigned to Jesus, upon which the three evangelists drew but reshaped for their respective purposes. The conception that merely because an ancient story-teller says someone said or did something does not mean he really said or did it goes back before the Enlightenment. After all, the beginnings of modern biblical studies surely reach into the mind of Spinoza. He was not the only truly critical intellect in the field before Voltaire. But as a powerful, socially rooted frame of mind, historical-critical and literary-critical work on the ancient Scriptures is the attainment of the late eighteenth and nineteenth centuries. And for the founders of talmudic history, Graetz, Frankel, and Krochmal, what had happened in biblical and other ancient historical studies was either not known or not found to be useful. And it was not used.

No German biographer of Jesus by the 1850s could have represented his life and thought by a mere paraphrase and harmony of the Gospels, in the way in which Graetz and Frankel and their successors down to the mid-twentieth century would paraphrase and string together talmudic tales about rabbis, and call the result "history" and biography. Nor was it commonplace, by the end of the nineteenth century, completely to ignore the redactional and literary traits of documents entirely, let alone their historical and social provenance. Whatever was given to a rabbi, in any document, of any place or time, was forthwith believed to provide evidence of what that rabbi really said and did in the time in which he lived. Even Christian "Fundamentalism" approaches the Biblical literature with greater shame than this!

III

Now why these people did what they chose to do is no more important than why they refrained from doing what they chose not to do. Just as they chose to face the traditionalists with the claim that the Talmud was historical, so they chose to turn their backs on the critical scholarship of their own day with that very same claim that the Talmud was historical. I think the apologetic reason is self-evident and requires no amplification. We may now answer our first two questions. The Talmud was first studied as a historical document because, in the war for the reform of Judaism, history was the preferred weapon. The Talmud was the target of opportunity. The traditionalists trivialized the weapon, maintaining that history was essentially beside the point of the Talmud: "The historians can tell us what clothes Rabh wore, and what he ate for breakfast. The Talmudists can report what he said." But, it goes without saying, polemical arguments such as these, no less than the ones of the Reformers, were important only to the people who made them up.

The weapon of history in the nineteenth century was ultimate in the struggle for the intellect of Jewry. And the intellectuals, trained as they were in the philosophical works of the day, deeply learned in Kant and Hegel, made abundant use of the ultimate weapon. The Reformers similarly chose the field of battle, declaring the Hebrew Scriptures to be sacred and outside the war. They insisted that what was to be reformed was the shape of Judaism imparted by the Talmud, specifically, and preserved in their own day by the rabbis whose qualification consisted in learning in the Talmud and approval by those knowledgeable therein.

But the shape of the subject and its results, paradoxically, also reveal the mind of the traditionalist Reformers, Graetz and Frankel. Their intellectual program consisted of turning the Talmud, studied historically, into a weapon against the specific proposals and conceptions of the Reformers. And for the next hundred years, with only one important additional area of study, the history of the "talmudic period" would be the story of rabbis, paraphrases of talmudic and midrashic units strung together with strings of homilies -- where they were strung together at all.

This additional area of study need not detain us for long, for what is done in it is essentially what is done in biography. I refer to the study of what was called "talmudic

theology" or "talmudic thought" or "rabbinic theology." In English the pioneering work is
Solomon Schechter's Studies in Judaism, three volumes beginning in essays in the Jewish
Quarterly Review, 1894 through 1896. The next important work in English is George F.
Moore's Judaism, published in 1927, then C. G. Montefiore's and H. Loewe's Rabbinic
Anthology, 1938, and Ephraim Urbach's The Sages. Their Concepts and Beliefs, in Hebrew
in 1969 and English in 1975. There were parallel works in German as well.[7] In all of these
works the operative method is the same as in biography, but the definitive category shifts
to theology. Each work takes up a given theological category and gathers sayings relevant
to it. The paraphrase of the sayings constitutes the scholarly statement. Urbach
correctly defines the work which was not done: "the history of the beliefs and concepts of
the Sages against the background of the reality of their times and environment" (italics
his) (1975:5). The use of evidence for the theological character of talmudic Judaism is
just as gullible and credulous as it is for biographies of talmudic rabbis. What is
attributed to a given rabbi really was said by him. What he is said to have done he really
did. No critical perspective is brought to the facts of the Talmud. And the Talmud
always supplies the facts, all the facts, and nothing but the facts.

We need not dwell on the historical study of the Talmud for theological purposes,
therefore, because the methods were no different from those taken to be essentially sound
for the study of the Talmud for biographical purposes. And these two purposes --
biography and theology -- define the character of nearly all of the historical work done in
talmudic literature for the century from the decade of foundation onward. Graetz set the
style for such history as was attempted; Frankel for biography. The greatest achievements of the next hundred years -- I think of the names of Buechler and Alon, for
example[8] -- in no way revised the methods and procedures or criticized the fundamental
suppositions laid forth in Graetz and Frankel. When we realize the conceptual and
methodological history of biblical studies in that same century, when we gaze upon the
stars which rose and the stars which fell, when we remember the fads and admire the
lasting progress, we realize that the Talmud as history is a world in which the clock
started in 1850 and stopped in 1860. That of course is an exaggeration. Even those who
could find no better methods and suppositions than those used for a hundred years could at
least propose better questions. A clearly historical, developmental purpose is announced,
though not realized, for example, by Urbach, when he says:

> The work of the sages is to be viewed as a protracted process aimed at the
> realization of the Torah and the ideals of the prophets in the reality and
> framework of their time... (1975:17).

Now while this is a clearly apologetic and theological proposal, it does make a place for
the notion of change and development, that is, a genuinely -- not merely a superficially --
historical proposal.

At the end let me quote Schorsch's (1975:61-62) judgment of Graetz, which forms a
devastating epitaph to the whole enterprise of talmudic history from the 1850s to the
1950s:

Above all, Graetz remained committed to the rejuvenation of his people. His faith in God's guiding presence throughout Jewish history, as witnessed by two earlier instances of national recovery, assured him of the future. His own work, he hoped, would contribute to the revival of Jewish consciousness. He succeeded beyond measure. As a young man, Graetz had once failed to acquire a rabbinic pulpit because he was unable to complete the delivery of his sermon. There is more than a touch of irony in the remarkable fact that the reception accorded to Graetz's history by Jews around the world made him the greatest Jewish preacher of the nineteenth century.

IV

The second century of the historical study of the Talmud and related literature is marked by the asking of those questions ignored in the first: What if not everything in the Talmud happened as it is narrated? What if the attribution of a saying to a given rabbi does not mean that the rabbi really said what he is supposed to have said? Then what sorts of historical work are we able to do? What sorts can we no longer undertake?

At the outset let me specify the answers to my third and fourth questions, raised earlier: What is the intellectual program of the people who today do the work? Why is the Talmud studied today as a historical document?

Answering these questions requires attention to the character of the people who do the work. These are all university people. Talmudic history may be taught in some Jewish theological institutions -- not in Yeshivas at all -- but no books or articles in talmudic history emerge from these schools. The books and articles in this field over the past twenty years have been written by university professors in America, Canada, Europe and the State of Israel. The reason this particular aspect of talmudic studies is important to professors in diaspora-universities should be made clear.

Among those engaged in the teaching of the "Jewish humanities," the Talmud is a particularly important document. It is distinctively Jewish. The Hebrew Scriptures are not; they are a splendid literature and a self-evidently important one. Much of the medieval philosophical and mystical literature is of very special interest. The Talmud, by contrast, speaks of the formative years of Judaism as we know it; and it addresses itself, also, to the centuries in which the two other religions of the West (Christianity, for the earlier phases of the Talmud, and Islam, for the very last phases) were taking shape. Consequently, there is a genuine interest in talmudic learning among a wide audience of scholars and students. It is natural, therefore, for people in the setting of secular universities to turn to talmudic studies as a distinctively Jewish, important, and welcomed topic.

But what people in universities want to know has little to do with the ritualistic repetition of hagiography. They are not apt to sit still very long for edifying tales of ancient rabbis (or other sorts of holy men either). There is a contemporary program of research, a set of questions which just now appear urgent and pressing, as much as the issues of the reform of Judaism through historicism appeared urgent and pressing a century ago.

Of still greater importance for the present part of the argument, there is a considerable and shared program of criticism, historical, literary, anthropological and philosophical, as well as religionsgeschichtlich. This program is naturally attractive. One question which to New Testament scholars is deemed unavoidable is how to tell what, if anything, Jesus really said among the sayings attributed to him, and what Jesus really did among the deeds assigned to him. There is no way that what is perceived as "fundamentalism" will find a serious hearing in the study of Judaism when that same attitude of mind is found irrelevant in the study of Christianity of the same place and nearly the same time. It follows, as I indicated at the outset, that the pressing problems of this second century of talmudic studies for historical purposes are not, Did Rabbi X really say what is attributed to him? but, What do we know if we do not know that Rabbi X really said what is attributed to him? What sort of historical work can we do if we cannot do what Frankel, Graetz, and Krochmal thought we could do?

V

Since the contribution of the nineteenth and early twentieth century historians in the talmudic area was to biography, let me now report the results of a considerable scholarly program of the past nearly two decades. I refer, specifically, to the study of the lives and thought of the rabbis -- "Tannaim" -- who are supposed to have flourished between the destruction of the Second Temple in 70 and the advent of Bar Kokhba in 132 and who are therefore associated with the period, if not the locus, of Yavneh. My Life of Yohanan ben Zakkai (1962) marks the end of an old epoch in methodology, and my Development of a Legend: Studies on the Traditions concerning Yohanan ben Zakkai (1970) signals the beginning of the new one in this area of study. A series of studies and dissertations has been successfully accomplished. These have repeatedly produced a few significant results.

First, in the study of the traditions attributed to, and stories told about, the earlier rabbis, we have to take account of three wholly distinct types of material which seem to have no influence upon, or connection with, one another. These are legal, exegetical, and "biographical."

The legal materials attributed to all of the rabbis of Yavneh occur in the earliest rabbinic documents, Mishnah and Tosefta. In general they unfold, where the history can be assessed, in a disciplined and orderly way. As I showed in Eliezer ben Hyrcanus, what is attributed to Eliezer b. Hyrcanus in the names of his immediate disciples and contemporaries will unfold and be subject to development in later strata, literary or attributive. But it will never then be contradicted. Moreover, pericopae bearing evidence of later origination in documents after Mishnah, or bearing attestations of authorities of the third and fourth century, fall nearly wholly within the thematic framework established by materials bearing names of earlier attestations or occurring in Mishnah. This means that in the area of legal sayings there was no tendency promiscuously and without clear warrant to attribute to Eliezer whatever people wanted. On the contrary, there seems to have been a rather disciplined effort to amplify and augment materials assigned to him solely within the conceptions and principles already established in his name. This is a sign that the unfolding of the legal tradition in the three of four hundred years after the turn of the second century was governed by attention to what is said in the name of the earlier authorities and will not be characterized by attribution to an early authority of an idea first invented later on, for instance, for the purpose of securing for that new idea the prestige of the name of the revered and ancient master.

When, by contrast, we come to exegetical materials, that is, sayings on the meaning of Scriptural verses given in the name of Yavnean authorities, we find it simply impossible to relate what is said on Scripture to what is said on law. Time and again, the students of the traditions assigned to Yavnean rabbis have been stymied by the problem of how to relate the exegetical to the legal corpus. What they find in Genesis Rabbah or Leviticus Rabbah, the earliest complications of exegetical sayings, and what they find in Mishnah and in Tosefta, or even in the two Talmuds, are simply without apparent relevance to one another. Nor are the exegetical materials themselves susceptible to the sort of study of development and disciplined amplification referred to in connection with the legal ones. In the exegetical compilations, Eliezer, Ishmael, Tarfon, and Gamaliel simply supply names to which exegeses are assigned without (as-yet-perceived) rhyme or reason. The exception will be reference in the legal exegetical compilations, particularly Sifra and Sifre, to legal rulings of Mishnah-Tosefta, in which case the point is to demonstrate that said rulings derive from exegesis, not from reason. These self-evidently are secondary to, and dependent upon, Mishnah-Tosefta and in no way change the picture.[9]

As to "biographical" materials, by which are meant sayings or stories in which a rabbi's name is mentioned, these are of two kinds. In the first, a rabbi's name is used without any clear claim that a particular individual and his intellectual or moral traits come under discussion. There will be set sequences of names, e.g., Eliezer, Joshua, Gamaliel, Aqiba. But what is said about, or done with, those names bears no relationship whatever to biography, that is, to what a particular individual said or did. In the second, a particular rabbi's name is used in a clearly homiletical story, e.g., how Tarfon tended to his mother's needs. Even if we were to believe all of the stories presented to us as "biographical," we should have very little biography for the earlier rabbis. The reason is that the homilies all together add up to no effort, even casual and unsystematic, to record what a given authority really said or did through a significant part of his lifetime. The blatant homiletical purpose precludes nineteenth century biography in these "biographical" materials.

A further insuperable barrier to biography is the absence of a generally accessible framework of biography for individual rabbis. There is no effort to report the outlines of a single authority's career, beginning to end. Because of that fact, even if all the sayings could be shown really to have been said by the rabbi in whose mouth they are set, and all the deeds really to have been done by him, we still should not have a hope of writing the sort of biography which Graetz and Frankel and their successors proposed to do. Their failure was apparent even at the outset: they really had nothing much to say and, when the sermons came to an end, so did their biographies.[10]

Since the three kinds of materials given in the name of a particular rabbi bear virtually no internal interrelationships, on the one hand, they must be used for purposes other than the composition of biographies. For even if we concentrate on the legal sayings, inclusive of the stories of various types, whether precedents or illustrations, we come to insuperable problems. These are generated by the documents in which said sayings occur. If we were to propose to describe a given authority's legal ideas, that is, his religious philosophy expressed through concrete teachings on the conduct of ordinary life, we should want to begin with some evidence that what a given authority is supposed to have said really has been said by him. Otherwise, our account of his legal ideas is really not intellectual biography at all. But when we approach the diverse documents of the law, we find that the sayings attributed to all authorities are given in highly patterned and stereotype language, so that it is hardly possible to claim that, to begin with, we have in our hands anything like ipsissima verba. We may have access to what an authority thought. That has yet to be demonstrated, and I think it is beyond proof. But we rarely can show, and therefore do not know, that what he thought has been preserved in the words in which he expressed his thought.

We often can demonstrate the opposite. For Mishnah and Tosefta are documents formulated in the processes of redaction. What the redactors have done to create Mishnah, in particular, is to revise the whole of the received corpus into the language and redactional constructions of their own preference.[11] I am inclined to think that, prior to the time of "Our Holy Rabbi," Judah the Patriarch, materials were collected along the lines of a single authority's name, or of a single formal pattern, or of a single principle of law affecting diverse topics of law. But Rabbi's preference clearly is to group materials not in the name of a given authority, form, or abstract principle, but, essentially, topically, even though the sherds and remnants of materials brought together along other lines do remain in our hands. It follows, in any event, that while what is attributed to a given authority may or may not derive from him or his circle of disciples, we have no hope of presenting sizable bodies of sayings in the exact words spoken by a given authority.

VI

Since these are the facts, it must be concluded that the effort to recover the biographies of individual rabbis of the late first and early second centuries is not feasible. It seems to me that the same conclusion holds for the rabbis who lived in the later second century, since the literary facts pertinent to Aqiba apply without much variation to Judah, Simeon, Meir, or Yosé. The state of the question of the rabbis of the third and fourth century is apt to be shaped by the nature of the quite different processes of literary formulation and transmission which produced the Talmuds in which their materials in the main are preserved, on the one side, and those same processes which yield the Midrashic compilations, on the other. These have not been critically assessed in detail, so we cannot yet come to conclusions on the promise of rabbinic biography for the "Amoraic" period.

We hardly are justified, however, to conclude that we learn nothing about earlier Rabbinic Judaism from the study of the sayings and stories assigned to its founding generations. On the contrary, once we ask the correct questions, we find we learn much worth knowing. In the study of the history and character of the traditions in the names of Yavneans, for example, we learn what it was important to say about those authorities in the times in which those responsible for the later compilations did their work. We notice, first of all, that in the third and fourth and later centuries, the telling of stories about earlier rabbis was deemed an important part of the work of traditioning and handing on the Tannaitic corpus. Men who, in their own day and for a century thereafter, are important, e.g., in Mishnah-Tosefta, principally in connection with opinions in their names on mooted topics of Mishnah-Tosefta, now, in the strata of the Talmuds and in the Midrashic compilations require yet another treatment entirely. They must be turned into paragons of virtue and exemplars of the values of the growing rabbinic movement. Long after their legal traditions had come to closure, their "biographies" continue to grow in response to a self-evident need to expand the modes by which Rabbinic tradition would express itself and preserve and impart its teachings. The histories of the traditions of the several authorities of Yavneh prove beyond doubt that it is in the third and fourth centuries that the telling of stories about rabbis of the first and second centuries, the making up of homilies about their deeds, and the provision of a more human visage for the ancient authorities became important to Rabbinic circles of both Palestine and Babylonia.

It furthermore should not be supposed that the attribution of sayings to authorities of the late first and second centuries bears no consequences for the study of the history of earlier Rabbinic Judaism. The contrary is the case. For we are able to devise a method by which we may test part of what is alleged in those attributions, which is that the saying belongs at a given point in the history of Rabbinic legal thinking, and not later. If to Aqiba is assigned a saying which in conception and logic is prior to one attributed to Judah or Meir, of the next generation, and which furthermore appears to generate the conception attributed to Judah or Meir, then we may fairly conclude that to the time of Aqiba belongs the conception of the saying given in his name. That sort of conclusion may not appear so satisfying, but upon that basis a fairly firm and solid history of the law and its religious and philosophical conceptions is to be worked out.

That kind of history in no way depends upon whether or not Aqiba really said what is attributed to him, but only whether we are able to find evidence that what is assigned to Aqiba or any other Yavnean is prior in conception or principle to what is assigned to Judah or Meir or any other Ushan after Bar Kokhba. Upon that basis a history of the unfolding of the law is to be founded. The consequent history of ideas further may be correlated with the great events of the age to which, it would seem reasonable, rabbis' thinking upon any important question necessarily responded, for instance, the Temple's destruction or Bar Kokhba's catastrophe. Once the history of the law is worked out for the Mishnah-Tosefta, we should have a fair picture of the foundations of the earlier stages of Rabbinic Judaism. These in turn will delineate the work which must follow.

VII

A sign of a field of study in flux is the incapacity of scholars to find common grounds for disagreement. At the present time the Talmud is read as history in two completely different ways. Those who do it one way cannot communicate with those who do it the other. For example, those who maintain the established theory of the character of the talmudic sayings and stories as facts of history, pure and simple, will present to those who do not the following arguments: 1) the rabbis were scrupulous about the truth; 2) facts incorrectly reported were challenged; 3) the holy rabbis of the Talmud surely would not lie. To these assertions, a master of the contrary viewpoint -- that talmudic stories, like biblical ones, have to be read in a critical spirit -- will reply with such words as "sometimes" and "probably." That is, the rabbis sometimes were scrupulous about the truth. Facts sometimes were challenged when reported incorrectly. The holy rabbis of the Talmud probably would not lie. But, this master will add, "Rabbinic literature is full of obviously contradictory and grossly false statements. Contradictory reports stand unchallenged as often as they are corrected. The rabbinic literature contains innumerable nonsensical and obviously incredible statements." So, this master concludes, "If the rabbis were so scrupulous and painstaking as you pretend, how do you account for the enormous mass of claptrap they handed down?"[12]

Clearly, an argument phrased in the language of piety provokes the language of anti-piety, as well it should. But it appears to me that the argument is poorly phrased when the "veracity" of "the rabbis" is made the issue. What really requires attention is the identification of the things we shall concur to regard as facts and the questions to which these facts are claimed to be relevant. An Israeli graduate student (of American origin) who attended a conference at which issues such as those under discussion here were raised made the following comment:

> I am used to historians who argue with one another by showing that the hypothesis suggested by competitors is either contradicted by some known datum or necessarily involved or extravagant to explain the known data, as a simpler hypothesis would equally do. That is, everyone assumes that the few known data, which by themselves do not give us an understandable picture, are the surviving fragments of a 'building' which once stood. The historian's job is to suggest what the building looked like.

Now this conception of the writing of history confuses history with mathematics. It is, indeed, a conception possible only for a graduate student who has heard lectures but given none, read and criticized many books but not yet formulated even his own thesis-topic.[13]

But the insight that no longer is there any agreement whatever on what constitutes facts and how facts are discovered and defined is significant. I think it is entirely sound and accurate, not only for the conference on which the student comments, but also for the state of the field of the Talmud as history. That is why the sort of discourse about "the holy rabbis' not telling lies" is possible. For, as I think is clear from the perspective of historical studies, we are not entirely sure what we mean by the truth. That is why we cannot say what is an untruth. We in the humanities do our work in an age of powerful, conflicting currents of thought. There is little argument on fundamental issues of method and theories of knowledge. It is no wonder that the character of the work done in this first quarter of the second century of the study of the Talmud as history should appear to be diverse and lacking a common core of consensus and concurrence. Since that is so of society at large, why should it not be so of scholarship?

WORKS CONSULTED

Alon, Gedelia

1954-1955   Toledot hayyehudim be'eres yisra'el betequpat hammishnah vehattalmud. 2 vols. Tel Aviv.

1957-58   Mehqarim betoledot yisra'el. 2 vols. Tel Aviv. Trans. Israel Abrahams: Jews, Judaism and the Classical World. Studies in Jewish History in the Times of the Second Temple and Talmud. Jerusalem, 1977.

Biderman, Israel M.

1976   Mayer Balaban. Historian of Polish Jewry. New York.

Boyce, Mary

1975   A History of Zoroastrianism. Leiden: E.J. Brill.

Cherniss, Harold

1935   Aristotle's Criticism of PreSocratic Philosophy. New York: Octagon.

1944   Aristotle's Criticism of Plato and the Academy. New York.

1945   The Riddle of the Early Academy. Berkely and Los Angeles: University of California Press.

Gereboff, Joel

1973   "The Pioneer: Zecharias Frankel." pp. 59-75 in The Modern Study of the Mishnah. Ed. J. Neusner. Leiden: E.J. Brill.

1979   Tarfon. Brown Judaic Studies. Missoula: Scholars Press.

Ginzberg, Louis

1955   "The Significance of the Halachah for Jewish History." On Jewish Lore and Law. Philadelphia: The Jewish Publication Society of America (orig. 1929).

Green, William S.

1977   Men and Institutions in Earlier Rabbinic Judaism. Brown Judaic Studies. Missoula: Scholars Press.

1978   "What's in a Name? -- The Problematic of Rabbinic 'Biography.'" pp. 77-96 in Approaches to Ancient Judaism. Missoula: Scholars Press.

1979   Joshua ben Hananiah. Leiden: E.J. Brill.

Kadushin, Max

   1964   Worship and Ethics. A Study in Rabbinic Judaism. Evanston:
          Northwestern University Press.

Kanter, Shamai

   1979   Gamaliel of Yavneh. Brown Judaic Studies. Missoula: Scholars
          Press.

Lasch, Christopher

   1977   Haven in a Heartless World. The Family Besieged. New York:
          Basic Books.

Moore, George Foot

   1921   "Christian Writers on Judaism." Harvard Theological Review
          14:197-254.

   1927   Judaism. 3 vols. Cambridge: Harvard University Press.

Neusner, Jacob

   1962   A Life of Yohanan ben Zakkai. Ca. 1--80 C.E. Leiden: E.J. Brill.

   1965-70   A History of the Jews in Babylonia. 5 vols. Leiden: E.J. Brill.

   1970a   Development of a Legend: Studies on the Traditions Concerning
          Yohanan ben Zakkai. Leiden: E.J. Brill.

   1970b   Formation of the Babylonian Talmud: Studies on the Achieve-
          ments of Late Nineteenth and Twentieth Century Historical and
          Literary-Critical Research. Leiden: E.J. Brill.

   1971   The Rabbinic Traditions about the Pharisees before 70. 3 vols.
          Leiden: E.J. Brill.

   1973a   Eliezer ben Hyrcanus. The Tradition and the Man. 2 vols.
          Leiden: E.J. Brill.

   1973b   The Idea of Purity in Ancient Judaism. Leiden: E.J. Brill.

   1973c   Invitation to the Talmud. A Teaching Book. New York: Harper &
          Row.

   1973d   Modern Study of the Mishnah. Leiden: E.J. Brill.

   1974-77   A History of the Mishnaic Law of Purities. 22 vols. Leiden: E.J.
          Brill.

Porton, Gary

   1976   The Traditions of Rabbi Ishmael. 4 vols. Leiden: E.J. Brill.

Primus, Charles

   1977   Aqiba's Contribution to the Law of Zera'im. Leiden: E.J. Brill.

Saldarini, Anthony J.

   1976   "Review: History of the Mishnaic Law of Purities I-III." Journal
          of Biblical Literature 95/1:151.

Sandmel, Samuel

   1978   Judaism and Christian Beginnings. New York: Oxford University
          Press.

Sarason, Richard S.
1979   A History of the Mishnaic Law of Agriculture. Demai. Leiden:
            E.J. Brill.
Schechter, Solomon
1970   Studies in Judaism. 3 vols. Paterson, NJ: Atheneum.
Scholem, Gershom
1960   Jewish Gnosticism, Merkabah Mysticism, and Talmud
            Tradition. Based on the Israel Goldstein Lectures, Delivered at
            the Jewish Theological Seminary of America. New York: Jewish
            Theological Seminary of America.
Schorsch, Ismar
1975   Heinrich Graetz. The Structure of Jewish History and Other
            Essays. New York: Jewish Theological Seminary of America.
Smallwood, Mary
1976   The Jews under Roman Rule. Leiden: E.J. Brill.
Smith, Jonathan Z.
1978   Map is Not Territory. Studies in the History of Religions. Studies
            in Judaism in Late Antiquity. Leiden: E.J. Brill.
Smith, Morton
1963   "A Comparison of Early Christian and Early Rabbinic Tradition."
            Journal of Biblical Literature 82:169-76.
1968   "Historical Method in the Study of Religion." History and
            Theory. Studies in the Philosophy of History, Beiheft 8. On
            Method in the History of Religions. Ed. James S. Helfer.
            Middletown: Wesleyan University Press.
Zahavy, Tzvee
1977   The Traditions of Eleazar ben Azariah. Brown Judaic Studies,
            Missoula: Scholars Press.

NOTES

[1]Compare my History of the Mishnaic Law of Purities (1977, XVII:202-220) on the Houses of Shammai and Hillel as represented by second-century authorities such as Meir, Judah, Simeon, and their contemporaries. I am able to show that attributed to the ancient Houses are positions on issues moot after Bar Kokhba's War, and that the opinions assigned to the Houses by the second century authorities are suspiciously similar to those held by the second century masters. The second century figures play an active part in the formation of the "tradition" of the Houses. Since the same authorities give in their own names what they also state in the names of the Houses, there can be little doubt that the attributions to the Houses are, in fact, invented and fictitious. This is especially likely because the authorities of the period after 70, which intervenes between the Houses and their

epigones, are remarkable ignorant of the principles espoused by the Houses and even of the basic issues debated by them. A gap of over a century in a continuous tradition is curious.

[2]See S.C. Humphreys (1975). She states:

One of the factors influencing the intellectual to adopt a transcendental perspective appears to be the need to make his work comprehensible to an audience widely extended in space and continuing indefinitely into posterity. How far is our own appreciative response to these works -- and especially to the rationalism of the Greek philosophers -- due to the authors' deliberate intention of transcending limitations of social structure and temporal horizons? How far is this successful transcendence due to content and how far to form, to the structuring of the communication in such a way that it contains within itself enough information to make it immediately comprehensible? Is this a common quality of rational discourse and of "classic" works of art?

[3]I pay little attention to Geiger in what follows because his work had little influence on the course of talmudic historiography. The main lines of research followed from Frankel, for biography, and Graetz, for narrative history.

[4]Ibid. Historical study also served as an instrument in the attack on talmudic tradition and defense of Reform Judaism in Poland in the same period. See Biderman (1976:19-44).

[5]Ibid.

[6]Gereboff concludes as follows:

For Frankel Rabbi was the organizer and the law-giver. He compiled the Mishnah in its final form, employing a systematic approach. The Mishnah was a work of art; everything was "necessary" and in its place. All these claims are merely asserted. Frankel gives citations from Mishnaic and Amoraic sources, never demonstrating how the citations prove his contentions. Frankel applied his theory of positive-historical Judaism, which depicted Jewish life as a process combining the lasting values from the past with human intelligence in order to face the present and the future, to the formation of the Mishnah. The Mishnah was the product of human intelligence and divine inspiration. Using their intelligence, later generations took what they had received from the past and added to it. Nothing was ever removed. Frankel's work has little lasting value. He was, however, the first to analyze the Mishnah critically and historically; and this was his importance.

[7]These are briefly summarized and criticized by Urbach (1975:1-18).

[8]See A. Buechler (1956, 1912, 1928) and G. Alon (1957-58). Alon's lecture notes were published as Toledot hayyehudim be eres yisra el betequfat hammishnah vehattalmud (1954-55). These are uneven, and most of the work on ancient history is seriously out of date.

[9]Compare my History of the Mishnaic Law of Purities. VII. Negaim. Sifra (1975:1-12, 211-30).

[10]I owe this point to Morton Smith.

[11]This is demonstrated at some length and systematically in my History of the Mishnaic Law of Purities. XXI. The Redaction and Formulation of the Order of Purities in Mishnah and Tosefta (1977:Chap. VII).

[12]I here paraphrase a correspondence between a distinguished American scholar and an equally accomplished Israeli one about the veracity of talmudic stories about rabbis and attributions of sayings to rabbis. Language in quotation marks is drawn from the actual correspondence. I am not free to reveal the names of the participants. The argument did take place in precisely the terms in which I represent it.

[13][The graduate student is now a junior faculty member at the Hebrew University of Jerusalem. Where else!]

23. THE RABBINIC TRADITIONS ABOUT THE PHARISEES
IN MODERN HISTORIOGRAPHY
[CCAR Journal, 1972, 19:78-108 = Method and Meaning in
Ancient Judaism (Chico, 1981) 3:185-216]

Four sources of information about the Pharisees come down from antiquity; the
pertinent materials in the Gospels, the references of Josephus, the various sayings
attributed to, and stories about, pre-70 "rabbis" in talmudic and related literature, and the
Apocryphal and Pseudepigraphic books attributed -- generally without adequate reason --
by modern scholarship to Pharisaic authors. Of these sources, the third is by far the
largest. In Rabbinic Traditions about the Pharisees before 70 (Leiden, 1971, I-III) I
analyzed those traditions from various critical perspectives and suggested what use may
be made of them by critical historians. In doing so I have attempted to close the immense
culture-gap separating contemporary historical method from the way in which even
contemporary talmudic historians make use of the talmudic literature for historical
purposes.

I
HISTORICAL STUDY OF TALMUDIC LITERATURE

The study of talmudic and related literature for historical purposes stands
conceptually and methodologically a century and half behind biblical studies. While
biblical literature has for that long been subjected to the criticism of scholars who did not
take for granted the presuppositions and allegations of the text, talmudic literature was
studied chiefly in yeshivot, whose primary interests were not historical to begin with, and
whose students credulously took at face value both the historical and the legal sayings and
stories of the talmudic sages. Here the influences of literary and historical criticism
emanating from universities were absent. The circle of masters and disciples was
unbroken by the presence of nonbelievers; those who lost the faith left the schools. When
talmudic literature was studied in universities, it was mainly for philological, not
historical, purposes.

Those Talmudists, such as Abraham Geiger and Louis Ginzberg, moreover, who did
acquire a university training, including an interest in history, and who also continued to
study talmudic materials, never fully overcame the intellectual habits ingrained from
their beginnings in yeshivot. Characteristic of talmudic scholarship is the search, first,
for underlying principles to make sense of discrete, apparently unrelated cases, second,
for distinctions to overcome contradictions between apparently contradictory texts, and
third, for hiddushim, or new interpretations of particular texts. That exegetical approach
to historical problems which streses deductive thought, while perhaps appropriate for
legal studies, produces egregious results for history, for it too often overlooks the problem

of evidence: How do we know what we assert? What are the bases in actual data to justify new ideas in small matters, or, in large ones, the postulation of comprehensive principles of historical importance? Ginzberg's famous theory (cited below) that the disputes of the Houses of Shammai and Hillel and the decrees of the earlier masters reflect economic and social conflict in Palestine is not supported by reference to archaeological or even extra-talmudic literary evidence. Having postulated that economic issues were everywhere present. Ginzberg proceeded to postulate to "explain" a whole series of cases. The "explanations" are supposed to demonstrate the validity of the postulate, but in fact merely repeat and illustrate it. What is lacking in each particular case is the demonstration that the data could not equally well -- or even better -- be explained by some other postulate or postulates. At best we are left with "this could have been the reason," but with no concrete evidence that this was the reason. Masses of material perhaps originally irrelevant are built into pseudohistorical structures which rest on nothing more solid than "we might suppose that." The deductive approach to the study of law ill serves the historian. One of the most common phrases in the historical literature before us is, "If this supposition is sound, then..." I found it in nearly every historian who wrote in Hebrew. It is Talmudics extended to the study of history.

I do not unreservedly condemn Talmudics, except in connection with historical studies. It is a great tradition, interesting and important as a phenomenon of intellectual history, beautiful and fascinating as an intellectual exercise, and a powerful instrument for apologetics and for the reinterpretation necessary to make ancient laws and doctrines apply to modern problems. I should not even deny that it may be a valuable instrument for philosophical research. For instance, Morton Smith comments on the work of Harry A. Wolfson, "Wolfson's achievements by his 'hypothetico-deductive method' are justly famous. But when Wolfson uses the method, the hypotheses are made from a minute study of the primary sources, and the deductions are checked at every point by careful consideration of the historical evidence, and those which cannot be confirmed are clearly indicated as conjectural." My objection is that when used by men without Wolfson's historical training, mastery, and conscience, the method lends itself easily to abuse, to the invention of imaginary principles and distinctions for which there is no historical evidence whatsoever, and to the deduction of consequences which never appear in the texts. It can too easily be used to obscure real differences of opinion or practice, to explain away the evidences of historical change, and to produce a picture of antiquity which has no more similarity to the facts that the Judaism of contemporary New York does to that of ancient Palestine.

A further, even more serious impediment to the development of the historical study of talmudic literature was the need for apologetics. Talmudists with university training encountered the anti-Pharisaic, anti-Judaic, and frequently anti-Semitic attitudes of Christian scholars, who carried out polemical tasks of Christian theology in the guise of writing history. The Jewish historians undertook the defense. Two polemical themes recur.

First, the Christians' account of the Pharisees ignores rabbinic sources, therefore is incomplete. The reason is that the Christian scholars do not know the rabbinic literature, therefore whatever they say may be discounted because of their "ignorance."

Second, the Pharisees were the very opposite of what Christians say about them.

The former polemic produced the Christian response that the rabbinical materials are not reliable, because they are "late" or "tendentious." Many Christian scholars drew back from using rabbinic materials or relied on what they presumed to be accurate, secondary accounts of them, because they were thoroughly intimidated by the claims of the Jewish opposition as to the difficulty of properly understanding the materials, and because they had slight opportunity to study the materials with knowledgeable scholars of Judaism.

The latter polemic -- to prove the Pharisees the opposite of what had been said of them -- was all too successful. When Christian scholars became persuaded that the earlier Christian view had been incorrect, they took up the polemic in favor of the Pharisees. In doing so, they of course relied on Jewish scholarship and took over uncritically its uncritical attitude toward the material. Consequently, on both sides, sources were more often cited as facts than analyzed as problems. We commonly find a source cited without attention to how the citation is supposed to prove the "fact" it purportedly contains. Systematic analysis of texts is rare; allusion to unexamined texts is commonplace.

Reservations about the method and results of previous scholars should not be taken as evidence that I consider their work to be utterly worthless, except as history. On the contrary, I have learned from earlier writings and rely upon some of their results. But I should not have done my work if I had not considered all previous studies of the rabbinic traditions about the Pharisees to be seriously inadequate, because, in general, the historical question has been asked too quickly and answered uncritically. The inadequacy results from the false presumption that nearly all sources, appearing in any sort of document, early, late, or medieval, contain accurate historical information about the men and events of which they speak. The historians are further to be blamed for allowing the theologians to set the issue: Were the Pharisees really hypocrites? On the part of the Jewish scholars, the issues were, What shall we say in response to the Christian theological critique of Pharisaism? How shall we disprove the allegations of the Christians' holy books? On the Christian side, there were few "historians" worthy of the name, for most served the Church and not the cause of accurate and unbiased historical knowledge. Since the Christian theological scholars set the agendum, the Jewish ones can hardly be condemned for responding to it, especially since contemporary anti-Semitism was both expressed and aided by the Christian scholarly assessment of Pharisaism. In fact the European Jewish scholars turn out to have been fighting for the lives of the Jews of their own day and place. They lost that fight. It was a worthy effort, but it was not primarily an exercise of critical scholarship, and it seriously impeded the development of scholarly criticism.

The history of scholarship on the Pharisees thus cannot be divorced from the history of Judaism and Christianity in the nineteenth and twentieth centuries, from the sociology

of the Jews in Europe and the USA, and from the interrelationships between the two
religious traditions. It is not my problem to describe the course of those complex and
inter-related histories. Instead, I have to demonstrate in detail how those handicaps
pointed out above -- anachronistic presuppositions, talmudic method, and apologetic
purpose -- have vitiated previous studies of the Pharisees. To do so, I shall rely upon the
device of substantial quotations from some important and influential studies on the
Pharisees. The reader will observe two recurrent faults: first, the claim that a story
contains an exact historical record of what actually happened; second, the tendency to say
far more than all the data together permit. It might have been better to state the
essential argument of each book or article, then to point out what is wrong with it. But to
do so, I should have had to enter into the discussion of issues defined by historians to begin
with not competent to formulate worthwhile issues for argument. I thereby should have
implicitly suggested that the modern historiographical tradition had formulated arguable
questions, and that its fundamental grasp of the evidence was sound. This is the opposite
of the truth. I therefore cannot attempt to refute, point by point, statements which are
made upon no foundation other than a false conception of the character of the evidence
and of the nature of historical inquiry.

II

APOLOGETIC

Two examples of the apologetic literature suffice, R. Travers Herford, The
Pharisees (repr. Boston, 1962) and Leo Baeck, The Pharisees and Other Essays (N.Y.,
1949). They mark the high point of the apologetic movement. Herford observes that the
German and other non-Jewish scholars "all seem to have the contrast with Christianity
more or less consciously present in their minds, not realizing that two things cannot be
rightly compared until it has first been ascertained what each of them is in itself... To
call the New Testament as the chief witness upon the question who the Pharisees really
were is false in logic and unsound in history." The Jewish scholars "know what Pharisaism
is like from the inside" -- as if the rationalistic Judaism of the nineteenth century were
still Pharisaism! For his historical account, Herford turns to Josephus (a prejudiced and
unreliable source), whose story he embellishes with some talmudic stories (mostly late
second and third century A.D.). The descriptions of "Pharisaic religion" then draw upon
the whole corpus or rabbinic literature, most of it relevant to a much later period than
that considered by Herford.

For Baeck, the Pharisees were "a movement within the Jewish people," "not a party
or a sect [manifestly false]. They were ascetics, Essenes [certainly not], and separatists."
They were committed to the "search for the exact meaning and the ultimate [?] law," and
were primarily a movement of exegetes of Scriptures. "The Pharisaic trend found its
leaders in the scribes." The Pharisees were "prominent figures, especially in the spriritual
life." We have "hardly any names of Sadducean scribes." The Pharisees were also "the
men of the synagogue," against the Sadducees, "the men of the Temple." Baeck concludes
"Pharisaism represents a great attempt to achieve the full domination of religion over

life, both over the life of the individual and the life of the collectivity... It took the idea of saintliness in earnest... Pharisaism was a heroic effort to prepare the ground for the kingdom of God." One could make an equally good case for the proposition that the Pharisees were concerned to limit as precisely as possible the claims of religion upon life. Various Tannaim -- whom Baeck would have considered Pharisees, though they were not -- were notoriously hostile to preparations for the coming of the Kingdom, for one thing.

III

CRITICAL STUDIES

From the late nineteenth century onward, a few historians have made intelligent use of talmudic materials. They have avoided assuming that rabbinic texts always are accurate accounts of things that really happened. They have compared various versions of a story without supposing that every detail of every version contributes to a factual picture. They have used common sense. The pseudorthodox reading of the materials therefore had to compete with the dispassionate historical evaluation of sources, item by item. Israel Lévi, and his student M. Stourdzé in France, and E. Schürer in Germany at the turn of the twentieth century are the most important early representatives of the critical approach. Lévi and Stourdzé examined a few specific pericopae. Schürer, by contrast, wrote a complete history of the period before 70 A.D. Characteristic of both is a certain reserve, a distance from the values and beliefs of the storytellers.

Israel Lévi, "Les sources talmudiques de l'histoire juive. I. Alexandre Jannée et Simon ben Schetah. II. La rupture de Jannée avec les Pharisiens," REJ 35, 1897, pp. 213-223, observes that many stories used by historians for the reconstruction of Pharisaic history are no more than aggadot, imaginary anecdotes for edification and amusement. This observation then is illustrated by the stories of Simeon, Jannaeus and the Nazirites. Lévi compares the texts and notes a few of the differences among them. He finds it incongruous that the Persian embassy wants nothing more than to hear wise teachings of the rabbi. The king is represented as naive. The whole is in the spirit of a fable: "It would not be difficult to uncover in medieval literature numerous parallels, not to mention equivalent fables in Midrashic literature, to which no one assigns historical value."

George Foot More, "Simeon the Righteous," Jewish Studies in Memory of Israel Abrahams (N.Y., 1927), pp. 348-364, alludes to the rabbinical stories, concluding only that Simeon "stands out in the memory of the age from which the legends come as the end of an epoch." He looks in second century A.D. problems for the animus of the stories of Meir and Judah about the Egyptian temple and treats the context in which the stories stand. None of these pericopae serves Moore as the basis for his comments on the historical Simeon. At best, he argues, the "Simeon... of the rabbinical sources" is to be put in the period located on the basis of other, more persuasive evidences. Moore's account of Simeon stands out. He both mastered and respected the talmudic materials, but he read them in a critical spirit.

Morton Smith, "Palestinian Judaism in the First Century," Israel: Its Role in Civilization, ed. Moshe Davis (N.Y,. 1956), pp. 67-81, observes that Josephus's picture of the predominance of the Pharisees is drawn not in War but in Antiquities, written twenty years after the War. "Every time he mentions them he emphasizes their popularity. It is almost impossible not to see in such a rewriting of history a bid to the Roman government... The Pharisees, he says again and again, have by far the greatest influence with the people. Any government which alienates them has trouble... Josephus's discovery of these important political facts (which he ignored when writing the Jewish War) may have been due partly to a change in his personal relationship with the Pharisees... But... the more probable explanation is that in the meanwhile the Pharisees had become the leading candidates for Roman support in Palestine and were already negotiating for it." But much of Palestinian Judaism was not Pharisaic. Further, "the influence of the Pharisees with the people... is not demonstrated by the history he records." Third, "even Josephus' insistence on their influence 'with the multitude' implies a distinction between them and the people whom they influenced." Smith demonstrates how one must read and make use of all sources, showing the importance of asking, Why does the narrator wish to tell us this history? What does he want to prove by it? How does the story fit into the larger narrative, and what is the purpose of that narrative? The historians who take for granted the "historicity" of talmudic stories tend also to treat New Testament and Josephus narratives in the same way. Smith's brief essay teaches the proper approach.

The comparative study of talmudic and Hellenistic literature is in the hands of Henry A. Fischel, for example, "Studies in Cynicism and the Ancient Near East: The Transformations of a Chria," in J. Neusner, ed., Religions in Antiquity, Essays in Memory of Erwin Ramsdell Goodenough (Leiden, 1968), pp 372-411. In "Story and History: Observations on Greco-Roman Rhetoric and Pharisaism," in American Oriental Society, Middle Western Branch, Semi-Centennial Volume. Asian Studies Research Institute, Oriental Series, no. 3, ed. Denis Sinor (Bloomington, 1969) pp. 59-88, Fischel observes (p. 65), "If we find... that the political fable plays a role in both [Greco-Roman and Near Eastern] cultures, we are fully aware of the fact that the animals never actually did what they are said to have done in the narrative... If, however, this genre is transformed into a type of anecdote in which the clever or good animal is replaced by a Sage and the dumb or wicked animal by his antagonist... the modern scholar has too often been tempted to consider every detail as true history." Further, "The cynicizing chria with many of its major motifs, forms and elements is found also in Tannaitic literature. Without exception, all the stories on Hillel and Elder... prove to be Greek-chriic, representing either (a) a complete Greek chria; (b) a composite of several chriic parts; or (c) an aggregate of the smallet meaningful chriic elements... Furthermore, some Hillel chriae are joined to one another within a narrative framework precisely as in Hellenistic sources." The motif, for instance, of the sage's forgetting the essentials of his teaching, or of his suddenly and unexpectedly becoming the head of the academy, is commonplace.

Fischel further noted, "Similarly, another startling phenomenon is found in both cultures. The same gnome... may be quoted in the name of several different Sages, thus making for contradictory features in the overall portrait of a particular Sage. Further, and more important, the same gnome may occur: (1) as the punch-line of a chria; (2) as an independent unit, without a story; (3) anonymously, often as a popular proverb;

(4) occasionally as the moral of a fable. It thus seems that the ascription of a *sententia* to a Sage might merely have been another means of stressing his importance and does not reflect an actual teaching of his." The Golden Rule is best example: "The point... is that Greco-Roman rhetoric reactiviated and reformulated older original materials in the Near East" [Note: "Lev. 19:18 may thus have been the original form of the Golden Rule in earlier Jewish culture."] Fischel counts thirty to thirty-five examples of cynicizing chria in talmudic literature, "whereas there are probably more than 1,000 in Hellenistic literature and the papyri." In the chria "all Sages were once slaves, all were abjectly poor, and almost all once did menial work. Only on these grounds can the interdependence of Cleanthes items and Hillel anecdotes be fully established and their probably non-historicity be suggested."

Fischel has not yet fully presented his result and evidence, so it is difficult to comment on the larger implications of his monumental conception. In general I am much impresssed by the dazzling erudition, breadth, and originality of his published account. One may wonder whether he occasionally slips into the state of "parallelomania," such as is described by Samuel Sandmel, "Parallelomania," JBL 81, 1962, pp. 1-13. In time to come Fischel may find occasion to reflect upon the distinctions among parallels and their meanings discovered by Morton Smith, Tannaitic Parallels to the Gospels (Philadelphia, 1951), and also alluded to in my Aphrahat and Judaism. The Christian-Jewish Argument in Fourth-Century Iran (Leiden, 1970), pp. 187-196. These several studies of the nature and meaning of parallels will serve not to contradict the significance of Fischel's work, but to refine his conceptional framework. Fischel's undertaking is unique. While others have noted various parallels between Hellenistic and talmudic literature, Fischel has carried out the work not on a sporadic or episodic basis, but thoroughly.

Another important area of critical study concerns the legal principles underlying discrete materials. Here the elucidation of the data has produced persuasive and striking results, especially when not accompanied by grandiose claims. Among the legal historians, Solomon Zeitlin seems to me to stand out. In his "Studies in Tannaitic Jurisprudence," Journal of Jewish Lore and Philosophy, 1, 1919, pp. 297-311, Zeitlin states, "Intention as a factor in Jewish law was first recognized and given a status by Hillel, who insisted that we ought to take into consideration not only the primary act of a man, but also his intention. This innovation is strenuously opposed by his colleague Shammai." Numerous Houses-disputes are explained in terms of this disagreement. Intention in laws of the Sabbath explains the Houses' differences. Work is forbidden "in which a man intends a particular result: any ML'KH-act in the doing of which the man contemplated no particular result is not forbidden."

S. Zeitlin, "Les principes des controverses halachiques entre les écoles de Schammai et de Hillel," REJ 93, 1932, pp 73-83, refers to four principles on which the Houses differed: 1. rabbis have the right to interpret and amend the laws through legal fictions; 2. rabbis may interpret the law according to its spirit, rather than its letter; 3. one should build a fence around the law; 4. intention is taken into account in the application of the law. In all four the Shammaites took a negative position, the Hillelites a positive one. As to M. Pe'ah 6:1, the difference of opinion pertains to the law of res nullius: if a person renounces his property rights, expressly stipulating that certain persons may not acquire that property, the object is regarded by Meir (a Shammaite) as res nullius, for at the moment that the rights are abandoned, the object becomes ownerless. Yosi (a Hillelite) does not consider the object as res nullius, for in abandoning his rights the owner has not lost his title or his responsibility for the object. The disputes in M. Ed. 1:3 pertain to the same issue. Zeitlin assembles a number of other disputes in which the same principle recurs. Zeitlin concludes, "J'ai essaye de montrer que les controverses entre les écoles de Schammai et de Hillel sont fondées sur des principles légaux bien définis." What impresses me in these and related papers of Zeitlin is his careful and judicious use of the legal materials for essentially legal purposes, that is, the elucidation of the underlying principles of various discrete cases. Zeitlin here makes no historical claims (if we discount his assumption that attributions invariably are correct, and that assumption plays no significant role in his argument). He shows that concrete issues of specific cases reflect underlying disputes on important legal issues.

IV

TRADITIONAL STUDIES

Without doubt the most ambitious and impressive traditional historian of the rabbinic traditions about the Pharisees -- as of every other topic in "talmudic history" -- is Yishaq Isaak Halevy, Dorot HaRishonim (German title: Die Geschichte und Literatur Israels. Ic. Um fasst den Zeitraum von Ende der Hasmonäerzeit zur Einsetzung der römischen Landpfleger, Berlin-Vienna, 1923), I call him "traditional" because Halevy makes no pretense of approaching materials as a participant in the wissenschaftliche or scientific tradition. He enjoys destroying the results of those who do. But his thoroughness, profound knowledge of law, willingness to analyze texts in depth and to criticize all authorities, ancient and modern -- these mark Halevy as the greatest master of "talmudic history" of his or any other generation. Obviously, one cannot assent to his ridiculous conclusions. He regards as facts the allegations of the tradition as to its own history -- it begins at Sinai, or, least, before Ezra -- and of course takes for granted that what stories tell is what really happened, what laws prescribe is what actually was done. For him these are natural assumptions, but not impediments to the critical analysis of all problems.

V

PSEUDOCRITICAL STUDIES

I share Halevy's negative view of the result of "the science of Judaism," though my reasons are not the same as his. Halevy ridicules the misleading impression given by "the German sages" that they possess more acurate information than they actually have. What seems to me equally absurd is the gullible and uncritical use of talmudic traditions, combined with the pretentious claims that, for the first time, something both new and "scientific" is being done with them. All of the studies we are about to consider (and many others not alluded to) take for granted what should be the problem, namely, the facticity or "historicity" of the source. Frequently, they merely allude to a pericope, without citing or analyzing it. For example, one will find Hillel ousted the Bathryans by citing his masters Shema'iah and Abtalion, with an accompanying footnote, B. Qiddushin 66b. We hear nothing of the existence of several versions of how the author understands the introduction of new materials, the rearrangements of old, the inclusion of inter-polations of various sorts (including the names of S + A), and so on. The unwary reader will therefore assume that the historian has facts, and that the task is to interpret or explain facts. He will not see the frail foundations beneath such "facts."

In this respect, I carry forward the study of 'pseudorthodoxy" of Morton Smith, in "The Present State of Old Testament Studies," JBL 88, 1969, pp. 19-35. Smith defines pseudorthodoxy as "the attempt to reconcile the traditional beliefs about the OT with the undeniable results of scholarship." Of greatest interest here are Smith's remarks about higher criticism, "which has always been the bête noire of the pseudorthodox. They were clever enough to see that its results had to be accepted. On the other hand, to attack higher criticism was the accepted way of vindicating pseudorthodoxy. Therefore higher criticism had to be both attacked and accepted. What could be done? The solution was: to concentrate the attack on the greatest and most famous representative of higher criticism, to announce to the public that his 'system' had been destroyed, and to appropriate privately its elements." Smith's pseudorthodox, and our pseudocritical, scholars have only the "pseudo" in common. The pseudocritical scholars claim to accept a critical approach, but in pretending that the sources are accurate historical records, and in failing to articulate and defend that notion, they reveal the fundamentalist convictions which they both hold and claim to transcend. They do not argue with the critical scholars. They either villify or ignore them. [The fate of the essay at the beginning of this book is a case in point. Invite, then disinvite -- the best of all worlds.] Schürer is attacked; Moore's article on Simeon the Just and the full implications of Smith's on Josephus's picture of the Pharisees are simply ignored. Or the pseudocritical scholars will allege that they grant the presuppositions of the opposition, then completely bypass them, pretending nothing has changed. It comes down to the same thing. Ironically, we face the opposite of Smith's pseudorthodox: the pseudocritical scholars announce to the public that they are "critical" but privately they appropriate nothing whatever of the literary and historical-critical advances of the past century and a half of biblical studies.

What commonly characterizes the pseudocritical school are some or all of these qualities: first, deductive reasoning; second, arbitrary and groundless judgments as to the "historicity" and the lack of "historicity" of various individual pericopae; third, failure to bring to bear a wide range of evidence external to the talmudic materials; fourth, the assumption that whatever is alleged in any source is as well attested as what is alleged in any other; fifth, the endless positing of untested, and untestable, "possibilities"; sixth, the recurrent, and groundless claim that a story "must have been supported by tradition"; seventh, the repeated argument that if a story were not true, no one would have told or preserved it; eighth, the spinning out of large theories to take account of stories and sayings under some grand philosophical scheme (which is not much different from the next); ninth, a love of homiletics; tenth, the invention of new definitions for old data, e.g. the use of proto-Pharisees, to describe the dim figures who link the Pharisees we know about to the alleged, earlier men of the Great Assembly about whom we know nothing. But above all, presumably, must or may have been and perhaps, a few sentences later magically converted into was and certainly, everywhere recur. The pseudocritical scholars claim to write history, but the "historicity" of their histories is superficial, not profound. They concentrate on the exegesis of discrete pericopae. Further, they merely take up one rabbi after another in chronological order and describe as historical facts the stories and dicta attributed to him by any and all sources. The best they can do with disparate sources, e.g. Josephus and the Talmud, is to weave one together with the other, both are true, or one is false and the other true -- that exhausts their powers of historical imagination. They never get behind such sources to events or situations indicated by both but different from either.

Abraham Geiger, HaMiqra veTargumav (Hebrew translation by Y. L. Barukh of Urschrift und Übersetzungen der Bibel in ihrer Abhängigker von der innern Entwicklung des Judentums, Jerusalem, 1949) pp. 69-102, discusses the Sadducees and Pharisees, whom he sees as aristocrats versus republicans. Geiger stands at the beginning of modern Jewish scholarship on the Pharisees. His picture affected nearly every subsequent treatment of the subject, except for Halevy's. Abraham Geiger, Judaism and Its History (trans. by Charles Newburgh, N.Y., 1911) pp. 90-121, treats the Pharisees and related questions. The Pharisees were separatists (whatever that means), opposing the Sadducees, "the descendants of the priest estate in connection with the families of rank." The Pharisees "objected to having the sanctity of the priesthood placed so much in the foreground." The Pharisees managed "all institutions that were of great importance in the popular life." The Pharisees "were the very core, the brain and the brawn of the nation: their exertions were directed toward the establishment of equal rights for all [!] -- their fight was the fight that was repeated in all times when great interests are at stake, the fight against priest-craft and hierarchy, against privilege of individual classes, the fight for the very truth that not outward qualities alone, but inward religious conviction and consequent moral conduct constitute the proper worth of the man." "Hillel is a fully historical person." Legends... "emanate from his character, so that we must acknowledge that even if they did not actually come to pass, they are yet in full harmony with his character." He came from Babylonia as a poor man. He was meek and mild. For him "the essence of Judaism consists in love of man and mutual regard, in this respect of the dignity of man and the equality of all men..." The adherents of the School of Shammai "maintained in perfect accordance with their gloomy ways that it would be better for man never to have been born..." Pure credulity, in all.

Henrich Graetz, History of the Jews, II. From the Reign of Hyrcanus (135 B.C.E.) to the Completion of the Baylonian Talmud (500 C.E.) (trans. H. Szold, repr. Philadelphia, 1949) follows and paraphrases Josephus's narrative, into which he mixes talmudic materials, the whole then being embellished with homilies. The Pharisees, "the very center... of the nation, having above all things at heart the preservation of Judaism in the exact form in which it had been handed down, insisted upon all political undertakings, all public transactions, every national act being tried by the standard of religion." The Pharisees were not a party, "for the mass of the nation was inclined to Phariseeism..." They received their name "from the fact of their explaining the Scriptures in a peculiar manner, and of deriving new laws from this new interpretation." This repertoire of lugubrious homilies masquerading as historical facts set the fashion from Graetz's time onward.

The account of the Houses given by S. Mendelsohn shows an even more gullible approach, in "Bet Hillel and Bet Shammai," JE 3, pp. 115-116. He sees the Shammaites as restrictive, the Hillelites as moderate. Three hundred sixteen [exactly!] controversies are preserved in the Talmud, "affecting 221 halakot, 23 halakic interpretations, and 66 guardlaws; and out of the whole number only 55 present the Shammaites on the side of leniency." This pseudoprecise number marches from book to book. The Hillelites were "like their founder -- quiet, peace-loving men, accommodating themselves to circumstances and times... The Shammaites... stern and unbending like the originator of their school, emulated and even exceeded his severity." "They were intensely patriotic and would not bow to foreign rule. Their principles were akin to those of the Zealots" -- who were not notorious for loving peace. "As all the nations around Judea made a common cause with the Romans, the Zealots were naturally inflamed against every one of them; and therefore the Shammaites proposed to prevent all communication between Jew and Gentile..." The Hillelites did not agree: "Eleazar ben Ananias invited the disciples of both schools to meet at his house. Armed men were stationed at the door, and instructed to permit everyone to enter, but no one to leave. During the discussion that was carried on under these circumstances, many Hillelites are said to have been killed; and then and there the remainder adopted the restrictive propositions of the Shammaites, known in the Talmud as the 'Eighteen Articles.' On account of the violence which attended those enactments, which the Shammaites thus triumphed over the Hillelites was thereafter regarded as a day of misfortune." The ritual obeisance to "historical criticism" takes the form of said to have. But the phrase has not affected Mendelsohn's "historical" picture.

Our next example of the pseudocritical school must be taken more seriously. Louis Ginzberg, "The Significance of the Halachah for Jewish History," On Jewish Law and Lore (Philadelphia, repr. 1961), pp. 77-126, proposes "to demonstrate that the development of the halachah... is not a creation of the House of Study but an expression of life itself."

The decree of the Yosi's about the uncleanness of foreign countries and of glass was imposed "at the time when, as a result of the persecution by Antiochus Epiphanes, emigration from the Holy Land began. During that period contemporary leadership feared the threat of mass evacuation as a great danger to the nation and its land. Therefore, as a preventive measure, they ruled that foreign lands were impure." Ginzberg claims that glass was very expensive, though it seems to have been cheap. Many preferred glass vessels, "which could not become ritually impure, to locally produced earthenware and metal dishes, which required safeguarding against ritual impurity... When ritual impurity was decreed for glassware this competition was partially lessened, since glassware from

Tyre and Sidon no longer possessed the advantage of being free from the liability to ritual impurty" -- as if the masses kept the purity-laws!

Joshua's decree about what from Alexandria is similary accounted for: "It is... well known that the competition between the Holy Land and Egypt in the grain trade, and particularly in wheat, was very great indeed; when, consequently, Joshua ben Perahya became aware that some apprehension of impurity existed with respect to Alexandrian wheat, he used it as the reason for a restrictive decree intended for the benefit of Jewish farmers. He hoped that the majority of buyers would prefer the wheat of the Holy Land, which was not conditioned to receive impurity, to impure foreign wheat. His colleagues... disagreed, for they preferred for the sake of the general good to encourage competition in foodstuffs."

Simeon b. Shetah's decree on metal vessels came because "people began to import into the Holy Land other metals... In order to protect native products, the susceptibility to ritual impurity was also decreed on these foreign metals, lest they be preferred to the metals of the Holy Land..." To be sure, Palestine had no metals to speak of.

Before the Houses, "it is established... that there were not many conflicts of opinion among the sages of Israel." The differences between the Houses cannot be systematized. Many factors caused them. Shammai and Hillel did not found the Houses: they date back to the beginning of the Pairs. But then from the beginnings there were many conflicts of opinion, or Ginzberg contradicts himself.

The Pharisees were split into two wings, right and left, conservatives and progressives. The controversy about laying on of hands "stems from the differences between the conservatives and the progressives." "It is my view that the conflict among the Pairs was over the issue whether obligatory burnt-offerings and obligatory peace-offerings required the laying on of hands only in connection with votive burnt-offerings and votive peace-offerings or in the cases of a guilt-offering or sin-offering." The controversy involved four questions.

1.   The extent to which scholars were empowered to derive new enactments by means of biblical exegesis: The conservatives wanted to limit the authority of biblical exegesis as a source of new law. Therefore, laying on of hands was not required, since the Bible does not mention it.

2.   The participation of the public, not merely priests, in the Temple service: The progressives favored increasing the influence of the people on the Temple, therefore said the people may lay on hands.

3.   Use of laying on of hands as a means of increasing the return of the Jews to the Holy Land: The progressives wished to use the ritual as propaganda towards that end.

4.   Equality between Jews of the Holy Land and those of the diaspora in offering their sacrifices: The conservatives said it was sufficient for the Jews to send obligatory burnt-offerings. The Progressives said in favor of the diaspora that there is no distinction between votive and obligatory burnt-offerings; in both instances laying on of hands is required.

As to the differences between the Houses, "the usual interpretation is that these two Schools expressed the personalities of their founders, the conciliatory Hillel and the unyielding Shammai." But this is not so. The real difference goes back before the two masters: the differences were over social and economic policy. For example, Ginzberg cites M. Ber. 6:5, "If one pronounces a benediction over the bread, he need not recite one over the side-dishes..." "The reason for the disagreement was that bread was the main dish of the poor man's meal, and, therefore, once he recited a benediction over the bread, he thereby blessed the entire meal; for the rich man, however, who ate meat, fish, and all kinds of delicacies, bread was not the main dish. The school of Shammai... maintained that even cooked foods were not included in a benediction over bread." Other differences concerning the meal were "based on the class difference between the Schools."

As to the several cases in which the Houses differ on the matter of intention: "Primitive man reckoned only with the act, and not with the intention; a man was judged by his deeds and not by his thoughts... We therefore find the School of Shammai, the representatives of the conservatives, considered deed more important than thought. In many cases involving laws of things prohibited and permitted... they declared that deed is paramount, as over against the progressive view of the School of Hillel, who taught that an act not accompanied by intention is not to be considered an act."

Ginzberg's picture depends upon the presupposition, not only that the decrees were made by those to whom they were attributed, but also that they were enforced. The Pharisees were in control of the government. Whatever they decreed had the force of law. The Hasmoneans were subservient to their wishes even at the very outset of their rule (the Yosis). The decrees of the Yosis were confirmed by the monarch, who presumably "sat humbly" before the Pharisaic masters. The government was, moreover, both sophisticated in matters of economics, and also able to carry out sweeping decrees pretty much as the Pharisaic masters issued them. One could argue in Ginzberg's behalf that the Pharisees might have decided their legal questions by considerations of public interest even though they knew their decisions would produce no practical consequences. If the presupposition that the law made by Pharisees was enforced were false, that fact would not render the rest of the structure impossible. What is weak is that Ginzberg never raises the question of whether and how the Pharisees enforced their rulings.

He does not bring a shred of evidence to substantiate any of his theories, e.g. that there was mass emigration at the time of the Maccabees, that everyone kept the purity laws, that many preferred glass vessels, that Joshua had the power and knowledge to help out the farmers, and that they needed help; that people began to import other metals in the time of Simeon b. Shetah, and that he had the power to prevent it. The House's disputes go back a century and a half before the establishment of the Houses, even though we have no hint of that fact in the sources attributed to antecedent authorities. The Pharisees were split into conservatives and progressives; so too the Sadducees were conservative and the Pharisees progressive, and so on. Wherever we find two parties, the difference between them will be explained in the same way. Everything is argued on the basis of what sounds reasonable.

Louis Finkelstein, HaPerushim veAnshé Kenneset HaGedolah (N.Y., 1950: The Pharisees and the Men of the Great Synagogue) and The Pharisees: The Sociological Background of Their Faith (Philadelphia, 1962) carries forward the economic-sociological thesis of Ginzberg. For him the plebians are urban workers, against the rural gentry. Differences in wealth were secondary. The Houses did not debate old vs. new law. The real differences were between provincials and metropolitans; they reflected differences of habitat. The struggle was "carried on in Palestine for fifteen [!] centuries." For example, the Hillelites were sympathetic to the Judean grape-growers; the "patrician Shammaites" favored Galilean olive-producers accounting for the difference of opinion between the masters recorded in b. Shab. 17a. Likewise, Shema'iah, a plebeian, believed in the merit of the fathers. The patricians denied predetermination. "Abtalyon, the patrician, maintains that the miracle was caused by the merit of the Israelites themselves."

Isaiah Sonne, "The Schools of Shammai and Hillel Seen from Within," Louis Ginzberg Jubilee Volume. On the Occasion of his Seventieth Birthday. English Section (N.Y., 1945), pp. 275-293, observes, "Granted that the two schools represented two classes [rich and poor], we must not overlook the fact that the schools had to settle their class differences not on a purely practical, but primarily on an academic theoretical ground... the schools were compelled to exert their objective thinking faculties beside seeking the mere calculation of class interest." Sonne proceeds to elucidate the "immanent dialectic of the controversies." This had been the contention of A. Schwarz, Die Erleichterungen der Schammaiten und die Erschwerungen der Hilleliten (Vienna, 1893), who held that the differences between the Houses were based upon the Shammaites' rejection of Hillelite hermeneutic principles of interpretation. For Sonne, too, the Shammaites were more literal than the Hillelites. For example, the Shammaites opposed the use of the principle of analogy. Sonne posits, however, that the fundamental difference is between "the one and the many, which constitutes the fundamental rhythm of human thinking in general... To lay stress on context [=Shammaites] means... to see the unity in diversity and multiplicity, to think in concepts and to defy sense perceptions... To lay stress on the word [=Hillelites], on the other hand, means to dissolve the unity and the continuity into an infinite multitude of fragments."

Sonne, referring to M. Miq. 5:6, says, "The unity in the continuous change of the stream" is in line with the view of the Shammaites, but denied by "the disruptive tendency of the Hillelites." Shammai holds that if a man sends another to commit murder, the instigator is guilty. "The long range causation asserted by the Shammaites accounts for series of their restrictions with regard to the starting of work on Friday which cannot be completed before the Sabbath." The same differences relates to intention: "The Hillelites require the intention to accompany the act; the Shammaites... extend considerably the range of the intention, so as to reach acts accomplished after a certain interval in time." The difference about grounds for divorce has to do with causation: "...from the point of view of the Hillelites, causation in general is something contingent and external, and therefore any 'unseemly thing,' even if it has nothing to do with marital life, may be the cause of divorce." In general the Shammaites "see the conceptual unity in the diversity and multiplicity... [while] the Hillelites' tendency [was] towards disintegration of conceptual units..." Sonne concludes that the Hillelites' "atomic-nominalistic tendency bears also unmistakably germs of disintegration and anarchy." So one man's progressives turn out to be another's anarchists.

While I find much to admire in Zeitlin's legal-historical studies, I regret to observe that the more narrowly historical articles and books uniformly exhibit unparalleled dogmatism, joined with the allegation that no one else understands talmudic literature. Zeitlin's papers confidently and repeatedly present as fact a wide range of quite dubious notions.

For example, S. Zeitlin, "Prosbol, A Study in Tannaitic Jurisprudence," JQR 37, 1946, pp. 341-362, takes for granted the literal, historical accuracy of the prosbol-stories. He does not analyze the literary traits of the stories and sees no historical problems in them. The primary issue is legal, but what the law describes is taken for granted as social and historical fact. Here that assumption is central to the argument. Zeitlin claims, "Before his [Hillel's] time, the creditor in order not to lose the money which he had loaned to his fellow men on account of the sabbatical year, deposited with the court a promissory note given to him by the debtor. Such a promissory note had a clause to the effect that the real property of the debtor was mortgaged to the creditor. In such a case, the creditor had the right to collect the debt even after the sabbatic year... According to the opinion of the school of Shammai, anything which ultimately has to be collected is considered as already collected [Footnote: "b. Git. 37a" -- which contains an Amoraic interpretation offered centuries after the incident]. However, that was only a custom and had not as yet been sanctioned. Hillel introduced the Takkana that the creditor may write a Prosbol, even without the knowledge of the debtor, in which he declares that he will collect all the debts people owe him. The Prosbol is valid, whether or not the creditor has a promissory note, and whether or not the note was deposited with the court. This Takkana Hillel made a law by supporting it by a verse in the Pentateuch. A Takkana must always be based on the Pentateuch." Zeitlin thus takes for granted that the Sabbatical laws were everywhere enforced. It was moreover possible for the Pharisees to effect changes in the administration of commercial (and real estate) law. Further, Zeitlin claims that the Prosbol was in existence before Hillel's time, which is not what the story says. He claims this was merely a "custom," but the story says Hillel introduced that custom. Zeitlin has imposed a theory upon stories which in their present form contradict his theory. It hardly serves to argue that Hillel "really" did introduce the Prosbol as the stories say, against the view that all he did was to find a Scriptural basis for a rather minor alteration of existing practice. Indeed, one can hardly argue with this sort of allegation, without being drawn into the conceptually primitive framework of discussion. What Hillel "really" did or did not do is not a suitable subject for analysis, given the character and condition of the sources.

Solomon Zeitlin, "The Pharisees and the Gospels," Essays and Studies in Memory of Linda R. Miller, ed. Israel Davidson (N.Y., 1938), pp. 238-286, now regards as "historically

accurate" only the controversies between the Pharisees and the Sadducees. "The Halakot
of the Schools of Hillel and Shammai, Akiba and Eliezer, etc., belong to the history and
the development of the halakah, but have nothing to do with the Pharisees." So the
Houses and presumably their founders were not Pharisees! The Sadducees ended at 70,
"and thus the Pharisees likewise disappeared as opponents." But the Pharisees "had great
influence on the Halakot of the Schools of Hillel and Shammai." There was "no such sect
as the 'Pharisees.'" This is very confusing. The difference between the teachings of Jesus
and the teachings of the Pharisees is accounted for as follows: "The Pharisees, leaders of
the Jewish people, although maintaining that ethical teachings are important for the
development of human nature, insisted on the fulfillment of the law... A state cannot
exist unless it is maintained by law and order. On the other hand, Jesus, not being
interested in the State, appealed to his fellow men to refrain from doing evil..."

Another characteristic of pseudocriticism is the resort to facile emendations to
solve historical problems. Since the facticity of the historical stories is taken for
granted, emending the sources will supply the answer to any difficulty and forthwith
create a new fact. For example, Solomon Zeitlin, "Sameias and Pollion," Journal of
Jewish Lore and Philosophy 1, 1919, pp. 61-67, reviews the references of Josephus and
then asks, "Who are the two men...?" He forthwith reviews various suggestions and
possibilities, rejecting each in turn. In the end he concludes the references of Josephus
are not always to the same men. In one passage Sameias is Shammai; in two others, he is
Shema'iah. The consequences of this theory are then spelled out. The passages are
treated as literally true and accurate accounts of what was really said and done. Zeitlin
then turns to Pollion the Pharisee, who must be Hillel. Josephus's Pollion is represented
as teacher of Sameias. "But Hillel was not the teacher of Shema'iah -- he was his pupil.
This reversing of relations can be explained as due to a scribal error."

Zeitlin's most ambitions work is The Rise and Fall of the Judean State. A Political,
Social and Religious History of the Second Commonwealth (Philadelphia, I, 1962; II,
1967). He holds that the Pharisees "stressed the principle of the universality of God..."
which the Sadducees held "that Yahweh is an ethnic God...." He does not cite the
Saducean documents on this matter; there are no evidences on their views. The
Pharisees go back to earliest Second Temple times: "The original Pharisees supported
Zerubbabel" (!). They were the "main factor in the revolt against the domination of the
Syrians." The Sadducees demanded rigid observance of the Pentateuchal law. "The
Pharisees, however, strove to amend the Pentateuchal law in order to bring religion into
consonance with life. They were ready to modify the Pentateuchal law in order to enable
it to accord with the requirements and demands of everchanging life." The Pharisees
disapproved of class distinctions. The Houses represented conservative and liberal
viewpoints, respectively. As with Ginzberg (not cited [!]), Zeitlin holds the differences
had begun with the first pairs, but Hillel and Shammai gave their names to the schools.
Shammai followed the established law, while Hillel was the innovator. He introduced
another new concept, the principle of intention. He made a legal distinction "between
happenings which stem from volition and those which do not." "Four controversies are

recorded between Shammai and Hillel. In all tannaitic controversies recorded in the Talmud, the name of the person who adhered to the conservative point of view is given first. Shammai's name, however, is given first in three of the disputes... while in the controversy of Semikah, that is, the transmittal of authority to introduce new laws, Hillel's name is given first. This is due to the fact that this principle had already been accepted. Shemayah and Abtalion had already debated this issue, and the name of Shemayah, who adhered to this principle, was recorded first." All of this is axiomatic. No evidence backs up these statements, other than allusion to the (unanalyzed) sources. And, as we note, Zeitlin cites whom Zeitlin chooses to cite. The notion that bibliographies record the literature is alien, not alone to Zeitlin. People cite books they like and pretend the others do not exist. But whom are they kidding?

Alexander Guttmann not only takes for granted the "historicity" of the various talmudic stories; he also seems to believe in the heavenly echoes, or voices, mentioned in them. In "The Significance of Miracles for Talmudic Judaism," HUCA 20, 1947, pp. 363-406, Guttmann holds that the Houses ended with the destruction of the Temple. Eliezer and Joshua refer to them. The "echo that settled their controversy must have appeared at the time when these controversies had not yet been settled, i.e. during the first Tannaitic generation (between 70 and 90 C.E.)." In "The End of the 'Houses,'" The Abraham Weiss Jubilee Volume, ed. Samuel Belkin et al. (N.Y., 1964), pp. 88-105, Guttmann asks, "When did the Bath Qol [echo] make this sweeping verdict [in favor of the Hillelites]; 2. did both Houses continue their existence after that verdict; 3. what was the extent of the authority this Bath Qol possessed?" Guttmann takes as fact the opinion of R. Yohanan that the echo came at Yavneh: "This information is repeated several times in the Palestinian Talmud, thus confirming its accuracy [sic!]." The echo came shortly after 70: "Few controversies of the Houses refer to conditions existing after the destruction of the Temple." Joshua and Eliezer disagree on the interpretation of controversies between the Houses. "Had they [the Houses] existed, a simple inquiry with the respective schools would have sufficed." The "fundamental decision in favor of Beth [The House of] Hillel was made at the end of a three year's dispute by a Bath Qol, a Heavenly Voice. The immediate effect of the Bath Qol was the doom of Beth Shammai. The Bath Qol was not effective retroactively."

Like Louis Ginzberg, Jacob Z. Lauterbach enjoyed wide influence for several decades. Herford says that he revised his own views of the Pharisees after reading Lauterbach. Lauterbach posits his own set of theories to account for various disputes. In general, he falls in line with the opinion of Reform Jewish scholars, beginning with Geiger, that the Sadducees were reactionaries, the Pharisees liberals. The whole then is embellished with sermons of various kinds. Lauterbach, in "The Sadducees and the Pharisees," and "The Pharisees and Their Teachings," Rabbinic Essays (Cincinnati, 1951), pp. 23-50, 51-86, 87-162, respectively, postulates that the Sadducees were the older, more conservative party, the Pharisees the younger, "broader and more liberal in their views, of progressive tendencies and not averse to innovations." Lauterbach treats the division of the two parties, which he assigns to early (!) in Second Temple times. Pharisees emerge from lay teachers, the Sadducees were formed by the priestly aristocracy. Lauterbach draws upon the whole corpus of rabbinic literature for his description of the Pharisees (called "sages of Israel").

The "significant controversy" between the parties concerned the manner in which the high priest should bring in the incense into the Holy of Holies on the Day of Atonement. "The Sadducees said it must be prepared outside the Holy of Holies. The Pharisees said it should not be put into the censer outside, but the high priest should enter the Holy of Holies carrying the censer with the fiery coals in his right hand and the spoon full of incense in his left hand. Only inside the curtain should he put the incense upon the fiery coals on the censer and thus offer it there." Lauterbach asks how the Pharisees could have known the law, when the Sadducees were in control of the Temple. The Pharisees, he claims to prove, introduced "a radical reform." The Sadducees retained "many of the primitive notions both about God and the purpose of the Service offered to Him in the Temple." The Pharisees had a "purer God conception and less regard for the sacrificial cult.... They tried... to democratize and spiritualize the service in the Temple and to remove from it the elements of crude superstition and primitive outworn conceptions." They were the Founders of Reform Judaism. "Preparing the incense outside was a measure of precaution; the smoke would protect the priest from "the danger of Satan's accusations...." Further, the smoke would prevent the high priest from "involuntary looking the Deity in the face...." These "primitive theological views" were rejected by the Pharisees.

"The Pharisees and their Teachings" makes the point that the Pharisees offered a "more spiritual" conception of religion than did their opposition. Their victory "had to result in a broad liberal universalism." Christianity sprang from Pharisaic Judaism. "Jesus and his disciples did not belong to the priestly aristocratic party of the Sadducees. They were of the plain humble people who followed the Pharisees." Each of the ancient sources, the Talmud, Josephus, and the New Testament, preserves "some accurate information about these two parties." The Pharisees were the newer party, the Sadducees the older; they were conservative, strict interpreters of the Torah. The Pharisees were "the younger, progressive party composed originally of democratic laymen who outgrew some of the older notions, cherished modern and liberal ideas, and therefore became separated from the older group and formed a distinct party. They were the liberal separatists, the dissenters who rejected some of the ancient traditional conceptions of religion and who broke away the primitive traditional attitude toward the Torah.... The Pharisees were heirs of the prophets and disciples of the priests" (even though elsewhere Lauterbach sees the Sadducees as the priests!).

Armand Kaminka exhibits a commmendable skepticism about some materials, but thorough-going gullibility about others. The traditional hiddush (novella) often involved the claim that what everyone took for granted was false, but the very opposite was true. In Kaminka's case, this meant turning Hillel from a Babylonian into an Alexandrian -- "perhaps" a provincial judge from Jericho (!). His sayings can be set at particular historical times and made to refer to particular events. So behind the facade of skepticism lies the usual pseudocritical attitude. In "Hillel's Life and Work," JQR 30, 1939-40, pp. 107-122, Kaminka recognizes that some of the Hillel-materials are unhistorical. Any priest in Jerusalem "could have testified with certainty as to how the ritual of the Passover sacrifice had been performed through long generations when the 14th day of Nisan fell in a Sabbath." The stories are spun out of "public addresses containing fables with ethical conclusions." The rise-to-power-story proves a haughty man loses his wisdom. The story of Hillel's hardships shows "poverty is no excuse for neglecting the study of the Law." Other materials likewise are for didactic purposes and should not be treated as historical. It is unlikely that Hillel, a poor man from abroad, "should have been suddenly chosen for a high position."

Hillel's sayings, "A name made great is a name destroyed," and "Those that drowned you will be drowned" refer to a great historical event, the battle of Pharsalus (48 B.C.E.). Hillel's saying alluded in fact to Pompey, and "It is to the skull of the latter that he addressed the verse..." (!). A. Kaminka, "Hillel and his Work," in Hebrew, Zion 4, 1939, pp. 258-266 (=JQR 30, 107-122) says Hillel came from Alexandria and had been "perhaps a judge in Jericho when this city was under the rule of Cleopatra." Again, the story about the skull floating on the water "was told about Pompey who drowned near Alexandria after the battle of Pharsalus."

VI

THEOLOGY IN HISTORICAL GUISE

If I have neglected accounts of Pharisaism by Christian theologians, the reason is that most are beneath criticism. What they lack are concern to portray the Pharisees accurately and dispassionately and willingness to abandon theological interests in favor of historical ones. To take one recent example, Reginald H. Fuller writes (in The Book of the Acts of God. Contemporary Scholarship Interprets the Bible, by B. Ernest Wright and Reginald H. Fuller [N.Y., 1960], pp. 229-231), "The dominant concern of the Pharisaic movement was to preserve inviolate the Mosaic law and its way of life against the encroachments of alien cultures. Since that law had been given once for all through Moses there could be no new laws. Instead, the ancient laws, which had been intended for a more primitive society, had to be reapplied to later situations. In this reapplication there was no thought of introducing novelties; rather, the idea was to extract the real meaning of the law." In the rabbinic traditions about the Pharisees, one will look in vain for the articulate expression of Fuller's "dominant concern." As to not making new laws, Fuller seems not to have noticed the taqqanot, and more especially, the later rabbinic interpretations of the authority of taqqanot. Certainly, some rabbis are accurately represented by Fuller, namely, those who sought or supplied Scriptural foundations for taqqanot. But others are misrepresented, for considerable efforts were made to change the law, and not merely through reinterpretation of casuistry. Here Fuller shows that he has neither examined the evidence nor read the scholarly literature.

Further, he reveals a theological bias: "There was little attempt to search for an underlying principle behind the numerous commands and prohibitions. The two great commandments, love of God and love of the neighbor, were of course part of the law, but even in combination they were not accorded that central and unifying position which they were given in the New Testament. All this naturally led to legalism and scrupulosity, to a belief in the saving value of good works, and the consequent sense of pride which a doctrine of merit inevitably entailed." [He writes of the Pharisees, but surely he means the Roman Catholics as caricatured by the Reformation.] The stories of Hillel, some of them made up at the same time the Gospels were composed, make precisely the point Fuller denies was central in the Pharisaic tradition. To Hillel, just as to Jesus, is given the saying that Lev. 19:18 was "the whole Torah," thus surely "central" and "unifying." (To be sure Hillel may never have said any such thing, but such critical considerations do not enter Fuller's argument.)

Fuller thus misrepresents the Pharisaic Judaism by the theology of classical Christianity. Legalism is a bad thing; belief in the saving value of good works obviously is inferior to "faith." The theological bias natural to a Protestant Christian theologian has prevented Fuller from carefully examining the Pharisaic literature and accurately representing what he finds there.

What is wrong with the Pharisees is that they were not Christians. Therefore one may do with the evidence anything he likes. For example, Fuller writes, "Hellenistic Judaism became a missionary religion. The statement in Matthew 23:15: '...you traverse sea and land to make a single proselyte...' may be an exaggeration, as far as Palestine is concerned, but it was certainly true of the dispersion." Fuller carefully omits the opening part of the saying: "Woe unto you, Scribes and Pharisees." For Fuller, the verse therefore testifies about "Hellenistic Judaism," of which it does not speak, and not about Pharisaic Judaism, to which it refers. This sort of "revision" of evidence may suit theological purposes, but hardly suggests that the canons of critical historical inquiry come into play at all. Fortunately for Fuller, there are no Pharisees around to sue him for his libellous misrepresentation. But fraud is fraud, and bigotry is unChristian.

Fuller's account of the Pharisees is brief and plays no important role in his picture of early Christianity. I use it to exemplify traits which occur in grosser form in other works of the same origin. What it shows is that the large number of Christian scholars of Pharisaism, even in very recent times, first, do not see differences between theology and history and, second, do not take the trouble to examine the rabbinic evidences, either accepting or rejecting the whole without careful, thorough study. Of these faults, the second seems from a scholarly viewpoint the more damning, for it means scholars have not even bothered to do their homework.

Fuller's Pharisees are unimportant in his book, and his account cannot be thought of much consequence. Matthew Black, "Pharisees," in George Arthur Buttrick et al., ed., Interpreter's Dictionary of the Bible (New York and Nashville, 1962), III, pp. 774b-781a, by contrast appears in a widely used handbook. To his credit, Black supplies a reasonably accurate account of Josephus's picture of the Pharisees. His references to Pharisaic law, which, he claims, is characterized as "legalism and apartheid," derive only from the New Testament. He seems entirely ignorant of the rabbinic traditions about the Pharisees, though he lists in his bibliography various works which make copious (if uncritical) use of those traditions. What alone renders his account noteworthy is his conclusion:

> There is no reason to doubt that the Pharisees still exercised a powerful influence within the Judaism of our Lord's time. But it is doubtful if they still enjoyed the same popularity with the masses as in the heydey of their political power in the previous centuries. By the first century A.D.... Pharisaism had become a bourgeois rather than a popular movement, a predominantly Jerusalem "city" party. No doubt the Jerusalem Pharisees also had their followers in the country districts, but their attitude to the 'Am Ha'ares suggests that the gulf between the Pharisees and the peasants who formed the bulk of the population was as great as that between the Sadducees and the small traders in the cities from whom the Pharisees drew their main support.

One would be curious to know how Black knows the Pharisees "still enjoyed the same popularity..." etc. He does not cite opinion polls or other hard data to that effect -- and I know no such data. That the Pharisees were "bourgeois" seems to me not merely a groundless, but a quite meaningless statement. In the materials before us and in the stories in Josephus's writings and the New Testament, one will look in vain, moreover, for their "attitude to the 'Am Ha'ares."

Thus far Black shows merely questionable historical judgment. One may wonder at the editors' selection of an incompetent in the study of Pharisaism for the composition of the article. However, the concluding paragraph passes from the study of Pharisaism to the judgment of Judaism, and from history to (prejudiced) theology -- that is, pure anti-semitism:

> This loss of influence with the broad masses, especially in the provinces and the countryside, applied to Pharisaic religion no less than to the membership of the sect [sic]. Pharisaism is the immediate ancestor of rabbinical (or normative) Judaism, the arid and sterile region of the Jews after the fall of Jerusalem and, finally, the Bar Cocheba debate (A.D. 134). In Jesus' time, no doubt with certain differences, the broad picture of Pharisaism cannot have been so far removed from that of rabbinical Judaism of the post-Jamnia period, the Judaism of the Tannaites. It is a sterile region of codified tradition, regulating every part of life by a halachah, observing strict apartheid, and already as entrenched in its own conservatism as that of the Sadducees. Its golden age lay in the second and first centuries B.C., from which its main literary monuments come [sic], and where its important ideals and conceptions are to be found.

We have already observed that Black has no evidence as to the influence or loss of influence of the Pharisees. His "no doubt with certain differences," like the "perhaps" and "may be" of the pseudocritical talmudic historians, changes nothing; the Pharisaism of Jesus's time is what he is talking about, and the Gospels supply the evidence. The "important ideals and conceptions" of the Pharisaism of which Black approves cannot derive from the evidence of Josephus, the Gospels, or the rabbinic traditions about the

Pharisees, for none of these sources supplies a picture of that "golden age" in terms of "ideals and conceptions." It evidently is based upon Apocryphal and Pseudepigraphical books attributed to the Pharisees, for no good reason, by obsolescent scholarship. Black has taken these attributions at face value.

As to his obiter dicta about post-70 Judaism -- which is not the topic of his article -- one need not comment. This is the sort of anti-Judaism which has nothing to do with either historical facts or lack of historical facts. The choice of prejudicial language -- "sterile" (twice), "arid," "strict apartheid" (!), "entrenched conservatism" -- is familiar in the anti-Semitic writings of every age, particularly in Germany, to which historical facts are quite irrelevant. Abingdon had no business publishing this anti-Semitic claptrap.

Rudolf Bultmann's knowledge of rabbinic Judaism derives entirely from secondary sources. Except for his claim to compare rabbinic literature with Hellenistic and Christian literary forms, that hardly matters. His Primitive Christianity in its Contemporary Setting (N.Y., 1965) does matter, for it is widely read and heralded by his American followers as scholarship, not as what it is, namely apologetics of a rather crude sort. Bultmann on Judaism tells us the following:

P. 60: There was no possibility of science and art, nor could there be any cultural intercourse with other nations. Israel (apart from Hellenistic Judaism) cut herself off from the outside world and lived in extraordinary isolation. As a result she cut herself adrift from history.

p. 64: The scribes regarded the foundation as immutable for it consisted in the holy scriptures themselves. Their method of exegesis was primitive, and, despite certain variations, stereotype. The progress of scientific knowledge was limited to painstaking exegesis. But there was no attempt to reach a deeper understanding of the context, to discover the ideas underlying the text itself, or the circumstances in which it took shape. The only kind of progress they recognized was the accumulation of possible interpretations.... New interpretations were simply recorded side by side with the old, and no attempt was made to decide which was the true one. It is the function of learning to preserve as many existing interpretations as possible. In teaching there was no attempt to ask questions of the pupil and thus train him to think for himself. The Greek method of seeking the truth in the cut and thrust of argument was entirely unknown.... [!] [Surely he was joking.]

p. 68: Radical obedience would have involved a personal assent to the divine command, whereas in Judaism so many of the precepts were trivial or unintelligible that the kind of obedience produced was formal rather than radical. The equality of importance attached to ritual and moral precepts was no less conducive to formalism...

p. 69: With the unintelligibility of many of the precepts and the scope for works of supererogation, it was impossible to entertain a radical conception of obedience....

p. 70: A further consequence of the legalistic conception of obedience was that the prospect of salvation became highly uncertain. Who could be sure he had done enough in this life to be saved.... It is a remarkable fact that side by side with this sense of sin and urge to repentance we find the 'righteous' proud and selfconscious.... In the end the whole range of man's relation with God came to be thought of in terms of merit, including faith itself.

Now what is wrong with all this (and much more not quoted) is that Bultmann simply does not know what he is talking about, in part because of his demonstrated lack of direct knowledge of the rabbinic traditions about the Pharisees, but in larger measure because no one has data on the basis of which "historical" statements such as these may be made.

Obviously the "extraordinary isolation" is groundless: here we may justly excuse Bultmann for what is evidently mere carelessness. But how would anyone be able to show, upon the basis of evidence now in our hands, whether or not the Pharisees "attempted to reach a deeper understanding of the context"? How does Bultmann or anyone else know what "kind of progress" the Pharisees recognized or did not recognize?

My criticism is not solely that Bultmann is ignorant of rabbinical traditions about the Pharisees, but that he makes statements which cannot be founded upon any evidence now available or likely to become available. It is as if, like other scholars, he accused the Pharisees of being "hypocrites" or "the brood of Satan." Without knowledge of their true feelings, shown, for instance, by diaries or personal interviews, how are we to know whether the Pharisees were, or were not, characterized by hypocrisy? Nor do historians accurately know who Satan's children really are. A work on historical problems, moreover, cannot rightly introduce considerations irrelevant to the historical inquiry. "Radical obedience" may serve as a fruitful theological category, but helps not at all to understand the nature of life under the law.

As to the triviality or unintelligibility of "many of the precepts" and the consequent "obedience" produced by them, one need only observe Bultmann does not know what seemed trivial to a Pharisee, nor, given the state of his talmudic knowledge, can one take seriously his judgment of what was intelligible in first century life.

The three instances of theology in historical guise are not of the same order. Fuller has merely repeated what he read in some books, decorating the picture with a few of his own embellishments. His emendation of Matt. 23:15 is adequate evidence of his historical reliability. Black, by contrast, presents an on-the-whole creditable encyclopedia article. It is only at the end that Black introduces post-70 rabbinic Judaism, in order to parade his contempt and hostility to it. Perhaps better editing would have left us with a less biased and therefore more respectable article. Bultmann is most influential of the three, and rightly so; his History of the Synoptic Tradition is apt to guide many students of talmudic literature in the method of literary-critical and historical-critical analysis of traditions. It is, therefore, to be regretted that in his journalistic works, for a wide audience, he has written theology in the past tense of a historical essay. This is pure bigotry.

VII

SUMMARY

First, we observe that few students of Pharisaism or of the rabbinic traditions about the Pharisees have thoroughly examined all pertinent sources. Second, a consistently critical, truly <u>historical</u> approach characterizes only a small number of scholars. What makes a scholar pseudocritical, third, is the claim that he follows the normal canons of historical inquiry while at the same time he advances arguments alien to that inquiry; or that he credulously takes as fact allegations contained in literature he has not actually analyzed; or that he may ignore the conceptual and methodological achievements of other scholars, both in the field of talmudic studies and in cognate areas of inquiry. One looks in vain, fourth, for the awareness that scholarship reflects the scholar's own sociological and historical situation. The Reform Jewish scholars who see the Pharisees as Reform Jews and the Conservative ones who claim the Pharisees were economic liberals (in the New Deal sense) exhibit scarcely a trace of selfconsciousness.

Admittedly, historians of Pharisaic Judaism face a very knotty problem. Information on the Pharisees derives from difficult sources. These sources are quite different from one another and in some measure entirely discrete. Many historians were baffled by the evidences of talmudic literature; the New Testament materials have not been critically examined by the Talmudists, who read the New Testament in exactly the same literal way in which they read the Talmud; and only Smith has subjected Josephus's information on the Pharisees to careful analysis. The attributions of various Apocryphal and Pseudepigraphical books to Pharisaic authors seem based upon shaky assumptions, but these attributions have yet to be carefully reconsidered in the light of recent advances of scholarship in Qumram, New Testament and the varieties of early Christianity and Judaism and the like. In any case reference to supposedly Pharisaic, Apocryphal, and Pseudepigraphical books is rare among the Jewish scholars of the Pharisees. Finally, the fact that Pharisaism was a sect, not "normative" or "popular" or "democratic," while now widely acknowledged, has scarcely entered the historical understanding of the Jewish scholars, even in recent times.

The following outline summarizes the chief historical faults found in the surveyed materials.

I.   Faulty Scholarship
    1.   Neglect of some or all of the rabbinic traditions about the Pharisees:
        a)   Houses-materials not used at all.
        b)   Houses-materials not thoroughly consulted.
        c)   Rabbinical traditions rejected without close examination.
        d)   Reliance on secondary accounts of rabbinic traditions.
    2.   Neglect of non-rabbinic evidences about the Pharisees on materials contained in rabbinic traditions.
        a)   No reference to archaeological data pertinent to historical interpretation.
        b)   Failure to follow the development of New Testament scholarship.
        c)   No consistent reference to Hellenistic literary and cultural parallels.

3.   Failure to consult relevant secondary literature.

4.   Failure to articulate and examine (questionable) presuppositions.

II.   Faulty Use of Evidence

1.   Attributions of sayings are always reliable.

2.   What a story says happened actually did take place (credulousness).

3.   Even miracle stories are of historical value in their own terms.

4.   "If the story were not true why should the tradition have preserved it?" Variation: "They must have had a good reason to tell the story."

5.   Construction of narrative by paraphrase of rabbinic stories about Pharisees (gullibility, similar to no. 2).

6.   Presumption of unitary pericopae.

7.   Use of emendations of texts of solve historical difficulties.

8.   Invention of historical settings or motives for exegetical materials.

9.   Claim of exact chronological or historical accuracy even for fables.

10. All versions of a story are correct and must be harmonized and unified (unitary tradition).

11. "No real evidence has been produced against the historicity of the accounts" (similar to no. 4).

12. Evidence contrary to one's theory is ignored. Books one does not like are not mentioned at all.

13. All stories deriving from all compilations are equally valid testimonies (parallel to no. 10).

III. Faulty Narrative

1.   False, inappropriate, or misleading analogies.

2.   Incompetent question-framing.

3.   Overinterpretation, or going beyond the limits of the evidence.

4.   Deductive reasoning.

5.   Homiletics.

6.   Postulates unsupported by evidence.

7.   Arbitrary definition to solve historical difficulties (similar to no. II.7).

8.   Use of critical form to hide pseudocritical presuppositions.

Among the historiographical errors of pseudocritical scholars, three are so serious as to render their historical results useless:

first, the failure carefully and critically to analyze the literary and historical traits of every pericope adduced as evidence;

second, the assumption that things happened exactly as the sources allege;

third, the use of anachronistic or inappropriate analogies and the introduction of irrelevant issues.

One or more of these three fundamental fallacies may account for every one of the specific faults listed above, as well as for many not specified. The historians might have learned the need for literary- and historical-critical analysis from classical and biblical scholarship of the past century and a half; second, they might have proved less gullible and credulous had they taken seriously the historical and philosophical achivements of the Enlightenment, at least its skepticism; and the study of the history of historical scholarship and of the sociology of knowledge ought to have suggested the dangers of anachronism, moralizing, and didacticism.

24. JEWS AND JUDAISM UNDER IRANIAN RULE:
BIBLIOGRAPHICAL REFLECTIONS
[History of Religions 1968, 8:159-177]

From the Parthian conquest of Babylonia, in 140-120 B.C., to the Moslem victory over the Sasanians in 640 A.D., almost eight centuries later, Babylonian and much of Mesopotamian Jewry lived under Iranian governments. Our interest here is in the political, religious, and cultural consequences of that long period of symbiosis.

I

David Winston, "The Iranian Component in the Bible, Apocrypha, and Qumran: A Review of the Evidence," History of Religions, V (No. 2), 183-216 (to which I have replied briefly in V (No. 3), 176-78), has provided a partial summary of the extensive literature which deals with the Iranian influence upon Palestinian Judaism. Just what one means by Iranian "influence" remains to be more closely defined. Many have supposed that any evidence of dualism, such as a reference to light and darkness, or Jewish conceptions similar to Mazdean ones of any period, for example, concerning Satan, Gayomart/Adam, eschatology, angelology, demonology, and the like, indicate Iranian influence. For instance, Winston supposes that the undeniable similarity between Zurvanite and Qumranian dualism is proof of "interpenetration." It might, however, be the result of parallel, independent developments. We must try to determine the circumstances which may have led to the introduction of Iranian religious ideas or forms into Judaism. Who were the intermediaries on each side? When and where did they meet? Is there no other explanation for the existence in each culture of parallel concepts, institutions, beliefs, or structures, but "interpenetration," or "influence," of one upon the other? If, as between Qumran and Zurvanism, we find striking similarities, we may satisfactorily account for them without positing reciprocal influence. Both constitute dualisms within monotheist systems. Zurvanism was a Zoroastrian monotheist "heresy" within dualism, following R.C. Zaehner, Zurvan, A Zoroastrian Dilemma (Oxford, 1955); and the Qumran sectarians were a Jewish dualist "heresy" within monotheism. Both, therefore, represent dualistic structures within a monotheist framework. Indeed, the sources within Israelite mono-theism from which such a dualism may have emerged have hardly been explored. One hardly need turn to Iran to account for Israelite ethical, anthropological, or metaphysical dualism. It would, by contrast, be simple enough to argue that Achaemenid political domination of Palestine from circa 540 to 333 B.C. made a profound impact upon Palestinian Judaism. But if so, what were the means by which such influence was mediated? Was Palestine so inundated by Persian officials, tradesmen, priests, and the like, that the Jews were likely to have had intimate contact with, and knowledge of, their traditions? In fact, both Achaemenid and Israelite life had come under Hellenistic influence long before Alexander's conquest of the Near and Middle East.

A further issue is: What was the state of Iranian religion in Parthian and Sasanian times? Are the contents of Avestan, Pahlavi, and Pazend texts, cited as evidence for Zoroastrian beliefs, valid evidence for the earlier periods? A view of the severe problem of dating book-Pahlavi texts will be found in W.B. Bailey, Zoroastrian Problems in the Ninth Century Books (Oxford, 1943), pp. 149-77, which should be compared to Jacques Duchesne-Guillemin, "La Fixation de l'Avesta," Indo-Iranica: Mélanges présentés à l'occasion de son soixante-dixième anniversaire (Wiesbaden, 1964), pp. 62-67, and J.-P. de Menasce, Une encyclopédie mazdéenne, le Denkart (Paris, 1958), 56 ff. The best recent popular critical studies of Achaemenid and Sasanian religion include J. Duchesne-Guillemin, La religion de l'Iran ancien (Paris, 1964), and R.C. Zaehner, Dawn and Twilight of Zoroastrianism (London, 1961), to mention only two important works. But for Zoroaster himself, studies begin, I think, with W.B. Henning, Zoroaster: Politician or Witchdoctor? (Oxford, 1951).

The broader issue of Judaic-Mazdean relationships is this: If one discovers a significant parallel, such as the perfectly obvious one between Judaic and Mazdean eschatology, as traced by R.H. Charles, A Critical History of the Doctrine of Future Life in Israel, in Judaism, and in Christianity (London, 1899, reprinted in New York, 1963, with an Introduction by George W. Buchanan), what are we to make of it? Who borrowed from whom? Or have both borrowed from a single anterior source? The usual answer given in recent times is that Israel must have borrowed from Iran, though Moulton, J. Darmesteter, Scheftelowitz, and others earlier thought that Israel had influenced Iran. The question of an anterior source is almost never raised to begin with. Both probably drew, however, from common Middle Eastern sources. The Babylonian roots in cuneiform culture of postbiblical Judaism have never been fully examined. We have helpful studies by philologists, tracing relationships between Hebrew and Akkadian words, and by biblical and cuneiform scholars on the earlier period, such as J.J. Finkelstein, "Bible and Babel," Commentary, XXVI (1958), 431-44. Qualified Assyriologists, however, have yet to explain systematically what was Babylonian about Babylonian Judaism and what was Babylonian about the syncretistic Babylonian-Iranian-Hellenistic culture of later times. Scholars of ancient Near Eastern law, such as Yohanan Muffs, Studies in Elephantine Papyri (Leiden, 1968), and Baruch A. Levine, "Mulugu-Melug: The Origins of a talmudic Legal Institution" (Journal of the American Oriental Society), have persuasively shown the Babylonian roots of some talmudic legal forms and expressions. But broader cultural phenomena, such as the ancient Middle Eastern common law, have yet to be traced. It seems to me premature to try to decide the relation of Iranian to talmudic law or religion before an extended preliminary inquiry into the roots of both in cuneiform law has been undertaken. (A helpful example of what can be accomplished is W.W. Hallo, "Akkadian Apocalypses," Israel Exploration Journal, XVI [No. 4], 231-42.) Similarly, is it not equally premature to try to decide the relationships between other aspects of Iranian and Jewish culture? Parallels may indicate a common root or a common response to a shared condition, rather than a reciprocal influence. This is not to suggest the informed and specific accounts of Iranian words, ideas, and institutions do not illuminate Babylonian talmudic data. Quite to the contrary, works such as Ezra Spicehandler, "Dina de Magista and Be Davar: Notes on Gentile Courts in Talmudic Babylonia," Hebrew Union College Annual, XXVI, 333-54, are all too rare.

If we must make premature hypotheses, let me here hypothesize that Iranian "influences" on the culture and religion of Babylonian Jewry, and all the more so of Palestinian Jewry, have been for the most part exaggerated and overrated.[1] Examining just what the talmudic rabbis actually knew about Iranian culture, we can hardly be impressed by the depth of their knowledge. Some could understand Pahlavi when it was spoken but could not read it. The Talmud preserves a thoroughly garbled account of Persian festivals, and two of the three Mazdean holidays the rabbis mention were in fact days upon which taxes had to be paid, so their knowledge does not prove to have been very profound. The exchanges between various third-century rabbis and magi recorded in the Talmud center upon astrology and medicine, the two indigenous, autochthonous sciences of Babylonia cultivated in the Babylonian schools down to the first century A.D. and studies by sages of other groups settled in the region. Evidences for these statements will be found in my History of the Jews in Babylonia, I: The Parthian Period (Leiden, 1965); II: The Early Sasanian Period (Leiden, 1966); III: From Shapur I to Shapur II (Leiden, 1968); and IV: The Age of Shapur II (Leiden, 1969). I do not know how much the talmudic rabbis knew about, or inherited from, cuneiform law and other aspects of Babylonian civilization. Babylonian Jewry lived side by side with the ancient Semitic peoples of the region, so that by the turn of the fourth century, more than nine hundred years of symbiosis had gone by. One should therefore expect to find many examples of borrowing. But I know of no comprehensive work providing such examples. Even the legal data have been rather fragmentarily and unsystematically considered.

Attention has focused upon Iranian and Jewish relationships, but most of those who studied such matters knew little about the problems of working with book-Pahlavi and other Iranian sources. The great philologians. W. and B. Geiger, were exceptional. The latter's signed articles in the revised printing of A. Kohut's edition of Arukh Completum (New York, 1956) are of primary importance, as are his scattered articles in the Wiener Zeitschrift für die Kunde des Morgenlandes. His "The Synagogue, Middle Iranian Texts," in C.H. Kraeling's The Synagogue ("Excavations at Dura Europos," Vol. VIII, Part I [New Haven, Conn., 1956]), pp. 283-317, provides a model for such studies. Among the cultural historians, Geiger has no counterpart. Most contemporary historians of religion and theologians normally have considerable training in Semitic and Hellenistic languages and culture but are usually quite uninformed about problems of Iranology, which facilitates their reaching neat and easy conclusions. By contrast one may note Richard N. Frye, "Reitzenstein and Qumran Revisited by an Iranian," Harvard Theological Review IV (1962), 261-68, and his "Problems in the Study of Iranian Religions," in Jacob Neusner (ed.) Religions in Antiquity: Essays in Memory of Erwin Ramsdell Goodenough (suppls. to Numen, Vol. XIV, Leiden, 1968), pp. 583-89.

II

The writing of the history of the Jews under Parthian and Sasanian rule began with Nahman Zvi Gezav, 'Al Naharot Bavel (Warsaw, 1876), a work which in general has been curiously neglected. Gezav studied Iranian history and culture as best he could, and given the primitive state of knowledge in his day, he made a singular contribution. But he had no successors. The next really historical work, not merely a collection of clever exegeses of talmudic texts or a kind of secular hagiography listing leading rabbis and recounting as history talmudic stories of their careers and virtues, is Salo W. Baron, A Social and Religious History of the Jews (Philadelphia, 1952), Vol. II. Baron's contribution to this subject has never received adequate appreciation. It was Baron who transformed a literature mostly used for exegesis into a historically useful body of documents, who redefined "talmudic history" in coherent and significant sociological and historical categories.

Previous historians -- such as H. Graetz, History of the Jews (reprinted in Philadelphia, 1948), Vol. II; Salomon Funk, Die Juden in Babylonien (Berlin, 1902) Vols. I and II; I.H. Weiss, Dor Dor ve Dorshav (4th ed.; Vilna, 1904), Vol. III; Ze'ev Yavz, Sefer Toledot Yisrael (Tel Aviv, 1935), Vols. VI and VII; and I.Y. Halevy, Dorot HaRishonim (Vienna and Berlin, 1923), Vol. I, Parts 3 and 5, and Vol. II — saw Babylonian Jewish history under the Arsacids and Sasanians as "talmudic history." That is to say, they used a literary category to define a historical period. Such was the method of nineteenth-century German historiography in the path of Hegel and Kant. The underlying philosophy assumed that what was historical about history was politics and the creations of the "spirit." "Spiritual creations" were enshrined in the literature produced by great minds. The doings of ordinary people, as preserved in social and economic history, the development of other than political institutions -- these were not worthy of the historian's attention.

Since politics was understood as the affairs of nations, the Jews were not supposed to possess a political life, for they had no national government; all that was therefore left for them was literature. And it was more than sufficient. The presupposition that whatever was important had been recorded in the Babylonian Talmud and other rabbinic documents, moreover, conformed to the theological conviction that the Pharisees and their Tannaitic and Amoraic heirs had constituted "normative Judaism." What they said was Judaism, and whoever diverged represented heresy. This question was hardly asked: What was the relationship between a rabbinic law or saying and the actualities of everyday life? It was assumed that merely describing rabbinical laws and sayings would constitute satisfactory history. Depicting the rabbis not as striking examples of religious and political leadership but rather as authoritative teachers and embodiments of Judaism was the content of that history. Since the Talmud and cognate literature had become normative over the centuries, it was assumed that they represented all that was important in Judaism during the period in which they took shape -- hence, "talmudic history."

Talmudic history was understood to extend roughly from Ezra to the Moslem conquest, for historians found in the talmudic stories, whether verifiable or not, data relevant to those centuries. The great dividing points, such as the destruction of the

Temple in Jerusalem, or the Bar Kokhba War, or the conversion of Constantine, or the rise of the Sasanians, were noted, to be sure. But history was divided into "the biblical period" and "the talmudic period." Within "talmudic history," the nineteenth- and early twentieth-century historians naturally focused upon what seemed to them historically interesting materials within talmudic and cognate literature. They were, excepting Halevy, not well trained in legal studies, nor did they find much of merit in theological or exegetical lore. But the Talmud contains many stories about rabbis. So "talmudic history" was written in terms of generations, of rabbis, of academies, and, in a limited measure, of the character of the ideas and literature produced in a given place and time.

Both the need to criticize and verify sources and the task of recovering some sort of sustained narrative lay beyond the concern and methodological capacity of the earlier historians. Whatever the text said happened actually did happen. One had to compare and contrast various accounts, where available, but the sources were never subjected to searching criticism of either lower or higher varieties. In the positivist tradition, the earlier historians supposed they could report what had "really" happened. Since the sources contain many details contrary to what rational, modern men expect to happen -- such as letters dropped from heaven into the laps of academicians, resurrections of the dead, and other exceptional events -- the historians would simply omit reference to such details and use the rest of the account as if they did not exist to begin with. The philological historians imagined that once they had properly established, understood, and interpreted a text in its own setting, they then knew pretty much what happened. I cannot think of a less likely supposition. On the other hand, the weaving of various stories into paragraphs and chapters required a sort of historical exegesis of texts, which in Graetz's and Yavez's hands turned into out-and-out sermonizing. Halevy's exegesis was far more impressive, in my opinion. He concerned himself mostly with the misconceptions of earlier historians, whom he called contemptuously "German sages," and in the midst of his fiery polemic, he produced many thorough and penetrating accounts of specific problems. He is by far the hardest to follow, however. One needs to read a given section four or five times before the train of thought emerges clearly.

Historians thus conceived talmudic history as a category of talmudic literary studies. They rarely consulted non-Jewish sources, and when they did, they merely read popular-scientific accounts, as in the cases of Gezav, Graetz, and Yavez. The Jews were people who suffered, wrote books, and produced great and holy leaders. They lived inside a test tube, and the history and culture of the "surrounding peoples" played no role in their development. And most strikingly, the Jews and the rabbis were one and the same. That the rabbis' laws did not necessarily describe the social life of ordinary people, that their theological and moral dicta did not fill the minds of the common folk, that the academy and the street were not one and the same -- these possibilities are not considered. So "talmudic history," "the history of the Jews," and "Judaism" were identified with one another in the minds of the historians.

Baron is the first major Jewish historian to see the historical task in this period as a social-scientific one. In studying talmudic and cognate documents, he raised basically social-scientific questions and answered these questions, as best he could. Baron's A Social and Religious History of the Jews, Vol. II, is the best account known to me of the state of our knowledge up to 1952. But that is not high praise.

One would want a secure knowledge of the framework of political history. For this purpose, N.C. Debevoise, Political History of Parthia (Chicago, 1938), remains most satisfactory. Jozef Wolski of Cracow is presently writing a new Parthian history. Anyone familiar with his recent articles, for example, "L'état Parthe des arsacides," Palaeologia, VII (1959), 91 ff., and "Decay of the Iranian Empire of the Seleucids and the Chronology of the Parthians' Beginnings," Berytus, XII (1956), 35-52, will anticipate a definitive statement. For Sasanian times, Arthur Christensen's L'Iran sous les sassanides (2d ed.; Copenhagen, 1944) is basic. I find George Rawlinson, Seventh Great Oriental Monarchy (London, 1876), of continuing value. Rawlinson extensively quotes the Greek and Latin historians. For the Persian, Arabic, Armenian, Manichaean, and Christian-Syriac sources, Christensen is, of course, of greater use.

Some Iranists working in pre-Islamic materials take a keen interest in Jewish data, though few are adequately trained to make much use of it. Among these, Geo Widengren, "The Status of the Jews in the Sassanian Empire," Iranica Antiqua, I (1961), 117-62, and his Iranisch-semitisch Kulturbegegnung in parthischer Zeit (Cologne, 1958) and "Quelques rapports entre juifs et iraniens à l'époque des Parthes," Supplements to Vetus Testamentum, Volume du congrès, Strasbourg, 1965, IV (Leiden, 1957), 197-242, are of greatest importance. Widengren's contribution is to bring to bear a wide range of knowledge of Babylonian and Iranian data upon specific Jewish issues. In his Iranica Antiqua paper, he surveys Pahlavi and Oriental Christian sources in Syriac, Armenian, and Greek, providing a compendium of references to the Jews and Judaism. Some of the material was known before his time, but he called attention to many items previously not properly appreciated. Apart from many philologists, only one other Iranist has consistently attended to Jewish materials and done so with appropriate care -- Otakar Klima. He makes excellent use of the German translation of the Talmud and the original texts as well. His work shows continuing interest in questions of Jewish cultural and religious history, both in Mazdak: Geschichte einer sozialen Bewegung im sassanidischen Persien (Prague, 1957) and in the accompanying "Mazdak und die Juden," Archiv Orientalni, XXIV (1956), 420-31. Similarly, his Manis Zeit und Leben (Prague, 1962) is exceptional among books on Mani and Manichaeism for its careful use of relevant Jewish sources. Many Iranists cite the well-known data in Graetz, and some refer to J. Newman (below), to the exclusion of weightier studies. Their discussion of the Jews and Judaism reflects a rather passing concern at best, as in M.-L. Chaumont, "Les sassanides et la christianisation de l'empire iranien au IIIe siècle de notre ère," Revue de l'histoire des religions, CLXV (1964), 165-202. Were Judaism not mentioned, it would hardly matter. Since Chaumont does raise the question of why Kartir persecuted the Jews, circa 272-92 (on pp. 192-93), it is deplorable that she has apparently not read important monographs on the subject. Her reference to the exilarch does not even indicate knowledge of Lazarus (below) nor of the excellent Jewish Encyclopedia article of W. Bacher ("Exilarch," Jewish Encyclopedia, V,

294 ff.). Iranists quickly recognize the limitations of non-specialists attempting to make use of Iranian data. It is time they perceived how superficially they have studied so rich a resource of information on Sassanian Iran as the Talmud. It constitutes a document of far more than narrowly philological interest for Iranian studies. [But the Arabists are worse. Current studies of early Islamic times are still citing Rodkinson's translation of the Talmud — by volume and page in Rodkinson no less!]

III

The monographic literature on Babylonian Jewish history in Arsacid and Sasanian times is not rich. We are, nonetheless, fortunate in having some excellent, entire reliable guides to geographical and political data. Let us note, first of all, the truly definitive works. One must begin with Jacob Obermeyer, Die Landschaft Babylonien im Zeitalter des Talmuds und des Gaonats (Frankfurt, 1929), which rendered obsolete all former work on the geography of Jewry in Babylonia and has never been superseded. Obermeyer's researches involved travel throughout the region, conversation with local inhabitants, and careful study of sites as well as of literary evidences, while he worked as tutor for a Persian pretender. Two other works of exceptional value are Felix Lazarus, "Die Haüpter der Vertriebenen: Beiträge zu einer Geschichte der Exilfurst in Babylonien unter den Arsakiden und Sassaniden," Jahrbücher für jüdische Geschichte und Literatur, X (1890), 1-183, and N. Brüll, "Adiabene," in the same journal, I (1874), 58-86; both provide a thorough account of the sources. M. Beer's article on the exilarchate in Ziyyon, XXVIII (1963), 1-33, represents an important supplement to Lazarus, and his dissertation on the Social and Economic Status of the Babylonian Amoraim, in Hebrew (Ramat Gan, 1963, in mimeographed form), is a useful compilation of sources and opinions. What I find most useful in Lazarus' monograph is his thorough and systematic presentation of the primary sources and careful study of Geonic traditions. Beer copiously cites evidence on the economic, political, and administrative aspects of the exilarchate and rabbinate. Neither work fully elucidates the relationship between the rabbi and the exilarch or the political theories underlying their conflicting claim to rule Jewry. And, unfortunately, Lazarus and Beer both suppose that evidence pertaining to one period applies equally to the whole three or more centuries under study. So neither describes the development, growth, and change of the exilarchate over a long period of time.

We have no systematic philological study showing the Iranian background of talmudic language, but the nearest thing to a full catalogue of Persian words in the Talmud is found in S. Telegdi, "Essai sur la phonétique des emprunts iraniens en araméen talmudique," Journal Asiatique, CCXXVI (1935), 177-257. The Geigers' contributions, noted above, cannot be overestimated. Apart from Beer's dissertation on one limited aspect, economic history remains to be written. Julius Newman's volumes on The Agricultural Life of the Jews in Babylonia, 200-500 (London, 1932) and the mimeographed pamphlet, "Commercial Life of the Jews in Babylonia," provide an arrangement by topic of whatever data Newman found of interest. No one supposes that they provide, or replace, rigorous and thorough economic history, for they are merely neat arrangements of relevant sayings. F.M. Heichelheim, "Roman Syria," in Tenney Frank (ed.), An

Economic Survey of Ancient Rome (Baltimore, 1938), IV, 121-258, contains much important information and has been unaccountably ignored. Just now, we are gaining access to the brilliant work of Soviet Iranists, in particular, N. Pigulevskaja, Les villes de l'état iranien aux époques parthe et sassanide (Paris, 1963). Those unfortunates who, like myself, do not yet know Russian will be glad, also, for the occasional remarks on social and economic history found in Vladimir G. Lukonin, Persia II (Cleveland, 1967), which is mainly devoted to archeological and artistic issues.

An exemplary recent work in legal history is R. Yaron, Gifts in Contemplation of Death in Jewish and Roman Law (Oxford, 1960). Yaron helpfully stresses aspects of legal development and change. A. Gulak, Yesodei HaMishpat Ha'Ivri (Berlin, 1922), Vols. I-IV, and Boaz Cohen's collected essays, Jewish and Roman Law, a Comparative Study (New York, 1966), Vols. I and II, provide accounts of Jewish law. None of these works concentrates specifically upon Babylonian Jewish law, nor would it have been possible to do so. I do not know why the interest in comparative law has centered upon the Mediterranean and not the Middle Eastern world. Since Babylonian talmudic data are used, one would suppose that the Matigan-i Hazar Datistan, studied by C. Bartholomae in Zum sasanidischen Recht, Sitzungsberichte der Heidelberger Akademie der Wissenschaften, Vol. I (1918), Vol. II (1918), Vol. III (1920), Vol. IV (1922), and Vol. V (1923), and also reprinted in an unscientific edition and translation by Sohrad Jamshedjee Bulsara as The Laws of the Ancient Persians (Bombay, 1937), would have been at least as interesting for comparative purposes as Justinian's Code. J.-P. de Menasche has published a brief study of it in his Feux et fondations pieuses dans le droit sassanide ("Travaux de l'Institut d'Etudes Iraniennes de L'Université de Paris" [Paris, 1964]). A.G. Perikhanian, the Soviet Iranist, will soon publish a complete edition and translation. Jozef Wolski recently published a bibliographical account, "Elam, Perse, Arménie (Achéménides, Arsacides, Sassanides)," in Introduction bibliograhique à l'histoire du droit et à l'ethnologie juridique, Part A/5 (Brussels, 1965), where many other important items are listed. In his 1955 Hebrew Union College Annual article, mentioned above, Spicehandler cites (p. 334, note; p. 336, note 6) the studies of Antonio Pagliaro, in Rivista degli studi Orientali, Vol. X (1910), Vol. XV (1935), Vol. XIX (1941), Vol. XXII (1946), Vol. XXIII (1948), Vol. XXVI (1951); and calls attention to A. Christensen, "Introduction bibliographique à l'histoire du droit de l'Iran ancien," Archives d'histoire du droit oriental, II (1938), 243-57.

Babylonian Jewish literature, meaning the Babylonian Talmud, has been studied for many centuries, but only in the present age have literary historians begun to undertake the task of form and tradition criticism. This is the first step toward a systematic, historical appreciation of the literature. Y.N. Epstein's Mevo'ot leSifrut Ha'Amora'im (Jerusalem, 1962) is especially relevant to the historian's interest, though he does not spell out the historical consequences of his literary inquiry and indeed seems to have had slight, if any, interest in history. Babylonian talmudic literature cannot be studied apart from contemporary Palestinian documents, and so S. Lieberman's Tosefta Kifshuta (10 vols.; New York, 1956-68) and other modern scientific works require close attention. Lieberman's Greek in Jewish Palestine [New York, 1942], Hellenism in Jewish Palestine

(New York, 1950), and "Palestine in the Third and Fourth Centuries," Jewish Quarterly Review, N.S. XXXVI (1946), 329-70, and XXXVII (1947), 31-54, contain much important information on Babylonia as well. The several volumes of Abraham Weiss, such as Hithavut HaTalmud beShelemuto (New York, 1943), center upon problems of literary history. In my view, the articles of Hyman Klein on the Saboraic strata of talmudic literature, such as "Gemara and Sebara," Jewish Quarterly Review, N.S. XXXVIII (1947), 67-91 (and see JQR, XLIII [1953], 341-63, and Journal of Semitic Studies, III [1958], 363-72), provide a very important key to understanding the formation of the talmudic sugya. Nonetheless, we are at the very beginning of historical criticism of talmudic literature, including the study of how it reached its present form. All of our studies of the history of Babylonian Judaism and Jewry, based as they are upon talmudic evidences, must therefore be seen as tentative and primitive, for only when we fully comprehend both the way in which our sources took shape and the later concerns which have selected and shaped traditions about earlier figures will we be able to criticize, if not to verify, our historical sources. We are a very long way from such a critical understanding of talmudic literature as a historical source, perhaps a century behind equivalent studies of New Testament and cognate literature.

IV

The history of Judaism in Babylonia is yet to be written. I do not know of a single systematic, methodologically sophisticated, and historically reliable account. Indeed, what would constitute such a history is still by no means clear to me. It would certainly have to include attention to the development of academic, rabbinic ideas from one generation to the next. Babylonian data are mixed indiscriminately with Palestinian ones in the various accounts of "talmudic Judaism." These provide little insight into the thought peculiar to the Babylonian academies in any one age or place, or in all of them put together. We are, however, fortunate to have a number of very helpful biographical studies, upon the basis of which the history of Babylonian rabbinic Judaism may eventually be constructed. The most important, comprehensive, and useful work is A. Hyman, Toledot Tanna'im ve'Amora'im (3 vols.; London, 1909), which is far more thorough than the brief entries in the Jewish Encyclopedia. Monographs on specific rabbis include David Hoffman, Mar Samuel (Leipzig, 1873), and Y.S. Yuri, Rav (Paris, 1925). Zuri's rather tendentious works on the relationship betwen Judean and Galilean culture with Sura and Nehardea, such as Tarbut HaDeromim (Tel Aviv, 1924) and Toledot Darkhei HaLimud bishivot Darom, Galil, Sura, veNeharde'a' (Jerusalem, 1914), remain interesting, and frequently his ideas about different methods of study in various schools bear rich fruit. A compendium of sayings, Abayye veRava, was published by Y.L. Maimon (Jerusalem, 1965), for what purpose I cannot fathom. Wilhelm Bacher, Die Agada der babylonischen Amoräer: Ein Beitrag zur Geschichte der Agada und zur Einleitung in den babylonischen Talmud (Frankfurt, 1913), provides brief accounts of some of the agadic sources, arranged by generations, and frequently adds important observations. But that work is not of the same depth or value as his studies of the Palestinians. I do not yet know how to make sense of the data he provides in Tradition und Tradenten in den Schulen Palastinas und Babyloniens (Leipzig, 1914), on which see J.Z. Lauterbach in Jewish Quarterly Review, N.S. VIII (1917), 101-12. One may note also S. Baer, "Leben und Wirken des tannaiten Chija," Magazin für die Wissenschaft des Judentums, XVII (1890), 28-49 and 119-35, one of the very small number of monographs dealing with specific Babylonian masters. The first modern effort at writing a history of the schools was that of M.D. Judelovitz, "The City of Nersh in Babylonia in the Time of the Talmud" (in Hebrew), Sinai XV (1945), 93 ff.; "The City of Sura" (in Hebrew), Sinai, I (1937), 168 ff.; Ha'Ir Pumbedita bimei ha'Amora'im (Jerusalem, 1939), and other works. This latter work was subjected to a searching, but unusually kindly, review by G. Allon, now reprinted in his Mehqarim beToledot Yisra'el (Tel Aviv, 1958), II, 298-302. A history of the talmudic academies ought to pay attention to the differing emphases and principles of Mishnah study and biblical exegesis, following Zuri; to the various results of such study of the Bible, following Bacher; to the external setting of the schools as well as to their personnel, following Judelovitz; but most important, to their contributions to the formation of the Babylonian Talmud.

Among the many works on the relationship between "talmudic Judaism" and Mazdaism, I should list, for bibliographical completeness only, the following of special interest: James Darmesteter, "Les six feux dans le Talmud et dans le Bundehesh," Revue des études juives, I (1880), 186-96; Moses Gaster, "Parsism in Judaism," Encyclopedia of Religion and Ethics, IX, 64 ff.; Alexander Kohut, "Parsic and Jewish Literature on the First Man," Jewish Quarterly Review, O.S. III (1890-91), 231-50, and his "Über die jüdische Angelologie und Dämonologie in ihrer Abhängigkeit vom Parsismus," Abhandlungen für die Kundes des Morgenländes, IV (1866), No. 3; S. Krauss, Paras veRomi baTalmud uvaMidrash (Jerusalem, 1947); A. Marmorstein, "Iranische und jüdische Religion," Zeitschrift für neutestamentliche Wissenschaft, XXVI (1927), 231-42 and S.H. Taqizadeh's definitive "Iranian Festivals Adopted by the Christians and Condemned by the Jews," Bulletin of the School of Oriental Studies, X (1939-40), 632-53, as well as the works of Geo Widengren cited above. So, while we have no history of rabbinic Judaism in the Babylonian academies, for which our data are so abundant, we do have a few Vorstudien on relevant issues of rabbinic Judaism and its relationship to Mazdean religion, as well as biographical and academic studies of value.

The other forms of Judaism are still less accessible. The religion of the ordinary Jews left only a few, mostly negative, remains in talmudic sources. The rabbinical elite preserved the religion of common folk only by criticizing it. On the other hand, the Dura synagogue contains a vast, if mute, testimony to what occupied the minds and souls of a small but cosmopolitan frontier community. Kraeling's report (cited above) is definitive for all but the interpretation of the art. Erwin R. Goodenough devoted volumes IX, X, and XI of his Jewish Symbols in Greco-Roman Times (12 vols.; New York, 1952 ff.) to that question, emphasizing the Hellenistic and Iranian motifs to be uncovered. I do not believe that E.J. Bickerman, "Symbolism in the Dura Synagogue," Harvard Theological Review, LVIII [1965], 127-52, has said the last word on Goodenough's researches. Morton Smith's

"Goodenough's Jewish Symbols in Retrospect," Journal of Biblical Literature, LXXXVI (1967), 53-68, provides a list of some of the more important reviews of Goodenough's work, a careful and penetrating critique of his conclusions, and a very thoughtful appreciation of his lasting achievements. A more constructive approach to the broader issue of the Hellenization of Judaism, with important implications for Babylonian Judaism, is Morton Smith, "The Image of God: Notes on the Hellenization of Judaism, with Especial Reference to Goodenough's Work on Jewish Symbols," Bulletin of the John Rylands Library, XL (1958), pp. 473-512, and his "On the Shape of God and the Humanity of Gentiles," in Jacob Neusner (ed.), Religions in Antiquity: Essays in Memory of Erwin Ramsdell Goodenough (suppls. to Numen, Vol XIV, Leiden, 1968), pp. 315-26.

A further testimony concerning popular religion is to be found in the Mandaean incantation bowls, of which some were prepared for or by Jews. The classic text is James A. Montgomery, Aramaic Incantation Texts from Nippur (Philadelphia, 1913); Cyrus H. Gordon published many articles on the subject, including "Aramaic and Mandaic Magical Bowls," Archiv Orientalni, IX (1937), pp. 95-106. We are now fortunate to have the comprehensive dissertation of Edwin Masao Yamauchi, Mandaic Incantation Texts ("American Oriental Series," Vol. XLIX [New Haven, 1967]). The bowls' implications for the history of religions, including Judaism, have yet to be explored. In this regard, Yamauchi hardly makes a beginning. My preliminary study is "Archaeology and the Jews of Babylonia," in J.A. Sanders and G.E. Wright (eds.), Nelson Glueck Festschrift (1970). The theme of the complicated relationship of the rabbis' religion to that of ordinary folk is explored in the several volumes of my History; the problem of the rabbis' control of synagogue life in general, and of Dura's synagogue in particular, is discussed in my "Rabbis and Community in Third-Century Babylonia," Religions in Antiquity (cited above), pp. 438-62.

Finally, we take note of the book-Pahlavi testimonies concerning what the Mazdeans thought of Judaism, found in the Denkart and in the Skand Gumanik Vicar, and translated by Lewis H. Gray, "The Jews in Pahlavi Literature," Actes du XIV Congrès International des Orientalists (Paris, 1906), pp. 161-92, and reprinted in the Jewish Encyclopedia. My translation, based upon the text and translation of J.-P. de Menasce, Une apologétique mazdéenne du IXe siècle (Fribourg, 1945), is "A Zoroastrian Critique of Judaism: Skand Gumanik Vicar Chapters Thirteen and Fourteen. A New Translation and Exposition," Journal of the Oriental Society LXXXIII (1963), 283-94, with additions, in Journal of the American Oriental Society, XXXVI (1966), 414-16. How accurately the Zoroastrian text observed the faith of ordinary Jews before the ninth century we do not know. But its stress upon fatalism and astrology certainly contradicts what we should have expected if we only had talmudic evidences and the later philosophical writings to go on. So the Iranian and archaeological sources are not unequivocal. The former are late, and the latter as yet are not wholly explicated for the history of religions. I think it likely that significant numbers of Babylonian Jews converted to Christianity in the second half of the third century, despite the persecutions of the latter community at that time. About Judaism in Mesopotamia (Edessa, Nisibis), Adiabene, Armenia, Mesene, Khuzistan, Elam,

Khorasan, and other satrapies of the Western Iranian Empire in Sasanian times where Jews lived, we know practically nothing. All we know is that there <u>were</u> Jews in these satrapies.

All our literary evidence (except scattered references in Christian Syriac literature) pertains to Babylonia; and most of it derives from, and testifies concerning the state of, the rabbinical academies alone. Indeed, the Babylonian Talmud, which makes possible a study of Babylonian Judaism, presents a monumental impediment to the study of that very history. It is mostly a commentary upon the Mishnah, and the historically useful data are limited by the concentration on what was relevant to Mishnah and other legal study, interpretation, and application. So the available literature leads us to suppose that we know more than we actually do. One could learn as much about American history and culture from approximately similar sources: minutes of some learned societies and faculty meetings of Harvard and Yale Universities, pious stories of Parson Weems, fragments of the Congressional Record and some court reports, and, chiefly, Blackstone's Commentaries in an American-annotated edition. Our knowledge would be partial and impoverished for America, as it is for Babylonian Jewry.

V

I have by no means attempted to offer a full bibliography of relevant works, as is obvious to the reader. In my <u>History,</u> I, 191-213, II, 291-302, III, 359-65, IV, 437-442, and V, 476-487, the reader will find bibliographies of works I found relevant to my study. Many of these books and articles contain long bibliographies as well, at least as extensive on specific problems as are mine. I call attention, for example, to the extraordinary bibliographies on oriental Christianity of Arthur Vööbus, <u>History of Asceticism in the Syrian Orient, I: The Origin of Asceticism: Early Monasticism in Persia</u> (Louvain, 1958); <u>II: Early Monasticism in Mesopotamia and Syria</u> (Louvain, 1960); and his <u>History of the School of Nisibis</u> (Louvain, 1965). W.B. Henning published <u>A Bibliography of Important Studies on Old Iranian Subjects</u> (Tehran, 1950). Of Jewish bibliographies containing references to our subject there is no end. I found very helpful Moise Schwab, <u>Repertoire des articles rélatifs à l'histoire et à la littérature juives parus dans les périodiques de 1665 à 1900</u> (Paris, 1914-1923).

In the face of the difficult, almost intractable, state of our archeological evidence; of the impossible necessity of preparation in many languages, including Hebrew and Aramaic (especially Syriac and Mandaean), Armenian, Avestan, book-Pahlavi, Parthian, Manichaean, and other Middle Iranian languages and dialects, Arabic and Modern Persian, as well as the usual scholarly languages, French, German, Italian, and <u>without question,</u> Russian; of the primitive state in which most of the literary sources are still found -- in the face of all these, among many, difficulties, one wonders whether the study of Babylonian Jewish history and religion under Parthian and Sasanian rule is really worth both giving the effort and accepting the inevitable certainty of one's own insufficiency and ultimate failure. I think it is. First, the sources are invariably interesting, and the problems they pose are engaging. Second, what we may learn will illumine the history of

Judaism and provide useful data for historians of religion and of Near and Middle Eastern civilization. Third, we are ignorant, and that is, after all, the best reason for wanting to learn.

VI

I should like to specify two among many themes which I believe will be particularly fruitful for the historian of religion. These are, first, the nature of rabbinic leadership and, second, the relationship between rabbinic law and theology on the one hand and the religion of ordinary people on the other. The rabbis were, to begin with, employed by the exilarch, or Jewish satrap, who was appointed, I think, by the Parthians and confirmed in office by the Sasanians later on. He hired them because he needed good lawyers, judges, and public administrators. That the rabbis had other aspirations interested the exilarch less than it ought to have. It turned out that they sought to shape many areas of popular life which hardly concerned political and administrative necessities, and in time they acquired so vast an influence that the exilarch became little more than a puppet of the rabbinate and its academies. The means by which the rabbis attained such vast influence were twofold. First of all, they controlled many of the courts, the academies that trained the future lawyers, and also the administrative posts of the Jewish community. Second, they were holy men, as I have said earlier (History of Religions, VI [1966], 169-78), who were believed by virtue of their knowledge of "Torah" to possess truly amazing powers. Indeed, in volumes III, pp. 95-195, and IV of my History, I have argued that one can hardly distinguish between "Torah" and magic, except by accepting the rabbis' own distinctions between the one and the other. From a historical viewpoint, the two were the same, and only for theological reasons have the vast numbers of stories about rabbinical magicians, sorcerers, astrologers, faith healers, and the like have been suppressed, ignored, or, mostly, explained away. In W.B. Henning's categories they were both politicians and witch doctors. An anthropologist might call them "the lawyer-magicians of Babylonia."

The study of these issues, which may contribute to phenomenological studies, seems to me rendered quite feasible by the sources even in their present condition. We are so obsessed with the positivistic historical questions as to ignore the incontrovertible facts always in our hands. So we have asked whether a given rabbi "really" did or said such-and-such.[2] We have generally ignored the fact that people really believed such was the case and that belief renders accessible, at least for interpretation, the structure of their perceptions of reality. The academies controlled by the rabbis thought it important to tell, to preserve for later generations' edification, and to repeat magical accounts alongside legal and theological ones. They were not only not embarrassed by stories about the magical prowess of one or another rabbi, but they were obviously eager to relate them, or otherwise we should not have them at all.

I am struck by the greater usefulness of talmudic data for the study of such matters than for the recovery of "hard" facts. As I said, the Babylonian Talmud contains limited and one-sided information about public affairs. On the other hand, it is a rich and hardly tapped resource for the study of questions of interest to historians of religion. First, of course, one needs to identify just what these questions are and to consider which ones may be fruitfully considered in talmudic studies.

NOTES

[1] All the more so for Babylonian Jewish "influence" on Palestinian Judaism. For example, C.S. Mann, "The Jerusalem Church in Acts," in Johannes Munck, The Acts of the Apostles ("The Anchor Bible," Vol. XXXI [New York, 1967]), p. 282, states: "The Parthian invasion about 140 B.C., with the resulting disruption of ordered life, meant that the old irrigation systems could no longer be maintained, and the complex system of retaining dykes... quickly broke. As a result, the Euphrates and Tigris rivers both changed their courses. This disastrous break with previously ordered ways of life... must have brought with it wholesale emigration of Jews." I do not know the basis for Mann's allegation. In his Diyala studies (Land behind Baghdad, a History of Settlement on the Diyala Plains [Chicago, 1965], pp. 61 ff.), Robert McC. Adams does not refer to such widespread destruction in the nearby Diyala basin. It is true that Babylonia changed hands several times between 140 and 120, but evidence of destruction so widespread as to lead to forced migration, let alone emigration, is not known to me. In any event, no source refers to such an emigration, and while an argument based upon silence may not be impressive, it is still stronger than an allegation based upon no direct, pertinent evidence whatever. (The only substantial attempt at emigration from Babylonia to Palestine, excluding the small band of Zamaris [Zimri], took place about 362-63, in consequence of Julian's promise to rebuild the Temple, when a passing messiah urged Jews to return. According to Christian Syriac hagiographical sources, many thousands of Mahozan Jews did in fact try to emigrate but were slaughtered by the troops of Shapur II. But this has no relevance whatever to Mann's point.)

[2] See, for example, the difficulties discussed in my "In Quest of the Historical Rabban Yohanan ben Zakkai," Harvard Theological Review LIX (1966), 391-413.